UNSOLVED MYSTERIES

OF

AMERICAN HISTORY

✳ Deluxe Edition ✳

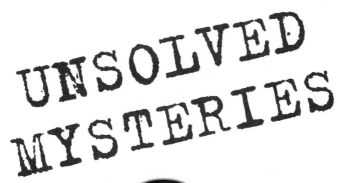

UNSOLVED MYSTERIES OF AMERICAN HISTORY

✳ Deluxe Edition ✳

**An Eye-Opening Journey through
500 Years of Discoveries, Disappearances,
and Baffling Events**

PAUL ARON

Reader's
Digest

The Reader's Digest Association, Inc.
Pleasantville, New York / Montreal

The material in this book was originally published as *Unsolved Mysteries of American History* (1997) and *More Unsolved Mysteries of American History* (2004) by John Wiley & Sons, Inc. This special deluxe edition was compiled and published by The Reader's Digest Association, Inc. by permission of John Wiley & Sons, Inc.

Library of Congress Cataloging-in-Publication Data

Aron, Paul, 1956 Sept. 15-
  Unsolved mysteries of American history : an eye-opening journey through 500 years of discoveries, disappearances, and baffling events / Paul Aron.-- Deluxe ed.
      p. cm.
  "The material in this book was originally published as Unsolved mysteries of American history (1997) and More unsolved mysteries of American history (2004) by John Wiley & Sons, Inc."
  Includes index.
  ISBN 0-7621-0716-2

  1. United States--History--Miscellanea. 2. America--History--Miscellanea. I. Aron, Paul, 1956 Sept. 15- More unsolved mysteries of American history. II. Title.
  E179.A75 2005
  973--dc22

Address any comments about *Unsolved Mysteries of American History, Deluxe Edition* to:

The Reader's Digest Association, Inc.
Editor-in-Chief, Reader's Digest Books
Reader's Digest Road
Pleasantville, NY 10570-7000

To order copies of *Unsolved Mysteries of American History, Deluxe Edition* call 1-800-846-2100.

Visit our Web site at **rd.com**

Printed in the United States of America
1 3 5 7 9 10 8 6 4 2
US 4768/L

COVER PHOTO CREDITS
Button: *Time & Life Pictures*; Richard Nixon, Abraham Lincoln, and Christopher Columbus: *Hulton Archive/Getty Images*; Pocahontas: *Bettmann Archives/Corbis*

Acknowledgments

For much useful advice, thanks to Jae Aron, Stephen Aron, John Kingston, Robert Thompson, and David Wolff. Thanks also to Rusty Carter and Bill O'Donovan of *The Virginia Gazette* and John Thornton of the Spieler Agency.

Thanks to everyone at Wiley, especially Chris Jackson, Elaine O'Neal, Chip Rossetti, John Simko, Mike Thompson, and my editors Judith McCarthy and Stephen S. Power.

Finally, I am grateful to my wife, Paula Blank, for her perceptive readings of the manuscript and its author.

Introduction

Ellery Queen's 1934 novel *The Chinese Orange Mystery* presents us with a murder scene that's completely backwards. The rug and table are upside down, the grandfather clock and bookcases face the wall, a set of Hebrew books (Hebrew being a language written from right to left, i.e., backwards) is missing.

It turns out the murderer has turned around everything in the room just to conceal the one thing which would normally be backwards: the dead man's collar. (The dead man was a priest, and priests always wear their collars backwards.) At this point, the rest of the puzzle pieces easily fit together and the mystery is solved.

"The detective," wrote Ellery Queen, "is a prophet looking backwards."

So is the historian. Like a detective, he or she must look backwards, trying to figure out what happened and why. And, like the detective in Queen's story, the historian must examine evidence which is often not what it seems.

Take, for example, the mystery of whether Leif Ericsson and his band of Norsemen (and Norsewomen, too, if one is to believe the ancient Icelandic sagas) discovered America, about five hundred years before Columbus. By the early nineteenth century, Leif's advocates had scoured the east coast of North America; no stone was left unturned in the search for evidence of Leif's settlement. And a remarkable number of those stones turned out to have Norse inscriptions on them. In towns from Newfoundland to Florida, the claim that "Leif Ericsson was here" was as common as the claim that "George Washington slept here." Alas, both claims were equally improbable; on closer examination most of these reputed Norse relics turned out to be crude hoaxes.

Then, in 1964, near a small fishing village in northern Newfoundland, the Norwegian archaeologist, Helge Ingstad, uncovered an ancient Norse spindle whorl. Here, at last, was genuine proof of Leif's settlement. This was better than finding a Viking sword, for it proved that the sagas were right not only about Norsemen coming to America but about Norsewomen, too. (It was the women who would have used the spindle whorl to spin wool.)

Case closed?

By no means. According to the sagas, Leif had named the country he found Vinland (or Wineland), after the wild grapes he found there. But: botanists assure us that grapes can't grow any farther north than Massachusetts—and a glance at any map shows Newfoundland atop Massachusetts. So how could Vinland have been in Newfoundland?

To make sense of something so backwards—or, in this case, so upside down—required a detective of Ellery Queen's ingenuity. Was Ingstad up to the task? To find out, see chapter 3 in part 1.

And that, as they say, is just the beginning. Did Pocahontas really rescue John Smith? Was Daniel Boone a traitor? Was Sally Hemings the mistress of Thomas Jefferson? Was Amelia Earhart a spy? Were the Rosenbergs guilty? Who killed JFK? How much did Reagan know about the Iran-contra affair? These are mysteries that have intrigued, sometimes baffled, but never deterred our most resourceful historians. These are mysteries with all the twists and turns, all the intellectual challenges, all the espionage and murder that you could hope for from Ambler or Chandler, Parker or Paretsky.

After all, these are the greatest mysteries of our history.

Contents

Part 1
Enduring Riddles of a Strange New World

Part 2
Unexplained Happenings in a Young Republic

☆ Contents ☆

Part 3

Unanswered Questions About a Divided Nation

Part 4
Lingering Puzzles from the Early Modern Era

☆ Contents ☆

Part 5
Baffling Events of More Recent Times

☆ Contents ☆

Part 1
Enduring Riddles of a Strange New World

Up to 1700

Chapter 1

When Did the First People Arrive in America?

Soon after Columbus landed in America, Europeans began speculating about the people of this New World. To Columbus himself there was no mystery: since he assumed he'd reached some island off the shore of India (as all of Asia was then sometimes known), he had few doubts about who these people were (or what to call them). But once it became clear that the Indians were not, in fact, Indians, theories about who they were and where they came from abounded.

One theory which was especially popular in Spain was that the Indians were survivors of the lost continent of Atlantis. Atlantis, according to stories dating back as far as Plato's dialogues, once stretched from Spain to America but had sunk in a great flood. The first to tie the people of Atlantis to those of America was Francisco López de Gómara; in 1552 he explained that the Indians had been stranded in America when Atlantis sank. As evidence, Gómara pointed out that the Mexican Indians used the word "atl" for water.

Another persistent theory was that the Indians were descendants of the lost tribes of Israel, whose exile to Assyria had been chronicled in the Old Testament and who hadn't been heard from since. A Dutch theologian named Joannes Fredricus Luminus seems to have been the first to make the connection between Jews and American Indians, arguing in 1567 that both had big noses and strange burial customs.

The first to move beyond such myths toward a serious study of American Indians were Spanish friars, among them the Jesuit missionary José de Acosta. In 1589 Acosta hypothesized that the Indians had reached the New World via an overland route from Asia. Here was a man ahead of his time; by the twentieth century, most scholars agreed he was right on the mark.

This consensus began to emerge in the mid-nineteenth century after Charles Darwin theorized that human beings first evolved in Africa, then spread around the rest of the world. Fossil evidence seemed to bear Darwin out: Africa and Europe could boast of numerous archaeological sites indicating the presence of humans tens of thousands of years ago; America had none (or at least none that weren't strongly disputed). Advances in geology strengthened the case for an overland route by demonstrating that a land bridge once existed between Siberia and Alaska, where today the waters of the Bering Strait are found.

So it seemed the mystery had been solved. Native Americans were not *truly* native; they had come from Asia. But an equally intriguing mystery remained: *when* had they arrived?

Until the 1960s and 1970s this mystery also seemed nearly solved. The consensus was that people crossed into America about 12,000 years ago.

This was near the end of the last Ice Age, when so much of the earth's water was locked up in glaciers that the Bering land bridge, also known as Beringia, was left exposed. Beringia had, to be sure, an inhospitable climate—worse even than that of Alaska and Siberia today. But the climate had warmed up enough for humans to survive in the area. Fossils found there indicate that woolly mammoths, steppe bison, wild horses, and caribou all lived in the region, and their human hunters might very well have followed them onto and across the land bridge. So the 12,000-year estimate made sense: any earlier, and it would have been too cold for people to survive so far north; any later, and the water from the melting glaciers would have submerged the land bridge and blocked the passage across.

This geological logic was buttressed by archaeological evidence. In 1908 a black cowboy named George McJunkin was riding near the small town of Folsom, New Mexico, searching for a lost cow. Instead, he came across some bones with a stone spearpoint beside them. The bones were much too large to belong to a cow; intrigued, McJunkin

Stone spearpoints found between the ribs of Ice Age mammoths prove people were living in America 10,000 to 12,000 years ago. If human hunters arrived in America about that time, that might also explain—according to some paleoecologists—why such Ice Age animals as mammoths (like this one, from an Arizona State Museum diorama reconstruction) quickly became extinct. (By permission of the Arizona State Museum.)

took them back to the ranch house. There they stayed until 1925, when they landed on the desk of Jesse Figgins of the Colorado Museum of Natural History. Figgins easily identified the bones as those of a long-extinct form of bison that had roamed the plains at the end of the Ice Age. But it was the stone spearpoints McJunkin had found beside the bones that had the more far-reaching implications. If these spearpoints were man-made weapons used to kill the bison, that meant humans had been hunting (and living) in America during the Ice Age.

More indications of Ice Age hunters followed soon after. In 1932 two amateur collectors exploring near Clovis, New Mexico, found the bones of some animals with stone spearheads between the ribs. In this case, the animals turned out to be woolly mammoths, also extinct since the Ice Age. And with the spearpoints right between the ribs, there could be little doubt that people were in America during the Ice Age.

In the 1950s a University of Chicago scientist named Willard Libby developed "radiocarbon dating," which allowed scientists to determine the age of the Folsom and Clovis finds more precisely; they turned out to date back between 10,000 and 11,500 years ago—thus fitting in very neatly with the puzzle being pieced together.

So, too, did evidence that came right from the prehistoric Indians' mouths—or rather, teeth. After examining more than 200,000 prehistoric teeth from the remains of about 9,000 prehistoric Indians, anthropologist Christy Turner determined that all Native American teeth shared certain genetic traits with northeast Asian teeth. These traits were unique—no other people had them besides the North American Indians and the northeast Asians. From this, Turner concluded that the Indians' ancestors must have come from northeast Asia. What's more, by examining the differences between northeast Asian and American Indian teeth and by comparing them to general dental evolution patterns, Turner calculated that the two populations must have separated in the vicinity of—you guessed it—12,000 years ago.

If people first entered America about 12,000 years ago, that explained another mystery as well: the rapid extinction of mammoths, mastodons, saber-toothed cats, native camels, giant beavers, and other large animals that roamed North America until about 10,000 years ago. When the bones of these animals were found at sites dated 12,000 years or older, there were no human artifacts nearby. When human artifacts less than 10,000 years old were found at similar sites, none of these animals' bones were around. Only in finds dating back between 12,000 and 10,000 years ago, such as those at Clovis and Folsom, did human artifacts (for example, spearheads) and these bones appear together. From this, paleoecologist Paul Martin formulated his hypothesis of "Pleistocene overkill" in 1967. Martin was convinced that human hunters crossed the Bering land bridge about 12,000 years ago and then moved south through an ice-free corridor just east of the Canadian Rockies. Here they found mammals so completely unadapted to human predators that they quickly hunted them to extinction.

Not all scientists accepted Martin's arguments. Some countered that climatic changes, or at least some combination of human hunting and climate, could better account for the extinctions. But there was no denying that the extinctions were yet another indication that people had crossed the Bering land bridge about 12,000 years ago. The mystery of when the first Americans arrived was, it seemed, solved.

☆ ☆ ☆

In the 1970s and 1980s this consensus fell apart as not one, but many, archaeologists claimed to uncover evidence of a human presence in America earlier—in some cases, *much* earlier—than 12,000 years ago.

Between 1973 and 1977 James Adovasio excavated Meadowcroft Rock Shelter in southwest Pennsylvania. There he found remnants of baskets and small stone blades at levels that radiocarbon dating indicated were occupied almost 20,000 years ago.

In 1976 in a Chilean peat bog called Monte Verde, Tom Dillehay unearthed the wooden foundations of huts that were occupied 13,000 years ago. At even deeper levels he found three hearths and some tools made from pebbles that radiocarbon dating showed to be about 34,000 years old.

Also in 1976 the husband-and-wife archaeologist team of Alan Bryan and Ruth Gruhn found the skeleton of a mastodon with a stone point inside it, at a site called Taima-taima in Venezuela. Radiocarbon dating placed the kill 13,000 years ago.

And in 1978 Niede Guidon dated some prehistoric art from a Brazilian rock shelter called Pedra Furada back to about 32,000 years ago, making it among the oldest art in the world.

How could these people have traversed a continent still covered with glaciers? And how did they get to America in the first place—before there was a land bridge across the Bering?

Proponents of a pre-12,000-year-old human presence in America have suggested a couple of possibilities. Some have suggested that people crossed into America during an earlier period when the land bridge was exposed but when conditions had warmed somewhat. And even during the heart of the Ice Age there may have been an ice-free corridor along which people might have headed south.

Another hypothesis, this one championed by the Canadian archaeologist Knut Fladmark, was that people traveled across the Bering Sea and down the west coast of the Americas by boat. The boats would have been very primitive, but perhaps the Pacific coast of North America might have sustained enough life for people to make it far enough south, after which they could have headed inland. After all,

Fladmark pointed out, people reached Australia about 40,000 years ago—also from Asia—and there was never a land bridge between those continents.

Proponents of the traditional 12,000-year date have sharply attacked all of these findings and theories. One traditionalist, Brian Fagan, mockingly referred to the ice-free corridor as a "prehistoric superhighway" beckoning the Paleo-Indians south from Beringia into warmer climes. Even at the warmest points during the Ice Age, Fagan argued, this corridor could barely support animal or human life, and people had little incentive to venture into it.

As for Fladmark's boat theory, traditionalists responded that, though the distance between Asia and America across the Bering Strait was about the same as between Asia and Australia, the trip to Australia was across fairly placid, tropical seas. In contrast, the Bering Strait—even during the warmer times of the Ice Age—was full of dangerous ice floes, hardly an appealing trip for people who, from all other evidence, survived by hunting and not fishing.

How, then, have traditionalists explained the pre-12,000-year-old finds? Many have claimed that the findings were simply wrong. In some cases the artifacts supporting earlier dates may have been natural and not man-made: trees may have fallen in ways that could be mistaken for human dwellings, natural deposits may appear to be hearths, pebbles eroded by streams may seem to be tools. In other cases the dating process may have been corrupted; radiocarbon dating depends on finding organic material (which can be carbon-dated) at the same level as human artifacts (which can't be carbon-dated), and then assuming that the latter are the same age as the former—but all sorts of geological disturbances could result in older organic matter ending up in the same layer as more recent human artifacts.

The majority of archaeologists today still stand by the 12,000-year date. Besides questioning the validity of the claims for sites like Monte Verde and Pedra Furada, these archaeologists point to the relatively small number of such sites. In Europe and Asia, on the other hand, there are thousands of well-documented sites that have yielded numerous and indisputably human artifacts dating back more than 30,000 years. If people lived here more than 12,000 years ago, most archaeologists insist, there ought to be more record of it. Or, as some traditional archaeologists have put it, the absence of evidence is evidence of absence.

But—to a much greater extent than was the case just a few years ago—archaeologists are willing to entertain the possibility that at least a few people might have arrived here earlier than 12,000 years ago. And even the most conservative archaeologists can't preclude the possibility that someday someone will find definitive proof that people were in America long before the Ice Age ended.

☆ To investigate further:

Fladmark, Knut. "Getting One's Berings." *Natural History,* November 1986. This and the following articles from *Natural History* were part of a series on the first Americans written by specialists and reporting on their original research but in nontechnical terms. Fladmark's article considers the likelihood of Ice Age Americans migrating by boat.

Adovasio, J. M. and Ronald Carlisle. "Pennsylvania Pioneers." *Natural History,* December 1986. A report on the Meadowcroft Rock Shelter excavations.

Turner, Christy. "Telltale Teeth." *Natural History,* January 1987. Dental evidence of Indians' Asian ancestry.

Ruhlen, Merritt. "Voices from the Past." *Natural History,* March 1987. What Indian languages reveal about the migrations to and in the Americas.

Dillehay, Tom. "By the Banks of the Chinchihuapi." *Natural History,* April 1987. A report on the Monte Verde excavations.

Grayson, Donald. "Death by Natural Causes." *Natural History,* May 1987. Considers whether human hunters or climate caused the extinction of North America's Ice Age animals.

Bryan, Alan. "Points of Order." *Natural History,* June 1987. A report on excavations in Venezuela and Colombia by a leading proponent of Americans' greater antiquity.

Guidon, Niede. "Cliff Notes." *Natural History,* August 1987. A report on the Pedra Furada excavations.

Martin, Paul. "Clovisia the Beautiful!" *Natural History,* October 1987. A summary of the conservative case against New World peopling prior to 12,000 years ago.

Fagan, Brian. *The Great Journey: The Peopling of Ancient America.* New York: Thames and Hudson, 1987. A scholarly but nontechnical overview of the subject by an archaeologist who is conservative in his assessment of the site data but open to the possibility of pre-Clovis finds. (This chapter is much indebted to Fagan's work.)

Dillehay, Tom and David Meltzer. *The First Americans: Search and Research.* Boca Raton, FL: CRC Press, 1991. A collection of essays that go beyond discussions of particular sites to discuss general issues relating to the peopling of the Americas, and which compare the migrations to America with those of other places and other times. Technical but readable.

Dixon, E. James. *Quest for the Origins of the First Americans.* Albuquerque: University of New Mexico Press, 1993. A highly speculative but fascinating analysis by a proponent of early settlement.

Chapter 2

Did St. Brendan Discover America?

St. Brendan was running a monastery in Ireland when a visiting abbot told him of his voyage across the ocean to the "Promised Land of the Saints." Brendan decided to see it for himself.

So, sometime in the middle of the sixth century, Brendan and seventeen other monks set sail in a small boat they framed with wood, then covered with ox hides, much like the curraghs still sometimes seen in Ireland. Their adventures were many and marvelous.

They came, for example, to one island filled with giant white sheep, and another covered by hymn-singing birds. They found a huge pillar of crystal floating in the ocean, surrounded by pieces of marble, and a whole island on fire, from which they were pelted by hot rocks. Brendan told his fellow monks they'd reached the edge of hell.

Another island appeared rocky and black, and the monks went ashore to cook a meal. As soon as the cauldron began to boil, the island started to move, and the monks scrambled back into their boat. Turns out, Brendan figured, the island was actually the ocean's largest fish.

More pleasantly, there was a spacious and woody island, and one with luxurious colors and fruit unlike anything the monks had seen before. And finally, after seven years, there was the Promised Land of the Saints, where a young man told the monks the land would be given to their successors. Brendan then returned to Ireland.

This is Brendan's story, as told in the *Navigatio Sancti Brendani Abbatis,* a Latin manuscript by an anonymous author. Scholars date the *Navigatio* back to sometime after A.D. 800, at least a hundred years after Brendan's death. The story was tremendously popular throughout the late Middle Ages—understandably, given its mix of maritime romance and Christian theology.

Also understandably, most modern scholars viewed the *Navigatio* as a work of literature, not history. Brendan seemed to have more in common with King Arthur, or perhaps with Odysseus, than with an actual historical figure. Many placed the work in a genre of early Irish literature known as *imrama;* these were generally filled with fantastic sea stories.

But there was a key difference. Unlike *imrama,* the *Navigatio* contained navigational directions and detailed descriptions of the places the monks visited. By plotting their course on a map and comparing the descriptions to actual islands, historians sought to reconstruct Brendan's journey. Some concluded that the Promised Land of the Saints was in North America.

If so, Brendan reached America about a thousand years before Christopher Columbus.

☆ ☆ ☆

Among those who tracked Brendan's voyage were Geoffrey Ashe in the 1960s and Paul Chapman in the 1970s. Ashe was a medieval historian, Chapman a World War II navigator familiar with the North Atlantic from ferrying planes across the ocean.

Some of the islands were fairly easy to identify, and most historians agreed which of these was which. The sheep and the birds were most likely in the Faroes, an archipelago in the North Atlantic between Scotland and Iceland. True, the sheep there aren't giant and the birds don't sing hymns, but there are plenty of both. *Faeroes,* in fact, is Danish for sheep, and the island of Vagar is known for its kittiwakes and arctic terns.

The crystal pillar could have been an iceberg, a likely sight as the monks headed north. What appeared to be marble could have been patches of ice that had broken off from the berg. The hot rocks? Molten slag from an erupting volcano near Iceland, according to some speculation, or farther south near the Azores, according to others. Both are areas of volcanic activity.

The moving island is surely a tall tale. But whales are common north of the Faroes, and there were undoubtedly more of them around in the seventh century. So, for Brendan enthusiasts, the story could be seen as confirmation that the monks were in that area.

Now it gets trickier. Brendan and company drifted for twenty days, then were swept west for another forty before reaching the large, wooded island. Chapman concluded this must have been the heavily forested Barbados. Heading north from there, the fruit he soon found may have been grapefruit, which was native to the Caribbean and unknown in Europe. Ashe was less certain of all this, saying only the "effect of the whole passage is West Indian."

The Land of the Promised Saints is even more amorphous. There were another forty days at sea—a number whose recurrence makes one suspect its significance is more biblical than nautical. Equally problematic, Brendan was at this point, according to the *Navigatio,* sailing east, presumably *away* from America.

Ashe concluded the Land of the Promised Saints was a "literary-religious figment," one that fulfilled the promise of the opening chapter but not the demands of historical reality. Chapman agreed that the *Navigatio* did not prove Brendan reached the mainland. He figured Brendan probably stopped at the West Indies, just as Columbus did.

The *Navigatio* alone, then, could not make the case for the Irish in America. Nor could other medieval Irish texts. Brendan had a minor role in a ninth-century *Life of St. Machutus,* another saint; there was also a tenth-century *Life of St. Brendan.* Both texts were useful in confirming Brendan was a real person, renowned for many sea voyages, but neither offered anywhere near the detail of the *Navigatio.*

There were, however, three medieval texts that did place the Irish in North America. Surprisingly, these came not from Ireland but from Iceland.

☆ ☆ ☆

For most of American history, historians treated the Icelandic sagas much as the Irish *imrama.* They were ancient stories, not quite as ancient as the Irish ones perhaps, but equally inadmissible as historical evidence. All that changed when a Norwegian archaeologist, Helge Ingstad, uncovered a Norse spindle whorl amid the remains of a village in northern Newfoundland. Here was proof that the Norse had reached—indeed had settled in—America hundreds of years before Columbus.

On his way to the "promised land," according to the Navigatio Sancti Brendani
Abbatis, *St. Brendan celebrated mass on the back of a whale. This illustration comes
from an early edition of the* Navigatio. *(Mary Evans Picture Library.)*

The Icelandic sagas, of course, told the stories of Eric the Red
and Leif Ericsson and other Norsemen, not of Brendan or the Irish.
Yet the Irish did appear in three of the sagas, and each time they were
in the New World.

In the *Saga of Eric the Red,* the Norse reached America, captured
some natives, and taught them their language. The natives then told
the Norse of a land whose people wore white clothes and marched
with poles that had cloths attached to them. To the Norse who heard
this story, according to the saga, this sounded a lot like a procession of
Irish monks. A second saga mentioned a land west of the Norse settlement in America, "which some call Ireland the Great." And a third had
a lost Norseman wash up on American shores, where natives spoke a
language that he thought sounded like that of the Irish.

In one sense, these stories made a lot of sense. The Norse knew
well that the Irish monks were accomplished seamen. The Irish had
beaten them to the Faroes and Iceland and Greenland, so why not

America? Indeed, it was the Norse who pushed the Irish monks out of Iceland, perhaps prompting them to head west. This was sometime in the ninth century, too late for Brendan to be the first Irishman to reach America, but still well before Leif Ericsson, let alone Columbus.

There were a number of problems with this theory, however. First, the sagas were vague about the location of "Ireland the Great." If the ninth-century Irish monks headed west from Iceland, they would have come to Greenland before America, and they might very well have founded a colony there. Second, there's no archaeological evidence that the Irish made it to America; no one has found an Irish equivalent of Ingstad's Norse spindle whorl.

And third, Leif Ericsson and the Norse didn't reach America before the end of the tenth century, more than a hundred years after the Irish monks left Iceland. So either these monks had reached Old Testament-like ages, or they had met some Native American women and abandoned their vows of chastity.

Most modern historians, therefore, would deny Brendan's claim. Even some of those who believed the Irish reached the West Indies weren't sure it was Brendan.

"Over a period of two or three hundred years, many Irish monks besides Brendan made actual voyages," wrote Ashe. "And as so often in legend-making, the most famous figure came to be credited with deeds not authentically his."

Ashe concluded the *Navigatio* was not so much the record of a specific voyage as an amalgam of knowledge the Irish accumulated, not only from their own travels but from studying traditions and legends from Plato's Atlantis to the Celtic "otherworld."

Samuel Eliot Morison, the premiere chronicler of the European voyages across the ocean, would grant neither Brendan nor any Irishman an American landing, even in the West Indies.

"We are not straining the evidence to conclude that Brendan sailed for several trips . . . on the circuit Hebrides-Shetlands-Faroes-Iceland, possibly as far as the Azores," Morison wrote in 1971. "But, discovery of America—no!

"The imagination of certain modern . . . writers, no whit less than that of the early storytellers, has brought Brendan to Newfoundland, the West Indies, Mexico, and even the Ohio River!" Morison continued. "They do not even boggle at peppering the Antilles with Irish monasteries which have disappeared, or ascribing to Brendan's curragh the speed and endurance of a clipper ship."

Tim Severin, a British explorer and writer, believed Morison was wrong, at least about the capabilities of the boat. To prove it, Severin stitched together forty-nine ox hides, stretched them over a wooden frame, put together a crew, and in May 1976, set sail from the west coast of Ireland. The ship—christened *Brendan*—reached the Faroes in June and Iceland in July. There *Brendan* rested until May 1977, when Severin and his crew headed west. Less than two months later, they reached Newfoundland.

Granted, Severin equipped the boat with some modern equipment, including a radio. But the medieval equipment, such as extra hides with which the crew patched leaks in the middle of the North Atlantic, came in just as handy and proved a lot more durable than, for example, the plastic food bags that were quickly inundated by seawater.

The trip did not, of course, prove that the Irish monks had reached America; merely that it was technologically possible.

"A leather boat that some had feared would disintegrate in the first gale off the Irish coast had successfully crossed the Atlantic. *Brendan* had demonstrated that the voyage could be done," Severin wrote. "But in the final analysis the only conclusive proof that it had been done would be if an authentic relic from an early Irish visit is found one day on North American soil."

☆ ☆ ☆

Assume for the moment that Brendan reached America. Or, as Ashe did, that the Irish monks at least knew about America. The question then arises: What did Columbus know about Brendan and the Irish?

Since the *Navigatio* was so widely known, Columbus may very well have read it, or at least heard about it. A pre-1492 globe includes "the Isle of St. Brendan," in what could be construed as the West Indies. Chapman believed Columbus followed Brendan's route, and intentionally hid that fact so that he could claim the New World for Spain.

That seems a stretch, especially since most of Columbus's biographers—including his own son Ferdinand and, more recently, Morison—maintained that the admiral was searching for a new route to Asia, not a New World. Indeed, even after Columbus reached America, he continued to describe it as an island, or perhaps a peninsula, off the Asian mainland.

Still, even the most skeptical historians, such as Morison, don't deny that Brendan may have been an inspiration—and therefore in some sense a forerunner—to later explorers, including Columbus.

"No, here is not a discovery of a New World," Morison wrote of the *Navigatio*, but then added that it was "a captivating tale which led men of later centuries to sail into the unknown, hoping to find Brendan's islands, confident that God would watch over them."

☆ To investigate further:

Selmer, Carl, editor. *Navigatio Sancti Brendani Abbatis*. Dublin: Four Courts, 1989. A reconstruction based on 18 of the 120 known Latin versions.

Ashe, Geoffrey. *Land to the West*. New York: Viking, 1962. Ashe focuses on what the Irish monks *knew*, as opposed to what Brendan *did*.

Morison, Samuel Eliot. *The European Discovery of America: The Northern Voyages*. New York: Oxford University Press, 1971. Morison's elegant prose is informed by his extensive knowledge not just of history, but also of the sea.

Chapman, Paul H. *The Man Who Led Columbus to America*. Atlanta, Georgia: Judson Press, 1973. The title has two meanings: Brendan came first, and Columbus used the *Navigatio* as a guide.

Severin, Tim. *The Brendan Voyage*. New York: Modern Library, 2000. Regardless of its historic import, this is a dramatic and well-told sea story in the tradition of Thor Heyerdahl's *Kon-Tiki*. Originally published in 1978.

Chapter 3

Did Leif Ericsson Discover America?

If one is to believe the ancient Icelandic sagas, the first European to discover America was not Christopher Columbus, nor was it Leif Ericsson. It was none other than Biarni Heriulfson.

Biarni was a trader who regularly crossed the part of the Atlantic between Norway and his home in Iceland. In the summer of 985 he left Norway to spend the winter with his father. He arrived to find his father had departed for Greenland—a land recently discovered by Eric the Red. Biarni set off after him. But on his way to Greenland he got lost and came upon some new land. This new land was America—at least according to those who believed the sagas to be historical documents and not just literary epics.

The discovery didn't excite Biarni. "To me this land looks good for nothing," he told his crew, and then he headed back to Greenland. There he was reunited with his father, thus securing his place in history as the world's most devoted son and least venturesome explorer.

Others, however, found Biarni's stories intriguing. These new lands sounded appealing, especially compared to Greenland; in spite of Eric the Red's efforts to attract other settlers by giving the land an attractive name, Greenland was anything but green. Among those stirred by Biarni's stories was Eric's son, Leif Ericsson. He bought Biarni's ship, assembled a crew, and set sail for the land that he would call Vinland. He lived there for a year before returning to Greenland.

Other Norse expeditions soon followed, including one led by Leif's brother, Thorvald. Thorvald spent the winter of 1004–1005 at Leif's settlement but, the sagas say, was killed by "Skrellings." (Presumably these were Indians or Eskimos.) The surviving members of his party then returned to Greenland. Yet another brother of Leif, Thorstein, and a sister, Freydis, then tried to colonize Vinland, but again, the Skrellings drove the intruders away. Only Freydis showed any Viking spirit: after failing to rally the fleeing men, she slapped a sword across her bared breasts and screamed so loud that the Skrellings retreated. But the men had had enough: This land may have been more hospitable than Greenland; its inhabitants, on the other hand, were not. For another five hundred years, the Indians had America to themselves.

Or so the story went. To most historians, however, it was just that—a story. Granted, there were some scholars who argued it was true, but these were mostly Scandinavians whose conclusions were tainted by chauvinism. For the sagas to be accepted as history, there had to be proof.

The search for that proof began in earnest in 1837 when the Royal Danish Society of Antiquaries published the original saga texts. The book's editor, Carl Rafn, also included in the book the results of his correspondence with Americans about various ruined towers and inscribed stones found along the east coast of North America and reputed to be of Norse origin.

Alas, Rafn's enthusiasm overwhelmed his judgment. He included almost anything anyone claimed might be Norse, even though he himself had never even been to America, let alone examined the evidence. On closer examination most of these finds turned out to be crude hoaxes. In towns from Newfoundland to Florida, the claim that "Leif Ericsson was here" became as common and as improbable as the claim that "George Washington slept here."

Among the evidence discovered was the Newport Tower. In one sense the tower couldn't really be discovered: it stood about 25 feet high on top of a hill in Newport, Rhode Island, so you didn't need an archaeologist to find it. The tower certainly *looked* medieval; with thick floors and round arches, it would have seemed at home in eleventh-century France or Belgium—or Norway. The case for the tower's Norse origins was strengthened when its measurements turned out to be readily divisible by old Norse measures. But something just didn't make sense: if the tower dated back to medieval times, how could Rhode Island's first English settlers have failed to notice it when they arrived? Not one of their writings makes any mention of it. In fact the earliest mention of the tower is in the 1677 will of Benedict Arnold (not the traitor—this Benedict Arnold was the governor of Rhode Island). Arnold referred to it as "my stone built wind mill," and later investigations confirmed it was built, probably by Arnold, around 1675.

The next major find was the Kensington Stone, uncovered in the roots of a 500-year-old tree on Olof Ohman's farm in Minnesota. In an alphabet that was used in medieval Scandinavia, the stone told of "8 Swedes and 22 Norwegians on an exploration journey from Vinland westward." It was dated 1362.

But the word *opdagelsefard* (exploration journey) didn't occur in any Scandinavian language until hundreds of years after 1362. The stone had to be a forgery. As one Icelandic linguist put it: "If a telephone book for the year 1957 were to be found under the roots of a 500-year-old tree, one would admire the skill with which it had been placed there; but one should not find it necessary to accept the antiquity of the volume in question."

By this point most of Leif's boosters were despairing of ever proving their case. One archaeologist—granted, a *Norwegian* archaeologist—refused to give up. During the 1950s Helge Ingstad traveled thousands of miles up and down the North American coast in search of Vinland. If the sailing times recorded in the sagas were accurate, he reasoned, then the land Leif called Vinland ought to be northern Newfoundland. The sagas' descriptions of these lands also fit.

In 1960, close to the small village of L'Anse aux Meadows near Epaves Bay in northern Newfoundland, Ingstad noted some indistinct overgrown elevations in the ground. They appeared to be sites of houses—very old ones. Their shapes were similar to ancient Norse buildings uncovered in Iceland and Greenland. Could these houses have been built by Leif Ericsson and his crew? Ingstad began excavating.

Supposedly drawn 50 years before Columbus set sail, the Vinland Map (with Vinland in the upper left corner) would—if it's authentic—be proof that the Norse reached America first. (By permission of Yale University Press.)

In 1964 he found exactly what he'd hoped for. In the southernmost room of the largest house site, one of Ingstad's colleagues found a small ring of stone which was clearly a Norse spindle whorl. It was exactly the kind of spindle whorl that Norse women had used in Sweden, Norway, Iceland, and Greenland, and it was unlike anything the Indians and Eskimos of Newfoundland would have used. This was as dramatic a find as a Viking sword would have been; in fact it was even better since it proved that the sagas were right—not just about Norsemen reaching America, but about a settlement with Norsewomen (who would have been the ones to use the spindle whorl) and sheep (whose wool the women would have spun).

There was no question that Ingstad had found a pre-Columbian Norse settlement. But a big problem remained. This was the name Vinland, sometimes translated as Wineland. Leif had named the country after the wild grapes found there. Yet botanists assert that the northern limit for wild grapes along the east coast is somewhere in Massachusetts. Which means: *there are no wild grapes in Newfoundland.*

And one cannot simply ignore the name, since *The Greenlanders' Saga* describes in detail how it was given. Leif, the saga tells us, was very worried when one of his company, a German named Tyrkir, disappeared. When Tyrkir finally returned, the following exchange took place:

> "Why are you so late . . ." Leif asked him, "and parted this way from your companions?"
>
> By way of a start Tyrkir held forth a long while in German, rolling his eyes all ways, and pulling faces. They had no notion what he was talking about. Then after a while he spoke in Norse. "I went no great way further than you, yet I have a real novelty to report. I have found vines and grapes."
>
> "Is that the truth. . . ?" Leif asked.
>
> "Of course it's the truth," he replied. "I was born where wine and grapes are no rarity."

Given how sure Tyrkir was that Vinland was a land of wild grapes, how could it be in Newfoundland?

Historians have ventured a number of guesses.

Farley Mowat, a botanist and climatologist as well as a historian, suggested that even though grapes don't grow in Newfoundland today, they may have grown there between 1000 and 1200. We do know that the vineyards of western Europe at that time extended farther north than they do today.

Ingstad himself offered a number of explanations: that Vinland might be translated as Meadowland rather than Vineland or Wineland or Grapeland; that Tyrkir, for all his apparent certainty, may have mistaken wild berries for grapes; that the saga-writers, in an effort to make Vinland more appealing, may have exaggerated its fertility. (After all, Eric the Red had no qualms about giving Greenland its very misleading name.)

Most historians were convinced for one reason or another. And even if L'Anse aux Meadows isn't Vinland and is simply a different Norse settlement, it's still incontrovertible evidence that the Norse did discover and settle North America five hundred years before Columbus.

☆ To investigate further:

Jones, Gwyn. *The Norse Atlantic Saga.* New York: Oxford University Press, 1986. The most widely respected translation of the sagas, along with a history of the Norse voyages. The translation from *The Greenlanders' Saga* is Jones's.

Haugen, Einar. *Voyages to Vinland,* New York: Knopf, 1942. The history is dated, and the translations have been superseded in scholarly circles by Jones's, but Haugen's account and translations are still the most dramatic.

Holand, Hjalmar. *Explorations in America Before Columbus.* New York: Twayne Publishers, 1956. The case for the authenticity of the Newport Tower and the Kensington Stone; generally discredited but still fun.

Wahlgren, Erik. *The Kensington Stone.* Madison: University of Wisconsin, 1958. The case against the authenticity of the stone; definitive but dry.

Mowat, Farley. *Westviking.* Boston: Atlantic Monthly Press, 1965. A fascinating combination of climatology, anthropology, zoology, seamanship, and various other disciplines. Mowat claims he's located Vinland in Newfoundland, though not at L'Anse aux Meadows. He also argues—contrary to generally accepted opinion—that Columbus knew of and was influenced by the Norse discoveries.

Skelton, Raleigh, et al. *The Vinland Map and the Tartar Relation.* New Haven: Yale University Press, 1965. The book features a map from 1440 which included Vinland. If authentic, the map would be the only pre-Columbian document, besides the sagas, to include Vinland. But whether it's "the most exciting cartographic discovery of the century" or a twentieth-century fraud remains a source of heated scholarly debate.

Ingstad, Helge. *Land Under the Polar Star.* New York: St. Martin's Press, 1966. Ingstad's account of his expedition to Greenland, during which he came to the conclusion that he should search for Vinland in Newfoundland.

———. *Westward to Vinland.* New York: St. Martin's Press, 1969. Ingstad's account of his discoveries at L'Anse aux Meadows. Scholarly but exciting.

Pohl, Frederick. *The Viking Settlements of North America.* New York: Clarkson Potter, 1972. Uses the sailing directions and topographical descriptions in the saga to locate Vinland in New England, contrary to most current thinking.

Morison, Samuel. *The European Discovery of America.* New York: Oxford University Press, 1971. The section on the Norse voyages is a concise yet comprehensive history and historiography. While you're at it, read the rest of the book—there's no better historian of the sea than Morison.

Chapter 4

Why Did Cahokia Fall?

In 1811, Thomas Brackenridge visited St. Louis to look at some ancient mounds and ruins just east of the city.

"When I reached the foot of the principal mound," Brackenridge wrote to his friend Thomas Jefferson, "I was struck with a degree of astonishment, not unlike that which is experienced in contemplating the Egyptian pyramids. What a stupendous pile of earth!"

Earthen mounds of various shapes and sizes were scattered across the eastern half of the country, but these were exceptional. More than a hundred mounds could be found within just a few miles of St. Louis, along with other remains from what appeared to have once been a great city. The mound about which Brackenridge wrote to Jefferson covered fourteen acres and rose nearly one hundred feet, making it by far the largest man-made structure in the United States. It looked, as Brackenridge noted, like a pyramid, though with a flat top. This could have supported "a real palace," speculated George Rogers Clark, who had visited the site a few years before Brackenridge (and whose brother, William Clark, was better known for his expedition with Meriwether Lewis). Brackenridge speculated the mounds "were sites of great temples, or monuments to the great men."

Who built these mounds? And what happened to them?

No one even knew what to call the mounds. The largest was known as Monks Mound, for a monastery erected on top. But the monks arrived just before Brackenridge, and even if they hadn't taken a vow of silence, they couldn't have told him anything about the mound's origins.

As for the city, it was known as Cahokia, for a local tribe, but not one with a particularly long history or significant population in the area. By the time French explorers sailed down the Mississippi in the late 1600s, only a few Indians lived nearby. Whoever built Cahokia, it was clear, was gone long before these Indians, let alone any white men, reached the area.

A popular nineteenth-century theory was that the mounds were built by a prehistoric race that the Indians had somehow eradicated. "The magnitude of the works will ever remain a marvel," wrote Charles Joseph Latrobe in 1835. "They [the builders] were more civilized, more powerful, more enlightened than the Indian races of our day." Among the nominees were people from the lost continent of Atlantis and the lost tribes of Israel. A preacher named Joseph Smith even managed to create a new religion—Mormonism—based on the belief that a race of white Christians had built the mounds before being driven off, in A.D. 400, by the "red sons of Israel."

There was no archaeological evidence for any of this, of course, but such theories were a good way to justify America's westward expansion. After all, if the Indians had displaced some other civilization, they were no more entitled to the land than white settlers. Indeed, since the moundbuilders were presumed to be white, pushing the Indians onto reservations could be seen as restoring the land to its rightful owners.

Another early but less biased theory was that the moundbuilders came from, or migrated to, Mexico. The pyramids of Mexico looked a lot like these pyramidal mounds, and some scientists still postulate a connection. But the Toltecs and Mayans and Aztecs all built their pyramids of stone, and since there was plenty of limestone near Cahokia, no one could explain why, if these cultures were related, the moundbuilders in Cahokia had chosen instead to use dirt.

Some scientists concluded the mounds hadn't been built by people at all; they were, instead, natural phenomena, perhaps the remains of glaciers or floods. This theory was especially popular in the late nineteenth and early twentieth centuries, when developers found the mounds very inconvenient, except as landfill. Around Cahokia, for example, almost half of the mounds were destroyed, including "Big Mound," which stood until the 1860s in what is now downtown St. Louis.

What all these ideas conveniently ignored was the most logical explanation for the mounds: Native Americans built them. Jefferson himself came up with this answer, after excavating some mounds near

Monticello. He found three carefully laid out layers of skeletons, and concluded that the mounds, like the pyramids, were burial sites.

Over the next fifty years, more digs confirmed Jefferson was right. Even the destruction of the St. Louis Big Mound turned out to be helpful in this sense, since just before it was razed, archaeologists uncovered twenty to thirty bodies there. But the question remained: Where did the builders go?

That question became all the more intriguing as excavations turned up all sorts of evidence that the moundbuilders had built a lot more than mounds. The seashells covering the skeletons in Big Mound, for example, came from the Gulf Coast, indicating that Cahokia had traded with, perhaps ruled over, a vast realm. At other mounds, archaeologists found pieces of finely crafted ceramics, statues, and ornaments.

A 1961 dig by a team of archaeologists hinted that the Cahokians were not just rich and powerful, but scientifically sophisticated. Working just ahead of the bulldozers, which this time were there to make way for a new interstate highway, Warren Wittry noticed several bathtub-size oval pits in a circle near Monks Mound. Some contained remnants of cedar, leading Wittry to conclude wooden posts had once been set in the pits. He calculated that when the sun rose due east, it was, viewed from the circle, directly over Monks Mound. Wittry concluded the posts served as a sun calendar, much like Britain's Stonehenge. He named Cahokia's version Woodhenge.

Other archaeologists found other woodhenges around Cahokia, and came up with other explanations for them. Some suggested their function was architectural, others religious. In any case, the woodhenges were further evidence that Cahokia was once a major Native American center.

Melvin Fowler's 1973 dig into a comparatively small mound near Monks Mound added an unsettling element to our understanding of Cahokian power. Of the three hundred or so skeletons he found, four were headless and more than fifty were those of young women. It was unlikely so many young women would have died naturally at the same time, and the headless skeletons were even more telling. Fowler concluded the Cahokians believed in human sacrifice. Its chiefs, it seemed, held the power of life and death over their subjects.

The most powerful statement of Cahokian power remained, of course, the mounds themselves. Back in 1814, Brackenridge had commented to Jefferson that "to heap up such a mass must have required years and the labors of thousands," and the archaeologists who followed were no less impressed.

This photo was taken in 1907, more than 500 years after the moundbuilders abandoned Cahokia. (Library of Congress.)

Carbon dating allowed archaeologists to set Cahokia in its historical context. Moundbuilding began as early as 500 B.C., as prehistoric Indians established themselves across the eastern part of North America. Indian villages around Cahokia dated back to about A.D. 700, and Monks Mound was probably begun about 950. Work on Monks Mound continued for about two hundred years.

Cahokia's "golden age" came between 1050 and 1200. This was the period when the area was, as J. W. Porter wrote in 1969, a "prehistoric megalopolis." In 1975, Michael Gregg counted how many houses had been identified in sample sections of Cahokia, and extrapolated that the city's population at its peak must have been more than 25,000—more than London or Rome at the time. Others came up with estimates of up to 40,000.

By the late twentieth century, Cahokia's place in history was firmly established. No longer could serious scientists suggest that its mounds were natural phenomena, or that its builders were not Native Americans. The Cahokian empire was perhaps less famous than the Incan or Aztec, but historians and archaeologists considered it the North American equivalent. Yet this understanding of Cahokia's tremendous power made its fall all the more mystifying. Unlike the Incas or Aztecs, the Cahokians did not fall to Spanish conquistadors. The first Europeans to explore the Mississippi River were the French, and they sailed right by Cahokia, probably assuming that, since there were so few Indians around, the mounds must have been natural hills.

Archaeologists estimated that by 1200, the population of Cahokia was already starting to decline; by the mid-1300s the area was virtually abandoned.

What, they continued to wonder, had happened?

☆ ☆ ☆

There were plenty of theories.

Some scientists blamed a change in the climate. Temperatures in the Midwest became distinctly colder around 1250, and this may have shortened the growing season. Changing rain patterns could have exacerbated the problem. "The evil twins Flood and Drought alternated their devastating work," wrote William Iseminger, sounding more like a prophet of doom than the archaeologist hired by the state of Illinois to supervise the site.

Others argued the growth of Cahokia was itself responsible for a spate of environmental problems. The Cahokians cut down trees for farms and lumber, causing erosion and rapid runoffs that flooded the crops. Clearing the forests would also have driven away much of the wildlife, increasing their dependence on corn and causing protein deficiencies. Cahokians, William Woods said, committed "an unintended suicide."

Another theory was that war did in Cahokia. Archaeologists have not uncovered any evidence of widespread warfare in Cahokia, but they have turned up some skeletons found with arrowheads embedded in them. Fowler's sacrificial victims could also be interpreted as evidence of warfare. And the discovery of the remains of a massive wooden palisade, apparently built between 1200 and 1250, was the clearest indication that the Cahokians were worried about an attack.

The enemy could have come from within Cahokia, according to some archaeologists. The huge wealth and power of Cahokia's chiefs may have fundamentally changed the city's social structure. Thomas Emerson counted bowls and jars found in the area's largest buildings, and noted that, starting around 1100, there were fewer of the former and more of the latter. Emerson interpreted this to mean there were fewer communal feasts, perhaps a sign that Cahokia's leaders were increasingly aloof. Beheadings wouldn't have endeared them to their public either. Porter surmised a "peasant revolt."

These various theories, their proponents readily admitted, were not mutually exclusive. Warfare could have been accompanied by civil unrest. Environmental problems could have increased political tensions within Cahokia, or with other tribes. And war would surely have exacerbated environmental problems; the palisade, for example, required a lot of trees. But some combination of these elements was undoubtedly to blame.

☆ ☆ ☆

If Cahokia could fall so quickly, declining from its peak population to complete abandonment in not much more than a hundred years, maybe it wasn't so powerful after all.

During the last years of the twentieth century and the first ones of the twenty-first, Cahokia's place in history has again come into question. Though a majority of historians still see it as the most powerful civilization of prehistoric North America, many are increasingly skeptical.

"Much is made about very little," wrote George Milner in 1998. "Nothing found at or around Cahokia is out of line with . . . developments elsewhere, except for the number of mounds and the size of some of them, particularly Monks Mound."

Milner and others have argued that Cahokia was not nearly as large as conventional wisdom would have it. Gregg's population estimates, though arrived at honestly, could have been inflated by a dense population in the sample areas, or by counting the remains of houses from a range of periods. In 1997, Timothy Pauketat estimated a peak population of 15,000; a year later, Milner suggested it was in the low thousands.

As for the sophisticated knowledge required to build the wood-henges or mounds, Milner was equally dismissive. "Despite claims to the contrary," he wrote, "the people directing the moundbuilding did not have to be especially knowledgeable to make great piles of dirt."

Are Milner and Pauketat a throwback to the nineteenth- and early twentieth-century scientists who couldn't believe Native Americans built anything of import?

Hardly.

Neither they nor any archaeologist today would advocate razing the mounds, nor would they denigrate the value of Native American history and culture. What they are saying is that Cahokia was just one of many moundbuilding societies that rose and fell prior to the Europeans' arrival. Cahokia was the largest, maybe the most powerful, but in many ways more like these others than what Milner referred to, somewhat derisively, as "the mighty Cahokia scenario."

Many who would defend that scenario would agree that an exclusive focus on Cahokia's fall has tended to diminish our appreciation of the various ways Native Americans adapted to their changing environment. That goes not only for the other moundbuilders, but also for Cahokia's descendants. For whatever happened to the city, its people did not vanish. Archaeologists believe some moved north, where they cultivated new strains of corn that grew better there. Others probably noticed the growing population of buffaloes to the west, and followed them there.

Cahokia's descendants were undoubtedly among the Indians whites encountered as they settled the West. Like these whites, many Cahokians were pioneers who left the city behind to find a new way of life.

☆ To investigate further:

Emerson, Thomas, and R. Barry Lewis, editors. *Cahokia and the Hinterlands.* Urbana: University of Illinois Press, 1991. Seventeen essays by (and for) specialists on Cahokia and its relationship to neighboring cultures.

Kennedy, Roger. *Hidden Cities.* New York: The Free Press, 1994. How America's founding fathers interpreted the mounds and tried to fit them into their views of the Indians. The portrait of Jefferson is fascinating and complex; not only did he correspond with Brackenridge, but he also excavated a burial mound on his estate and recognized its Indian origins.

Emerson, Thomas. *Cahokia and the Archaeology of Power.* Tuscaloosa: The University of Alabama Press, 1997. Emerson uses Cahokia's "architecture and artifacts of power"—material remains from the mounds to figurines—to trace the increasing power of its chiefs.

Milner, George. *The Cahokia Chiefdom.* Washington, D.C.: Smithsonian Institution Press, 1998. Milner's provocative thesis: "The presence of mounds and fancy artifacts, even lots of them, does not require a society as populous, organizationally complex, or powerful as conventional wisdom would have us believe." His writing, though technical, is more readable than that of most archaeologists.

Young, Biloine Whiting, and Melvin Fowler. *Cahokia.* Urbana: University of Illinois Press, 2000. An entertaining history of Cahokia's archaeology, full of politics and personalities as well as science.

Chappell, Sally A. Kitt, with William Iseminger and John Kelly. *Cahokia.* Chicago: The University of Chicago Press, 2002. Despite its New Age flavor, this is a comprehensive, readable, and beautifully illustrated overview.

Chapter 5

Why Did the Anasazi Abandon Their Cities?

The first white men to explore Chaco Canyon, in northwestern New Mexico, arrived in 1849, led by Army Lieutenant James Simpson. What Simpson found there convinced him that the Aztec empire of Mexico must once have extended this far north. Only such an advanced civilization, he concluded, could have constructed the massive and beautiful buildings whose ruins he now surveyed. The largest of them—Pueblo Bonito—stood five stories tall and had several hundred rooms. It was larger than any apartment building in North America (and it remained so until 1882, when it was surpassed by one in New York City).

Simpson was wrong: in the twentieth century, archaeologists dated the Chaco Canyon buildings to the end of the tenth century, well before the rise of the Aztecs. From numerous other sites in the area, archaeologists were able to chronicle the rise of the civilization that culminated in these buildings. This was, they determined, a homegrown civilization, one which had been built by a people called the Anasazi by the Indians Simpson encountered.

But who could blame Simpson for looking outside of Chaco Canyon for its architects? The ruins at Chaco Canyon bore little resemblance to the buildings of the Hopi or Zuni or any other Indians then living in the area. At least Simpson, in attributing the Chaco Canyon buildings to the Aztecs, was willing to give the credit to Native

Americans, albeit the wrong ones; others would later argue that the buildings must have been a Roman outpost.

In the eleventh century all roads did not lead to Rome; many led—quite literally—to Chaco Canyon. Straight, broad avenues connected Pueblo Bonito to nine "Great Houses" and to some 75 other settlements in and around Chaco Canyon. Archaeologists have mapped more than four hundred miles of roads, many of them 30 feet wide, radiating out from the canyon center. The Anasazi must have used these roads to carry the timber that made up the vast roofs and support systems of their buildings. Judging from the tremendous quantities of turquoise found in the area, the roads were also used to transport the gems from distant mines to Chaco Canyon. After being made into small tiles, the turquoise was then sent as far away as California and Mexico.

The Anasazi were remarkably wealthy: along with exotic gems, archaeologists have found huge quantities of discarded pots—at one Chaco building, a single trash heap contained 150,000 broken pots. This must also have been a remarkably egalitarian society, for there were no palaces or special buildings mixed in among the huge apartment buildings. Supporting all this was a sophisticated irrigation system that used dams and dikes, contoured terraces, and reservoirs to make the most of the sandy soil and limited rainfall.

About one hundred years after they built the Great Houses of Chaco Canyon, the Anasazi moved north into southwest Colorado, creating an architecture that was, if possible, even more stunning. Here they built their homes right inside the caves that sculpt the steep cliffs of the area's canyons. Protected by the caves, many of these cliff dwellings (including the huge Cliff Palace at Mesa Verde) are still largely intact.

But the civilization that built these houses was not nearly so durable. By 1200 Chaco Canyon's houses were empty; by 1300 Mesa Verde's cliff dwellings were, too. Why did the Anasazi abandon their great cities, in many cases only a hundred or so years after they built them? And where did they go? This is a mystery that has intrigued historians—not to mention archaeologists, anthropologists, demographers, biologists, and visitors to the American Southwest—ever since James Simpson and his men first stumbled upon Chaco Canyon.

☆ ☆ ☆

To the historian and archaeologist Harold Gladwin, writing in 1957, the solution was obvious: the Anasazi were under attack. This would

Built 900 years ago, the Cliff Palace in Mesa Verde, Colorado, has proven a lot more durable than the civilization that built it. (By permission of the Arizona State Museum.)

explain why people who had been widely scattered came together in the huge apartment buildings of Chaco Canyon. The large pueblos offered more protection than smaller, scattered villages—hence the building spree in Chaco Canyon at the end of the tenth century. It would also explain why they had abandoned the Chaco Canyon buildings so soon after they'd built them. When the Chaco Canyon towns failed to hold off their attackers, the Anasazi retreated to the cliff dwellings of Mesa Verde, built during the eleventh and twelfth centuries. The cliff dwellings were, to put it mildly, inconvenient—but at least that made them inaccessible to enemies as well.

So, protected by deep canyons and sheer escarpments and warned of the dangers by refugees from Chaco Canyon, the Anasazi held out for another hundred years. But eventually their attackers wore them down, and by the end of the thirteenth century the cliff dwellings of Mesa Verde had gone the way of the pueblos of Chaco Canyon.

Who were the people who drove away the Anasazi? Gladwin believed they were the people who later became known as the Navajo and Apache. Sweeping down from western Canada, they were the last people to reach the Southwest before the Spanish invasion. Navajo tradition seems to confirm this theory: the word "Anasazi" comes from the Navajo word for "ancient enemies." Other historians have proposed it was the Southern Paiute or Ute, not the Navajo or Apache. (Ute legends, too, tell how they conquered people as they moved south.) Whoever their enemies were, the Anasazi outnumbered them, but the raiders' hit-and-run attacks against their settlements and fields eventually took their toll.

But there was one major problem with these "military" solutions to the mystery: there is no archaeological evidence that the Apache or Navajo or Ute or Paiute entered the area until long after the pueblos and cliff dwellings had been abandoned. Granted, the Apache and Navajo were traditional enemies of the Pueblo people of the Southwest, but some historians argued that this tradition originated in the seventeenth century after the Indians acquired horses from Europeans (giving them a tremendous tactical advantage). Finally, if the Anasazi went down in battle, why didn't archaeologists find any mass graves or other signs of war? Anyone looking at the ruins of Pueblo Bonito or Cliff House today can see they were deserted—not burned or sacked.

☆ ☆ ☆

And so we turn to an alternative solution to the mystery of the Anasazi: the great drought.

This theory depends on advances in the science of dendrochronology, which uses the growth rings of trees to supply precise information about past climates. Each year a tree produces a growth ring; the wider the ring, the more rain there was that year. It was A. E. Douglass, on a National Geographic expedition to the Southwest in 1929, who developed new techniques of tree-ring dating, then charted the tree rings in living trees and overlapped and matched them with those found in wooden beams from increasingly older archaeological sites. Douglass found there was a severe drought in the area between 1276 and 1299—exactly the time the Anasazi cities were finally and fully abandoned.

But Gladwin's followers struck back: there had been previous droughts in the area, they pointed out, and the cities hadn't been abandoned. And there were nearby areas with more rainfall—but there was no evidence that the Anasazi had moved there.

So the environmental explanations became more complex, taking into account not just rainfall amounts but the times of the year the rain fell, water table levels, land-clearing practices, the changing mix of subsistence strategies.

Other explanations emerged as well.

Could there have been a massive epidemic? Unlikely: there was no sign of large burial areas.

Could there have been a disruption of the turquoise trade? Perhaps Lieutenant Simpson wasn't so wrong after all; if the Anasazi were dependent, not on the Aztecs, but on some earlier Mexican civilization, then might not the Anasazi demise be tied to problems down south? Also unlikely. Most archaeologists are skeptical of this explanation for the same reason they originally rejected Simpson's theory: the only pre-Aztec Mexican civilization that might have extended so far north was that of Teotihuacán, and that had declined long before the rise of the Anasazi. Although there was trade between the Anasazi and Mexico, there is no evidence that the Anasazi civilization depended on it.

Could there have been a civil war among the Anasazi? Perhaps. But there were still no signs of massive burials or sacked cities. And why wouldn't the victors have stayed on?

Could there have been some sort of religious upheaval? Some archaeologists have argued that the Anasazi may have been drawn south by the emerging Kachina religion. But others question whether the archaeological record of Kachina icons and artifacts puts the religion in the area early enough to have attracted the Anasazi. Besides, why would the religion have required the Anasazi to leave their cities?

And so the debate goes on.

☆ ☆ ☆

There are some signs, though, that it may someday be resolved. Most of the archaeologists, anthropologists, and historians working on the mystery today agree that there will never be a single solution, whether military, environmental, or social. Rather, they believe a variety of factors came into play. Perhaps, for example, drought or crop failures set off internal fighting, or undermined people's religious faith. Perhaps a combination of many factors chipped away at a complex system until it could barely maintain itself, and then some final force—a massive drought, an outside attack—was just the last straw.

Almost all scholars agree on one point: the Anasazi did not simply vanish into the sands. Whatever the reason for abandoning their cities, the Anasazi went somewhere. Some probably settled along the Rio Grande, some at the foot of Black Mesa. Some may even have stayed on in Mesa Verde or Chaco Canyon, but in a less structured society that built nothing new to reveal its presence to archaeologists. After all, before Chaco Canyon and Mesa Verde were built, the Anasazi had survived for hundreds of years in smaller, more nomadic groups. That type of life may have seemed as natural and appealing to them as their more complex, urban society seems to us.

Part of the problem, historian Kendrick Frazier points out, is the use of the term "Anasazi." It sounds like a particular tribe of Indians, just like the Navajo or Hopi, and since there are no Anasazi today we think of its people as having disappeared. But they didn't disappear. The Anasazi merged with the tribes who became the modern Pueblo Indians and—though the passage of eight hundred years may make it difficult for us to recognize them—the descendants of the Anasazi are living today in Arizona and New Mexico. To think otherwise is to repeat the mistake James Simpson made almost one hundred and fifty years ago.

☆ To investigate further:

Douglass, A. E. "The Secret of the Southwest Solved by the Talkative Tree Rings," *National Geographic,* December 1929. How Douglass advanced the science of dendrochronology and discovered the great drought.

Gladwin, Harold. *A History of the Ancient Southwest.* Portland, ME: Bond Wheelwright Co., 1950. One of the first comprehensive histories, and still the most dramatic, to make the case that the Anasazi were attacked by outside tribes.

Colton, Harold. *Black Sand.* Albuquerque: University of New Mexico Press, 1962. The case for an epidemic.

Pike, Donald and David Muench, *Anasazi.* New York: Crown, 1974. Striking photos of Anasazi ruins.

Euler, R. C., T. N. V. Karlstrom, J. S. Dean, R. C. Hevley, "The Colorado Plateaus: Cultural Dynamics and Paleoenvironment." *Science*, September 1979. A multidisciplinary approach arguing that though the causal relationships were not as direct as previously supposed, environmental factors led to the abandonments. Technical but compelling.

Cordell, Linda S. *Prehistory of the Southwest*. San Diego: Academic Press, 1984. An anthropology textbook with a useful synthesis of research.

Frazier, Kendrick. *People of Chaco*. New York: Norton, 1986. A history of Chaco archaeology that succeeds in capturing the mystique as well as the mystery of the Anasazi.

Ambler, J. Richard and Mark Sutton, "The Anasazi Abandonment of the San Juan Drainage and the Numic Expansion." *North American Archaeologist* 10, no. 1 (1989). One of the most recent revivals of the case that outside attackers (in this case the southern Ute and Paiute) drove away the Anasazi.

Rafferty, Kevin. "The Anasazi Abandonment and the Numic Expansion." *North American Archaeologist* 10, no. 4 (1989). The author makes the case that the disruption of ties with the Toltec empire in Mexico precipitated the Anasazi collapse.

Gumerman, George, ed. *Themes in Southwest Prehistory*. Santa Fe: School of American Research Press, 1994. A multidisciplinary collection including a provocative essay on the need to focus on "push" as well as "pull" factors, i.e., what drew the Anasazi to new locations as well as what drove them away from old ones.

Chapter 6

Where Did Columbus Land?

Leif Ericsson beat him here and perhaps others did as well. But it was Christopher Columbus's discovery of America that mattered most; once Columbus set foot on American soil, the New World and the Old were forever linked. Columbus's landfall was arguably the most momentous occasion in western history. Yet more than five hundred years later, historians are still arguing about where it took place.

☆ ☆ ☆

To most historians the solution to the mystery was to be found in the *Diario*, a summary of Columbus's own shipboard log of the journey. Unfortunately, the original version of the *Diario* has been lost; when Columbus returned to Spain, he presented it to Queen Isabella, and it hasn't been seen since. Fortunately, two copies of the log were made. One ended up in the hands of a Dominican friar named Bartolomé de Las Casas, who included it in his *Historia de las indias;* that same copy (or the other one) was also at some point in the hands of Columbus's son Fernando, who used it as a source for his biography of his father.

With the *Diario* in hand, historians have attempted three ways of solving what's become known as the "landfall problem." First, they've tried to track Columbus's westbound journey, starting from the Canary Islands, off the coast of Africa, and following the log's directions

Columbus's first encounters with Native Americans most certainly did not include naval battles or cannibal barbecues (as portrayed in this 1621 illustration by the Venetian artist Honorario Philopono). (By permission of the Houghton Library, Harvard University.)

to see where he ended up. Second, they've tried going backward, taking as their starting point the north coast of Cuba (which is the first place Columbus visited whose identity is certain) and reconstructing his track between there and his first landing. And third, they've tried to match the log's descriptions of the islands Columbus visited with the current topography of the various possible landing places.

Using all three methods, historians have come up with about a dozen serious candidates for the honor of being the site of the first landfall. Foremost among them is San Salvador, a small island in the northern Bahamas. San Salvador was first cited as the landfall by the Spanish historian Juan Bautista Muñoz in 1793. And San Salvador was also the name Columbus gave to the island of his landfall—but that's irrelevant to the case for this particular island because it was known as Watlings Island until 1926. At that time the island's British colonial government, trying to preempt other claimants, gave it the name San Salvador.

What mattered much more than the local government's endorsement was that of Samuel Eliot Morison in 1942. That was the year Morison published what is still considered the standard biography of Columbus. In it he stated in no uncertain terms that only San Salvador/Watlings fit Columbus's course and description as set down in the log. Morison's prestige as both historian and navigator—he was a rear admiral in the navy and he scoffed at "dryadusts" who studied Columbus's voyages from their armchairs—all but ended the discussion for 40 years.

Gradually, however, other claimants chipped away at Morison's and San Salvador's position. In 1986 *National Geographic*, after spending one million dollars on a new study, lent its considerable prestige to the case for Samana Cay, a Bahamian island about 65 miles southeast of San Salvador. Samana Cay, too, had had many previous advocates, among them Gustavus Fox, who had been Lincoln's assistant secretary of the navy. (Morison and Fox were just two of the many admirals to be found on Columbus's track.) The *Geographic* study argued that Morison had failed to take into account the effects of currents and leeway (a ship's slow skid downwind), and it enlisted the aid of a computer to resail the routes electronically.

In 1991 other researchers, arguing that neither Morison nor the *Geographic* study had taken into account the effects of magnetic variation (don't ask!), located the first landfall farther southeast, on the island of Grand Turk. Grand Turk, too, had had many early advocates, the first being Martin Fernández de Navarette in 1825.

As the landfall's quincentennial approached, the debate intensified, with proponents of one island or another seizing upon different passages in the *Diario* to demonstrate why no other island besides their choice fit the bill. San Salvador, which remained the orthodox position, came under the most attack, but strong cases were made for and against all the leading candidates. The only thing everyone agreed on was that Columbus's landfall took place somewhere in the Bahamas.

Why couldn't all these sophisticated historians and mariners come to some sort of consensus? What was so difficult about comparing Columbus's words with the locations and characteristics of Bahamian islands?

For one thing, it's not so clear what Columbus's words were. Only 20 percent of the *Diario* is in his words; the rest consists of summaries and paraphrases by Las Casas. We can't even be sure that what Las Casas used hadn't been altered before it got to him.

Furthermore, even when you take the words that we're fairly sure are Columbus's own, you run into problems. To take just one example, the *Diario* says the landfall island has *una laguna en medio muy grande*—a very large lagoon in the center. Advocates of Watlings have been especially vehement in pointing out that only Watlings, of all the leading candidates, has a large body of water in the middle of the island. Advocates of Grand Turk and Samana Cay have argued that their islands may have dried up in the past five hundred years, that groundwater is seasonal in the Bahamas, and that we can't know for sure how much water there was on any given island then. But undeniably these are efforts to make the best of a description that favors Watlings.

What neither supporters nor detractors of Watlings take into account is that we have no idea what Columbus meant by a "large lagoon." Large compared to what? Landfall advocates compare the size of their various islands' waters but Columbus couldn't compare them; this was the first New World island he'd seen. What's more, the rest of the phrase—*en medio,* or in the middle—has been taken to mean in the middle of the island as it would be viewed from above, that is, a lake in the middle of the island. But what if you take "in the middle" to mean halfway up the shoreline? Then "laguna" might not mean lake, but "lagoon," as we use the word today. Suddenly Watlings, which has a lake but no lagoon, has lost its most compelling piece of evidence.

The point here is not to make a case *against* Watlings, or *for* any other island. Rather, it is to show, as the historian David Henige did most thoroughly in his 1991 book, that all these cases are based on a primary source that may be unreliable and is certainly vague. One revisionist historian has even speculated that Columbus was intentionally vague. Kirkpatrick Sale, a writer who admittedly doesn't like Columbus (he blames him for just about every instance of exploitation of land and people that has taken place in America since 1492), suggests that Columbus's descriptions were vague because he wanted to keep the location secret. If gold and glory were to be found on the landfall island or any other, Columbus wanted it for himself. As evidence, Sale points to a September 1493 letter from Ferdinand and Isabella to Columbus, in which the sovereigns demand more details about "the degrees within which the islands and land you discovered fall and the degrees of the path you traveled." There's no record of Columbus ever answering that letter.

But one needn't attribute Columbus's vagueness to greed to admit the *Diario* isn't as useful a source as we'd like it to be. Perhaps it was that Columbus was (understandably) preoccupied. Perhaps he just didn't care about this island; had he returned to it during any of his three subsequent voyages to the New World, this mystery might be easily solved. Alas, the first time Columbus stepped on the landfall island was also the last time he did so.

So, we can't help asking: if this island didn't matter to Columbus, why should it matter to us?

One answer is that it shouldn't. Neither our understanding of American or European history, nor our understanding of Columbus's character, have changed the slightest bit as the result of conclusions on behalf of one island or the other. Except for a minor blip in a few islands' tourist trade, not much is at stake.

Many historians have, therefore, put the landfall question behind them, moving on to other questions. Perhaps the most hotly contested issue in recent Columbus scholarship has been not where the landfall island is, but where Columbus *thought* it was. Morison maintained that Columbus died believing that he'd found a new route to the Far East, and that the islands he visited were somewhere off the coast of Asia. This remains the majority view. Nonetheless, an increasing number of historians have been convinced that Columbus knew that he'd discovered a truly New World, and some have even argued that this was always his goal.

And yet, even as other questions about Columbus have taken precedence, the landfall mystery has continued to intrigue historians, mariners, and others. With its tantalizing mixture of just enough evidence to get us close but not quite enough to get us there, it has again and again proved an irresistible challenge. Columbus's San Salvador, the natives' Guanahani: this was, after all, the place where two worlds first collided.

☆ To investigate further:

Fuson, Robert. *The Log of Christopher Columbus*. Rockport, ME: International Marine Publishing Co., 1987. Like most translations of the log, this one has an agenda: it was prepared in conjunction with the *National Geographic* case for Samana Cay. Still, it's a lively version.

Morison, Samuel Eliot. *Admiral of the Ocean Sea.* New York: Little, Brown, 1942. Still the definitive biography, with the case for Watlings/San Salvador.

De Vorsey, Louis, Jr. and John Parker, editors. *In The Wake of Columbus.* Detroit: Wayne State University Press, 1985. A wide-ranging collection of scholarly essays, with a concise historiography by Parker.

Judge, Joseph and James Stanfield. "The Island Landfall." *National Geographic,* November 1986. The case for Samana Cay.

Marvel, Josiah and Robert Power. "In Quest of Where America Began." *American History Illustrated,* Jan/Feb 1991. The case for Grand Turk.

Sale, Kirkpatrick. *The Conquest of Paradise.* New York: Knopf, 1990. Even if you don't buy Sale's argument that Columbus embodies everything wrong with America, from enslaving blacks and Indians to destroying the environment, you'll still find him lively and provocative.

Henige, David. *In Search of Columbus.* Tucson: The University of Arizona Press, 1991. A critique of the flaws of the *Diario* as a primary source, and of the way it's been misinterpreted and manipulated.

Wilford, John Noble. *The Mysterious History of Columbus.* New York: Knopf, 1991. A readable review of the ways historians from Columbus's time on have mythologized, debunked, and otherwise interpreted the man and his journeys.

Chapter 7

How Did Cortés Conquer the Aztecs?

ernán Cortés and his band of four hundred or so Spanish adventurers first sighted Tenochtitlán, the capital of the Aztec empire, in November 1519. With its busy canals, bustling markets, and beautiful buildings, Tenochtitlán might have reminded some of the Spaniards of Venice. For most of them, though, this was a far larger city than any they'd seen; Tenochtitlán's population of about 250,000 was larger than that of any city in Europe. The city was built on an island in the middle of a large lake near present-day Mexico City. Broad causeways stretched many miles across the lake, connecting the island to the mainland and to an Aztec empire that ruled over nearly four hundred cities and more than 125,000 square miles.

Two years after the Spaniards first set foot in Mexico, Tenochtitlán was in ruins and the remains of the empire were presided over by Cortés. How Cortés defeated the Aztecs is one of the greatest mysteries of history. For unlike the other Native American groups encountered by Europeans, the Aztecs were a highly organized, highly militarized people. Montezuma II, the Aztec emperor, commanded an army of more than 200,000 warriors, many seasoned in the far-reaching campaigns that had gained the Aztecs their empire. How was it possible for a few hundred Spaniards—acting on their own, with no support or supplies from the Crown, and operating in territory that no European had even seen before—to conquer the Aztec empire?

Most of our knowledge of the conquest comes to us from the conquistadores themselves. Cortés described the events in a series of letters to the Spanish king, Charles I. So did a number of others, most notably the foot soldier Bernal Díaz del Castillo, who participated in the conquest and wrote his recollections twenty years later, and Francisco López de Gómara, who wasn't a witness to the events but who later became private secretary and chaplain to Cortés.

Cortés set off for Mexico in March 1519 under the auspices of the Spanish governor of Cuba, Diego Velázquez. Velázquez ordered him to explore the Mexican coast and trade with any Indians he found there. Cortés, however, had bigger things in mind. Upon reaching Mexico's east coast, he announced (through an interpreter he'd picked up along the way) that he'd been sent by Charles I of Spain, the greatest king on earth, to speak to their leader. This was Montezuma, he learned. Cortés added that he'd also like some gold because, "I and my companions suffer from a disease of the heart which can be cured only with gold." Montezuma's messengers carried this message to Tenochtitlán and then returned with lavish gifts—including gold. But the emperor regretted he would not be able to meet with Cortés, they said.

If Montezuma thought gold would get rid of Cortés, he was tragically mistaken. The gold only whetted Cortés's appetite. He and his motley crew set off for Tenochtitlán, discovering to their delight that many of the cities en route deeply resented the tribute they were forced to pay the Aztecs. Far from resisting the Spanish advance, these people were happy to join forces with Cortés. Most significant of these allies were the Tlaxcalans, fierce enemies of the Aztecs whom the latter had never subdued.

And so it was that on November 8, 1519, Cortés, now accompanied by about five thousand Indian allies, reached the causeway leading to Tenochtitlán. Again, Montezuma chose a policy of appeasement; he welcomed Cortés and his army into his city, put them up in a luxurious palace, and served them sumptuous feasts. Still, after a few days, Cortés became uneasy. Though Montezuma continued to play the generous host, Cortés could sense the growing hostility of

A map of Tenochtitlán and the Gulf of Mexico, made for Cortés in 1524. Although the European-style houses are certainly not authentic, the map does show Aztec temples, causeways across Lake Texococo, and other features of the city prior to its conquest. (Courtesy of the British Museum.)

other Aztecs. Whatever its emperor's policies, this was, after all, a nation of warriors.

Cortés then came up with one of the most audacious plans in the history of war: he would take the emperor hostage in his own city. In the midst of one of the emperor's social calls, Cortés and his men did just that. For the next six months, with Montezuma as their prisoner, the Spaniards had the run of the city. But trouble was brewing on two fronts. The more hawkish Aztecs, uniting under the emperor's brother Cuitláhuac, seemed increasingly willing to attack the Spaniards, even if it meant risking Montezuma's life. Then, to make matters worse, a Spanish fleet sent by the Cuban governor Velázquez arrived on the Mexican coast. Velázquez was not at all happy that Cortés had turned his little trading mission into a major expedition; if there were riches to be had in Mexico, the governor felt, they were for *him* to discover, not Cortés.

So Cortés headed back to the coast, taking about 120 soldiers with him. He left just a hundred or so at Tenochtitlán under the command of Pedro de Alvarado. Once he reached the coast, Cortés put to work the same admirable powers of persuasion that had won over so many Indians. And again he succeeded: after some minor skirmishes with Velázquez's soldiers, Cortés convinced most of them to join him. So he headed back to Tenochtitlán with his new recruits.

Alas, in leaving Alvarado in charge in Tenochtitlán, Cortés had erred as greatly as Velázquez had when he chose Cortés. Alvarado had none of Cortés's subtlety, and in the midst of an Aztec religious festival he'd attacked and massacred the celebrants. The Aztecs, led by Cuitláhuac, counterattacked, and full-scale fighting had broken out. When Cortés reached Tenochtitlán, he discovered that his carefully cultivated Indian allies had fled, leaving the Spaniards trapped in the palace. Again, Cortés tried to use Montezuma to quell the Aztecs: he sent the emperor up to the palace roof to speak on behalf of the Spaniards. But by now the Aztecs would have none of this, and Montezuma was killed by stones thrown by his own people.

Cortés then decided his best chance was to sneak out at night and, on June 30, 1520, the Spaniards stuffed their pockets with Aztec treasure and headed for the causeways. But the Aztecs discovered them and attacked, killing more than half of the Spaniards. Many drowned in the waters around Tenochtitlán, weighed down by the gold in their pockets. "Those who died," Gómara wrote, "died rich."

Cortés regrouped at Tlaxcala, with his most loyal allies. He set to work building boats, which would cut off all access to Tenochtitlán. In late April 1521, the Spaniards set siege to the city, then began a bloody, house-by-house advance. Three months later, they again ruled Tenochtitlán—or what remained of the once great capital.

☆ ☆ ☆

This was the Spanish version of the conquest. The Spanish won because they were braver, more tenacious, more resourceful and, when necessary, ruthless in the service of their king and God; the Aztecs, and Montezuma in particular, were indecisive and cowardly. Still, a mystery remained. Why would Montezuma, whose past included many battlefield victories, suddenly lose all heart when faced by the Spaniards? Cortés's letters to the king of Spain contain his answer. When Montezuma first welcomed the Spaniards into Tenochtitlán, the emperor spoke to Cortés, and Cortés's letter quotes him as follows:

> For a long time we have known from the writings of our ancestors that neither I, nor any of those who dwell in this land, are natives of it, but foreigners who come from very distant parts; and likewise we know that a chieftain, of whom they were all vassals, brought our people to this region. And he returned to his native land . . . and we have always held that those who descended from him would come and conquer this land and take us as their vassals. So, because of the place from which you claim to come, namely, from where the sun rises, and the things you tell us of the great lord or king who sent you here, we believe and are certain that he is our natural lord. . . . So be assured that we shall obey you and hold you as our lord in place of that great sovereign of whom you speak.

Montezuma, Cortés explained, had first mistaken Cortés for the Aztec god, Quetzalcoatl, who, according to Aztec legend, would someday return to rule his people. Later, as in the above speech, Montezuma realized Cortés was not a god but still thought he was the god's emissary. Either way, Montezuma's superstitious nature prevailed over his military judgment, and Cortés took full advantage of it.

It was not just the conquistadores themselves who explained the conquest thus. Most historians followed suit, admiring Cortés for his courage and strategy, and ridiculing Montezuma's superstition-induced paralysis. Even those historians who have denounced Cortés as a greedy imperialist, the destroyer of Indian culture, could only pity Montezuma.

And yet, to many historians today, the above portraits of Cortés and Montezuma don't ring true. Cortés's letters to King Charles I ought not to be considered an accurate historical narrative, they argue. Rather, Cortés had a very specific purpose in mind: to convince Charles that Cortés, and not Velázquez, ought to be granted the right to explore (and conquer) Mexico. To make his case, Cortés was capable of grossly distorting history: for example, according to some historians, the speech about Quetzalcoatl that Cortés put into Montezuma's mouth is entirely apocryphal. Quetzalcoatl was indeed an Aztec god, but he was worshipped in Cholula, not Tenochtitlán. Cortés may have heard the legend on his way to Tenochtitlán and used it in his letter to show Charles how well he—as opposed to Velázquez—had mastered and manipulated the Aztecs on the king's behalf.

Alternative explanations for Montezuma's behavior have come from recent studies of the Indian accounts of the conquest. To be sure, these accounts are also problematic; they're fragmentary and, since the Aztec language was not a written one, they've come down to us in versions recorded by Spaniards soon after the conquest. Still, the Aztecs' own accounts, along with other studies of Aztec culture, do present another side of the story. The Montezuma who emerges from these studies is reluctant to fight, but not because he's superstitious or cowardly. This Montezuma shies away from battle with the Spaniards for many reasons: he's not sure whether to trust the Spaniards' talk of peaceful intentions, but he's very aware that they've arrived toward the end of the harvest season, and that many of his warriors are busy in the fields. At the very least, he may have been biding his time, hoping his emissaries could break up the alliances between the Spaniards and other Indian groups.

Historians have spent a great deal of energy debating what was going on in Montezuma's head. At this point we must admit that we can't know for sure why he let the Spaniards enter Tenochtitlán. In one sense, however, this debate is irrelevant to explaining the conquest: whatever Montezuma's motives, whatever the efficacy of his appeasement strategy, a better understanding of these issues could only help explain the *first* phase of the conquest—up until the death of Montezuma. After Montezuma's death, the Aztecs were ruled by the openly anti-Spanish Cuitláhuac. There was no longer any question that this was war, and that the Aztec empire was at stake. Yet even at this point, with the massive Aztec forces mobilized by a brave and competent chieftain, it took the Spaniards only a bit more than a year to regroup and return to besiege and overrun Tenochtitlán. To explain this second phase of the conquest, historians have had to shift their focus away from the debate about the relative merits of Cortés and Montezuma to other factors.

One obvious factor was the superiority of Spanish weapons. Against the Aztec arrows, the Spanish had cannons; while the Aztecs were on foot, the Spanish had horses. Yet the importance of this factor is easily overstated. The Aztecs were quick to figure out how to neutralize Spanish war technology. They would fall back to positions such as towns or ravines where the Spanish horses couldn't maneuver. And cannons were not so powerful an advantage as they might sound—the Spaniards only had a few of them and their supply of gunpowder was limited and at times too wet to be of much use. Besides, a few horses and cannons couldn't make up for the vast numerical advantage the Aztecs held.

Another factor was disease. A member of the crew sent by Velázquez had smallpox, and the disease swept across Mexico, whose people had never been exposed to the disease and who therefore had no resistance to it. By 1558, the population of Mexico had been reduced from a preconquest figure of about ten million* to a mere two or three million, and disease was undeniably a major factor in this. But smallpox struck down as many of Cortés's Indian allies as it did Aztecs, and it did not spread fast enough to account for the conquest on its own.

Yet another factor was the Aztec tradition of trying to capture, rather than kill, their enemies on the battlefield. This was hardly a compassionate tradition—many of those captured were later sacrificed to the gods and *eaten* by their captors, a practice that struck terror into the hearts of the most courageous Spaniards. But it did mean that in their efforts to capture rather than kill their enemies, the Aztecs often let them get away. And given the limited number of Spaniards, this undeniably aided Cortés's campaign.

All these factors played a role in the conquest. So, too, did Cortés's courage and strategy. Without a doubt, however, Cortés's greatest contribution to the Spaniards' success was his ability to enlist the support of Indian allies. More than anything else, this evened out the numbers on the opposing sides. Cortés admitted this; so did the Indian accounts of the conquest. Reliable numbers are hard to come by, but the Tlaxcalans alone added thousands of warriors to the Spanish ranks.

The empire that the Spaniards conquered was indeed a huge and powerful one. The Aztecs received tribute from far-flung cities and, in the absence of a major competing power, there was little these cities could do about it. But they deeply resented the Aztecs, and when the Spaniards arrived on the scene they offered a rallying point around

---

*The preconquest population of Mexico is itself a major source of debate. Estimates range from thirty million to four million, with those denouncing the conquest as immoral tending to favor the higher numbers (to make the Spaniards look guiltier) and those defending the conquest and the Spaniards coming up with lower numbers. Whatever the preconquest numbers, however, it is clear that by the late 1540s, when statistics were for the first time systematically gathered, the population had been considerably reduced.

which these disaffected cities could unite. For all of Cortés's efforts to portray himself as the only figure the king could trust to handle the Indians, it was not Cortés alone who brought down the Aztec empire; it was the Tlaxcalans and their allies, as much as the Spaniards, who were the *conquistadores*.

☆ To investigate further:

Pagden, Anthony, translator and editor. *Hernán Cortés: Letters from Mexico.* New Haven: Yale University Press, 1986. This translation of Cortés's letters includes a fascinating introduction in which J. H. Elliott convincingly demonstrates how Cortés's accounts of the conquest were slanted by his efforts to gain the king's support.

del Castillo, Bernal Díaz (translated by A. P. Maudslay). *The Discovery and Conquest of Mexico.* New York: Farrar, Straus and Cudahy, 1956. A Spanish soldier's account of the conquest, written in 1555.

de Gómara, Francisco López (translated by Lesley Byrd Simpson). *Cortés.* Berkeley: University of California Press, 1964. Cortés's secretary and chaplain's account of the conquest, written with Cortés's cooperation.

de Fuentes, Patricia, editor and translator. *The Conquistadors.* Norman: University of Oklahoma Press, 1993. A handy volume of excerpts from all the major first-person Spanish accounts of the conquest (except Díaz's).

de Sahagún, Bernardino (translated by Howard Cline). *Conquest of New Spain.* Salt Lake City: University of Utah Press, 1989. Sahagún, a Franciscan friar, wrote this history in 1585 based on his interviews with Indians who'd survived the conquest. Though the Aztecs' recollections may have been colored both by Sahagún's mediation and by their own feelings toward the conquest, this is nonetheless the most valuable source of knowledge on the Aztec world.

Leon-Portilla, Miguel, editor. *The Broken Spears.* Boston: Beacon Press, 1962. An English translation (from the Spanish, which was itself a translation from the Aztec language, Nahuatl) of surviving Aztec descriptions of the conquest.

Prescott, William Hickling. *The Conquest of Mexico.* New York: Harper & Brothers, 1843; reissued by Modern Library (New York) 1936. Though dated by Prescott's nineteenth-century prejudices in favor of Cortés and against Indians, this remains a classic work of narrative history.

Todorov, Tzvetan. *The Conquest of America.* New York: HarperCollins, 1984. Todorov, a French critic, attributes the conquest to the superiority of the Spaniards, not as fighters or strategists, but as communicators.

Hassig, Ross. *Aztec Warfare.* Norman: University of Oklahoma Press, 1988. An ethnohistorian's view of the rise and fall of the Aztec empire, this makes clear the extent to which the empire's downfall was brought about by cleavages that preceded Cortés's arrival.

Clendinnen, Inga. "Fierce and Unnatural Cruelty." *Representations,* Winter 1991. A highly provocative essay emphasizing how both the Spaniards and the Aztecs misunderstood each other and misrepresented the conquest.

Thomas, Hugh. *Conquest.* New York: Simon & Schuster, 1993. While Thomas is not quite as masterful a writer as Prescott, this comprehensive narrative is as close as the twentieth century has come to Prescott's history, and the wide range of twentieth-century scholarship incorporated in Thomas's work certainly supplants Prescott's.

Chapter 8

What Happened to the Lost Colony of Roanoke?

90 men. 17 women. 9 children.

These were the colonists who landed on Roanoake Island, off the coast of what is now North Carolina in July 1587—20 years before John Smith reached Virginia and 35 years before the Pilgrims reached Massachusetts. Among them was Eleanor Dare, the daughter of the colony's governor, John White. She was about to give birth, and that child—the appropriately named Virginia Dare—would be the first European child born in the New World, assuming no anonymous Norse child had preceded her.

White stayed in America for the birth of his granddaughter, then set sail for England to arrange additional supplies for the colony. When he returned three years later, the colonists had vanished; the only clues to their whereabouts were the letters CROATAN, carved on a post, and CRO on a nearby tree.

Had the colonists quickly carved these messages while under attack from Indians? White thought not: he'd instructed them to carve a cross if they were in trouble. Did the colonists mean they'd gone to join the friendly Indians on nearby Croatan Island? That, too, perplexed White: he'd discussed with the colonists the possibility of heading north towards the Chesapeake Bay, but Croatan Island was south of Roanoke Island.

Bad weather prevented White from looking further and forced him to return to England, but by no means did that end the search. To the Jamestown settlers later on, the fate of the Roanoke colonists was no mere history exercise; they believed, quite reasonably, that it might be the key to understanding how they themselves could survive in the New World, and John Smith led a number of expeditions in search of his predecessors. More recently, historians and archaeologists have continued the search. And though no white person ever again saw the "lost colonists," those on their trail have turned up some tantalizing clues and proposed some engaging scenarios.

The fate of the Lost Colony is very much bound up with the fate of Sir Walter Raleigh. This was the same Walter Raleigh who, legend has it, spread his best cloak over a puddle before the queen. Perhaps, perhaps not. In any case, whatever he did to charm the queen was worth hundreds of cloaks—for Raleigh became such a favorite that in 1584 Elizabeth granted him an exclusive patent to colonize America.

Within a month he arranged a reconnaissance voyage to North America. It returned later in the year with enthusiastic reports of abundant Carolina resources and friendly Carolina Indians. Raleigh did not delay: in April 1585 he sent off one hundred colonists in seven ships. They arrived at Roanoke Island later in the year, built a fort, and appointed Ralph Lane as governor.

This, then, was the first Roanoke colony, and the first British colony in America. It was founded two years before the Lost Colony, and its fate, in contrast, is well-known.

It was a remarkably ill-conceived colony. Lane was a soldier, as were most of the colonists. What they had in mind for Roanoke was a base for attacking Spanish ships en route from South America. Their plan was to get rich on Spanish treasure; building houses and toiling in the American soil was not for them. They quickly came to depend on friendly Indians for food, and they almost as quickly alienated the Indians. (Lane's idea of diplomacy was to kidnap the favorite son of the powerful chief Menatonon and hold him hostage until the chief gave Lane information about other tribes' defenses.) By the spring of 1586 the colonists were out of supplies and allies and in desperate straits.

Fortunately, help appeared on the horizon in the form of a fleet of ships commanded by Sir Francis Drake. But Drake was as much a privateer as the Roanoke colonists. He had come in order to use the colony as a base for his attacks on the Spanish; he could offer the colonists guns but no butter. And when a storm sank four of his ships, he could barely offer them passage home. In fact, to make room for the Roanoke colonists, Drake had to leave behind some African slaves and Indians he had liberated from the Spanish. These slaves and Indians were never heard from again; they were as "lost" as the more celebrated "lost colonists" of John White.

A few weeks after Drake, Lane, and the rest of the colony set sail for England, a relief party sent by Raleigh arrived. (On the way they'd been delayed by an irresistible urge to attack some Spanish ships.) When they found the colony deserted, they turned around, leaving behind a holding party of 15 men. None of them were ever heard from again, either.

Now we get to the "real" lost colony, a colony which ironically was much better prepared to survive in the New World than Lane and company. However greedy a privateer Raleigh was, he was a man who could understand what had gone wrong and act to correct it. For his next colony, instead of the authoritarian Ralph Lane, he chose as governor the artist John White. (White was a superb artist; his drawings of Indian life are still among the best sources for anthropologists and historians.) Instead of soldiers, Raleigh chose colonists whose interest was in building a colony, and he granted them land as incentive to work and stay. Women and children came along, with more planning to follow. And instead of the sandy soil of Roanoke, this new group was to settle in the Chesapeake Bay, not far from where Jamestown would eventually take root. In short, the colony Raleigh sent to America in 1587 was, much more even than Jamestown, the prototype for later successful colonies.

So what went wrong?

To begin with, the ships somehow ended up at Roanoke again, instead of on the Chesapeake. Then the ships' pilot, a Portuguese named Simon Fernandes, announced it was too late in the year to take the colonists any further. According to White's letters (one of the primary sources for exploring the mystery of the Lost Colony), greed was the motive of Fernandes; like so many associated with the Roanoke ventures he was a privateer. He dumped the colonists at

If John White made an ineffectual governor of Roanoke, he was nonetheless a superb artist; witness his drawings of Indian life, such as these engraved in 1590 by Theodor De Bry. (Library of Congress.)

Roanoke so he could run off and attack some Spanish ships. More generous interpreters have argued that Fernandes might have been trying to do the colonists a favor. The pilot had had some previous experience in Chesapeake Bay while in Spanish service, and he may have told the colonists (quite accurately) how warlike the Indians in the area were, and how they had wiped out a Jesuit mission there in 1570.

Whatever reasons Fernandes had for staying at Roanoke, White acquiesced. Perhaps he felt Fernandes had the upper hand and there was nothing he could do about it. Perhaps, though he wouldn't admit it, he was happy to be back on familiar ground—despite the inadequacy of the site and the bad relations Lane had generated with the Indians. Perhaps—and this is the most likely explanation—White was an admirable artist but an ineffectual leader.

In any case, Fernandes stuck around for a month, departing in August 1587 and taking White with him. Here's another mystery: why would the colony's governor leave the colony, not to mention his newborn granddaughter? According to White, the colonists insisted that only *he* could be counted on to make sure that they were not forgotten by their backers. More likely, they were fed up with his vacillating leadership and decided he'd be more use to them back in England.

Again White let them down; it was not until three years later that he returned and by then, as we've seen, it was too late. For this, however, it's not really fair to blame White. He worked tirelessly on behalf of the colonists but his timing couldn't have been worse. For one thing, Raleigh's interest was waning: he had put a lot of money into the venture and didn't feel he could keep doing so, especially since the Earl of Essex had replaced him as the queen's favorite. More ominously, the Spanish had grown tired of British privateering and had decided to cut it off at its base. With the Spanish Armada on its way, Elizabeth was taking no chances. In April 1588 she ordered all ships capable of war service—including those White was putting together to go back to Roanoke—to stay put. Even after the Armada was defeated, Elizabeth feared a new attack and was reluctant to let ships go. And so it was not until 1590 that White finally returned to find—or rather, not find—his colony.

☆ ☆ ☆

What happened to the colonists?

White himself was sanguine. He knew they had planned to move eventually anyway. He found no cross anywhere, and he clearly remembered instructing them "that if they should happen to be distressed in any of those places, that they should carve over the letters or name, a Crosse." White couldn't explain why they would have changed plans and gone south instead of north, nor did he explain how they were supposed to carve a cross at Roanoke if they ran into problems elsewhere. Still, everything seemed pretty much in order at the fort and there definitely was no cross there. White was relieved.

Meanwhile, back in England, Raleigh's position was deteriorating. He'd secretly married, and when Elizabeth found out, she did not take it well, imprisoning both groom and bride in the Tower of London. When he was finally released, he found himself exiled from the court. In 1595 Raleigh finally made it to America—but now it was the South American coast that attracted him. Roanoke seemed far away and unimportant. Some historians have argued that Raleigh intentionally abandoned the search to protect his patent, which required him to have a settlement. As long as he could claim the colonists were alive somewhere in the area, his patent was safe; further searches might risk proving they were dead. In 1602 Raleigh did send a party to search further but it turned up nothing new.

It was not until after Jamestown was settled in 1607, therefore, that the search continued in earnest. That same year George Percy of Jamestown described seeing an Indian with "a head of haire of a perfect yellow and a reasonable white skinne, which is a Miracle amongst all Savages." And John Smith, in *A true relation of such occurrences and accidents of noate as hath hapned in Virginia*, told of meeting an Indian chief who told him "of certaine men cloathed at a place called Ocanahonan, cloathed like me." William Strachey's 1612 *Historie of Travell Into Virginia Britania* describes how Indians told him of "howses built with stone walls, and one story above another, so taught . . . by the English."

Strachey also told of the slaughter of the lost colonists by Powhatan, the father of Pocahontas. Strachey's story went as follows: The colonists did head north, as White planned, eventually finding their way to the Chesapeake Bay. There they lived in peace for about 20 years with the Chesapeake Indians. Then, just about the time the first Jamestown colonists were arriving, Powhatan went to war with the Chesapeakes, slaughtering both the Indians and the settlers.

This was the story the Jamestown settlers settled on. It explained both the persistent rumors of lost colonists in the area and the failure to actually find them.

Other solutions to the mystery have been proposed in the centuries since then. Some suggested the colonists were lost at sea, trying to get back to England. But that's unlikely—they didn't have a large enough boat to cross the Atlantic. Others have suggested they were killed by Spaniards. Also unlikely—since Spanish documents show they were still looking for the English colony as late as 1600. Still others claim today's Croatan Indians are the direct descendants of the lost colonists, pointing to some linguistic similarities between the Indians' language and English. But these can more easily be explained by hundreds of years of contacts with European immigrants.

So Strachey's story, which the Jamestown settlers believed, may very well be the truth. One modern historian, David Beers Quinn, has added a new twist. Most of the colonists, he believes, moved north, thus accounting for the rumors and reports that reached Jamestown. At least a few stayed behind for a while longer, however, perhaps to wait for White or to hold the fort, and these were the colonists who ultimately headed south to Croatan, thus accounting for the signs on the tree.

Archaeologists continue to search for clues and they may someday be able to tell us more about what happened to Raleigh's lost colonists, or Drake's lost freedmen. As for Raleigh himself, though he may have given up on his Roanoke colony, he never gave up on America. He found himself even more out of favor with Elizabeth's successor, James I, than he'd been with Elizabeth, and he spent twelve years in the Tower. He was released in 1616, tried to win back his wealth and power with another expedition to South America, failed, and was executed.

And the much maligned John White? A John White, "late of parts beyond the seas," was declared dead in Ireland in 1606. But his was such a common name historians can't be sure this was the former governor. The fate of John White, like that of his daughter and granddaughter, remains something of a mystery.

☆ To investigate further:

Harriot, Thomas. *A briefe and true report of the new found land of Virginia.* Frankfort, 1590, reprinted by Dover, NY, 1972. One of the greatest mathematicians of the Renaissance, Harriot accompanied the 1585 expedition and produced this report, which includes White's drawings.

Hakluyt, Richard. *The Third and Last Volume of the Voyages, Navigations, Traffiques and Discoveries of the English Nation*. London: George Bishop, Ralph Newberie, and Robert Barber, 1600; reissued by Viking (New York) 1965. What we know about the lost colony and about all the British expeditions to America is largely thanks to Hakluyt, who collected the narratives, letters, and reminiscences of Raleigh, White, Lane, and others.

Quinn, David Beers. *England and the Discovery of America, 1481–1620*. New York: Knopf, 1974. No one has devoted more time and pages to the mystery of the lost colony, or to the British explorations and settlements in general. Sometimes Quinn goes way out on a limb, as when he suggests that the British discovered America before Columbus, or (some say) when he explains what happened to the lost colonists. But Quinn always lets you see the evidence on which his theories are based and, given the evidence we have so far, his theory about the lost colony is more plausible than anyone else's.

Stick, David. *Roanoke Island*. Chapel Hill: University of North Carolina Press, 1983. One of a number of very readable histories to appear around the settlement's 400th anniversary.

Kupperman, Karen Ordahl. *Roanoke: The Abandoned Colony*. Totowa, NJ: Rowman & Alanheld, 1984. An attempt to present Quinn's ideas in a less academic, more popular style; as such, it's successful, but it's well worth the effort to read Quinn's own work.

Hume, Ivor Noël. *The Virginia Adventure*. New York: Knopf, 1994. The latest reports from the area's leading archaeologist; informative and entertaining.

Chapter 9

Did Pocahontas Save John Smith?

In December 1607, just a few months after the first permanent British colony in America was established at Jamestown, Captain John Smith led a trading party up the Chickahominy River. He was captured by Indians and taken before the great chief, Powhatan, who ruled over much of Tidewater Virginia. In *The Generall Historie of Virginia, New-England, and the Summer Isles*, Smith himself told what happened next:

> A long consultation was held, but the conclusion was, two great stones were brought before Powhatan: then as many as could layd hands on him, dragged him to them, and thereon laid his head, and being ready with their clubs to beate out his braines, Pocahontas the Kings dearest daughter, when no intreaty could prevaile, got his head in her armes, and laid her owne upon his to save him from death: whereat the Emperour was contented he should live to make him hatchets and her bells.

Is Smith's story true? Did the Indian princess throw herself between Smith and the tomahawks heading toward his "braines"?

Among the first and most adamant to call Smith a liar was Henry Adams in the mid-nineteenth century. He pointed out that Smith's ear-

From The True Travels, Adventures, and Observations of Captaine John Smith. *In this 1629 book, Smith himself described how Powhatan "commanded him to be slaine" but then "Pocahontas saved his life." (Library of Congress.)*

lier histories of Virginia made no mention of Pocahontas saving him; it was not until the 1624 *Generall Historie* that Smith published the story. By then, Adams argued, those who could have refuted it—such as Pocahontas herself—were dead. With no other English-speaking witnesses besides Pocahontas, it came down to Smith's word.

The rest of the *Generall Historie* didn't do much to increase the value of that word. Smith told some remarkable—some would say incredible—tales. Seemingly least credible of all was that Pocahontas was just one of four foreign ladies who, unable to resist Smith's charms, came to his rescue. Before coming to Virginia, Smith had joined the Austrian armies fighting against the Turks in Hungary. He was captured by the Turks and made a slave in Constantinople. There his luck improved: his mistress, "the beauteous Lady Tragabigzanda," took a liking to him, treated him well, and then sent him to her brother in Tartary, from where he escaped. He ultimately reached a Russian garrison where "the good Lady Callamata . . . largely supplied all his wants." And when Smith escaped some pirates, it was "the good Lady Madam Canoyes" who "bountifully assisted me."

All this from the *Generall Historie*—all this about a very short, bearded, battle-scarred man whose portraits are distinctly underwhelming. No wonder that some of Smith's contemporaries called him a braggart and a liar, and many historians agreed.

But then, in 1953, the tide of opinion turned. That year Bradford Smith's biography of Smith appeared, with an appendix on the captain's Hungarian adventures written by Laura Striker Polanyi. Polanyi carefully checked Smith's narrative of the wars against the Turks; to almost everyone's surprise, everything that could be checked turned out to be accurate.

The case for Smith was further strengthened by ethnohistorians. Their work showed that Smith's descriptions of Indian life and culture were realistic. In fact, his works are considered an important primary source for those studying Indian history and culture. Geographers, too, came to admire the accuracy of Smith's maps of Chesapeake Bay and New England.

Smith's defenders took the offense, accusing Henry Adams and his followers of denigrating the man because he was a Southerner. After all, Adams was the great-grandson of John Adams and the grandson of John Quincy Adams. Both Adamses were New Englanders to the core and were bitter political enemies of John Randolph, a Virginian—and a descendant of none other than Pocahontas. (Yet another noncoincidence: the first to answer Henry Adams in print was William Hirt Henry, grandson of Virginia's Patrick Henry.)

With Smith's reputation on the upswing, it was time to put aside sectionalist politics and Balkan adventures, and look anew at his relationship to Pocahontas.

The strongest case against the Pocahontas rescue story remained that Smith never published it until his 1624 *Generall Historie.* That he left it out of his 1612 work, *A Map of Virginia,* was fairly easy to explain: that dealt mostly with geography and ethnology and not with Smith's own explorations and adventures.

But why was the story nowhere to be found in Smith's 1608 work, *A True Relation of Such Occurrences and Accidents of Noate as Hath Hapned in Virginia?*

Smith's apologists have offered a number of suggestions. Perhaps, they've argued, it was for the sake of public relations. *A True Relation* was written to encourage investment and settlement in Virginia, and stories of hostile Indians didn't help that cause. Some speculated that the Pocahontas story might have been cut by an overzealous editor. But, Smith's detractors were quick to point out, *A True Relation* contained plenty of stories about Indians attacking Jamestown settlers—with endings much bloodier and unhappier than that of the Pocahontas story.

So the pro-Smith, pro-truth-of-the-story faction presented a variety of other arguments. In 1608, they said, Smith respected Powhatan; in 1609 he learned of Powhatan's role in killing the Roanoke colonists and his later works therefore portrayed the chief as much more bloodthirsty. Smith's supporters even used his reputation as a braggart to defend him, arguing that he might have left out the Pocahontas story simply because he was embarrassed that he needed an Indian princess—and an eleven-year-old at that—to save him. They also noted that the *Generall Historie* was a longer book with lots of details and stories that weren't in the earlier works. Perhaps Smith left out the Pocahontas story from his earlier works for no particular reason at all; his was a life full of hairbreadth escapes from death and, until Pocahontas later became a celebrity in England, Smith's encounter with her might not have seemed of much importance to him. He had no way of knowing that a few words in the *Generall Historie* were to become the basis of

America's version of Romeo and Juliet, or of what Henry Adams called "the most romantic episode in the whole history of his country."

Finally, Smith's supporters pointed out that Smith *had* included the Pocahontas story in at least one work prior to the *Generall Historie*. This was his letter to Queen Anne, dated June 1616. Pocahontas had by then married the Englishman, John Rolfe, and moved to England. With plans underway for her to meet the royal family, Smith took it upon himself to do the introductions. His letter to the queen tells a story much like that in the *Generall Historie*: ". . . at the minute of my execution, she hazarded the beating out of her owne braines to save mine, and not onely that, but so prevailed with her father, that I was safely conducted to James towne . . ."

The letter was dated 1616, when Pocahontas was still alive and presumably could have denied the story. But it did not appear in print until 1624, as part of the *Generall Historie*. By then, Pocahontas had died. So, again, we have only John Smith's word to go by.

Perhaps the best way to determine the truth of Smith's story is to ask, simply: does it make sense?

Some of the legend that's surrounded it makes no sense at all and can be summarily dismissed. For one thing, it is absolutely certain there was never a love affair between John Smith and Pocahontas. In 1607 Pocahontas was eleven years old; John Smith was 27. She may have had a crush on him but it was no more than that. It was John Rolfe, not John Smith, whom she married in 1614. If there was any sort of special relationship between Smith and Pocahontas—and, according to the *Generall Historie,* she did come to his aid and the colony's a number of other times—it was not a romantic one. Nor did Smith ever claim otherwise.

As for the claims Smith *did* make: do they make sense?

No.

Smith said he was spared "to make him hatchets, and her bells." Powhatan had no shortage of hatchets or bells; he knew very well that Smith was a leader of the English and worth a lot more than a few hatchets or bells. Nor is there any reason to believe a powerful warrior and chief would be swayed because of his daughter's plea.

But this does not mean Smith was a liar. More likely, the incident did take place much as Smith described but he misunderstood what was going on. According to Smith's account, Indians prepared to "beate out his braines" by feeding him extravagantly and parading him before the various tribes; right before they were to kill him one Indian woman brought him water to wash his hands and another brought feathers to dry them. All this sounds like a carefully orchestrated ceremony. In all likelihood, the "rescue" of Smith by Pocahontas was also part of the ceremony.

Many historians have suggested that the rescue was part of a traditional ritual of death and rebirth that accompanied adoption into an Indian tribe. Recently, the archaeologist and historian Ivor Noel Hume argued that it was not a traditional ritual but a conscious effort on Powhatan's part to try to turn Smith into an ally. To have executed Smith, Hume wrote, would have been to bring down on Powhatan the wrath of the English, and Smith had made clear there were plenty more Englishmen across the water. Better to stage a ceremony that might leave Smith both intimidated and grateful.

Smith, of course, understood none of this. He was indeed intimidated by Powhatan and grateful to Pocahontas. And who can blame him?

☆ To investigate further:

Barbour, Philip L., editor. *The Complete Works of Captain John Smith*. Williamsburg, VA: Institute of Early American History and Culture, 1986. Decide for yourself whether you believe him.

Kupperman, Karen Ordahl. *Captain John Smith*. Williamsburg, VA: Institute of Early American History and Culture, 1988. Selected writings for those who don't quite need all of the above.

Smith, Bradford. *Captain John Smith*. Philadelphia: Lippincott, 1953. Includes Polanyi's groundbreaking work on the Hungarian episodes and, until Barbour's, the best defense and biography of Smith.

Barbour, Philip L. *The Three Worlds of Captain John Smith*. Boston: Houghton Mifflin, 1964. Still the most widely respected biography, this argues that the Pocahontas episode was true (though Barbour later expressed some doubt about it).

————. *Pocahontas and Her World*. Boston: Houghton Mifflin, 1970. Adds little to the above.

Vaughan, Alden T. *American Genesis*. New York: Little, Brown, 1975. A short—and on the subject of the Pocahontas story, inconclusive—biography of Smith.

Gerson, Noel B. *The Glorious Scoundrel*. New York: Dodd, Mead, 1978. Argues that Smith not only made up the story but that he never even met Pocahontas until she came to England.

Lemay, J. A. Leo. *The American Dream of Captain John Smith*. Charlottesville: University Press of Virginia, 1991. Part of a backlash against the "politically correct" scholarship that has placed Smith at the front of a long line of Europeans who have exploited Native Americans, this polemic portrays Smith as a friend and admirer not just of Pocahontas but of all Indians. However, it doesn't add much substance to Barbour's work and even Smith, braggart that he was, might have been embarrassed by so much praise.

———. *Did Pocahontas Save John Smith?* Athens: University of Georgia Press, 1992. A history of the controversy, which concludes the answer is yes.

Hume, Ivor Noël. *The Virginia Adventure*. New York: Knopf, 1994. The latest report from the area's leading archaeologist.

Chapter 10

What Caused the "Starving Time"?

Entering the towne, it appeared rather as the ruins of some auntient fortification, then that any people living might now in habit it."

Thus did William Strachey describe Jamestown in May 1610, when supply ships from London finally reached the settlement. Famine was so widespread that, according to the colony's president, George Percy, one man "murdered his wife . . . and after chopped [her] in pieces and salted her for his foode."

Other colonists took to digging up corpses. They were, Percy explained, "driven through unsufferable hunger unnaturallie to eat those things which nature most abhorred."

Most historians put the English population of Virginia at about five hundred in the fall of 1609. By the time the supply ships arrived, it was down to sixty. No wonder that year's winter was known from then on as the "Starving Time."

So desperate was the situation that it was clear the supply ships did not carry enough to save the colony. The survivors clambered aboard for the return trip to England, abandoning Jamestown. The town appeared destined to join Roanoke Island to the south as another "lost colony."

Then, as the ships sailed down the James River toward the Chesapeake Bay, they ran into another fleet, this one commanded by

Thomas West who, as Lord Delaware, had been appointed the new governor of Virginia. Delaware brought with him enough food for a year, as well as a determination that Jamestown survive.

It did—and the rest, as they say, is history.

Yet for many historians the starving time was a mystery. *Why* were the colonists starving? There was sturgeon aplenty in the James River, and game in the surrounding woods. And the settlers could have planted corn, as the Indians did.

Instead, as the colonist Thomas Dale reported, they passed the time "at their daily and usuall workes, bowling in the streetes . . ."

Another contemporary account, this by Ralph Hamor, said the colonists "would rather starve in idlenesse then feast in labour." Strachey, too, described the colonists' "sloath."

This sloth, as historian Edmund Morgan wrote, was "more an accusation than an explanation." Why would people go bowling, if their lives depended on hunting game or planting crops? Were these colonists, Morgan quite reasonably asked, lunatics?

John Smith, the colony's first president, had no doubt what the problem was: the colony had too many gentlemen who "never did know what a dayes work was."

The numbers bore Smith out. Of the 105 settlers who first joined Smith in Jamestown, there were 36 gentlemen, and another 56 soon followed. Worse, many were accompanied by footmen whose jobs were to take care of the gentlemen, not to plant crops.

The colony's London sponsors compounded the problem by recruiting a variety of specialized craftsmen who also saw common labor as beneath them. These included jewelers and goldsmiths and even a perfumer. A hundred good laborers, Smith reported, "would have done more than a thousand of those that went."

Smith was also confident he knew the solution: strong leadership, namely his own. And Smith does deserve at least some of the credit he gave himself.

Confronted by rampant "idlenesse," Smith imposed an increasingly military discipline, assigning each colonist specific tasks and imposing a strict schedule. In 1608, still a year before the starving time, Smith gave the settlers an ultimatum: "You must obey this for a law, that he will not worke, shall not eate."

Smith was not always the most reliable of reporters. His various accounts of Virginia were not always consistent, and he had a reputation as a braggart. Many suspected he invented or exaggerated his exploits (including the story of how the Indian princess Pocahontas saved him from her father's tomahawks). Yet other colonists confirmed that most of his stories were at least partly true, and—until Delaware arrived—there seemed no one else capable of keeping the settlers or the Indians in line.

There's no doubt that Smith's bullying tactics (along with his timely trading for Indian corn) helped keep the colony alive through 1609.

Alas, Smith left Virginia that October, under somewhat murky circumstances. Smith's own account was that, on his way back from an expedition farther up the James River, a spark "accidentallie" set off a bag of powder, and he "was neare blowne to death." According to Smith, he left Virginia to seek medical treatment in England.

Possibly.

But it's also possible that Smith's enemies—and his military-style discipline had made plenty of them—tried to kill him. John Ratcliffe, definitely no friend to Smith, wrote that Smith was "sent home to answere some misdemeanors whereof I perswade me he can scarcly clear him selfe from great imputation of blame." And Henry Spelman wrote that Smith conspired with the Indians to kill a rival, then "was Aprehended, and sent abord for England."

Archaeologist Ivor Noël Hume doubted Smith's injury was an accident. "Perhaps," wrote Noël Hume, "because the mixing of gunpowder is not part of a historian's required education, none seems to have asked whether the story (at least as it has come down to us) really makes sense." Noël Hume argued that it was much more likely someone intentionally lit the powder.

In any case, Smith left Virginia, never to return. It was not until Delaware arrived the next spring that the colony again had a leader capable of instilling the discipline needed to survive.

☆ ☆ ☆

Smith's role aside, historians have proposed a variety of other explanations for the colonists' suicidal laziness.

During the heyday of the Cold War, for example, some historians compared the colony's economy to communism, noting that everyone was expected to work together to grow food, with everyone sharing the produce. This, they argued, removed the incentive to work. This may very well have been true, but seems insufficient to explain such extreme laziness.

More persuasively, in the 1970s, Morgan traced the colonists' attitudes toward work back to seventeenth-century England. It was not only gentlemen, Morgan found, who were used to very limited hours. English farmers put in long days at harvest time, but for much of the year they waited around for the crops to grow. Nor was manufacturing particularly efficient in England prior to the industrial revolution.

Moreover, many of the colonists had military backgrounds, and for them Virginia was another military expedition. Officers and soldiers were not expected to farm in Europe, and they saw no reason why it should be different in America.

Against these ingrained attitudes, Morgan argued, the discipline of a Smith or Delaware was bound to fail. That Virginia survived and ultimately prospered was no testament to a changing work ethic. Instead, it was because Virginians eventually imported a new work force—African slaves.

Also during the 1970s, a number of historians blamed various diseases, rather than starvation, for the Jamestown deaths. Anita and Darrett Rutman made a case that malaria weakened many colonists, making them susceptible to other diseases. Carville Earle argued that even if the colonists themselves thought they were starving, many of the symptoms they described—such as "bloudie Flixes" (diarrhea) and "Burning Fevers"—were more consistent with disease than starvation.

For these historians, the colonists' most disastrous decision was Jamestown's site. At first, the island in the James River seemed to make a lot of sense; it offered protection from any Spanish or Indian attacks, and it was a very pleasant environment, at least in the spring of 1607, when the colonists arrived. What they failed to realize was that, come summer, Jamestown became a swamp, surrounded by stagnant and brackish water.

This was the water the colonists drank, and it quickly made them sick.

"We cannot say conclusively that typhoid, dysentery, and salt poisoning were the principal causes of death in that winter," Earle concluded. "However, we can suggest that the case for massive starvation is far from proven."

John Smith had no doubt that, without him, the colonists would have starved. This illustration from his 1629 book, The True Travels, Adventures, and Observations of Captaine John Smith, *shows his capture by Indians in 1607. (Library of Congress.)*

Another defense of the colonists' apparent laziness came from historian Karen Ordahl Kupperman. Unlike Earle, she believed the colonists did starve to death, but she argued their apparent unwillingness to work was actually a physical symptom of their nutritional deficiencies. Their inactivity, in turn, intensified the food shortages, creating a vicious cycle that ended in death.

Perhaps the most significant new explanation for the Starving Time came in 1998, after scientists measured tree rings in southeastern Virginia. The width of tree rings indicates how much a tree grows in a year, so the rings are also a good indication of the annual rainfall. Data taken from bald cypress trees indicated that, in northeast North Carolina and southeast Virginia, the most severe droughts of the past eight hundred years occurred from 1587 to 1589 and from 1606 to 1612.

In one fell swoop, scientists had a new explanation for the failure not only of Jamestown but also of Roanoke. Stronger leadership, better planning, harder work—none of these could have overcome the devastating effects of arriving amidst two devastating droughts. The droughts affected the Indians as well, and while they were better able to cope than the colonists, it deprived them of a surplus they might otherwise have been willing to trade.

"If it weren't for bad luck, these English wouldn't have had any luck at all," said Dennis Blanton, an archaeologist who was one of the authors of the 1998 study.

Blanton and his fellow scientists were not environmental determinists. They conceded other factors played a role in the demise of Roanoke and near-demise of Jamestown. Nor were all historians ready to cede to drought the leading role. But after 1998, few could deny that it was a crucial factor, and one that exacerbated whatever other problems the colonists faced.

☆ ☆ ☆

Even more startling than the tree ring data, though less documented, was the theory of medical researcher Frank Hancock, presented in a 2000 BBC documentary.

Hancock noted that some of the symptoms the colonists described, such as skin peeling off, were not typical of typhoid or dysentery or starvation. All the symptoms, however, were consistent with arsenic poisoning.

Hancock's conclusion: the colonists were murdered.

The poisoners, he believed, were militant Catholics, furious that England's first colony was Protestant. In particular, Hancock suspected Thomas Arundell, a Catholic alchemist involved in the 1605 Gunpowder Plot, a failed effort to blow up the English Parliament.

The sensational charges stirred up some press attention; in nearby Williamsburg, the *Virginia Gazette* headlined its lead story, "Arsenic in an Old Place." But most historians considered murder unlikely, at least without a lot more evidence.

"While it is possible, it is not probable," said William Kelso, the head archaeologist at Jamestown. "There were plenty of ways to die here besides that."

☆ To investigate further:

Barbour, Philip, editor. *The Jamestown Voyages Under the First Charter.* London: Cambridge University Press for the Hakluyt Society, 1969. Documents relating to Jamestown's founding, including John Smith's 1608 *A true relation of such occurrences and accidents of noate as hath hapned in Virginia since the first planting of that Collony* and his 1612 *Map of Virginia.*

Morgan, Edmund. "The Labor Problem at Jamestown." *American Historical Review,* June 1971. How English attitudes toward work crossed the Atlantic.

———. *American Slavery, American Freedom.* New York: W. W. Norton, 1975. Slavery and freedom, uncomfortably and provocatively intertwined in colonial Virginia.

Vaughan, Alden T. *American Genesis.* Boston: Little, Brown, 1975. A colorful biography of John Smith.

Tate, Thad, and Ammerman, David, editors. *The Chesapeake in the Seventeenth Century.* Chapel Hill: University of North Carolina Press, 1979. Includes Carville Earle's influential essay, "Environment, Disease, and Mortality in Early Virginia," which makes the case for disease.

Kupperman, Karen Ordahl. "Apathy and Death in Early Jamestown." *Journal of American History,* June 1979. The psychological impact of malnutrition.

Noël Hume, Ivor. *The Virginia Adventure.* New York: Knopf, 1994. Noël Hume, the area's leading archaeologist, bounces back and forth between the history of Roanoke and Jamestown, and the excavations there, in an account both scholarly and witty.

Stahle, David, Malcolm Cleaveland, Dennis Blanton, Matthew Therrell, and David Gay. "The Lost Colony and Jamestown Droughts." *Science,* April 24, 1998. How climate changed the course of history.

Chapter 11

What Caused the Salem Witch Hunt?

In February 1692 in the town of Salem, Massachusetts, two children in the house of the Reverend Samuel Parris— nine-year-old Betty Parris and her eleven-year-old cousin Abigail Williams—began acting very strangely. They ran around the house, flapping their arms, screaming "Whish, Whish, Whish." They pulled burning logs out of the fireplace and threw them around the room. It was as if, another local minister observed, they "were bitten and pinched by invisible agents; their arms, necks, and backs turned this way and that way, and returned back again, so as it was impossible for them to do of themselves, and beyond the power of any Epileptick Fits, or natural Disease to effect." Local doctors were at a loss to explain what was going on. Finally, Dr. William Griggs suggested the girls were bewitched.

The authorities sprang into action, demanding that the children tell them who was tormenting them. The girls first named Tituba, the Parris family's West Indian slave. Then they added the names of two other local women, Sarah Good and Sarah Osborne. Tituba admitted she'd read palms and told fortunes and perhaps dabbled in some voodoo, but she denied harming the girls; that was the doing of Good and Osborne, she said. Good, in turn, said Osborne was the witch.

So far this was no big deal. There had been other accusations of witchcraft in other New England towns, usually resulting in a lot of gossip and perhaps an occasional arrest or even a conviction. But in Salem this was just the beginning. More and more of Salem's teenage and preteen girls began having fits; more and more of Salem's adults were accused of witchcraft. Even the four-year-old daughter of Sarah Good was accused and sent to prison with her mother, where she remained in heavy irons for nine months. By summer the town's jail was filled with more than a hundred accused witches; by the end of the year, 19 people had been hanged—more than in all the previous New England witch trials. Another victim was pressed to death under heavy stones because he refused to testify before the magistrates.

It was clear things had gone too far. Influential ministers and magistrates, many of whom had been quick to see the devil's work in the girls' behavior, now realized this had gotten out of hand (a realization aided no doubt by the fact that some of them and their wives were being accused). The trials came to a halt, as did the witch hunt. But the question did not go away: What drove the people of Salem to behavior so extreme that, ever since, Salem has been a metaphor for persecution and intolerance?

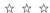

To the rationalists of the eighteenth and nineteenth centuries, the question barely merited analysis. Since there was obviously no such thing as a witch, the girls were simply liars. Those who supported the girls acted out of fear of being themselves accused; those who confessed to being witches and who named other witches did so only to save themselves from the gallows.

In the twentieth century, Freudian interpretations came to the fore. The girls' fits were a classic case of hysteria, the result of repressed adolescent and preadolescent sexuality. It is easy enough to believe the girls were repressed—the Puritans, after all, could be puritanical.

Freudian interpretations reigned until the early 1970s, when social historians began to probe the social and economic background of the witch hunts. The 1690s, they stressed, were years of extreme instability in Massachusetts. Indian wars had been devastating; so had epidemic illnesses. The king had revoked the charter under which the colony was governed, leaving the entire structure of the government unsettled. And the traditionally agrarian culture of the area was increasingly threatened by the influence of a more cosmopolitan merchant class.

What possessed the girls of Salem? Explanations for the witch hunt have included ergot poisoning, sexual repression, social tensions, family feuds, corrupt judges—and the devil. From Augustus Mason's 1883 book, The Romance and Tragedy of Pioneer Life. *(Library of Congress.)*

With their world seemingly coming apart, it was not so surprising that New Englanders, steeped as they were in Puritan theology, would blame Satan. Some people took all the fire-and-brimstone talk with a grain of salt, but others undoubtedly believed in witches. In any case, the particular people they accused fit the bill. Tituba was a black slave, an obvious pariah. Sarah Good was a beggar whose pleas had gotten on everyone's nerves. Sarah Osborne was more financially secure than Sarah Good, but she had been involved in some nasty disputes over land with her own sons and was widely suspected of having lived with her husband before they were married—no small transgression in Puritan society. To make matters worse, she hadn't been to church for more than a year. Many of the others accused early on were also conveniently vulnerable scapegoats.

But if all this illuminated the social strains and social divisions that led New Englanders to cry witch, it did little to explain why the witch-hunt materialized in Salem and not elsewhere in New England. To solve that mystery, two social historians, Paul Boyer and Stephen Nissenbaum, took a close look at Salem. What they found was that Salem was actually more like two towns. Near the coast stood Salem Town, a flourishing commercial center dominated by merchants and tradesmen; a little farther inland lay Salem Village, a traditional and increasingly impoverished agricultural hamlet. To a remarkable extent, the accusers and their supporters lived in the interior and the accused and their defenders lived near or in town; the former tended to be poorer and more devout; the latter tended to be richer and more secular.

Nowhere else in New England did these two ways of life confront each other so directly and so unavoidably. Had Salem Village been situated somewhat farther inland, its inhabitants might not have felt so threatened by Salem Town, nor would they have known its residents well enough to accuse them of anything, let alone witchcraft. Had this been the case, the name Salem might today conjure up nothing more than a pleasant coastal village. But with Salem's particular situation, daily contact meant a continual buildup of the villagers' resentment of their rich and godless neighbors. Worse, some of the villagers, Boyer and Nissenbaum found, had a particular grudge against their neighbors. In fact, underlying the Salem witch hunt was a family feud that made the Capulets and the Montagues seem the closest of friends.

On the one side were the Putnams, on the other were the Porters. Both lived in the village, but the Porters lived on the town side, and the Putnams farther inland. Trouble started brewing in 1686, when Thomas Putnam Sr. died, bequeathing the best part of his estate to his second wife, Mary Veren Putnam, and his only son by that wife, Joseph. Like the biblical Joseph, Joseph Putnam was deeply resented by his older half brothers. Thomas Putnam Jr., the eldest, was especially bitter as he watched Joseph become one of the richest men in town with money and land that Thomas felt was rightfully his. His bitterness only deepened in 1690, when Joseph Putnam married Elizabeth Porter, a member of the only town family that rivaled the Putnams' wealth and prestige. To the Putnams, the Porters personified the evils of Salem Town.

No wonder, then, that the Putnams and Porters could be found on opposite sides of almost every issue dividing the town. The Putnams and their wives belonged to the church of Samuel Parris (father and uncle, you'll recall, to the two girls who started the whole witch hunt). The

Porters, on the other hand, led a drive to replace Parris with a new minister. And throughout the witch trials, the Putnam name appeared again and again among the accusers. Eight Putnams were involved in the prosecution of 46 accused witches, and Ann Putnam, the 12-year-old daughter of Thomas Putnam Jr., was by far the most active of all the afflicted girls. Meanwhile, the Porters' friends and family were prominent among the accused.

Three years after the witch trials were over, the feud was still going strong. In 1695 Mary Veren Putnam died, leaving everything that was hers (and that had once belonged to Joseph Putnam Sr.) to Joseph. The Putnams challenged the will, claiming it had actually been written by Israel Porter, Joseph's father-in-law. Furthermore, the Putnams claimed, Mary Veren Putnam had not been of sound mind when she signed the will. And what doctor did they call to testify this was so? None other than William Griggs, the doctor who had first suggested the children in the Parris household had been bewitched.

The Putnam/Porter feud brings to mind not just Bible stories but also fairy tales. Think of Thomas Putnam Jr. and his brothers as Hansel and Gretel, exploited by their father's evil second wife, who abandons them to the forest and its witch. How did Hansel and Gretel survive? The Putnams knew the answer: *they killed the witch.*

Alas, for the Putnams, it was all in vain. Throughout his life, Thomas Putnam Jr. had to sell off what little land his father did leave him in order to pay his increasing debts. When he died in 1699, there was little left for his three sons, all of whom moved away from the area, or his five daughters, three of whom remained spinsters. Joseph Putnam, in contrast, remained rich, and his sons and daughters prospered in Salem. (The only son who moved away from Salem was Israel Putnam, who became a highly successful soldier, known best for his bravery at Bunker Hill, where he uttered the famous line "Don't shoot until you see the whites of their eyes.")

☆ ☆ ☆

Whether the Putnams consciously sought revenge, or whether they actually believed the accused were witches, is unclear. But the Boyer/ Nissenbaum analysis convinced most historians that the social tensions between the two families and communities were at the root of the witch trials. A few historians, however, disagreed.

As Bernard Rosenthal saw it, the trials could only be understood through a study of the surviving trial records. What he found there convinced him that the trials were part of a scam perpetrated by the county sheriff, George Corwin. Rosenthal backed up the charge by demonstrating that Corwin profited from the illegal seizure of the property of the wealthier defendants. More damning still, Corwin's uncle and father-in-law were both among the judges who sent the witches off to jail or to be hanged. Although no evidence exists that they conspired with Corwin, they must certainly have known what was going on, as did the other judges.

Rosenthal's close reading of the records revealed other motives were also at work. For example, the influential minister Cotton Mather backed the court proceedings because he felt that one of the defendants, the dissenting minister George Burroughs, was a dangerous threat to the religious hegemony. Mather, in spite of his fire-and-brimstone image, had mixed feelings about the trials in general, but he was willing to legitimize the other hangings to get rid of Burroughs.

Rosenthal strongly criticized social historians for focusing too much on the background and losing sight of the foreground; namely, the individual motives of people like Corwin and Mather. In this, he was not being entirely fair to Boyer and Nissenbaum; after all, although they certainly paid a lot of attention to socioeconomic factors, they also wrote about the very personal motives of the Putnams and the Porters.

Nor was the Boyer/Nissenbaum theory quite so at odds with Rosenthal's evidence as his criticism of it implied. The Salem witchhunts were caused by both the underlying patterns in the community (which the social historians brilliantly illuminated) and the more immediate motives of the participants (as revealed by Rosenthal). Not all of the participants were driven by the same motive, and some were undoubtedly driven by more than one. Corwin might have been driven by greed, Mather by theology, Putnam by jealousy and resentment, the girls by boredom or frustration. So many different problems converged in 1692 Salem that it didn't take much to cause an explosion. All that was needed was a spark—which appeared in the form of a West Indian slave who dabbled in voodoo.

☆ To investigate further:

Boyer, Paul and Stephen Nissenbaum, editors. *Salem-Village Witchcraft*. Boston: Northeastern University Press, 1972. A documentary record, including transcripts of the preliminary trial proceedings and much of the testimony. (The actual trial records have not survived.)

Upham, Charles. *Salem Witchcraft*. Boston: Wiggin and Lunt, 1867. This standard "rationalist" approach to the witchcraft was reprinted in 1959 by F. Unger Publishing Co. (New York).

Starkey, Marion. *The Devil in Massachusetts*. New York: Knopf, 1950. Though it preceded much of the modern scholarship, this remains the most dramatic narrative history of the crisis.

Hansen, Chadwick. *Witchcraft at Salem*. New York: George Braziller, 1969. In a society where most people believed in witchcraft and where many practiced black magic, spells might actually work—if only through the power of suggestion. So, at least according to this iconoclastic work, some of the accused might actually have been guilty of witchcraft.

Boyer, Paul and Stephen Nissenbaum. *Salem Possessed*. Cambridge: Harvard University Press, 1974. How social tensions between Salem Town and Salem Village led to the witch hunt.

Caporael, Linnda. "Ergotism: The Satan Loosed in Salem?" *Science,* April 1976. A biologist's proposal that the girls' fits and visions were symptoms of convulsive ergotism, a disease contracted from contaminated grain.

Spanos, Nicholas and Jack Gottlieb. "Ergotism and the Salem Village Witch Trials." *Science,* December 1976. Disputes Caporael's diagnosis by arguing that the fits and visions seemed to start and stop on cue, thus implying a social rather than physiological cause.

Demos, John. *Entertaining Satan*. New York: Oxford University Press, 1982. Though not exclusively about Salem, this is the most thorough and sophisticated study of New England witchcraft; Demos approaches the subject from the perspectives of biography, psychology, and sociology as well as history.

Karlsen, Carol F. *The Devil in the Shape of a Woman*. New York: Norton, 1987. A feminist investigation, which contends that many of the accused were singled out because they owned or were in line to inherit property that would otherwise go to men.

Gragg, Larry. *The Salem Witch Crisis*. Westport, CT: Praeger, 1992. A straightforward history of the crisis with an excellent chapter on how prison conditions led many to confess.

Rosenthal, Bernard. *Salem Story*. New York: Cambridge University Press, 1993. The case that systematic fraud caused the witch hunt; also includes fascinating discussions of how the Salem story has been used in American literature and culture.

Part 2
Unexplained Happenings in a Young Republic

1770s to 1850s

Chapter 12

Who Was to Blame for the Boston Massacre?

Despite a foot of snow on the ground, groups of Bostonians wandered the streets of the town on the evening of March 5, 1770. Some, responding to a fire alarm, carried buckets of water. Others carried clubs to defend themselves—or perhaps to threaten—the despised "lobsterbacks," the red-coated British troops who had been stationed in the town since 1768.

Near the Custom House on King Street, several wigmakers' apprentices taunted Private Hugh White, the lone British sentry. Words soon escalated to snowballs and stones, and White struck back with the butt of his gun. Captain Thomas Preston heard of White's predicament and rushed to the scene with seven other soldiers. By then, hundreds of Bostonians had gathered as well, some still holding their buckets.

There was no fire. But a piece of ice knocked down Private Hugh Montgomery, and when he stood up, he fired into the crowd. More shots followed. Three Bostonians were killed on the spot and two others mortally wounded.

Samuel Adams called the deaths a "bloody butcher," and Paul Revere quickly produced an engraving showing soldiers firing point-blank at citizens. Other patriot leaders published a pamphlet, "A Short Narrative of the Horrid Massacre in Boston," and more than ten thousand mourners paraded at the funeral.

Adams made sure the image of the Boston Massacre didn't fade from American memory. He set aside March 5 as a day of mourn-

*Paul Revere's 1770 engraving is riddled with errors, including the invented
"Butcher's Hall" sign and an inaccurate casualty list. (Library of Congress.)*

ing. Annual orations recalled the massacre as the direct and inevitable
result of British oppression, its victims the first heroes of the revolution to come. Until 1784, when the Fourth of July took its place, Americans celebrated their independence on March 5.

Not surprisingly, the British and Tories had a different view of
the day's events. Some London newspapers suggested the Bostonians
were after the king's coffers in the Custom House. Others accused patriot leaders of planning the incident, perhaps even with the hope of
turning its victims into martyrs. To loyalists, this was not the Boston
Massacre but "the riot on the King Street."

This was more than a contest of names. It was, as historian Alfred
Young wrote in a slightly different context (he was discussing the loyalist tendency to call the Boston Tea Party "the destruction of the tea")
"part of a larger contest for the public memory of the Revolution."

With patriot leaders like Adams and Revere fomenting rebellion, Massachusetts's royal governor Thomas Hutchinson moved decisively to calm the town. He ordered the British soldiers out of Boston, and he had Preston and the other soldiers arrested and charged with murder.

Preston's case came to court in November. The captain was defended by Samuel Adams's cousin John. Thirty years later, John Adams recalled sitting in his office the day after the massacre.

"Mr. Forrest [a loyalist merchant] came in," Adams wrote in his autobiography. "With tears streaming from his Eyes, he said I am come with a very solemn Message from a very unfortunate Man, Captain Preston in Prison. He wishes for Council, and can get none. I have waited on Mr. [Josiah] Quincy, who says he will engage if you will give him your Assistance.

"I had no hesitation in answering that Council ought to be the very last thing that an accused Person should [lack] in a free Country," Adams answered, somewhat pompously but no doubt sincerely.

Adams was one of Massachusetts's leading attorneys. His cross-examination undermined the credibility of the prosecution's key witnesses, who testified that they heard Preston order the soldiers to fire. Adams argued the captain might have said "fire by no means," even if some in the crowd heard only the first word. He also paraded to the stand a series of convincing defense witnesses; perhaps most effective was Richard Palmes, a revolutionary merchant who had attacked Preston and was standing right next to him when the shooting began, yet conceded he had never heard the captain order the soldiers to fire.

The jury took only three hours to acquit Preston.

Next came the trial of the rest of the soldiers. Here Quincy and Adams, again appearing for the defense, faced a tricky problem. Having established that Preston never gave the order to fire, they had eliminated the soldiers' best defense; namely, that they were just following orders.

Quincy's solution was, essentially, to take the British view of the massacre. He called to the stand a series of witnesses to testify about the hostility to the soldiers throughout Boston, the point being that the mob intentionally provoked the soldiers. This was too much for Adams; whether out of loyalty to the patriot cause or to Boston's reputation, he threatened to quit the case if Quincy continued in that vein.

Adams prevailed, and the remaining the defense witnesses focused on the immediate danger to the soldiers, rather than the generally hostile climate. Perhaps most effective was Dr. John Jeffries, a friend of Samuel Adams who had treated Patrick Carr, one of the massacre's victims. Jeffries testified he had asked Carr, as he lay dying, whether he thought the soldiers acted in self-defense. According to Jeffries, Carr answered, "he heard many voices cry out to kill [the soldiers]." Carr added, movingly, "that he did not blame the man, whoever he was, that shot him."

The jury acquitted six of the soldiers of murder and found the other two—Montgomery and Private Mathew Kilroy—guilty of the lesser charge of manslaughter. Kilroy and Montgomery were sentenced to having their thumbs branded, a painful punishment but one that avoided any jail time.

Samuel Adams, writing in the Boston *Gazette,* decried a miscarriage of justice and demanded revenge. For many patriots, though, the trials were more a propaganda victory than a legal defeat. If the massacre proved the evils of British power, the verdicts proved the power of American justice. They should, Samuel Adams's friend Samuel Cooper wrote Benjamin Franklin, "wipe off the imputation of our being so violent and blood thirsty a people, as not to permit law and justice to take place on the side of unpopular men."

For many historians, too, the trials became another symbol of American rectitude. Certainly this was the view enshrined in American textbooks for most of the nation's history. But in the 1960s and 1970s, amidst debate over whether antiwar protesters were peace lovers or rioters, both the massacre and the subsequent trials came under new scrutiny.

In the late 1960s, Hiller Zobel, a lawyer and legal historian, studied the trial records and noted that the jury was packed with British sympathizers, virtually guaranteeing the not-guilty verdicts. So, according to Zobel, the case John Adams later described as "one of the most, gallant, generous, manly and disinterested actions of my whole life," was fixed.

Why prosecutors didn't object to a pro-Tory jury remains a mystery. Some historians have pointed to a Tory bias on the part of at least one prosecutor. Others have maintained the prosecutors were patriots, but, like John Adams, eager to show the world how fair they were. Still others have speculated that the prosecutors simply weren't paying close attention, perhaps because they were overconfident that no Boston jury would dare let the soldiers off.

Another theory is that Governor Hutchinson might have pardoned any soldier convicted of murder, and prosecutors feared a pardon would lead to more violence. An acquittal, though hardly likely to satisfy radical patriots, would at least appear to be the result of a fair and legal process.

Whatever the reasons for the prosecution's lapses, the trial was clearly stacked in favor of the defense.

Zobel wasn't satisfied just to debunk the traditional view of the trial. His 1970 book on the massacre argued that the colonists were as much to blame for the violence as the British. He portrayed Samuel Adams as a "demagogic genius" eager to take advantage of the mounting tension between the townspeople and the soldiers.

Other revisionists, such as historian John Shy, went further. Shy resurrected the old loyalist claim that the massacre was a patriot conspiracy, masterminded by Samuel Adams and his fellow revolutionaries. Shy found the timing of the massacre suspicious, coming as it did at the end of a Parliamentary session. That meant, he pointed out, that Hutchinson could not count on a strong response from London, so would have no choice but to give in to the patriots' demand that the soldiers leave Boston. And, in fact, that's exactly what happened.

"Circumstances suggest there was as much purpose as spontaneity in the events leading up to the Massacre," Shy concluded.

Shy's evidence, like Zobel's, is largely circumstantial and ultimately unconvincing. What the revisionists failed to take into account was the fact that Boston's "mobs" were perfectly capable of acting on their own. Working-class Bostonians didn't need Sam Adams or Paul Revere to get them worked up about British soldiers in town. Indeed, laborers had more reasons than other colonists to resent the lobsterbacks. Army regulations allowed the soldiers to work part-time at civilian jobs, and many took work and pay away from Boston workers.

Tensions between soldiers and workers had been on the rise since 1768, and March 5 was by no means the first time that bands of workers had clashed with soldiers. As recently as March 2, a fight had broken out when some ropemakers asked a passing soldier if he wanted work, and then suggested he clean their outhouse.

Amid all the conflicting reports of the massacre, one fact stands out: none of the revolutionary leaders accused of planning a riot were on the scene until well after the five workers were shot. In fact, as Zobel himself noted, when the first of the prominent revolutionaries arrived on the scene, they immediately began negotiating with Hutchinson to remove the troops from Boston. Their goal was to avoid further bloodshed, not cause more.

Patriot leaders were on the scene for the massive funeral march a few days later, and they did help organize it. But the fact that more than ten thousand Bostonians turned out—the town's population at the time was only about sixteen thousand—seems more an indication of the depth of local anger than of the radicals' organizational skills.

The revisionists deserve credit for showing the not-guilty verdicts to be more than the result of an American sense of fairness or of John Adams's legal genius (though it seems unfair of Zobel not to give Adams some of the credit). More fundamentally, the revisionists put to rest the myth that the massacre was entirely the fault of the British. Workers provoked soldiers as often as the reverse, and when Hugh Montgomery shot into the crowd, he had every reason to believe his life was in danger.

But the revisionists failed to realize that the workers' anti-British fervor had outpaced that of patriot leaders like Sam Adams, not to mention his more conservative cousin John. The patriot leadership wanted the troops out of Boston, but they were not yet ready for all-out revolution. That was still six years in the future.

☆ ☆ ☆

In one sense, the traditional and revisionist views of the massacre were not so far apart. Both saw the American Revolution as an essentially conservative movement aimed at protecting the traditional rights of Englishmen, rights threatened by George III and Parliament. Most historians would agree that the Revolution, when it did come, was led by prominent colonists like the Adams cousins, or George Washington and Thomas Jefferson.

In the past thirty or so years, though, historians such as Alfred Young, Eric Foner, and Gordon Wood have highlighted some more radical elements of the Revolution, turning it into more of a preview of the one in France than a rerun of the Magna Carta. From this perspective, the five slain workers were not just martyrs (as in the traditional view) or puppets (as the revisionists would have them), but genuine revolutionaries.

Of the five, the most threateningly revolutionary was Crispus Attucks, the first man killed on the scene. During Preston's trial, one witness described Attucks waving "a large cord-wood stick" at the head of a group of "huzzaing, whistling" sailors. Another recalled Attucks grabbing two four-foot logs from a wood pile and handing him one.

Perhaps most threatening of all, Attucks was an escaped slave, the son of an African father and a Native American mother. John Adams was quick to use this against him, calling him a "stout Mulatto fellow . . . to whose mad behaviour, in all probability, the dreadful carnage of that night, is chiefly to be ascribed." Adams went on to describe the mob as "a motley rabble of saucy boys, Negroes and mulattoes, Irish teagues and outlandish jack tarrs."

Most patriot leaders managed to suppress any racist slurs in the interest of revolutionary solidarity, or at least revolutionary propaganda. Attucks was buried alongside the other four victims, in spite of laws prohibiting integrated burials.

In the 1850s, Attucks's radicalism resurfaced. By then, he had become a symbol not of American freedom but of African American emancipation. To abolitionists, he belonged in the company not of either Adams, but of Nat Turner. Black Bostonian leaders lobbied for a monument to commemorate the massacre and Attucks.

Wrote John Rock, an African American doctor: "The John Brown of the Second Revolution is but the Crispus Attucks of the first."

Again, an Adams spoke out against Attucks. This time it was Charles Francis Adams Jr., the president of the Massachusetts Historical Society. Echoing his great-grandfather, Adams called the "so called massacre" a riotous mob, not to be confused with the "peaceful, earnest, patriotic protest and resistance by our wise and resolute popular leaders."

In 1888, after a forty-year campaign by black Bostonians, the monument was erected on Boston Common. Attucks was immortalized as "the first to die, the first to defy."

This was not, by any means, an endorsement of a radical revolution, either for 1770 or 1776 or 1888. By the time the monument went up, Boston had again reimagined Attucks, this time as a symbol of American unity.

At the dedication, Mayor Hugh O'Brien declared "that all men are free and equal, without regard to color, creed, or nationality; and that the memory of the martyrs whose blood was shed in the cause of liberty in 1770 will thus be preserved and honored for all time." The inscription in the upper-right corner of the monument read: "On That Night the Foundation of American Independence Was Laid."

Those words were originally written by Attucks's first and foremost detractor, John Adams.

☆ To investigate further:

Wroth, L. Kinvin, and Hiller Zobel, editors. *Legal Papers of John Adams.* Cambridge, Massachusetts: The Belknap Press, 1965. Volume 3 includes the records of the massacre trials.

Shy, John. *Toward Lexington.* Princeton, New Jersey: Princeton University Press, 1965. How the British army—and the colonial response to it—led to the American Revolution.

Zobel, Hiller. *The Boston Massacre.* New York: W. W. Norton, 1970. Despite the above criticism, this is the most thorough study of the massacre.

Smith, Page. *A New Age Now Begins.* New York: McGraw-Hill, 1976. The revolution "from the bottom up."

Middlekauff, Robert. *The Glorious Cause.* New York: Oxford University Press, 1982. The best one-volume history of the revolution.

Browne, Stephen. "Remembering Crispus Attucks." *Quarterly Journal of Speech,* May 1999. A penetrating study of the politics behind the memorial in Boston Common.

Young, Alfred. *The Shoemaker and the Tea Party.* Boston: Beacon Press, 1999. At once a biography of a revolutionary shoemaker and an elegant essay on historical memory.

Chapter 13

Was Daniel Boone a Traitor?

Boonesborough, Kentucky. September 1778. To the east and north: the British army. To the west: equally hostile Shawnee Indians. Yet what entranced the people of Boonesborough was a drama of another sort. This was the court-martial, by authority of the Kentucky militia, of the man after whom the town had been named—Daniel Boone.

Boone, his fellow officers charged, had left the fort in February 1778 with 27 men, heading for some nearby salt springs. That was in itself perfectly reasonable. The Shawnee had burned the town's crops and kept the men pinned inside the fort, unable even to hunt. What little meat the townspeople had would spoil without salt to preserve it.

But then Boone had left his party, only to return leading a Shawnee war party and demanding that the salt-makers surrender. Worse, the salt-makers had then witnessed Boone conspiring with the Shawnee and their British allies, and agreeing to surrender Boonesborough to them. And when the Shawnee did attack Boonesborough later that year, Boone had persuaded the town's leaders to meet with the Indians outside the fort so that the Shawnee could ambush them.

And so it was that Daniel Boone, the man whose exploits on the frontier had already made him a legend, came to be charged with treason.

☆　☆　☆

Remarkably, Boone denied none of these acts. But the story he told put quite a different spin on them. This is how it went.

While scouting for the salt-makers, Boone was spotted by four Indians. He tried to flee but—for all his skills as a frontiersman—he was 45 years old and not as fast as he used to be. They caught him.

The Indians took Boone to their camp, where he found 120 warriors painted for war. The Shawnee chief, Blackfish, told Boone they had already seen the camp of the salt-making party and they planned to kill them and then attack Boonesborough.

Realizing that neither the salt-makers nor Boonesborough could withstand such an attack, Boone hatched a plan (or so he said—remember, this is all Boone's version of the story). He told Blackfish that he'd get the salt-makers to surrender, if Blackfish would promise to treat them well. And he convinced the chief that he couldn't take Boonesborough now, but that it would be weaker in a few months. Wait until then, Boone said, and he would turn the fort over to the Shawnee.

All this, Boone claimed, he did to buy time to build up the fort's defenses.

Blackfish agreed to the deal. So Boone convinced the salt-makers to surrender, and the prisoners and their captors headed north. Along the way Boone ingratiated himself further with Blackfish—so much so that by the time they reached the Shawnee village of Chillicothe, the chief had decided to adopt Boone as his own son. He named him Sheltowee. (The ceremony was no fun for Boone—it involved having his hair plucked out and his skin scrubbed to purge him of his whiteness.)

The Shawnee then took Boone and the other captives to the fort of their British allies in Detroit. There Boone again agreed to surrender Boonesborough, this time convincing the British commander, Lieutenant Governor Henry Hamilton, that both he and his fellow settlers were loyal to the Crown.

Having gained the trust of both the Shawnee and the British, and knowing they were readying their attack, Boone escaped and returned to Boonesborough. In September the Indians emerged in the meadow before the fort. A voice called for Sheltowee; it was Blackfish calling his

W

S

Boonesborough, as seen in this early drawing, was hardly an impregnable fortress—which might have accounted for some of Boone's questionable defensive strategies. (Library of Congress.)

son. The chief reminded Boone of the promises he'd made; Boone replied, truthfully, that he was no longer in command of the fort. Blackfish agreed to negotiate, if Boone and his fellow chiefs would do so in front of the fort.

Clearly this would be risky; Blackfish may have had a great deal of faith in his adopted son, but Boone's escape must surely have tested that. Everyone in the fort knew the offer to negotiate might be a trap. But the more they could prolong negotiations, the better chance they had to prepare the fort's defenses. So Boone convinced a delegation from the fort to meet with Blackfish.

In the midst of negotiations the Shawnee attempted to take members of the delegation prisoner, fighting broke out, and the siege of Boonesborough began. But siege warfare was not the Shawnee style; after ten days they withdrew. Boonesborough was saved, and Boone was its hero.

Or was he? Should we believe Boone's story?

His judges did. The verdict of the court-martial was not guilty. Further vindication came right after the court-martial, when Boone was promoted to major.

Given Boone's importance as a symbol of the winning of the West, it's not surprising that most early biographers also bought his story. His earliest biographer, John Filson, wrote *The Adventures of Col. Daniel Boone* in 1784, just six years after the siege of Boonesborough. Boone cooperated in the writing; in fact, the book was written in the first person, and if it wasn't so obvious that the language was too highfalutin to be Boone's, this might even be called his autobiography. Certainly it did much to establish the legend of Boone as frontier hero. And it's therefore hardly surprising that, though it recounts Boone's version of the captivity and siege, it doesn't even mention the court-martial which followed. Filson and Boone probably considered it too embarrassing.

Others followed in Filson's footsteps. Boone's first twentieth-century biographer, Reuben Thwaites, was a bit more objective than Filson, going so far as to concede that Boone's "services in defense of the West . . . were not comparable to those of George Rogers Clark or Benjamin Logan." But on the question of Boone's loyalty, there could be no doubt. To Thwaites, writing in 1902, it was obvious that Boone just pretended to like the Indian life. How could anyone want to eat food "prepared in so slovenly a manner as to disgust even so hardy a man of the forest as our hero"? And there were "many other discomforts intensely irritating to most white men," Thwaites added.

Thirty-seven years later, historians still could not entertain any doubt on the matter. Boone's 1939 biographer, John Bakeless, attributed the court-martial to jealousy and gossip.

☆ ☆ ☆

Today, however, Boone's actions and motives are more suspect. We know, for example, that Boone's wife, Rebecca, came from a leading

Tory family and that Boone had accepted a captain's commission from the British-appointed governor in 1774. (This commission came in very handy when the captured Boone met Hamilton in Detroit.)

John Mack Faragher, author of the definitive modern biography of Boone, concluded that Boone "aligned himself with neither ideological camp, a neutrality that became increasingly difficult to maintain as the conflict sharpened and grew bitter." While chauvinistic historians might have wished otherwise, this ambivalence was common throughout the country, especially in the western territories. For Boone and for many others in and around Boonesborough, loyalty to your immediate community was far stronger than loyalty to either America or Britain.

Just as the line between patriot and Tory has blurred, so too has the line between pioneer and Indian. Part of the Boone legend—at least the part that didn't become confused with Davy Crockett's—always included his ability to adopt Indian ways. And Boone was not alone in this. Appalling though it seemed to more genteel whites back east and to historians like Thwaites, pioneers and Indians had a great deal in common: they hunted the same game, they lived off the same land, they traded and made treaties together. Boone himself, in spite of his reputation as an Indian fighter, only killed one Indian in his entire life.

Blackfish and Boone could discuss turning over the fort because both could genuinely envision its inhabitants becoming Indians. Boone was just one of hundreds of European and American captives to be adopted into Indian tribes. Many refused to return to the white world, even when they were part of prisoner exchanges.

Does all this mean Boone was a traitor? By no means. Just because lines have been blurred does not mean that Boone crossed over them. Just because he could easily pass as a Tory or an Indian does not mean he betrayed either America or Boonesborough. We may never know for sure whether Boone's actions were all tricks, or treason, or something in-between.

What we do know is that the age of Boone was already passing. It had been an age when pioneers and Indians, in spite of all their clashes, had much in common, when Boone and Blackfish might at least consider making a deal. But soon the British, who supplied the Shawnee with arms, would be gone, as would the buffalo and other game that kept them alive. With the end of the Revolution, settlers flooded into Kentucky, changing forever the face of the countryside.

Blackfish's plan to convert all of Boonesborough to Indian ways went way beyond the scope of previous adoptions; it was a desperate effort to save a lost way of life. Ironically, it was also Boone's way of life that was lost. Though his judges exonerated him, Boone no longer had a place in Boonesborough. A year after his trial he left forever the town which bore his name.

☆ To investigate further:

Filson, John. *The Discovery, Settlement And Present State of Kentucke: . . . To which is added, An Appendix, Containing, The Adventures of Col. Daniel Boone.* Ann Arbor, MI: University Microfilms, 1966. Originally published in 1784, the primary source for much of the Boone legend.

Thwaites, Reuben G. *Daniel Boone.* New York: Appleton and Co., 1902. Dated, but lots of good stories.

Bakeless, John. *Daniel Boone.* New York: Morrow, 1939. Also dated, but fun.

Eckert, Allan W. *The Court-Martial of Daniel Boone.* New York: Bantam, 1973. A fictional account of the trial; the dialogue is invented but the rest of the story *could* be true.

Faragher, John Mack. *Daniel Boone.* New York: Henry Holt, 1992. The definitive modern biography.

Aron, Stephen. *How the West Was Lost: The Transformation of Kentucky from Daniel Boone to Henry Clay.* Baltimore: Johns Hopkins, 1996. A new revisionist approach from which are drawn this chapter's conclusions.

Chapter 14

Why Did Benedict Arnold Turn Traitor?

For most of America's famous turncoats—Aaron Burr, Alger Hiss, the Rosenbergs—there is at least some question and in some cases much doubt as to whether they were guilty. In the case of Benedict Arnold, there is no doubt: his name has justly become a synonym for traitor. Nor is there any doubt as to the magnitude of his treachery. Arnold commanded the American forces at West Point and his plan was to turn over the fort there to the British. Had he done so, the British might easily have captured George Washington (who was in nearby Peekskill meeting with the Marquis de Lafayette). Even if Washington had escaped, the British would have controlled the Hudson River crossings. This would have enabled them to cut off supplies to Washington's army, which was already underfed and underarmed. The American Revolution, in short, might very well have failed.

Yet if it's clear what Arnold did (or tried to do), *why* he did it is much less clear. Arnold himself, in a proclamation published soon after he switched sides, said the war had been "a defensive one until the French joined in the combination." Then his eyes had been opened and he saw how dangerous were "the insidious offers of France . . . the enemy of the Protestant faith." But few then or later bought this explanation. Never before had Arnold indicated any qualms about the French. Besides, the language of Arnold's proclamation was suspiciously similar to much else written by the Loyalist writer William Smith; clearly this was little more than propaganda. To understand what really motivated Benedict Arnold, therefore, historians had to look elsewhere, and the obvious place to start was Arnold's life prior to his treason.

By far the most striking aspect of his life prior to turning traitor was that Arnold had been a genuine hero of the Revolution. Along with Ethan Allen, in May 1775, he had captured Fort Ticonderoga on the northern New York frontier; with the fort came cannon and powder crucial to the American war effort. In September 1775 he'd led 1,100 men on a wilderness expedition from Massachusetts to Quebec City. There, though 40 percent of his men were lost to death or desertion, he besieged a city manned by twice his number of troops until May 1776, when 10,000 British reinforcements forced the Americans to retreat. Next, during the summer of 1776, Arnold supervised the construction of a fleet on Lake Champlain; under his command, the makeshift navy was largely destroyed but managed to hold out until winter set in and forced the British to return to Canada. A year later, when the British again swept down from Canada, Arnold led the crucial charge at the Battle of Saratoga that precipitated the British surrender there. Twice wounded, Arnold was honored and trusted by George Washington for his bravery and leadership.

And yet with each victory came frustration and disappointment. At Ticonderoga, Arnold clashed with Ethan Allen; each had independently conceived of the attack on the fort and each felt he should lead the charge. Arnold had the official backing of Massachusetts; Allen was backed by Connecticut and most of the troops. Their compromise—a joint command—was an uneasy one that was further marred by Allen's subsequent charges that Arnold had overstepped his orders and misappropriated funds. Arnold's invasion of Canada, though heroic, failed to capture Quebec. His enemies were quick to label it a failure and to accuse him of confiscating provisions and materials from Montreal merchants for his own profit. Even the Battle of Lake Champlain—which, in retrospect, is seen to have bought the American army the time it needed to prepare for its defense of Saratoga—was at the time seen only as a naval defeat. And Arnold's decisive victory at Saratoga came in defiance of his commanding

MAJ. GEN. BENEDICT ARNOLD.

Major General Benedict Arnold of, for the moment, the Continental Army. (Library of Congress.)

officer, Horatio Gates, who disliked him and had ordered him to stay in his tent; in Gates's official report, Arnold's name was omitted.

Understandably, Arnold was bitter. He must have been further shocked and angered when Congress promoted five others to major general, each one of whom was far less experienced than Arnold. Instead of the renown he felt he deserved, he found himself defending himself against Ethan Allen's charges that he had misappropriated funds.

Since Arnold's injuries left him unfit for field duty, in 1778 Washington appointed him military governor of Philadelphia. Here again, Arnold soon found himself at odds with other revolutionary leaders. He closed the city's shops to inventory all captured goods, and was promptly accused of doing so to line his own pockets. Then he was accused of using army wagons to haul private goods to Philadelphia and granting an illegal pass for a ship, again for his own profit. Arnold was indignant. In May 1779 he wrote Washington that he had "little expected to meet the ungrateful returns I have received from my countrymen."

In December the charges against Arnold culminated in a court-martial, the results of which must have frustrated both Arnold and his accusers. The court found there was insufficient evidence to convict him on most of the counts but did find him guilty of two misdemeanors. It recommended that Washington reprimand him, which he did.

Was Arnold's indignation justified? Was he (up to this point) a patriot or a profiteer? Most historians have concluded he was both: the Revolution offered him a chance for fame and fortune and he wasn't about to turn away either. There is little doubt that he used his positions, especially as military governor of Philadelphia, to further his moneymaking schemes. But his contributions to the revolutionary effort were undeniable, as was his courage under fire. Arnold must have felt unappreciated—and this must have been a factor in his decision to switch sides.

What, specifically, pushed him over the edge?

For 160 years, most historians assumed it was the court-martial, when Washington, once his great supporter, turned on Arnold. Then, in 1941, Carl Van Doren took a careful look at the recently rediscovered letters from the files of the British headquarters. To his surprise, he found that Arnold had been negotiating with the British *before* the court-martial. As early as May 1779 there are letters between the British commander in chief, Henry Clinton, and his adjutant general, John André, discussing Arnold's terms for turning traitor. The correspondence between André and Clinton, as well as that between Arnold and André, also made it very clear that Arnold was looking for money. Specifically, he wanted 20,000 pounds if his plan to turn over his new command at West Point succeeded, and 10,000 pounds if it failed. André countered with an offer of 6,000 pounds. This treason, it seemed, was a transaction motivated less by disillusionment than by sheer greed.

Arnold was especially eager for cash in May 1779 because he'd recently married. His new wife, the 19-year-old Peggy Shippen, had expensive habits; marriage meant new wardrobes for both of them, new furniture, and a continuing round of parties. Pointing as well to her Tory family and friends, many speculated that it was Shippen's influence that pushed Arnold over the brink. The British headquarters papers contain no hard evidence that Peggy Shippen influenced Arnold, but they did establish that she knew of the treason and had participated in its planning.

When the treason plot was discovered, however, with the capture of André, Arnold quickly ditched his wife. This was no time for chivalry. Arnold grabbed a boat and fled across the Hudson—leaving her behind. George Washington then paid her a visit. He found her hysterical and concluded she'd known nothing about her husband's treachery. Was her hysteria merely a show for Washington, this Lady Macbeth's latest act of deceit? Or was Peggy Shippen Arnold genuinely terrified because she feared her role in the treason would be discovered? No one can be sure.

As for Arnold himself, historians have continued to debate the particular mix of bitterness and greed that prompted him to turn traitor. These are not mutually exclusive motives—the British offered him both recognition and money. It's even possible that his love for Peggy was a factor in his decision. But there could no longer be any question that at the center of Arnold's treachery was his craving for money.

Characteristically, one of Arnold's first actions after putting on a British uniform was to present Clinton with a bill for 10,000 pounds. Two weeks after his coconspirator André was executed as a British spy,

Arnold again wrote Clinton insisting on the money. Clinton agreed to pay 6,000 pounds (André's final offer), plus 350 pounds for expenses. For some, especially someone as rich as Arnold, this might have been the end of the story. But not for Benedict Arnold: more than ten years later, with the Revolution over and both Arnold and Clinton living in England, Arnold was still writing to Clinton, and still insisting on being paid.

☆ To investigate further:

Van Doren, Carl. *Secret History of the American Revolution.* New York: Viking, 1941. The first examination of the British headquarters papers, including an appendix with the text of letters from Arnold, André, Clinton, and others.

Flexner, James. *The Traitor and the Spy.* New York: Little, Brown, 1975. Originally published in 1953, this dual biography of Arnold and André portrays Peggy as a Lady Macbeth manipulating her husband into treachery.

Wallace, Willard. *Traitorous Hero.* New York: Harper & Brothers, 1954. A balanced biography of Arnold.

Boylan, Brian Richard. *Benedict Arnold.* New York: Norton, 1973. Of all of Arnold's biographers, Boylan is the kindest to his subject.

Randall, William Sterne. *Benedict Arnold.* New York: Morrow, 1990. An able retelling of Arnold's life, though there's nothing particularly new here.

Brandt, Clare. *The Man in the Mirror.* New York: Random House, 1994. A psychological portrait of Benedict Arnold that attributes most of his actions, including his treachery, to feelings of insecurity stemming from his father's alcoholism and bankruptcy; that this was a factor is certainly credible, but Brandt's argument that it was the primary factor in almost everything Arnold did is unconvincing.

15

Was Sally Hemings the Mistress of Thomas Jefferson?

I t is well known that the man, *whom it delighteth the people to honor*, keeps, and for many years past has kept, as his concubine, one of his own slaves. Her name is SALLY. The name of her eldest son is TOM. His slaves are said to bear a striking although sable resemblance to the president himself.

So wrote James Callender in the September 2, 1802, issue of the Richmond *Recorder*. The charge that Jefferson had a slave mistress named Sally Hemings was picked up by other Federalist newspapers throughout the country; a Philadelphia magazine even commemorated it in verse, to be sung to the tune of "Yankee Doodle Dandy":

Of all the damsels on the green
On mountain or in valley
A lass so luscious ne'er was seen
As Monticellian Sally.

Stories of his slave mistress haunted Jefferson throughout the 1804 election campaign. Jefferson himself never commented on the charges publicly, though he denied them in a private letter to Robert Smith, his secretary of the navy. Other Republicans vehemently defended the president, however. They stressed that the stories were

MAD TOM in A RAGE

The Federalists accused Jefferson of more than having an affair with a slave; in this 1801 cartoon he and "Mad Tom" Paine are pictured trying to pull down the government. (The Huntington Library.)

politically motivated, and in this they were undeniably correct: not only was the *Recorder* a Federalist paper, but Callender had a personal grudge against Jefferson.

Callender had once been a leading propagandist for Jefferson's own Republican party. One of his earlier exposés had forced Alexander Hamilton to admit to an affair with a married woman; another of them had landed Callender in jail under the 1798 Alien and Sedition Acts. In 1801, when Jefferson became president, he pardoned Callender. But Callender felt his sufferings merited more than a pardon. He demanded that Jefferson appoint him postmaster at Richmond and that the president personally pay back the fines Callender had paid under the 1798 laws. When Jefferson refused, Callender threatened revenge; in switching to the Federalist side and writing the first of the Sally stories, he made good on that threat.

For Jefferson's defenders, then and since, Callender's blatantly malicious motives discredited his story. But to get to the truth, to determine whether or not Jefferson had a slave mistress, we must look beyond Callender's motives and examine the evidence.

Callender himself had little hard evidence to offer. He never visited Monticello, never talked directly to Sally Hemings or anyone else connected with the story. Nor, apparently, did any other writer of the period. But then, in 1873, an obscure Ohio newspaper, the *Pike County Republican*, published an interview with Madison Hemings, the son of Sally Hemings and—he claimed—Thomas Jefferson. Hemings, in fact, claimed that his mother had told him a great deal about her longtime relationship with Jefferson—namely that the two had first become lovers in Paris in 1787. Jefferson, a widower since 1782, was then minister to France; Sally Hemings was there as a servant to his daughter. Madison Hemings went on:

> During that time my mother became Mr. Jefferson's concubine, and when he was called home she was *enciente* [*sic*] by him. He desired to bring my mother back to Virginia with him but she demurred. She was just beginning to understand the French language well, and in France she was free, while if she returned to Virginia she would be re-enslaved. So she refused to return with him. To induce her to do so he promised her extraordinary privileges, and made a solemn

pledge that her children would be freed at the age of twenty-one years.

This promise Jefferson eventually kept. When Jefferson died, his slaves had to be sold to pay off creditors to whom he owed more than $100,000. But Jefferson made sure in his will that five of his slaves were to be freed; among these five were Madison Hemings and his brother Eston.

Madison Hemings's version of events was confirmed by another ex-slave memoir, that of Israel Jefferson. Israel Jefferson described how for fourteen years he'd cleaned and kept up Jefferson's bedroom and private chamber, and been on intimate terms with both Thomas Jefferson and Sally Hemings. Of Madison Hemings's claim to be the son of the president, Israel Jefferson said: "I can as conscientiously confirm his statement as any other fact which I believe from circumstances but do not positively know."

Israel Jefferson's memoir also confirmed another story that had been passed on for many years; namely, that Sally Hemings's mother, Betty Hemings, had been the mistress of Thomas Jefferson's father-in-law, John Wayles. This meant that Sally Hemings was the half sister of Thomas Jefferson's late wife, Martha Wayles Jefferson.

Strangely, many of Jefferson's defenders were quick to accept Israel Jefferson's testimony about the John Wayles-Betty Hemings liaison. Perhaps this was because the Wayles-Hemings affair provided an alternative explanation for why Thomas Jefferson treated the Hemings family so much better than other slaves, and why he eventually freed Madison and Eston Hemings. After all, if Jefferson knew they were related to his wife, then his special treatment of them might have had nothing to do with Sally Hemings in particular.

As for the rest of Madison Hemings's and Israel Jefferson's testimony, however, that they adamantly rejected. To discredit it, Jefferson's nineteenth-century biographer Henry Randall produced a letter from Jefferson's grandson, Thomas Jefferson Randolph, in which he revealed that Sally Hemings had indeed been the mistress of a white man—but it was Jefferson's nephew, Peter Carr, and not Jefferson himself who'd slept with her and fathered her children. One of Jefferson's granddaughters, Ellen Randolph Coolidge, came up with a similar story, this time placing the blame on Samuel Carr, Peter's brother, whom she described as "the most notorious good-natured Turk that ever was master of a black seraglio kept at other men's expence." If either Carr brother fathered Sally Hemings's children, that could account for the children's resemblance to Jefferson.

Further mitigating against the Madison Hemings-Israel Jefferson version of events was the fact that both memoirs were published in the *Pike Country Republican*. For a Republican newspaper in 1873, it was good politics to make the antebellum South—with which the Democrats could still be associated—look bad, and the *Republican* was almost as partisan a paper as Callender's *Recorder*. Also suspicious was the language in both the Madison Hemings and Israel Jefferson memoirs; it sounded a lot more like that of a newspaper editor than that of two ex-slaves, and Jefferson's defenders concluded that an editor might have worked on the content as well as the language. Furthermore, they argued, even if Madison Hemings had come up with the story himself, it was clearly in the interest of an impoverished ex-slave to turn out to be the son of Jefferson—and even if Sally Hemings had really told him Jefferson was his father, *she* might have made up the story for the same reason.

Of course, Jefferson's grandchildren had just as vested an interest in their version of events as his ex-slaves did in theirs. But most historians followed Randall's lead, or at least concluded the conflicting testimonies cancelled each other out. And in the absence of more hard evidence of the affair, most dismissed it as a nasty rumor.

☆ ☆ ☆

This genteel consensus received its greatest test with the 1974 publication of Fawn Brodie's "intimate history" of Thomas Jefferson. The first major biographer to accept the Hemings story, Brodie presented a portrait in stark contrast to the traditional image of a monkish Jefferson, a man who, after his wife's death, devoted himself to philosophy and politics. Brodie's Jefferson remained a passionate lover. In France, before the arrival of Sally Hemings, Jefferson met an artist named Maria Cosway, to whom he wrote a remarkable love letter consisting mostly of a debate between "My Head and My Heart." Most biographers have interpreted the letter as a victory for Jefferson's head; Brodie, however, saw the heart as the winner. Brodie was convinced the Cosway-Jefferson relationship was both passionate and sexual.

But it was her portrait of the Hemings-Jefferson relationship that generated the most controversy. In addition to her efforts to rehabilitate the reputations and credibility of Callender and of Madison Hemings, Brodie presented a great deal of "psychological" evidence. For example, she noted that in his 1788 diary of a tour of Germany, Jefferson used the word "mulatto" eight times to describe the color of the soil; in Brodie's interpretation, it was Sally Hemings's mulatto color and not Germany's soil that was on Jefferson's mind. In a 1789 letter to Cosway, Jefferson described himself as "an animal of a warm climate, a mere Oran-ootan"; Brodie points out that in his *Notes on the State of Virginia,* Jefferson had indiscreetly written that "the Oran-ootan preferred the black woman over those of his own species."

In another letter to Cosway, Jefferson described a painting he'd just seen of Sarah delivering Hagar to Abraham. Jefferson called the painting "delicious" and added: "I would have agreed to have been Abraham though the consequence would have been that I should have been dead five or six thousand years." Brodie was quick to remind readers of the significance of the biblical story: Sarah, who was barren, gave Hagar (whom most artists depicted as dark-skinned) to Abraham so that she could bear him a child. To Brodie, Jefferson's lustful description could only be an unconscious admission of his love for Hemings.

Brodie's book was the best-selling nonfiction book of the year, and many general interest newspapers, including the *New York Times* and the *Washington Post* reviewed it favorably. The historical establishment, however, was unconvinced. Dumas Malone, whose multivolume Jefferson biography won a Pulitzer Prize, said the book ran "far beyond the evidence and carries psychological speculation to the point of absurdity; the resulting mishmash of fact and fiction, surmise and conjecture is not history as I understand the term." Merrill Peterson, author of the most widely respected one-volume biography of Jefferson, called Brodie "obsessive" and concluded there was "no need to charge off in defense of Jefferson's integrity when we have no solid grounds for doubting it."

Indeed, much of Brodie's psychological evidence does seem farfetched and some of it is just outright wrong; for example, according to the *Oxford English Dictionary,* the use of the word "mulatto" to describe the color of soil was common in eighteenth-century America. Even scholars with no vested interest in any particular image of

Jefferson found Brodie's work long on speculation and short on hard evidence.

Still, the vehemence of the attacks on Brodie, and the even more vehement denials that someone of Jefferson's character could have slept with Hemings, were themselves revealing. Dumas, for example, wrote that "it is virtually inconceivable that this fastidious gentleman . . . could have carried on through a period of years a vulgar liaison." Clearly, Brodie had done more than repeat some old gossip; she'd touched a nerve.

What Brodie had done was to bring into the foreground of Thomas Jefferson's life the place of slavery and race, something most of his other biographers were loath to do. By focusing on his purported relationship with Hemings, she'd reminded readers that, regardless of whether or not he'd slept with her, he'd *owned* her. Brodie herself did not believe the relationship was an abusive one; on the contrary, she was convinced Jefferson and Hemings shared a deep and lasting love. But Jefferson most certainly was not in love with the other two hundred slaves he owned—and his treatment of them and attitudes toward them were not so different from those of other wealthy Virginian slaveowners.

This is not to deny that Jefferson hated slavery; his writings make that clear. Nor is it to deny the extent to which Jefferson's ideals inspired later antislavery efforts. But Jefferson's actions definitely did not live up to his ideals. Unlike Washington, whose will freed all his slaves on his death, Jefferson freed only the two Hemings brothers and three others. Jefferson's 1783 draft of a new constitution for Virginia provided for the freedom of all children born of slaves after the year 1800, but that unsuccessful effort was his last on behalf of emancipation. After his return from France, wrote David Brion Davis, "the most remarkable thing about Jefferson's stand on slavery is his immense silence." On one of the few occasions he did speak out, during the Missouri crisis of 1820, he threw his considerable weight behind slavery's expansion.

It is in this context that Jefferson's relationship with Sally Hemings must be viewed. Probably he did not have an affair with her; Brodie's evidence is far from convincing. But he was supported by a slave system under which owners routinely did far worse things to slaves than Jefferson was ever accused of. And, when the chips were down, Jefferson supported the system that supported him.

☆ To investigate further:

Peterson, Merrill D. *The Jefferson Image in the American Mind*. New York: Oxford University Press, 1960. The evolution of Jefferson's image in the American imagination.

Jordan, Winthrop. *White Over Black*. Williamsburg, VA: Institute of Early American History and Culture, 1968. A study of American attitudes toward blacks up to 1812 that includes arguments against the affair.

Malone, Dumas. *Jefferson The President, First Term*. New York: Little, Brown, 1970. Volume 4 of the Pulitzer Prize-winning set.

Peterson, Merrill D. *Thomas Jefferson and The New Nation*. New York: Oxford University Press, 1970. The best one-volume biography.

Brodie, Fawn. *Thomas Jefferson, An Intimate History*. New York: Norton, 1974. Unconvincing—but undeniably provocative and entertaining.

Adair, Douglass. *Fame and the Founding Fathers*. Williamsburg, VA: Institute of Early American History and Culture, 1974. Adair's 1960 essay, "The Jefferson Scandals," is included here and remains one of the most convincing refutations of the affair.

Davis, David Brion. *The Problem of Slavery in the Age of Revolution, 1770–1823*. Ithaca, NY: Cornell University Press, 1975. A wide-ranging study of the complex and contradictory factors that influenced opinions on slavery, including a very unforgiving analysis of Jefferson's role.

Smith, Page. *Jefferson*. New York: American Heritage, 1976. A pictorial biography which follows Brodie's lead on the affair.

Miller, John Chester. *The Wolf by the Ears*. New York: The Free Press, 1977. "We have a wolf by the ears, and we can neither hold him nor safely let him go," wrote Jefferson in 1820. "Justice is in one scale, and self-preservation in the other." In Miller's book you can see how Jefferson chose the latter.

Chase-Riboud, Barbara. *Sally Hemings*. New York: Viking, 1978. A novel about Hemings and Jefferson that is sometimes moving but ultimately unconvincing as a portrait of either.

Dabney, Virginius. *The Jefferson Scandals: A Rebuttal*. New York: Dodd, Mead, 1981. The most thorough and also the most sanctimonious refutation of Brodie's account.

Randall, Willard Sterne. *Thomas Jefferson: A Life*. New York: Henry Holt, 1993. The latest biography; competent and readable though nothing dramatically new.

Chapter 16

Was Aaron Burr a Traitor?

Aaron Burr's origins would seem to make him an unlikely traitor.

The grandson of Jonathan Edwards, the country's most famous theologian, Burr served gallantly during the Revolution (albeit under the command of Benedict Arnold). His political star rose steadily, and he was elected vice president under Thomas Jefferson in 1800.

The election turned out to be the high point of Burr's career. Though voters clearly intended Jefferson to head the ticket, the ballot did not distinguish between presidential and vice-presidential candidates. As a result, Jefferson and Burr each ended up with 73 electoral votes. Tradition called for one or two of Burr's electors to throw their votes elsewhere, assuring Jefferson the presidency. But Burr, undeniably ambitious, made no effort to see that happen. That threw the election into the House of Representatives.

The House was controlled by Federalists, who were no fans of Burr but who liked Jefferson even less. Suddenly it seemed that Burr, not Jefferson, could become the nation's third president. It was then that Alexander Hamilton stepped in, urging his fellow Federalists to vote for Jefferson. Jefferson, Hamilton said, at least had "solid pretensions to character."

"As to Burr there is nothing in his favour," Hamilton went on. "His public principles have no other spring or aim than his own aggrandizement."

Hamilton was persuasive, and Jefferson, of course, became president. And the Twelfth Amendment to the Constitution was quickly adopted, to make sure that from then on voters would distinguish between presidential and vice-presidential candidates.

Burr's star continued to plummet. Jefferson, understandably unhappy with the man who almost usurped his presidency, made sure that the vice president had no role in his administration. The enmity with Hamilton escalated until Burr challenged him to a duel. In July 1804, the two rowed across the Hudson River to a spot near Weehawken, New Jersey, where the vice president shot and killed Hamilton. Burr was indicted for murder in New Jersey, and for lesser charges pertaining to the duel in New York.

"In New York I am to be disenfranchised, in New Jersey hanged," Burr wrote his son-in-law. "Having substantial objections to both, I shall not, for the present, hazard either, but shall seek another country."

But where?

Dueling was illegal throughout the North. It was more acceptable in the South, but that was Jefferson country. That left the West, where gun fighting was common, and where many saw Hamilton as a symbol of the hated eastern establishment of bankers and land speculators. In April 1805, Burr headed west.

At first, it seemed just the right place for Burr. He began attracting followers for various military expeditions to Texas and Florida. Spanish rule was increasingly unpopular in both places, especially among westerners eager to expand America's (and their own) holdings. Burr bought about 300,000 acres in Louisiana, known as the Bastrop land, and promised a share to many of his followers.

Burr seemed destined to follow the likes of Lewis and Clark, or perhaps Andrew Jackson, another duelist-turned-military hero against Spain. He met with Jackson, as well as with James Wilkinson, commander of the U.S. forces in the West, and impressed both. He may even have received some encouragement from Jefferson, whose own expansionist tendencies were clearly revealed by the Louisiana Purchase.

Yet within a few months of his arrival out west, there were already unflattering rumors circulating about Burr's intentions. In August 1805, a front-page article in the widely read *Gazette of the United States* asked: "How long will it be before we shall hear of Col. Burr being at the head of a revolution party on the western waters?"

This 1881 illustration shows Burr addressing his troops. Jefferson was certain his vice president was plotting to lead them against the United States. (New York Public Library.)

The clear implication was that Burr was preparing, not to attack Florida or Texas, but to lead a western secession from the United States.

Throughout 1806, Burr gathered men and supplies on Blennerhassett Island, in the middle of the Ohio River, which was owned by the improbably named Irish immigrant and Burr follower Harman Blennerhassett. In October, Wilkinson received a coded letter, dated July and allegedly from Burr.

"I have at length obtained funds, and have actually commenced," the letter read, as Wilkinson decoded it. "The Eastern detachments, from different points and under different pretence, will rendezvous on Ohio on 1 November."

It continued: "Every Thing internal and external favor our view . . . Wilkinson shall be second to Burr only and Wilkinson shall dictate the rank and promotion of his officers. . . . Draw on me for all expenses.

"The gods invite us to glory and fortune. It remains to be seen whether we deserve the boons," the cipher letter concluded.

What the letter described was clearly more than a military expedition against Spain. It sounded suspiciously like a plot for a revolution in the West, with Burr setting himself up as emperor of a new nation and Wilkinson as his second-in-command.

Wilkinson quickly forwarded the letter to Jefferson, who had by then received reports from numerous others of Burr's alleged plots. Jefferson denounced Burr as the organizer of this "unlawful enterprise." He called his guilt "beyond question," and he ordered his arrest.

And so it was that in August 1807, Aaron Burr—who had come within a single electoral vote of being president of the United States—stood trial for treason.

The presiding judge was John Marshall, Chief Justice of the United States, and both Jefferson's cousin and political foe. Jefferson and Marshall had clashed over a number of constitutional issues, since Marshall was a Federalist and eager to protect the judiciary against Jefferson's efforts to expand the power of the executive branch. Not that this necessarily meant Marshall would be prejudiced in Burr's favor, for the Chief Justice also happened to be a great admirer of Alexander Hamilton.

The prosecution was at something of a disadvantage from the start, because of the dubious credibility of its star witness—Wilkinson. During the grand jury, defense attorneys were quick to point out that the general seemed to know a great deal about Burr's plots; Wilkinson answered, not very persuasively, that he'd pretended to go along with Burr to find out more about his plans. To many, Wilkinson appeared to have turned against Burr to protect himself. After all, the cipher letter named the general as "second to Burr only." Wilkinson further undercut the prosecution's case by admitting he erased portions of the letter that referred to his previous correspondence with Burr.

Still, the government had more than a hundred other witnesses ready to testify about Burr's plans. But they all became irrelevant on August 31, when Marshall ruled that treason required an *overt* act, and one witnessed by at least two citizens. That meant that Burr's plans, whatever they were, could not be brought into evidence.

Prosecutors now had to limit their case to the goings-on on Blennerhassett Island in December, when Burr's forces assembled and presumably committed some sort of overt act of treason. The problem was, Burr himself wasn't there; in December, he was in Frankfort, Kentucky, a day's journey away. So, Marshall ruled, none of that evidence was relevant either.

The next day, the jury took only twenty-five minutes to decide "that Aaron Burr is not proved to be guilty under this indictment by any evidence submitted to us." The phrasing clearly indicates it was a grudging acquittal, but Burr was free to go.

The question, again, was: where should he go?

The press and public thought he was a traitor, even if the jury wasn't sure. The treason trial left him with no base in the West, and in New York there were still charges against him from the duel. In June 1808, Burr sneaked out of Manhattan and set sail for England. He spent two years in Europe before deciding there was no place for him there, either.

Back in America, he continued to maintain his innocence. In Burr's 1836 memoirs, he emphasized that his intentions in the West were always, first, "the revolutionizing of Mexico," and second, "a settlement on what was known as the Bastrop lands." Matthew Davis, who co-authored the memoirs, reported that when Burr was asked if he'd ever thought of a "separation of the Union," he responded, "I would as soon have thought of taking possession of the moon, and informing my friends that I intended to divide it among them."

Burr felt somewhat vindicated in 1836, when Sam Houston defeated the Mexicans and Texas declared its independence. "You see? I was right. I was only thirty years too soon," he said. "What was treason in me thirty years ago, is patriotism now."

☆ ☆ ☆

In 1890, more than eighty years after Burr's treason trial, the historian Henry Adams uncovered new evidence pointing to his guilt. The evidence came not from anything in America, but from British archives.

Adams examined the letters of Anthony Merry, British ambassador to the United States between 1803 and 1806. Merry's letters home were voluminous; one contemporary remarked that if you asked Merry what time it was, he would write his government for instructions. Amidst this correspondence Adams found a short note to the British foreign secretary, dated August 6, 1804.

Wrote Merry: "I have just received an offer from Mr. Burr, the actual Vice President of the United States . . . to lend his assistance to His Majesty's Government in any Manner in which they may think fit to employ him, particularly in endeavouring to effect a Separation of the Western Part of the United States from that which lies between the Atlantick and the Mountains, in its whole Extent."

Merry warned his government of the "Profligacy of Mr. Burr's Character," but insisted that he could be of much use to the British. "He is now cast off as much by the democratic as by the Federalist Party," Merry wrote, "and where he still preserves Connections with some People of Influence, added to his great Ambition and Spirit of

Revenge against the present Administration, [this] may possibly induce him to exert the Talents and Activity which he possesses."

A March 29, 1805, letter from Merry home seemed even more damning. By then, Burr had already been west, and apparently had reported to Merry on the likely success of a revolution, adding that if England wouldn't help, France might.

"Mr. Burr . . . told me that the Inhabitants of Louisiana notwithstanding that they are almost all of French or Spanish Origins, as well as those in the Western Part of the United States, would, for many obvious reasons, prefer having the Protection and Assistance of Great Britain to the Support of France," Merry wrote. "If his Majesty's Government should not think it proper to listen to this overture, Applications will be made to that of France who will, he had reason to know, be eager to attend to it in the most effectual manner."

Surely, if Burr was attempting to enlist foreign support for a western revolution, this was treason, and that was Adams's conclusion. Yet Burr's defenders had an answer: Burr wanted money from the British, so he told Merry whatever he thought might get him the money. Burr's actual intentions, his defenders maintained, were always a perfectly patriotic (and typically American) expansionism.

"To secure the sum he conceived to be necessary for his purposes," wrote Walter McCaleb in 1903, "he never scrupled at discoursing of treasons, although at the moment every step he was taking looked toward an invasion of the Spanish territories."

More support for Burr was soon forthcoming, this time from Spanish archives.

Here historians found proof that Wilkinson—the man who sent Jefferson the cipher letter and who testified to Burr's treason—was himself a traitor. The Spanish records confirmed a rumor that had circulated even before the trial. Wilkinson, it turned out, was receiving $2,000 a year from the Spanish government, in return for which he regularly supplied the Spaniards with military intelligence. Indeed, just after Wilkinson sent the cipher letter to Jefferson, he sent another copy to the Spanish governor of Florida to let him know of Burr's plans (and to suggest a suitable reward for the information).

Wilkinson's credibility had been suspect during the trial, especially after he admitted to doctoring the letter. With the proof that Wilkinson was on the Spanish payroll, it seemed all the more possible that the general had turned on Burr to deflect suspicion from himself. At the very least, it was clear that the cipher letter to Wilkinson was not grounds for condemning Burr, and some scholars concluded the letter was forgery.

The most thorough analysis of the letter was by Mary-Jo Kline, who edited Burr's papers in the 1970s and early 1980s. Kline noted that the letter, which still exists in Chicago's Newberry Library, is clearly not in Burr's handwriting. Instead, she found a remarkable resemblance to the writing of Jonathan Dayton, a Federalist senator and Burr associate.

If Dayton was the author, that cleared up one mystery. It explained why the letter referred to Burr as well as Wilkinson in the third person, a usage that seemed strange, even for a letter in code.

But the greater mystery—whether Burr was or was not a traitor—remained unsolved. Sure, it now seemed clear, Burr didn't write the letter. But Dayton, unlike Wilkinson, was Burr's ally and friend. Burr might have asked Dayton to keep Wilkinson informed of the progress of Burr's plans, perhaps to make sure the general was willing to help. Or Dayton might have decided to do so on his own.

Either way, Dayton had no reason to make up stories about Burr's plans, and there's good reason to believe Dayton knew what those plans were.

☆ ☆ ☆

From the start, Burr's reputation has been tied to that of his adversaries.

The duel, ironically, gave Hamilton the last word on their feud. As dueling came to be seen as increasingly objectionable, so, too, did Burr. In spite of Burr's adamant denials, most historians believe Hamilton had no intention of shooting Burr, and that Burr shot first.

Similarly, Jefferson once seemed destined to have the last word on Burr's alleged treachery. He was, after all, the president and the author of the Declaration of Independence; of the founding fathers, only Washington's reputation seemed more unassailable.

A majority of historians continue to follow Jefferson in viewing Burr's guilt as "beyond question." But Jefferson's reputation has been tarnished by the now generally accepted evidence that a slave, Sally Hemings, gave birth to his children. More generally, historians have increasingly emphasized the extent to which Jefferson's slaveholding belied his democratic ideals.

Jefferson's fall from grace has meant a corresponding rise in his enemy's reputation, and the latest histories of the period have cast Burr in a decidedly more positive light. For all his character flaws, Burr was a committed abolitionist, and some historians have gone so far as to argue that's why Jefferson wanted him out of the way. When Jefferson called Burr a "threat to the Empire of Liberty," wrote Roger Kennedy in 2000, it was because Burr's plans for the West threatened "the liberty of . . . those who had slaves to sell into an expanding plantation system."

That's hardly proof of Burr's innocence. The driving force throughout Burr's life was not abolitionism but ambition, and his ambition may very well have encompassed a dream of becoming the Napoleon of the West. Recent revisionists like Kennedy, in their eagerness to cut Jefferson down to size, are perhaps a bit too eager to build up Burr's stature. But they are absolutely right to look at Burr anew, and through eyes other than Hamilton's or Jefferson's.

☆ To investigate further:

Kline, Mary-Jo, editor. *Political Correspondence and Public Papers of Aaron Burr.* Princeton, New Jersey: Princeton University Press, 1983. Includes essays on topics such as the cipher letter, as well as the papers themselves.

Reed, V. B., and J. D. Williams, editors. *The Case of Aaron Burr.* Boston: Houghton Mifflin, 1960. Documents pertaining to the conspiracy, arrest, and trials.

Davis, Matthew L. *Memoirs of Aaron Burr.* New York: Da Capo Press, 1971. Originally published in 1836, this is as close as we'll come to Burr's own version of his life, though it's in the words of his friend.

McCaleb, Walter Flavius. *The Aaron Burr Conspiracy.* New York: Argosy-Antiquarian, 1966. Originally published in 1903 and still one of the best cases for the defense.

Abernethy, Thomas Perkins. *The Burr Conspiracy.* New York: Oxford University Press, 1954. A persuasive case that Burr, at least initially, was planning to create a new nation in the West.

Lomask, Milton. *Aaron Burr.* New York: Farrar Straus Giroux, 1979, 1982. The definitive biography, in two volumes.

Fleming, Thomas. *Duel.* New York: Basic Books, 1999. An entertaining retelling of the fateful "interview" at Weehawken.

Ellis, Joseph J. *Founding Brothers.* New York: Knopf, 2000. Ellis's opening chapter offers an excellent analysis of the mysteries surrounding the duel, including whether Hamilton shot first, and whether Burr intended to kill him.

Kennedy, Roger. *Burr, Hamilton, and Jefferson.* New York: Oxford University Press, 2000. A provocative though sometimes disjointed defense of Burr as abolitionist and proto-feminist.

Melton, Buckner F. *Aaron Burr: Conspiracy to Treason.* New York: John Wiley & Sons, 2002. A Constitutional scholar's thorough overview of the legal and ethical issues surrounding the trial.

Chapter 17

Was Meriwether Lewis Murdered?

In September 1806 Meriwether Lewis—along with William Clark—received a hero's welcome as he entered St. Louis. Lewis and Clark had just returned from their epic journey across an unknown continent, a journey during which they had overcome Indians, grizzlies, mosquitoes, illness, and near starvation. At 33, Lewis was a national hero.

Just three years later he was dead, shot twice in a small cabin in the Tennessee wilderness. Who shot him has been one of the longest-lingering murder mysteries in American history.

If there was an official inquest into Lewis's death, we don't know of it; the records of Maury County, Tennessee, where the shooting occurred, have been lost. But we do know that Thomas Jefferson took it upon himself to investigate the death personally.

Jefferson's interest was not surprising. Lewis had grown up on a plantation only eight or nine miles from Monticello, Jefferson's Virginia home. Jefferson had plucked Lewis from the army to serve as his private secretary, and the president had then chosen him to lead the expedition across the continent. After investigating his friend's death, Jefferson concluded it was suicide. The story he pieced together went as follows.

Meriwether Lewis, from the Analectic Magazine, *1816. Jefferson concluded his friend committed suicide; so did Lewis's partner in discovery, William Clark. But others were convinced it was murder. (Library of Congress.)*

After returning to St. Louis, Lewis was appointed governor of Upper Louisiana. Alas, it turned out this was a man who coped better in the actual wilderness than in the political jungle. Early in his term Lewis reversed some of the Indian policies of his chief assistant, Territorial Secretary Frederick Bates, and Bates worked from then on to undermine Lewis's authority and popularity. Once Jefferson left office, Lewis also managed to alienate his bosses in Washington, in particular Secretary of War William Eustis.

Matters came to a head when Lewis paid five hundred dollars more than Eustis had authorized to return an Indian chief to his tribe. The chief had come east with Lewis on the expedition's return trip, and Lewis felt responsible for getting him back home. Eustis, however, saw this as an example of Lewis's disregard for his higher authority. In addition, he was convinced there was a conflict of interest involved, since the company Lewis had contracted with to escort the chief home was a company in which Lewis's brother had invested.

To make matters worse, Lewis was deeply in debt. When Eustis refused to pay Lewis's expenses, Lewis was near bankruptcy. (He had to borrow some money from Clark—his partner in discovery—to get by.) In September 1809 the much-vexed Lewis set off for Washington to make his case to Eustis in person.

Along the way, Lewis stopped at Fort Pickering, near what is now Memphis. By this time, Lewis was more than vexed; according to the fort's commander, Captain Gilbert Russell, he was "in a state of derangement." Russell also reported that members of Lewis's crew had told him that Lewis had made two attempts at suicide, and that he'd taken it upon himself to keep Lewis in the fort's sick bay.

In about six days, according to Russell, Lewis's condition improved and he again set off for Washington, this time accompanied by Major James Neelly, the United States agent to the Chickasaw nation. For what happened next, during the last 23 days of Lewis's life, we are mostly dependent on Neelly's report. According to Neelly, Lewis's condition again deteriorated and he again "appeared deranged in mind." On October 9, two of their horses escaped and Lewis proceeded on to a small inn, while Neelly stayed behind to track down the horses.

From this point on Jefferson (and future historians) could no longer rely on Neelly's own eyewitness report. Instead, we can only depend on the story which Neelly had to reconstruct from the words of the innkeeper, Mrs. Grinder. According to the innkeeper, Lewis arrived there deranged. Not wanting to be around him, she gave him the house and slept in another one nearby, along with Lewis's and Neelly's servants. At about three in the morning she heard two pistol shots, went to Lewis's room, and found he'd shot himself in the head and a little below the chest. Lewis's last words, according to Grinder, were: "I have done the business my good Servant, give me some water."

This, then, was the story which Jefferson believed. As further evidence of Lewis's suicidal tendencies, Jefferson recalled that "Lewis had, from early life, been subject to hypochondriac affections," as had his father and other family members. Jefferson concluded that "during his Western expedition, the constant exertion which that required of all the faculties of body and mind, suspended these distressing occupations." But back in St. Louis these "affections" had returned, and "he was in a paroxysm of one of these" when he committed suicide.

Another who knew Lewis well also appeared unsurprised on being told he had committed suicide. William Clark reacted to the news by saying: "I fear O! I fear the weight of his mind has overcome him."

With the prestige of the presidency behind it, the verdict of suicide seemed settled.

☆ ☆ ☆

Yet, from the start, there were doubters.

Grinder's cabin lay on the Natchez Trace, a trail already well-known for the presence of bandits who wouldn't hesitate to rob and kill well-to-do travelers. About $120 that Lewis had with him when he left Fort Pickering was never found. Could not one of the Trace's notorious bandits have killed Lewis?

Nor was Grinder an entirely credible witness. Over the years she recounted the story to a number of different visitors, and these stories differed in many details. In some versions Grinder immediately aroused the servants, in others not; in some she was alone, in others her children were present; in some she gave Lewis the water he asked for, in others she refused; in some she described Lewis as crawling around and then heading over to the Trace, while in others he stayed in the cabin. In one version, Lewis's dying words became: "I am no coward; but I am so strong, so hard to die."

Some historians have suspected that Grinder couldn't keep her story straight because she was covering up her role in Lewis's murder—or perhaps the role of her husband. Others have been more sympathetic. After all, finding a world-famous explorer dead in your home would fluster almost anyone, and Grinder was just a poor and uneducated innkeeper.

Neelly, too, has come under some suspicion, as have Lewis's and Neelly's servants. We know little about any of them, other than that Jefferson accepted their innocence (and in the case of Lewis's servant, Jefferson interviewed him at the White House).

Ultimately, with no eyewitnesses (unless Neelly or Grinder were lying), we can never know for sure whether Lewis was murdered or committed suicide. So, like Jefferson, historians have looked beyond the Grinders' cabin and into Lewis's psyche. And many, in contrast to Jefferson, concluded Lewis could *not* have killed himself.

How, they asked, could a man who had conquered the wilderness be so distraught by a few political and financial problems? In his 1947 dual biography of Lewis and Clark, John Bakeless wrote: "Though the government's financial methods drive men to distraction, they rarely drive them to suicide. If they did, the streets of Washinton would be littered with corpses." And in a 1965 biography of Lewis, Richard Dillon wrote: "If ever there is such a person as the anti-suicide type, it was Meriwether Lewis. By temperament, he was a fighter, not a quitter." For many of Lewis's biographers, especially his earlier ones, suicide just didn't make sense; it was the wrong ending to the epic tale they told.

Alas, Lewis was not bound by the need for an appropriately heroic ending to his life. Beset by debt and depression and perhaps disease, he may have seen no alternative to suicide. Perhaps he found it easier to escape Indians and grizzlies than his own despair. Perhaps, with his great adventure in the past, he saw nothing of promise in the future. Perhaps, even as he exhibited great courage during his expedition, he was courting death. Though Clark was certainly no coward, it was Lewis who unnecessarily climbed a dangerous cliff and nearly fell from it; it was Lewis who wandered off alone into country he knew was filled with grizzlies; it was Lewis who, with only two companions, went to meet the Shoshone, who had never before seen white people, and then, with only three others, ventured into the land of the Blackfeet, who he had been warned were hostile. Was he defying death—or embracing it? Did the same forces, however incompletely we understand them, drive him across the continent and then to his death?

We can't know for sure the answer to these questions; much about Lewis's death remains a mystery. But those who knew him best, Jefferson and Clark, concluded he committed suicide, and in the absence of more compelling evidence to the contrary, that seems the most likely solution.

☆ To investigate further:

Allen, Paul, editor. *History of the Expedition under the Command of Lewis and Clark.* Philadelphia: Bradford and Inskeep, 1814. This official account of the expedition, which Lewis was working on when he died, includes Jefferson's memoir and his conclusion that it was suicide.

Bakeless, John. *Lewis & Clark.* New York: Morrow, 1947. Includes a case for Lewis's murder.

Phelps, Dawson A. "The Tragic Death of Meriwether Lewis." *William and Mary Quarterly,* July 1956. A good summary of the case for suicide.

Fisher, Vardis. *Suicide or Murder?* Denver: Alan Swallow, 1962. The most thorough of the cases for murder.

Dillon, Richard. *Meriwether Lewis.* New York: Coward-McCann, 1965. Includes a case for murder.

Kushner, Howard. "The Suicide of Meriwether Lewis." *William and Mary Quarterly,* July 1981. A psychoanalytic case for suicide which argues that both Lewis's excessive risk-taking and his suicide stemmed from his feelings that his father had abandoned him.

Lavender, David. *The Way to the Western Sea.* New York: Harper & Row, 1988. A thorough if uninspired retelling of the Lewis and Clark expedition, including Lavender's leanings toward the case for suicide.

Chandler, David Leon. *The Jefferson Conspiracies.* New York: Morrow, 1994. Argues that Lewis was murdered by agents of General James Wilkinson, and that Jefferson covered up evidence of the murder to keep secret his own intrigues with Wilkinson. Chandler's evidence is *extremely* circumstantial.

Ambrose, Stephen. *Undaunted Courage: Meriwether Lewis, Thomas Jefferson, and the Opening of the American West.* New York: Simon & Schuster, 1996. The most recent and most readable account of the expedition, with a strong case for suicide.

Chapter 18

Was There a "Corrupt Bargain"?

For Henry Clay, the presidential election of 1824 was both a disappointment and an opportunity. Clay, with 47,217 popular and 37 electoral votes, finished fourth, behind Andrew Jackson (152,901 and 99), John Quincy Adams (114,023 and 84), and William Crawford (46,979 and 41). Since none of the candidates won a majority of electoral votes, it was up to the House of Representatives to choose the next president. The bad news for Clay was that only the top three were eligible. The good news was that, as Speaker of the House and by far its most influential member, it was up to him to choose from among the other three.

Supporters of Jackson, Adams, and Crawford converged upon the Speaker. "I am enjoying, while alive," Clay remarked just before the House vote, "the posthumous honors which are usually awarded tothe venerated dead."

Cutting the list to two was a cinch. Crawford's strict constructionist views of the Constitution precluded the strong federal government Clay envisioned. Besides, Crawford had taken only Virginia and Georgia, and had suffered a debilitating stroke. There was nothing his supporters could say to sway Clay.

Jackson had a far stronger case. Not only had he won the most popular and electoral votes, but he was, like Clay, from the West. In Clay's home state of Kentucky, Jackson finished a strong second, and once it was clear that its favorite son was out of the race, the Kentucky legislature passed a resolution supporting Jackson. But Clay was loath to go along. For one thing, it would be difficult for one westerner to follow another as president, and Clay had by no means given up his ambition. For another, Clay didn't like the idea of turning a "military chieftain" (Jackson's fame stemmed from his victories in the Creek War and the War of 1812) into a president.

"Remember," he had warned the House back in 1819, in words that enraged Jackson's supporters, "that Greece had her Alexander, Rome her Caesar, England her Cromwell, France her Bonaparte, and that if we would escape the rock on which they split, we must avoid their errors." By this thinking, Jackson's popularity just made him all the more dangerous.

That left Adams. Clay didn't think much of him, either. The two had served together on the American team negotiating an end to the War of 1812, and the puritanical Adams had refused to dine with the uncouth westerner. ("They . . . drink bad wine and smoke cigars," Adams wrote in his diary, "which neither suits my habits nor my health, and absorbs time which I cannot spare.") But Adams's ideas, at least, were ideologically compatible with Clay's; both supported road and canal projects, a protective tariff, and a centralized banking system. On January 9, Clay visited Adams's home, and emerged committed to supporting his host.

A month later, with Clay's help, Adams was elected president. Three days after that, Adams offered Clay the position of secretary of state, a traditional stepping-stone to the presidency. (Madison, Monroe, and now Adams were all secretary of state before becoming president.)

Much of the nation was outraged. This "monstrous union," wrote Congressman Louis McClane of Delaware, "is so unnatural and preposterous that the reports of no committees, nay all the waters of the sweet Heavens cannot remove the iota of corruption." Newspapers decried the "corrupt bargain" between Adams and Clay.

"The Judas of the West has closed the contract and will receive the thirty pieces of silver," proclaimed Jackson. "Was there ever witnessed such a bare faced corruption in any country before?"

For the rest of his life, Jackson maintained Adams and Clay had stolen the presidency that was rightfully his. Near his death, Jackson was asked if there was anything he had left undone. "Yes," he responded, "I didn't shoot Henry Clay." His logic was clear: "Clay voted for Adams and made him President and Adams made Clay secretary of state," Jackson wrote in 1844. "Is this not proof as strong as holy writ of the understanding and corrupt coalition between them?"

It was a question historians would ask as well.

Jackson made sure the question stayed in voters' minds as the next presidential campaign heated up. In 1827, Jackson said he had evidence of the corrupt bargain: prior to the 1824 election, he recalled, Congressman James Buchanan of Pennsylvania had approached him on behalf of Clay, offering the Speaker's support in return for the job of secretary of state. This was, of course, the same deal, according to Jackson, that Adams and Clay ultimately made. Jackson had indignantly turned it down.

Clay continued to deny any bargain, and he demanded Buchanan speak for himself. At this point Buchanan, who would himself go on to become one of the least renowned of American presidents, backed away from his story. Yes, he admitted, he had approached Jackson about a deal, but Clay hadn't known anything about it. Buchanan had been acting on his own. "I regret beyond expression," he wrote the furious Jackson, "that you believed me to be an emissary from Mr. Clay."

Gloated Clay: "Instead of any intrigues on my part . . . they were altogether on the side of General Jackson." Then, as was his wont, Clay pushed his luck too far. He demanded the Kentucky legislature clear him of any wrongdoing. The ensuing investigation revealed that Clay had written a series of letters about the election to a friend. Clay refused to show anyone the letters, leading Jackson's supporters to conclude that they included proof of the corrupt bargain. Finally, Clay had to make the letters public. They turned out to prove nothing, other than that Clay had plenty of embarrassingly insulting things to say about all the candidates, including Adams.

The mudslinging continued. Jackson's supporters accused Adams of being a gambler (the evidence was a billiard table in the White House) and a pimp (based on a completely false story that, while he was a diplomat in Russia, Adams had supplied American virgins to the czar). Adams's supporters countered with charges that Jackson's wife, Rachel, was a bigamist. (This was technically true, but it ignored the fact that both Rachel and Andrew Jackson believed, albeit incorrectly, that she had divorced her first husband before marrying her second.)

Clay also had to deal with the ranting of Virginia Congressman John Randolph about "the combination of the puritan with the blackleg."

"Are we babies?" Randolph asked. "Can't we make out apple pie without spelling and putting the words together?" Clay challenged Randolph to a duel in which both missed, satisfying Clay's honor but not Randolph's suspicions—when he died seven years later, he was buried facing west "so as to keep an eye on Henry Clay."

Adams, meanwhile, was doing little to help his cause, pushing various unpopular federal initiatives by arguing that America should not be "palsied by the will of our constituents." This was hardly the type of rhetoric to disarm critics who accused him of conspiring to undermine the democratic process. Adams's legislative program went nowhere, and in 1828 Jackson swept into the presidency with 56 percent of the popular vote and 68 percent of the electoral college.

Well into the twentieth century, most historians considered the election of 1828 an appropriate verdict on that of 1824. Adams's own diary buttressed the case against him. His entry for January 9, 1825, is the only contemporary account of his meeting with Clay.

"Mr. Clay came at six," Adams wrote, "and spent the evening with me in a long conversation explanatory of the past and prospective of the future." According to Adams, Clay said he had been approached by friends of Crawford and of Adams, each "urging considerations personal to himself as motives to his cause." Then Clay asked Adams "to satisfy him with regard to some principles of great public importance, but without any personal considerations for himself." Finally, Clay said, "he had no hesitation in saying that his preference would be for me."

To many historians, Adams's abrupt description of a lengthy and crucial meeting meant he had something to hide, even from his own diary. Why, they asked, would Adams record Clay's question but not his own answer? Jackson's biographer, Marquis James, wrote in 1938: "Whatever Mr. Adams replied . . . it was agreeable to the Speaker because from that day forth the two acted in concert."

James continued: "Before coming to Washington, Clay hoped to be able to bring about a situation whereby he could benefit himself by supporting Adams; upon his arrival there he assumed an attitude of aloofness designed to put the Adams people on the anxious seat and bring them to his terms; after which Mr. Adams met the terms. The alternative is an assumption that Clay's support of Adams and Adams's appointment of Clay were merely a coincidence."

George Dangerfield's classic 1952 history of the period also interpreted Adams's reticence as damning. "We are forced to conclude that the two men came to an understanding," Dangerfield wrote. "Clay's conscience was a political conscience: it was not necessarily bad or corrupt, it was simply elastic." As for Adams, "like a dram-drinker, whose ordinary life is usually spent in dull sobriety, he swallowed one intoxicating expedient after another; and the more intoxicated he grew, the more his doleful inner voice assured him that nothing good would come of it."

Indeed, Clay may not have been Adams's only corrupter. Dangerfield noted that Adams might have cut a deal with, among others, Missouri Congressman John Scott. In return for his vote, Scott asked that Adams ignore an effort to unseat Scott's brother, a judge who killed a colleague in a duel. As president, Adams reappointed Scott's brother.

Even Robert Remini, who has written generally complimentary biographies of Adams and Clay (as well as Jackson), suspected a deal, albeit not an explicit one. Remini speculated: "Nothing crude or vulgar, like declaring the terms of their political deal, passed their lips. No need. Both men understood one another's purposes. Both knew what was expected of them when their conversation ended. Surely they both realized that in exchange for House support Adams would designate Clay as secretary of state."

But Remini, like most recent historians, also stressed that Adams and Clay were motivated by more than personal ambition. Both genuinely believed that Adams was better qualified, by experience and temperament, than the "military chieftain." Both genuinely believed they were representing the interests of their constituencies, and that their union was in the best interests of the nation. Whatever else the two discussed in January 1825, they must also have discussed what Adams referred to in his diary as "some principles of great public importance," and they must have found a great deal of common ground there.

"It had to be Adams," Remini wrote. "Much as he personally disliked the man, Clay had little choice."

The election of 1828 was more than a personal rebuff to Adams and Clay and their bargain, corrupt or otherwise. It signaled the rise of what has come to be known as Jacksonian democracy, in which the White House was finally seen to belong not to a would-be aristocrat like Adams but to the common man. Resentment over the bargain

This 1827 drawing shows
Clay attempting to sew
Jackson's mouth closed.
(Library of Congress.)

sparked movements to change the system so that electors were chosen directly by voters rather than by state legislatures.

"The corruption involved in the presidential election," wrote Remini, "was not whether Adams and Clay met in secret and made a deal. . . . The corruption was the decision to hand the presidency to Adams in open defiance of the popular will." Clay could argue, legitimately, that the Constitution gave the House of Representatives the right to make the choice, regardless of what anyone in the Kentucky legislature or the country at large had to say. But that didn't make his appointment as secretary of state any less outrageous, in the minds of most voters. For America, between 1824 and 1828, was transforming itself from a republic to a democracy.

There were, to be sure, stark limits to that democracy. The Jacksonians' common man included neither blacks nor Indians nor women. Indeed, as many historians have pointed out, the rights of white men grew to a considerable extent at the expense of those of African Americans and Native Americans. And, of course, undemocratic features of the Constitution, such as the electoral college, survived not only the election of 1824 but also that of 2000.

But Jackson's call for reform was more than rhetoric. "There is no other corrective of these abuses but the suffrages of the people," he said in February 1825, and he believed it. Four years later, in his first message to Congress, Jackson announced that "the majority is to govern," and he never wavered in this belief.

Clay would never concede that point. In an 1842 speech, he repeated that his motives were "as pure and patriotic as ever carried any man into public office." By then, however, he recognized that, politically at least, he had erred. "It would have been wiser and more politic in me to have declined accepting the office of secretary of state," he said.

☆ To investigate further:

Adams, John Quincy. *Memoirs*. Freeport, New York: Books for Libraries Press, 1969. His diary from 1795 to 1848, originally published in 1874. The meeting with Clay is in volume 6.

Hopkins, James, and Robert Seager II, editors. *The Papers of Henry Clay*. Lexington: The University Press of Kentucky, 1972. Clay's own defense can be found in letters and speeches in volumes 4 and 9.

James, Marquis. *The Life of Andrew Jackson*. New York: Bobbs-Merrill, 1938. Dated, but still entertaining.

Schlesinger, Arthur Jr. *The Age of Jackson*. New York: Little, Brown, 1945. Portrays Jackson as "the Man of the People" and his election and administration as a key stage in the growth of American democracy.

Dangerfield, George. *The Era of Good Feelings*. New York: Harcourt, Brace & World, 1952. Good feelings were pretty scarce during Adams's administration, but the book remains a superb introduction to the period.

Peterson, Merrill. *The Great Triumvirate*. New York: Oxford University Press, 1987. Though Clay never made it to the presidency, through the Senate he (along with Daniel Webster and John C. Calhoun) did much to control the course of American history.

Remini, Robert. *The Life of Andrew Jackson*. New York: Harper & Row, 1988. A one-volume condensation of Remini's masterful three-volume biography.

Watson, Harry. *Liberty and Power*. New York: Hill and Wang, 1990. A concise survey of the period's politics.

Remini, Robert. *Henry Clay*. New York: W. W. Norton, 1991. Scholarly but readable.

Nagel, Paul. *John Quincy Adams*. New York: Knopf, 1997. An entertaining psychobiography.

Chapter 19

Was Rachel Jackson a Bigamist?

From the moment the 1824 election ended in victory for John Quincy Adams, supporters of his opponent, Andrew Jackson, cried foul. Jackson had received a plurality of the popular and electoral votes, but he fell short of a majority, thus throwing the election into the House of Representatives. There, Henry Clay's support for Adams was decisive. When Adams then selected Clay as his secretary of state, Jacksonians charged both with a "corrupt bargain."

Four years later, the Jacksonians were out for revenge, and the election was one of the nastiest ever. Jackson's supporters denounced Adams as a gambler (the evidence was a billiard table Adams purchased for the White House) and as a pimp (the story—completely false but nonetheless widely circulated—was that while Adams was a diplomat in Russia he had supplied American virgins to the czar).

Adams's supporters responded in kind. They countered Jackson's reputation as a military hero by portraying him as a brute likely at any moment to explode in violence. That Jackson had fought eight duels and in one notorious tavern brawl didn't help his reputation, nor did his execution of six militiamen to quell a mutiny under his command during the 1813–1814 war against the Creek Indians. By far the most widely circulated charge against Jackson, however, was that he was an adulterer and that his wife, Rachel, was a bigamist.

KING ANDREW THE FIRST.

In the eyes of his opponents, Andrew Jackson was a monarchist, a mulatto, a murderer
... and worst of all, married to a bigamist. The last charge may very well have been
true. (Library of Congress.)

This charge presented a particularly difficult problem for Jackson; namely, that—at least technically—it was true.

Jackson's supporters put together an eighteen-man committee to gather evidence and present his side of the story. Central to the Jacksonians' version of events was a narrative by John Overton, an eyewitness to much of what he reported.

Around 1787, Overton recalled, he became a boarder in the Kentucky house of the widow Robards; also living there were her son, Lewis Robards, and his wife, Rachel Robards—later to become Rachel Jackson. The Robardses' marriage was a disaster from the start. Lewis Robards was intensely antisocial and suspicious while Rachel, who loved to dance and ride horses and tell stories, was exactly the sort to bring out his jealous streak. At least once, Overton was called upon to intervene and bring about a reconciliation between the Robardses. All three—Lewis and Rachel Robards and John Overton—then moved to Tennessee, near Nashville, where they boarded with Rachel's mother, the widow Donelson.

Enter Andrew Jackson. Like Overton, he was a young frontier lawyer; like Overton, he became a boarder of the widow Donelson. On the Kentucky and Tennessee frontiers of 1789, this arrangement was not so unusual as it might sound: a widow would have been happy to have a couple of extra men around to fend off Indian attacks, and Overton and Jackson would have been happy to have someone to keep house for them. As boarders, Overton and Jackson shared a bed; this prompted one historian to comment, in light of how important Overton's account of what happened was to Jackson's 1828 campaign, that the saying that politics makes strange bedfellows ought in this case to have been reversed.

Inevitably, the tempestuous Jackson and the jealous Robards soon clashed. When Robards found Jackson talking with Rachel—a completely innocent meeting, Overton emphasized—Robards was incensed. Jackson attempted to reason with him but to no avail. The upshot was Robards stormed back to Kentucky, vowing never to live with Rachel again.

But sometime in the fall of 1790, he changed his mind—at least this was the rumor that reached Nashville at that time. On hearing that her husband intended to take her back to Kentucky—by force, if necessary—Rachel was understandably distraught. She decided to flee down the Mississippi River to Natchez, where she had friends who'd protect her.

Jackson was now "the most unhappy of men," according to Overton. Not because he'd done anything wrong, Overton emphasized, but for "having innocently and unintentionally been the cause of the loss of peace and happiness of Mrs. Robards." So Jackson decided to help out by joining the party going down the river. It was, after all, dangerous Indian country through which they'd pass.

In either the winter or spring of 1791, Overton continued, Rachel and Andrew set off for Natchez. By May, Jackson was back in Nashville, where he learned that the legislature had granted Robards a divorce. (Divorce was sufficiently rare that it required a legislative act.) Jackson then rushed back to Natchez, where in the summer of 1791 he married Rachel. They lived together there for a short time and in the fall of 1791 returned to Nashville together.

A happy ending, it seemed. But then, in December 1793—more than two years after they were married—the couple was horrified to learn that Robards hadn't gotten a divorce after all. The Virginia legislature had merely passed an act enabling Robards to take Rachel to court. That he had now done. Since Rachel and Andrew had been living together for more than two years, Robards had no problem convincing a jury that she was guilty of adultery. Worse, though the jury had no need to rule on this, if she had been married to Jackson during this period, she was also clearly guilty of bigamy.

But, Overton emphasized, this guilt was merely a technicality. When Rachel and Andrew married in 1791, both *thought* she was divorced. And when they learned that wasn't the case, they immediately got married again.

This was the story the eighteen-man Nashville committee put forth in the midst of the 1828 presidential campaign. And though it was clearly a political document (Adams's supporters were quick to label the committee the "Whitewashing Committee"), it included a great deal of supporting evidence.

But there were also a lot of holes in the story. Jackson's most prominent nineteenth-century biographer, James Parton, basically accepted the committee's story but admitted that Jackson's conversations with Lewis Robards were probably "not characterized by that moderation of statement and demeanor which might be inferred from a hasty reading of Overton's narrative." Still, the basic story stood.

In 1938 Marquis James's biography of Jackson expressed somewhat more skepticism. How could Jackson, a lawyer, have rushed into a marriage without actually checking out the legislative act which supposedly made that marriage possible? And how could the two live together for more than two years, undisturbed by the slightest suspicion that there'd been no divorce? But, James concluded, "one must believe these things for they are true." Communications on the frontier were both slow and inaccurate; an error like that of the Jacksons was by no means inconceivable. Again, the story stood.

In the most recent major biography of Jackson, completed in 1984, Robert Remini was most skeptical of all. First, he wondered about Jackson's decision to accompany Rachel on her flight from Nashville to Natchez. Surely there was someone who could have accompanied her other than the man her husband had accused of being her lover. Couldn't one of Rachel's ten brothers or brothers-in-law have protected her on her journey? For that matter, why couldn't they have protected her in Nashville as easily as in Natchez? The story just didn't make sense. Remini concluded Jackson was already in love with Rachel at this point, and that he planned the trip with her in order to provoke Robards into granting her a divorce—a plan which succeeded. Not that this was an immoral plan—Rachel was trapped in a horrible marriage and this may have been the only way out she and Jackson could imagine. Still, this was a far cry from the completely innocent mistake Overton described.

Next Remini turned to the marriage ceremony itself—the first one, that is. Overton didn't actually witness the wedding; he merely said that "in the Summer of 1791, General Jackson returned to Natches, & as I understand, married Mrs. Robards." But Natchez was under Spanish rule in 1791, so only Catholic marriages were permitted. Both Andrew and Rachel were Protestant. A Protestant minister could have secretly (and illegally) married them, but no record of that first marriage has ever been found.

Yet there *is* a court record of the Jackson/Robards party's arrival in Natchez—and here the plot really thickens. According to the Spanish records, Jackson and Robards arrived in January 1790, not 1791 (as Overton claimed). If this is the case, then Rachel and Andrew Jackson were married, or living together, months before the divorce proceedings were initiated, let alone completed. And the charges made in 1827—for example, the Cincinnati *Gazette's* claim that "Gen Jackson prevailed upon the wife of Lewis Roberts [*sic*] to desert her husband, and live with himself in the character of a wife"—were indeed true.

So why the big fuss? Who cares if they lived together before they were married, or before she was divorced, or even before she *thought* she was divorced? It is a telling commentary on the difference between the frontier mores of the early 1790s and the national morals of the late 1820s that the Jacksons' eighteenth-century Nashville neighbors clearly didn't disapprove of the marriage; all evidence points to the high esteem in which the couple was held. Frontier life called for all sorts of improvisation, and the Jacksons were hardly unique in not standing on ceremony. Thirty years later, things had changed.

In any case, the accusations against the Jacksons mattered a great deal to Rachel Jackson. Though she was shielded from much of the campaign rhetoric, she came upon some pamphlets during a shopping trip right after the election. What she read staggered her, and many felt it contributed to the heart attack she soon suffered. She died just before she was to set off with her husband for the White House.

The accusations were also relevant for the impact they had on Jackson's presidency. When the wife of Vice President John Calhoun refused to call on the notoriously promiscuous wife of one of Jackson's cabinet members, the president—seeing the attacks on her as comparable to those on Rachel—rose to her defense. The incident became a major scandal, occupying a great deal of cabinet time and ultimately leading to a rift between Jackson and Calhoun that cleared the way for Martin Van Buren, rather than Calhoun, to succeed Jackson.

Finally, the vehemence and prevalence of the charges and countercharges during the 1828 campaign signaled a change in the nature of American politics. True, American politics had always been personal and often been nasty; witness the Federalists' charges that Jefferson had a slave mistress. But by 1828 the press and the parties were much better organized to disseminate negative stories about candidates.

Jackson was a central figure in this transformation. Though he was not personally involved in organizing his party's campaign, he came to symbolize many of the issues that galvanized both his supporters and opponents. To the former, he was the champion of the people, the common man standing against the commercial and banking interests that threatened to corrupt the nation; to the latter, he was a frontier brawler and military chieftain who would upset the orderly improvement of America's resources. What Jackson *actually* stood for was less clear and has been the basis of much historical debate. After his resounding victory in 1828, however, at least one thing was clear: running as the "common man" is an effective route to the White House.

☆ To investigate further:

Parton, James. *Life of Andrew Jackson* (3 volumes). Boston: Houghton Mifflin, 1859. Though many of its stories are apocryphal, there is much essential source material here for any study of Jackson.

James, Marquis. *The Life of Andrew Jackson* Indianapolis: Bobbs-Merrill, 1938. Dated but still entertaining.

Schlesinger, Arthur, Jr. *The Age of Jackson.* New York: Little, Brown, 1945. A classic work of history, this volume portrays Jackson as "the Man of the People" and his election and administration as a key stage in the growth of American democracy.

Hofstadter, Richard. *The American Political Tradition and the Men Who Made It.* New York: Knopf, 1951. Disputes Schlesinger's thesis by portraying Jackson, not as a champion of urban workers or small farmers, but as more concerned with the interests of entrepreneurs and other capitalists.

Curtis, James. *Andrew Jackson and the Search for Vindication.* New York: Little, Brown, 1976. A fascinating psychological portrait of Old Hickory.

Remini, Robert. *Andrew Jackson and the Course of American Empire.* New York: Harper & Row, 1977. With Remini's *Andrew Jackson and the Course of American Freedom* (1981) and *Andrew Jackson and the Course of American Democracy* (1984), this is the most recent major biography, and in many ways a return to Schlesinger's view of Jackson.

Watson, Harry. *Liberty and Power.* New York: Hill and Wang, 1990. A broad but concise survey of the period's politics, this portrays the Jacksonians as attempting to roll back the market revolution.

Cole, Donald. *The Presidency of Andrew Jackson.* Lawrence: University Press of Kansas, 1993. A nuanced portrait of a man more controlled by than in control of the political and economic forces of the age.

Chapter 20

What Were Joseph Smith's Golden Plates?

merica, according to the Book of Mormon, was first settled by Israelites who crossed the Indian Ocean and then the Pacific sometime around 2250 B.C. Then they split into two warring tribes, one led by a prophet named Nephi and the other by his jealous older brother, Laman. For more than two millennia their descendants fought for control of the continent. About A.D. 400, in an epic battle at a hill in upstate New York, the Lamanites defeated the Nephites.

The Lamanites, whose evil ways God had cursed by turning their skin dark, spread throughout America, where they became known to white settlers as Indians. The Nephites were wiped off the face of the earth. But before that final defeat, the Nephite general, Mormon, wrote the history of the two peoples on a set of golden plates, and his son Moroni hid them at the site of the battle. There they remained buried for another fourteen hundred years.

In 1823 (this now according to Joseph Smith's autobiography) Moroni reappeared, this time as an angel. He told the seventeen-year-old Smith where he could find the plates, along with two "seer stones"—the Urim and Thummim—which would enable Smith to read the ancient hieroglyphics. Smith dug up the plates and the stones, and in 1830 published the Book of Mormon.

Thus was born the Church of Jesus Christ of Latter-day Saints, one of the world's fastest-growing religions and the only one whose

According to Joseph Smith, an angel named Moroni led him to the gold tablets that he translated into the Book of Mormon. (Library of Congress.)

holy text is set in America. America would also be the site of a new Zion, Smith promised his followers, and in search of it he led them from New York to Missouri and Ohio, then back to Missouri and on to Illinois. There, in 1844, he was gunned down by a mob incensed by his having destroyed the offices of an anti-Mormon newspaper, as well as by a general dislike of Smith's religion and politics. This martyrdom attracted more followers, who (now led by Brigham Young) established another new Zion, this time in Salt Lake City.

To back up his account of how he found the Book of Mormon, Smith allowed eleven witnesses to look at the golden plates. They couldn't keep them since, as Smith later explained, Moroni returned and took the plates with him. But the witnesses all agreed they'd seen the plates, and three swore they'd seen Moroni as well. One of these witnesses, Martin Harris, brought a copy of some of the hieroglyphic-like symbols to Charles Anthon, a professor of classics at Columbia University. This paper, too, has disappeared, amidst conflicting reports of Anthon's verdict. (Harris said Anthon identified the writing as some sort of ancient Egyptian; Anthon later denied this.)

For Mormons, all this was proof that the Book of Mormon was literal truth. For non-Mormons, of course, both the text and Smith's story of how it came to be were met with skepticism from the start. Let Mormon literalists beware: they need read no further in this chapter, since historians and archaeologists have uncovered no evidence whatsoever that would lead anyone to believe ancient Israelites immigrated to America, or fought a great battle in upstate New York. The Book of Mormon was not written by a general named Mormon, but rather by a farmer named Smith.

Does that mean there's no mystery here? On the contrary: for historians, the intriguing question is not *who* wrote the Book of Mormon, but *how* Smith did so. For as Mormon believers have pointed out from the start, Joseph Smith was an uneducated farmboy. His wife, Emma Hale Smith, said he could barely write a letter, let alone a complex literary work. Even his mother, Lucy Mack Smith, described Joseph as the least bookish of her children.

How, then, did Smith do it?

☆ ☆ ☆

The first and simplest explanation was: he didn't.

As early as 1834, Eber D. Howe argued that Smith had plagiarized the Book of Mormon. The true author, Howe argued in *Mormonism Unvailed* [*sic*], was an Ohio minister and novelist named Solomon Spaulding. Howe quoted neighbors of Spaulding, who said parts of the Book of Mormon were the same as a story Spaulding had read to them years before. This theory fell apart when Spaulding's papers were discovered and his unpublished manuscript was compared to the Book of Mormon. They had little in common.

Howe's book also provided evidence for another, longer-lasting theory. Much of *Mormonism Unvailed* consisted of testimony from Smith's neighbors, many of whom described how he and his father had tramped around upstate New York using all sorts of divining rods and seer stones to search for gold. This type of folk magic was fairly common in rural parts of the state, and there was nothing inherently disreputable about it. But the portrait of the prophet-to-be as a treasure hunter raised suspicions that, having failed to find gold, Smith chose instead to invent the golden plates.

Nineteenth-century commentators also noted that Smith absorbed many other aspects of rural culture besides magic and treasure hunting. This was a time of much religious revivalism. Just a year after the Book of Mormon was published, for example, another upstate New York farmer named William Miller began preaching to followers who later became known as Seventh-Day Adventists. Smith was thus to some extent just another preacher, albeit an extraordinarily successful one.

His story about Indian origins, too, was a product of his time. Indian mounds dotted much of the eastern half of the country, and were a source of much fascination and speculation. Distinguished preachers like Cotton Mather and Jonathan Edwards had already argued that the mounds were evidence that Indians were descendants of the lost tribes of Israel, and the same theory was espoused in an 1823 book, *View of the Hebrews,* by Ethan Smith (no relation). Joseph Smith could have read the book, or least have heard the theory. Indeed, with eight mounds within twelve miles of the Smith farm, it would have been surprising if he hadn't heard of it.

Lucy Mack Smith's 1853 family memoir provided more evidence that her son's theory about Indian origins predated his alleged discovery of the golden plates. "During our evening conversations Joseph would occasionally give us some of the most amusing recitals that could be imagined," his mother wrote. "He would describe the ancient inhabitants of this continent, their dress, mode of traveling, and the animals upon which they rode; their cities; their buildings, with every particular; their mode of warfare; and also their religious worship. This he would do with as much ease, seemingly, as if he had spent his whole life with them."

By the end of the nineteenth century, most historians had concluded that the source of the Book of Mormon was the popular culture of the time. Smith may not have been bookish, but his mother's description made clear he had plenty of imagination and intelligence. There was no need to steal Spaulding's manuscript; he was perfectly capable of creating the Book of Mormon himself.

The twentieth century brought the rise of psychology, and many historians were as eager as therapists to put it to use. Increasingly, they looked inside Smith as well as outside.

Woodbridge Riley's 1902 study was the first to do so. Riley concluded that "the psychiatric definition of the epileptic fits the prophet to a dot." Since then, others have diagnosed Smith as bipolar and manic-depressive. More convincingly, many historians have noted the similarities between the story of the Book of Mormon and Smith's own life, and explained the former as an expression of the latter. Like Nephi, Smith had five brothers, and he fought with them throughout his life. The Book of Mormon begins: "I, Nephi, having been born of goodly parents . . ." Smith's 1832 autobiography starts with: "I was born . . . of goodly parents."

Were Smith's revelations, then, the product of his unconscious mind rather than a conscious hoax? Neither option would please devout Mormons, but the question has shaped Mormon historiography into the twenty-first century.

No one has come closer to a definitive answer than historian Fawn Brodie, whose masterfully subtle biography of Smith, *No Man Knows My History,* appeared in 1945. Brodie brought together the nineteenth-century emphasis on Smith's environment and a twentieth-century understanding of his mind. To the former, she added new evidence that Smith had been an avid folk magician and treasure hunter before becoming a prophet. This evidence included an 1826 court case in which Smith faced charges that he had used these practices to defraud a neighbor. Brodie also noted that Smith's first autobiographical sketch, published in 1834, was decidedly sketchier about the origins of the Book of Mormon than his later versions. Perhaps, she speculated, Smith had started the Book of Mormon as a secular history of ancient America, and only later decided to sell it as holy scripture.

Brodie was also the first historian to count Smith's wives. She listed forty-eight, a figure that subsequent historians have argued is too high but is nonetheless a reasonable starting point. More importantly, Brodie placed Smith's polygamy in a psychological context, demonstrating how he used his religious doctrine to satisfy his sexual desires.

But Brodie's Smith was more than just a charlatan. She concluded that, gradually, he came to believe in his visions, such as seeing Moroni (and, at other times, God and Jesus Christ). Even his polygamy was in some sense an indication of how fully enveloped he became in his role as prophet. Brodie's 1971 revision added a section on his psychology, clearly implying that Smith was torn by inner conflicts and was not just some ordinary liar.

"The awesome vision he described in later years was probably the elaboration of some half-remembered dream stimulated by the early revival of excitement and reinforced by the rich folklore of visions circulating in the neighborhood," she wrote. "Dream images came easily to this youth, whose imagination was as untrammeled as the whole West."

Brodie's detractors attacked her on all sorts of grounds. Some accused her of focusing too much on Smith's charisma, instead of other causes of Mormonism's growth. (True, but the latter was never her subject.) Some charged she was motivated by her own religious alienation. (Brodie, who was born a Mormon, undoubtedly had a personal interest in her subject, but there's no indication that it affected her objectivity.) Some even criticized her superb writing style, claiming that her use of literary techniques made the book more like fiction than history. (If only all historians could write like her.) The church's review was in no way mixed: soon after the book was published, Brodie was excommunicated.

More moderate Mormons, including such well-known historians as Leonard Arrington and Davis Bitton, responded to Brodie by conceding much of the evidence was on her side but affirming the true nature of Smith's visions a matter of faith. "Historical research can never either confirm or disprove alleged supernatural experiences," the two wrote in 1979. For them, there was no point in arguing about whether Smith believed his own stories. The point was that they—and millions of other Mormons—did.

If Arrington and Bitton seemed to be signaling that the debate over the origins of the Book of Mormon was at an end, they were wrong.

The early 1980s witnessed the appearance of a spate of new documents, most of which further undercut the church's view of its own history. Over a five-year period, a rare documents dealer named Mark Hofmann made hundreds of thousands of dollars selling these documents, mostly to church leaders eager to keep them secret. Hofmann was, as another documents dealer said, "the Mormon Indiana Jones who could lead us to impossible treasures of information and wealth."

One document was a land deed linking Sidney Rigdon, a follower of Smith, to Solomon Spaulding. This reopened the question of whether Smith plagiarized Spaulding's manuscript.

Then there were two letters, not really having to do with the church's origins but nonetheless highly embarrassing. One was signed by Smith on June 23, 1844, just four days before he was murdered. It was addressed to two sisters and it demonstrated that, contrary to the church's claims that he was in the process of abandoning polygamy, he was still very much into it. In another letter, Smith named his son as his successor, effectively undermining Brigham Young's claim.

Worst of all, from the perspective of the church establishment, was what came to be known as the "salamander letter." In it, Martin Harris, one of the witnesses who testified he'd seen not only the golden plates but also the angel Moroni, recalled how Smith initially described to him the discovery of the golden plates: "I hear Joseph found a gold bible and I take Joseph aside & he says it is true I found it 4 years ago with my stone but only just got it because of the enchantment the old spirit come to me 3 times in the same dream & says dig up the gold but when I take it up the next morning the spirit transfigured himself from a white salamander in the bottom of the hole & struck me 3 times & held the treasure & would not let me have it because I lay it down to cover over the hole."

The problem wasn't the lack of punctuation, it was the lack of Moroni. Instead of an angel, there was this white salamander, placing Smith and the Book of Mormon squarely in the folk magic tradition and implying Moroni was a later invention. A loyal Mormon business-man named Steven Christensen paid Hofmann $40,000 for the letter, hoping it would never see the light of day.

Then, in October 1985, a bomb exploded, killing Christensen. An-other killed Kathy Sheets, the wife of Christensen's business partner. What had been a historical mystery became a murder investigation.

At first, detectives suspected the murderer was a disgruntled investor in Coordinated Financial Services, the Christensen-Sheets business. They also wondered whether it could have anything to do with the Hofmann deal, and they brought in forensic documents ex-perts to study the paper and ink. The experts concluded that Hofmann had forged the documents—not just the salamander letter but every-thing the dealer had sold to the church.

Under questioning, Hofmann confessed. He had forged the let-ters, and he had murdered Christensen because Christensen was on to him, or nearly so. He had intended to murder James Sheets to throw the police off track, hoping they'd assume both deaths had something to do with Coordinated Financial Services. Kathy Sheets just hap-pened to be the one who picked up the package with the bomb inside.

Hofmann, it turned out, was motivated by more than money. Raised in a devout Mormon family, he had come to hate the church. He had forged the documents to do double damage: first, by making the church pay him to keep them secret; second, by leaking the docu-ments to the press anyway.

Hofmann was sentenced to life in prison.

Was the church leadership also to blame? Obviously, they had not plotted any murders. But they had conspired to keep the documents secret, and the entire forgery and murder case, wrote journalists Richard and Joan Ostling, "could only have happened in connection with the curious mixture of paranoia and obsessiveness with which the Mormons approach church history."

And what about historians? Robert Stott, the chief prosecutor in the case against Hofmann, didn't hesitate to point fingers in their direction as well. "Mark Hofmann recognized those areas in which you would be the least objective," he told a conference of Mormon historians. "He recognized your interest in folk magic, he recognized that you better accept something in that area than something that wasn't. His deceptions, his creations, then, in part, were fashioned with that in mind, to meet what you wanted."

Stott's criticism certainly shouldn't be applied to all historians, Mormon or otherwise. But it is surely a clear warning that history's mysteries should be approached with the care and objectivity that mark any modern murder investigation.

☆ To investigate further:

Smith, Joseph. *The Book of Mormon.* Salt Lake City, Utah: Church of Jesus Christ of Latter-day Saints, 1981. "Chloroform in print," Mark Twain called it, and others have noted that the phrase "and it came to pass" occurs more than two thousand times. But for millions of people, it's the bible.

Brodie, Fawn. *No Man Knows My History.* New York: Alfred A. Knopf, 1945, revised 1971. The title comes from a line in an 1844 sermon, almost a challenge to future biographers. Perhaps no man does fully know his history, but this woman sure came close.

Arrington, Leonard, and Davis Bitton. *The Mormon Experience.* New York: Alfred A. Knopf, 1979. The authors' positions as official church historians obviously bias them, but this is nonetheless a thorough and readable history.

Bushman, Richard. *Joseph Smith and the Beginnings of Mormonism.* Urbana: University of Illinois Press, 1984. Bushman won deserved acclaim for his earlier work on Puritans and Yankees in New England. Here his Mormon faith undermines his objectivity, though not his stylish writing.

Bitton, Davis, and Leonard Arrington. *Mormons and Their Historians.* Salt Lake City: University of Utah Press, 1988. Portraits of Mormon historians, though the pro-church bias can be quickly judged by the fact that Brodie gets only five pages.

Lindsey, Robert. *A Gathering of Saints*. New York: Simon & Schuster, 1988. Like the best true crime stories, this is not just about a criminal (Hofmann) and detectives, but also about the society in which they lived.

Naifeh, Steven, and Gregory White Smith. *The Mormon Murders*. New York: Weidenfeld & Nicolson, 1988. Naifeh and Smith offer more detail about the crime and investigation than Lindsey does, and are also more critical of church leaders.

Bringhurst, Newell. *Reconsidering No Man Knows My History*. Logan: Utah State University Press, 1996. A collection of essays critiquing Brodie's biography, often unfairly but nonetheless interestingly.

Anderson, Robert. *Inside the Mind of Joseph Smith*. Salt Lake City, Utah: Signature Books, 1999. This psychobiography treats the Book of Mormon as, essentially, Smith's autobiography.

Bushman, Claudia, and Richard Bushman. *Building the Kingdom*. New York: Oxford University Press, 1999, 2001. A brief introduction to Mormon history, made even shorter by the Bushmans' tendency to airbrush most blemishes.

Ostling, Richard, and Joan Ostling. *Mormon America*. San Francisco: Harper-San Francisco, 1999. A balanced view of Mormonism, past and present.

Walker, Ronald, David Whittaker, and James Allen. *Mormon History*. Urbana: University of Illinois Press, 2001. A thorough historiography of Mormon history, biography, and social science literature.

Worrall, Simon. *The Poet and the Murderer*. New York: Dutton, 2002. Mormon documents weren't the only ones Hofmann forged. Among the other handwritings he faked were those of Daniel Boone, Butch Cassidy, Nathan Hale, John Hancock, Francis Scott Key, Abraham Lincoln, Paul Revere, Betsy Ross, Myles Standish, Mark Twain, George Washington, Walt Whitman, and—the poet of the book's title—Emily Dickinson.

Chapter 21

How Did Davy Crockett Die?

To the millions of Americans who remember Fess Parker in ABC's 1954 *Davy Crockett, Indian Fighter* series or John Wayne in the 1960 movie *The Alamo,* the answer to this chapter's question is no mystery: Davy died fighting at the Alamo, along with all its other defenders. In the television version, he is last seen swinging his rifle like a club, with the bodies of the Mexicans he has slain at his feet; in the movie version he is if anything more heroic, blowing up the fort's powder magazine to make sure a score of Mexicans die with him.

So clear was this image in Americans' minds that when historian Dan Kilgore presented evidence in 1978 that Crockett surrendered at the Alamo and was executed after the battle, Kilgore was branded un-American. Yet Kilgore's evidence was not new, nor were Hollywood's versions the first fictionalized accounts of Crockett's life and death. Crockett himself was famous as a teller of tall tales, and historians attempting to uncover the truth about his death had first to peel away many layers of legends, lies, and half-truths.

☆ ☆ ☆

The mythic "Davy"—as opposed to the real person historians prefer to call "David"—was at least in part a creation of Crockett's own making. Crockett's autobiography, *A Narrative of the Life of David Crockett,* is more admired by literary critics than by historians. Still, it does present many of the facts of his life and reveals something, at least, of whether he was the type of man who'd fight to the end, or who'd prefer to live to fight another day.

Like Daniel Boone, the Crockett in *A Narrative of the Life* is a great hunter, a superman from the backwoods of Tennessee who killed 105 bears in a single season. So famed was he as a hunter that, so the story went, once a treed raccoon recognized him, it would yell, "Don't shoot, I'm a comin' down!"

Above all, however, the real Crockett was a politician. Using his comic drawl and his log-cabin background as proof that he would fight for the interests of the common man and of the westerner in particular, he was elected to the Tennessee House of Representatives in 1821 and 1823, and to the U.S. House in 1827, 1829, 1831, and 1833. At first he was an ardent supporter of that other "man of the people," Andrew Jackson. But Crockett broke with the president over his policies for disposing of western lands and Indians, and was then embraced by the Whig party. The Whigs saw in Crockett someone who could match Jackson's image as the common man's protector—and who might even be able to challenge Jackson for the presidency. They began ghostwriting his speeches and books, including his *Narrative of the Life,* which was in one sense a campaign biography.

The Whig propaganda made Crockett a national figure—a sort of western Poor Richard, uneducated but rich in common sense and experience. But Crockett's own constituents were less impressed by him. They noted his failure to pass a land bill protecting the rights of poor settlers and squatters; they noted that, in fact, in his entire congressional career he'd failed to get a single bill passed. With the Jacksonians mobilized against him, the 1835 congressional election promised to be a tight one. Crockett promised his followers that he'd serve them to the best of his ability if they elected him. And if they didn't? "You may all go to hell," Crockett answered, "and I will go to Texas."

They didn't—and so he did.

Crockett was not alone: by the early 1830s, although Texas was a province of Mexico, Americans made up 75 percent of its population. Americans flocked there for land that was available at one-tenth the price of land in the United States. For Crockett, who for all his fame was short on cash, the opportunity to buy cheap land was undoubtedly a factor in his decision to immigrate to Texas. And as a politician,

Fall of the Alamo—Death of Crockett.

The 1837 edition of Davy Crockett's Almanac *contained, along with this illustration, the following report: "Colonel Crockett's body was found . . . with his big dagger in his hand, and around him were lying seventeen dead Mexicans, eleven of whom had come to their deaths by his dagger and the others by his rifle and four pistols." But those who were actually at the Alamo told a very different story. (Library of Congress.)*

Crockett was also undoubtedly attracted by the possibility that Texas voters would appreciate him more than Tennesseans had.

The Mexican government, on the other hand, didn't like the idea of these Texans voting for anyone at all. Quite reasonably, Mexico saw these increasingly assertive immigrants as a threat to its authority, and decided to outlaw new immigration and ban slavery in the province. The more militant Americans responded by declaring Texas an independent nation and appointing Sam Houston as commander in chief. Like Crockett, Houston was an ex-Tennessean and an ex-congressman; unlike Crockett, Houston remained tied to the Jacksonians in the United States.

By the time Crockett arrived in San Antonio in early February 1836, tensions were near the breaking point. Not only were the Mexican general Santa Anna and his 2,400 troops on the march toward the fort but the Texans at the Alamo were themselves split between those who acknowledged Houston's authority and those who did not. Houston, recognizing that the 183 men in the Alamo could not hold the fort against Santa Anna's troops, ordered its commander, Colonel William Travis, to blow up the Alamo and retreat. But Travis, as part of the opposition to Houston, refused, thus setting up the fateful battle.

It is amidst these political maneuverings that Crockett's decision to stay at the Alamo—and the likelihood of his fighting to the death as opposed to surrendering—must be considered. Crockett had come to Texas because it was a land of economic and political opportunity, not so that he could fight and die. Moreover, Crockett was no soldier. (In his autobiography he readily admitted that he'd hired a substitute to finish out an earlier term of enlistment.) But once he got to Texas he found his past political affiliations threw him in with the anti-Houston, anti-Jackson forces, and these were the forces defending the Alamo. He was stuck there.

Of course, this doesn't prove that Crockett surrendered, or that his heroic death scene is mere myth. Many have died heroically on the battlefield with less evidence of previous heroism than Crockett's life provided. What Crockett's past life proved was merely that he was the type of person who easily *could* have surrendered. To determine whether he actually did so, historians needed some actual witnesses.

☆ ☆ ☆

The obvious problem with witnesses, at least on the American side, was that they were dead.

Once Colonel Travis used his sword to draw his famous line in the sand, and all those willing to stay and fight to the death crossed the line, the fate of the Americans was sealed.* After 90 bloody minutes on the morning of March 6, 1836, they were all dead. (Not quite all: The Mexicans did spare the life of a slave, Joe, and a woman, Susannah

---

*The question of whether Travis really drew this line has intrigued historians almost as much as that of how Crockett died. The story went as follows: On March 3, Travis lined up his men and told them there was no escaping the Mexicans. He then drew a line with his sword and asked all those who would stand beside him and fight to the death to cross the line. Every man did so, but for one: Louis Rose, who would inevitably become known as "the yellow rose of Texas." Rose vaulted the walls of the Alamo and eluded the Mexicans.

The story was first written down in 1873, and by then it was at best thirdhand. Many historians have questioned not just the story, but whether Rose was even at the Alamo. Some have argued that the story didn't make sense: on March 3, Travis was still hoping reinforcements would reach the fort, so his heroic gesture would have been premature. But it's possible Rose was there, and it's also possible that the 1873 account got the story right but the date wrong. Perhaps Travis drew the line on March 5; by then it was all too clear that help could not arrive in time to save the Alamo.

Dickinson, and the latter's report of seeing Crockett's mutilated body has often been used to prove he died fighting. But she didn't see his body until well after the fighting had ended—and well after he might have been captured and executed.)

On the Mexican side, of course, there were many survivors. That their testimony was for so long ignored can only be attributed to American chauvinism. In 1975, however, Carmen Perry translated into English the narrative of José Enrique de la Peña, an aide to Santa Anna and an eyewitness to Crockett's death. According to de la Peña, Crockett most definitely did not go down fighting. Rather, he was captured along with six others and brought before Santa Anna. Drawing on his famous ability to tell tall tales, he attempted to talk his way out of his situation. He claimed that he'd merely been exploring the country around the Alamo when he'd heard of the Mexican advance. Then, "fearing that his status as a foreigner might not be respected," he'd sought refuge in the Alamo. But Santa Anna didn't buy it. He ordered Crockett and the others killed, and his officers (though not the horrified de la Peña) "fell upon these unfortunate, defenseless men just as a tiger leaps upon his prey."

Other Mexican witnesses offered briefer but similar versions of Crockett's death. Among them were Colonel Fernando Urissa, another aide to Santa Anna; General Martín Perfecto de Cos, Santa Anna's brother-in-law; Colonel José Sanchez Navarro, who led one of the assault columns against the Alamo; and Sergeant Francisco Becerra. Santa Anna's personal secretary also reported the capture and execution of some Americans (though he didn't mention Crockett). In spite of efforts to discredit the testimony of these Mexicans, the sheer number of witnesses to his surrender, and the lack of any reliable eyewitness to his death in battle, clearly favors the surrender story.

At the time, many U.S. newspapers reported the surrender, as did many nineteenth- and early twentieth-century histories. In fact, the story of Crockett's execution was often used as evidence of Santa Anna's barbarity, and it generated comparatively little controversy. Only after the Fess Parker/John Wayne versions were filmed did Crockett's death become a part of American mythology. But mythology, not history, is almost surely what it was.

The revisionist view of Crockett's death can be taken too far, however. Just because he wasn't Parker or Wayne didn't mean he died in vain. Even in its surrender and execution version, Crockett's death focused the attention of the United States on Texas, and money and volunteers rolled into the territory. Six weeks after the Alamo, Sam Houston's men, crying "Remember the Alamo!", overwhelmed the Mexicans. A day later Santa Anna surrendered.

Nor should Crockett's surrender be confused with cowardice: faced with insurmountable odds, Crockett made the only reasonable choice. De la Peña's account of the execution concludes by telling how "though tortured before they were killed, these unfortunates died without complaining and without humiliating themselves before their torturers." Or, to put it another way, Davy Crockett died like a hero.

☆ To investigate further:

Crockett, David. *A Narrative of the Life of David Crockett of the State of Tennessee.* Knoxville: University of Tennessee Press, 1987. This facsimile edition of Crockett's 1834 autobiography includes useful notes and an introduction by James Shackford and Stanley Folmsbee.

de la Peña, José Enrique. *With Santa Anna in Texas: A Personal Narrative of the Revolution,* translated and edited by Carmen Perry. College Station: Texas A&M University Press, 1975. Written soon after the battle, its translation and publication in 1975 set off the debate about Crockett's death.

Shackford, James. *David Crockett: The Man and the Legend.* Chapel Hill: University of North Carolina Press, 1956. Shackford was unaware of some of the Mexican sources on the Alamo; as a result, he argued that Crockett—who was certainly no coward—was likely to have been on the front lines and therefore was likely to have died very early on in the battle. Though he was wrong on this, he was right on most everything else, and his book remains the best biography of Crockett.

Kilgore, Dan. *How Did Davy Die?* College Station: Texas A&M University Press, 1978. A concise summary of the case that Crockett was captured and then executed.

Lord, Walter. *A Time to Stand.* Lincoln: University of Nebraska Press, 1978. Originally published in 1961 and still the most dramatic history of the Alamo.

Lofaro, Michael and Joe Cummings, editors. *Crockett at Two Hundred: New Perspectives on the Man and the Myth.* Knoxville: The University of Tennessee Press, 1989. Most of the essays here are somewhat specialized but the ones by Kilgore and Hutton contain interesting descriptions of the backlash that followed the publication of Perry's translation of de la Peña's book.

Long, Jeff. *Duel of Eagles.* New York: Morrow, 1990. The most recent history of the Alamo; worth reading but not quite up to the standard set by Lord's 1961 book.

Derr, Mark. *The Frontiersman: The Real Life and the Many Legends of Davy Crockett.* New York: Morrow, 1993. The most recent biography of Crockett; worth reading but not quite up to the standard set by Shackford's 1956 book.

Groneman, Bill. *Defense of a Legend,* Plano, TX: Republic of Texas Press, 1994. Claims the de la Peña diary was a forgery, and that Crockett *was* killed at the Alamo.

Part 3

Unanswered Questions About a Divided Nation

1860s to 1890s

Chapter 22

Did Lincoln Provoke the Attack on Fort Sumter?

From a strictly military viewpoint, Fort Sumter was hardly worth fighting over. Surely, neither side fought the Civil War for the sake of a tiny, man-made island about four miles off the shore of Charleston, South Carolina. Yet for the five months between the election of Abraham Lincoln and the opening shots of the war, this piece of rock commanded the attention of both North and South. The reason was simple: when South Carolina and six other states seceded, there were hardly any federal troops stationed in the South, or anywhere else for that matter. Confederate authorities quickly took over most federal possessions within their borders, leaving only Sumter—along with three forts off the coast of Florida—in federal control. With the Florida forts more easily defended, Sumter quickly became the symbol of the Union's dwindling authority in the South.

Still, both sides were loath to fire the first shot. For Jefferson Davis and the new Confederate government, the goal was independence, not war; if they could hold on to the former without the latter, that was all the better. Up north, the newly empowered Republicans included both militants and moderates, with the latter very concerned that the use of force in South Carolina would push into the Confederate camp the southern and border states, especially Virginia, which had not yet seceded. Lincoln's secretary of state, William Seward, was negotiating with Davis's ambassadors, convinced that given time, the Deep South would return to the fold. Northern moderates also pointed to the military difficulties involved in starting a war. Near the end of February, Major Robert Anderson, who commanded Fort Sumter, informed the secretary of war that it would take about twenty thousand more men to hold the fort against the South Carolina forces massed around Charleston; this would require an act of Congress and months of preparation. The army's top general, Winfield Scott, advised the president to withdraw Anderson's forces and turn over Sumter to the Confederates.

Lincoln was unwilling to do so, and the status quo held through March. It might have continued beyond that had Anderson not informed his superiors that he was running out of food. When Lincoln learned of this, he ordered assistant Secretary of War Gustavus Fox to put together an expedition to reinforce the fort, and on April 4 he ordered it to sea. Two days later, he sent a messenger to inform South Carolina Governor Francis Pickens "to expect an attempt will be made to supply Fort Sumter with provisions only." Lincoln added that "if such an attempt be not resisted, no effort to throw in men, arms, or ammunition will be made without further notice."

Now the choice was Davis's. If the Confederates waited, Sumter would be resupplied, and if Lincoln was lying, reinforced. Davis would not take that chance. He demanded that Anderson immediately withdraw. Anderson refused, and at 4:30 A.M. the first shot of the Civil War went soaring over Charleston Harbor.

That the South—specifically, Captain George S. James—fired that shot has never been questioned. But what led to the first shot has been much more contentious. Many Southerners immediately accused Lincoln of cynically manipulating the situation so that Davis had no choice.

"He chose to draw the sword," the Petersburg (Virginia) *Daily Express* wrote of Lincoln, "but by a dirty trick succeeded in throwing upon the South the seeming blame of firing the first gun."

Davis, not surprisingly, agreed. "He who makes the assault is not necessarily he who strikes the first blow," he wrote. "To have awaited further strengthening of their position by land and naval forces, with hostile purpose now declared, would have been as unwise as it would be to hesitate to strike down the arm of the assailant, who levels a deadly weapon at one's breast, until he has actually fired."

What was more surprising, in the years that followed, was how many historians agreed.

☆ ☆ ☆

This illustration appeared in the April 27, 1861, Harper's Weekly, *just weeks after the Confederates fired on Fort Sumter. (Library of Congress.)*

Lincoln gave his own explanation in a July 1861 address to Congress. Fully aware that many considered his decision to send Fox's fleet a provocation, he maintained that he had strongly considered evacuating Sumter and reinforcing Florida's Fort Pickens instead, since the latter would have served just as well as a symbol of federal authority. Just days before Sumter was attacked, he learned that troops could not reach Pickens before Anderson's garrison was starved out of Sumter. This, he said, left him no choice but to order Fox to South Carolina.

But, Lincoln insisted, his intentions remained peaceful—thus his message to the governor emphasizing that, if the Confederates allowed him to send in supplies, they would consist of food and not arms or men. "They were expressly notified," Lincoln reminded Congress, "that the giving of bread to the few brave and hungry men of the garrison was all which would on that occasion be attempted, unless themselves, by resisting so much, should provoke more."

Lincoln took pains, he continued, "not only to keep this declaration good, but also to keep the case so free from the power of ingenious sophistry, as that the world should not be able to misunderstand it."

It was not just Southerners, however, who understood his actions differently. Many Northerners, even many Republicans, cast Lincoln as the man who brought about the war, though they tended to admire rather than condemn the way he shrewdly provoked the South into firing the first shot. "The attempt at reinforcement was a feint," wrote the *New York Times* a few days after the battle. "Its object was to put upon the rebels the full and clear responsibility of commencing the war." The *Daily Pittsburgh Gazette* compared Lincoln's strategy to that of the Greeks' Trojan horse.

Just the day before giving his address to Congress, according to Senator O.H. Browning of Illinois, the president confided that he was pleased with the results of Fox's expedition, even though Anderson surrendered thirty-three hours after the Confederate bombardment began. "The plan succeeded," Lincoln told Browning, at least as Browning recorded it in his diary. "They attacked Sumter—it fell, and thus, did more service than it otherwise could."

A letter from Lincoln to Fox, written soon after Sumter fell, may have been meant to comfort the expedition's leader about his failure to resupply the fort, but it also provided evidence that the president's plan entailed more than feeding the hungry. "You and I both antici-pated that the cause of the country would be advanced by making the attempt to provision Fort Sumter, even if it should fail," Lincoln told Fox, "and it is no small consolation now to feel that our anticipation is justified by the result."

Lincoln's own private secretaries, J. G. Nicolay and John Hay, re-ported that the president was neither surprised nor excited when he learned of the attack on Fort Sumter, since that had been his "carefully matured purpose." In their 1890 history, Nicolay and Hay praised Lincoln for the "universal statesmanship" of his plan, but their description of Lin-coln's motives was not so different from that of Davis. "He was master of the situation," they wrote, "master if the rebels hesitated or repented, be-cause they would thereby forfeit their prestige with the South; master if they persisted, for he would then command a united North."

Among twentieth-century historians, the most Machiavellian portray-als of Lincoln came from Charles Ramsdell in 1937 and John Shipley Tilley in 1941. Ramsdell's Lincoln, in sharp contrast to the Nicolay-Hay universal statesman, was not particularly concerned about preserving the Union or ending slavery. He was a political animal whose primary concern was to mollify the radical Republicans who were clamoring for war without alienating more moderate Northerners.

To Ramsdell, Lincoln's message to Governor Pickens was better proof of his mastery of the language than the Gettysburg Address.

"He had the skill of an artist in so phrasing a sentence that it conveyed precisely the meaning he wished it to convey," Ramsdell wrote. "He could do more than that: he could make the same sentence say one thing to one person and something entirely different to another and in each case carry the meaning he intended."

In the Pickens letter, Northern moderates heard Lincoln say "an attempt will be made to supply Fort Sumter with provisions only"; this was merely a president fulfilling his humanitarian obligations to provide food for hungry men. Suspicious Southerners, on the other hand, worried that more than food would slip through, and that food alone would allow the garrison to hold the fort. They heard a clear threat to use force "if such an attempt be . . . resisted." For the Confederates, Ramsdell wrote, letting Fox's fleet through would be "a ridiculous and disgraceful retreat."

The message to Pickens left Davis no choice but to attack, thus uniting radicals and moderates behind Lincoln.

Tilley took this thesis even further, arguing that Lincoln invented the story of the starving garrison. Tilley noted he could find no copy of the letter Anderson allegedly sent informing his superiors of a food shortage. Indeed, Tilley pointed to earlier letters from Anderson in which he reported he had plenty of supplies.

Tilley's argument fell apart in 1947, when historian David Potter delved into the Lincoln papers in the Library of Congress and found Anderson's letter. Refuting Ramsdell proved more difficult, but Potter marshaled a great deal of evidence to demonstrate the sincerity of Lincoln's desire for peace. And peace was still possible in April 1861, Potter stressed. True, seven slave states had seceded, but eight had not, including Virginia. Potter's Lincoln was every bit as moderate as Seward, committed to negotiating with the Confederates and convinced they could be brought to their senses and back into the Union.

In February 1861, Potter noted, Lincoln told a number of leading Virginians that he would withdraw the troops from Fort Sumter if they would stay in the Union. A few days later, he told a German diplomat the same thing, explaining that "a state for a fort is no bad business."

Lincoln, according to Potter, was telling the truth in July 1861, when he told Congress that he would have called off the Sumter expedition if Fort Pickens could have been fortified instead. Once he was forced to resupply Sumter, Lincoln fashioned as unprovocative a message as possible to the Confederates, one designed to reassure them that he would not send in more arms or men.

Asked Potter: "Given Lincoln's determination to save the Union, and given his belief that the loss of Fort Sumter, without being sure of Fort Pickens, would make it impossible to save the Union, could he have followed any more peaceable course than he did? Was there any possible means of holding Sumter that would have been less provocative?" It was Davis, not Lincoln, who bowed to the political pressure from his own extremists and made the decision to go to war.

Potter's Lincoln bore no resemblance to the smug politician who confided in Browning and consoled Fox. This Lincoln considered his Sumter policy a failure, since it ended in war, and this failure haunted Lincoln to his death.

"In the months that followed, Lincoln exhibited great forbearance and charity toward the South," Potter wrote. "That he did so may not be entirely a consequence of his personal magnanimity. It may also have derived from a conviction that, if the matter had been handled differently—if, indeed, he had handled the matter differently—the conflict might have been averted."

☆ ☆ ☆

Could it really have been averted?

In contrast to Potter, many recent historians have portrayed the Civil War as inevitable, or as Seward put it, an "irrepressible conflict." More to the point, historians such as Kenneth Stampp and Richard Current have argued that Lincoln saw war as inevitable and acted accordingly.

"By January, 1861," Stampp wrote in 1970, "Lincoln had lost faith in a southern Unionist reaction and had come to the conclusion that he might have to use force to preserve the Union."

Stampp and Current accumulated a huge body of evidence demonstrating Lincoln's abiding commitment to preserve the Union and stop the spread of slavery. This was, after all, the man who declared in 1858 that "a house divided against itself cannot stand." This was the platform on which he was elected, and only someone much more naïve than Lincoln could have remained oblivious to the extent of Southern discontent. For Stampp and Current, the key was not Lincoln's July 1861 speech to Congress but his inaugural address four months earlier.

"In your hands, my dissatisfied countrymen," he said to the Confederates, "and not in mine, is the momentous issue of civil war. . . . You have no oath registered in Heaven to destroy the government, while I shall have the most solemn one to 'preserve, protect, and defend' it. You can forbear the assault; I can not shrink from the defense of it."

This Lincoln did not want war, but he was preparing for it—and that included making sure the onus of the first shot fell on the Confederates. "The Sumter project was designed to relieve Lincoln from the responsibility for initiating hostilities," wrote Stampp.

Was this, then, a return to the Ramsdell-Tilley thesis? Were Stampp and Current, for that matter, making the same points that Jefferson Davis had made a hundred years earlier?

Not quite. For one thing, Stampp and Current stopped short of accusing Lincoln of deliberately provoking the war, though the former conceded that "his Sumter policy revealed his willingness to risk one for the sake of the Union if the responsibility for aggression could be placed upon the South."

More importantly, unlike Ramsdell and Tilley and Davis, Stampp and Current *approved* of what Lincoln was doing. Their Lincoln was closer to the universal statesman of Nicolay and Hay than the Machiavelli of Ramsdell and Tilley.

"It may well be true that the outbreak of war saved the Republican party from disintegration," wrote Stampp. "But the . . . implication that he started the war to achieve that purpose remains unproved. The evidence makes equally valid the conclusion that he thought only in terms of what he understood to be the deep and enduring interests of the whole country."

Ultimately, neither Potter nor Stampp nor Current could prove beyond a doubt what motivated Lincoln. The documentary record provided plenty of examples of Lincoln seeking peace and of Lincoln preparing for war. Even Ramsdell's thesis, though rightly in disrepute, can't be entirely disregarded; as late as 1960, historian Ludwell Johnson revived it in an essay focusing on Confederate decision making.

For most historians, the question of Lincoln's motives couldn't be separated from their own feelings about whether the Civil War was worth fighting. In 1942, Potter was not so sure.

"The Civil War . . . saved the Union, and it freed 4,000,000 slaves," Potter conceded. "But it can hardly be said that these immense values were gained at a bargain. For every six slaves who were freed, approximately one soldier was killed; for every ten white Southerners who were held in the Union, one Yank or one Reb died. A person is entitled to wonder whether the Southerners could not have been held and the slaves could not have been freed at a smaller per-capita cost."

For Stampp, writing after the Civil Rights movement, the value of emancipation, incomplete as it was, outweighed the misery that followed Fort Sumter. "By 1860 white Americans had tolerated more than two hundred years of black slavery and still had discovered no peaceful way to abolish it," he wrote. "A person is entitled to ask how many more generations . . . should have been forced to endure life in bondage in order to avoid its costly and violent end."

As for Lincoln, the misery of the war was clearly etched on his face. But at no point did he ever express any doubts about the worthiness of his cause.

☆ To investigate further:

Nicolay, John G., and John Hay. *Abraham Lincoln.* New York: The Century Company, 1890. Volumes 2 and 3 of ten cover events leading to Sumter.

Ramsdell, Charles. "Lincoln and Fort Sumter." *Journal of Southern History,* August 1937. Lincoln as Machiavelli.

Potter, David. *Lincoln and His Party in the Secession Crisis.* New Haven, Connecticut: Yale University Press, 1962. Originally published in 1942, this remains the most persuasive portrait of Lincoln's efforts to maintain peace.

Stampp, Kenneth. *And the War Came.* Baton Rouge: Louisiana State University Press, 1970. Originally published in 1950, this takes the position that there was pretty much nothing Lincoln could have done to prevent war.

Current, Richard. *Lincoln and the First Shot.* Philadelphia, Pennsylvania: J. B. Lippincott, 1963. Reaches the same conclusion as Stampp, though on the basis of somewhat different evidence.

Boritt, Gabor, editor. *Why the Civil War Came.* New York: Oxford University Press, 1996. In his opening essay, Gabor argues, like Stampp, that war was virtually inevitable, but, like Potter, that Lincoln tried to avert it.

Klein, Maury. *Days of Defiance.* New York: Alfred A. Knopf, 1997. Klein writes in the tradition of Stampp, though he's less concerned with making his argument than with telling his story.

Detzer, David. *Allegiance.* New York: Harcourt, 2001. This latest history of the events leading up to the Civil War focuses on Anderson, who as commander of Fort Sumter was torn between his duty to the Union and his desire to avoid war.

Chapter 23

Who Was Emily Dickinson's "Master"?

In Cave if I presumed to hide
The Walls—begun to tell—
Creation seemed a mighty Crack—
To make me visible—

Thus did Emily Dickinson express her most desperate desire: to hide from the world. Even in her own lifetime, long before her posthumously published poems made her famous, her elusiveness made her the subject of local gossip.

"I must tell you about the character of Amherst," Mabel Loomis Todd wrote to her parents in 1881, just a couple of months after moving to the Massachusetts town. "It is a lady whom the people call the Myth. . . . She has not been outside of her own house in fifteen years, except once to see a new church, when she crept out at night, & viewed it by moonlight. . . . She dresses wholly in white, & her mind is said to be perfectly wonderful. She writes finely, but no one ever sees her."

One of Dickinson's first editors, Thomas Wentworth Higginson, was equally mystified. "I have the greatest desire to see you," he wrote her in 1869, "but till then you only enshroud yourself in this fiery mist & I cannot reach you, but only rejoice in the rare sparkles of light." Higginson did finally meet her, but later confessed that "she was much too enigmatical a being for me to solve."

From the start, her mystery revolved around a thwarted love affair, one whose end was so traumatic that it was the source of both Dick-

Taken soon after her six-teenth birthday, this is the only undisputed mechani-cally created print of the poet. (Amherst College.)

inson's withdrawal from the world and her remarkable poetry. Dickinson herself fueled such speculation by dropping hints about the affair in her poems and letters. In 1862 she wrote Higginson: "I had a friend, who taught me Immortality—but venturing too near, himself—he never returned—Soon after, my Tutor died—and for several years, my Lexicon—was my only companion."

Scholars in search of Dickinson's secrets have been especially drawn to the drafts of three love letters found among her papers after her death. Addressed only to "Master," they were undated and it's unclear whether they were actually sent.

The first, which on the basis of handwriting analysis has been dated 1858, was the most restrained. Dickinson wrote: "I wish that I were great, like Mr. Michael Angelo, and could paint for you. You ask me what my flowers said—then they were disobedient—I gave them messages. They said what the lips in the West say, when the sun goes down, and so says the Dawn."

The letter was apparently written in response to Master's questions about the meaning of some flowers—presumably poems—Dickinson had sent him. In typical fashion, she answered with a riddle, perhaps even a veiled criticism of Master for not having understood the "messages." She continued: "Each Sabbath on the Sea, makes me count the Sabbaths, till we meet on shore—"

In the second Master letter, which handwriting experts have dated to 1861, there is still longing, and more pain. Began Dickinson: "If you saw a bullet hit a Bird—and he told you he wasn't shot—you might weep at his courtesy, but you would certainly doubt his word." Dickinson clearly felt a bullet had struck her—perhaps in the form of a break-up—and that her lover ought to have seen her agony, even though she tried to cover it up.

"I heard of a thing called 'Redemption'—which rested men and women," she went on. "You remember I asked you for it—you gave me something else. . . . I am older—tonight, Master—but the love is the same—so are the moon and the crescent. . . . if I wish with a might I cannot repress—that mine were the Queen's place—the love of the Plantagenet is my only apology—" Her request for redemption has been interpreted to mean Master might have been a clergyman; her desire to take the place of the Plantagenet's queen that her king, whoever he might be, was already married.

Then: "Vesuvius . . . said a syllable—a thousand years ago, and Pompeii heard it, and hid forever—She couldn't look the world in the face afterward—I suppose—Bashful Pompeii!" Dickinson saw herself both as Vesuvius, whose passion once erupted, and as Pompeii, forever buried by the results of that eruption.

And finally this plea: "I want to see you more—Sir—than all I wish for in this world—and the wish . . . will be my only one . . . Could you come to New England—would you come to Amherst—Would you like to come—Master?"

By the time of the third letter, dated to 1862, Dickinson has apparently lost all hope: "I've got a cough as big as a thimble—but I dont care for that—I've got a Tomahawk in my side but that dont hurt me so much . . . Her Master stabs her more—"

No longer aspiring to be Michelangelo, Dickinson has now been reduced to begging: "Master . . . I will never be noisy when you want to be still. I will be your best little girl . . . I shall not want any more— and all that Heaven only will disappoint me—will be because it's not so dear."

The passion and frustration of the Master letters, especially the second and third, were rivaled only by her poems. Indeed, the letters and poems shared much of the same imagery, and many of the latter seemed written with Master in mind. So one could hardly blame read-ers for wanting to know who he was.

The prime candidate was Reverend Charles Wadsworth, a respected Philadelphia minister Dickinson met while passing through that city in 1855. Wadsworth's name first surfaced in a 1931 edition of Dickinson's let-ters edited by Mabel Loomis Todd. This was the same Todd who had once written to her parents about the "myth" of Amherst. In the inter-vening years, she learned a great deal more about Dickinson's reality, pri-marily through a longtime affair with Emily's brother Austin. Todd's edi-tion of Dickinson's letters made clear the latter's great admiration for Wadsworth, whom she described as her "dearest earthly friend" and a man "whom to know was Life." Wrote Todd: "Just what shade of ten-derer feeling to ascribe to her attachment, who would presume to guess?"

Wadsworth's name moved further front and center in the 1932 book *Emily Dickinson Face to Face,* by Martha Dickinson Bianchi. Bianchi was Dickinson's niece, the daughter of Austin and Susan Dickinson. According to Bianchi, everyone in the family always knew Wadsworth was her aunt's lover—this came from no lesser authorities than Bianchi's father (Emily Dickinson's only brother), her aunt (Dickinson's only sister), and her mother (one of Dickinson's closest friends).

Wrote Bianchi: "The testimony of her closest contemporaries leaves no doubt that during her visit to Philadelphia . . . my aunt met the man who was henceforth to stand to her for the Power and the Glory . . . . These contemporaries were agreed that any further development of what was stated to be their mutual recognition of each other was im-possible, owing to the fact that he was already married. According to them, the definite renunciation followed a brief interview in her father's house, and left a permanent effect upon my aunt's life and vision."

Wadsworth fit the bill: he was not just a minister but a renowned orator, which would have impressed someone with Dickinson's appre-ciation for language; he was married, so the place of his "Queen" was already filled; he briefly visited the Amherst area in 1860, around the time of the Master letters; he moved from Philadelphia to California in 1862, the same year the final Master letter manifested such despair.

The main problem with the Wadsworth-as-Master theory was that the reputed lovers could not have met more than once or twice. She may indeed have heard him preach when she visited Philadelphia in 1855, and he may have visited her in 1860 when he stayed in nearby

Springfield, but that was it. Nor, if you don't count the Master letters, was there anything in their correspondence that indicated any intimacy, let alone a grand passion.

Many scholars, therefore, looked elsewhere for Master. The next likely candidate was Samuel Bowles, editor of the nearby *Springfield Republican,* a close friend of Austin and Susan Dickinson, and a frequent visitor to their Amherst home. In contrast to her letters to Wadsworth, Emily Dickinson's letters to Bowles had, if nowhere near the passion of the Master letters, at least many more hints of an actual relationship.

Like Wadsworth, Bowles was married, which might explain this poem she sent him in 1862:

> Title divine—is mine!
> The Wife—without the Sign!
> Acute Degree—conferred on me—
> Empress of Calvary!
> Royal—all but the Crown!
> Betrothed—without the swoon!

It's hard to read this as anything but a love poem, in which the love was off limits (The Wife—without the Sign) and perhaps unconsummated (without the swoon).

There were, alas, as many problems with Bowles-as-Master as with Wadsworth. For one thing, Bowles and Dickinson most likely met sometime after 1858, the approximate date of the first Master letter. Then there was the plea in the second Master letter that he come to New England. This made perfect sense in the case of Wadsworth, who lived in Philadelphia and then San Francisco. Bowles, however, spent most of his life in nearby Springfield and frequently stayed in Amherst. Moreover, Dickinson's request for "Redemption" seemed a lot more appropriate for a minister than a newspaper editor.

With both Wadsworth and Bowles problematic, the search for Dickinson's lover continued. Starting in the 1970s, many feminist scholars concluded that one reason it had been so difficult to identify the man was that it wasn't a man at all.

☆ ☆ ☆

At the same time that Austin Dickinson was courting his future wife, so was his sister.

"I have but one thought, Susie . . . and that of you," wrote Emily Dickinson to Susan Gilbert in 1853. "If you were here—and Oh that you

were, my Susie, we need not talk at all, our eyes would whisper for us,
and your hand fast in mine, we would not ask for language." In 1858,
after Austin and Susan were married, Dickinson wrote her a poem:

> One sister have I in our house
> And one, a hedge away.
> There's only one recorded,
> But both belong to me.

This could easily be interpreted as nothing more than welcoming a new
sister-in-law to the family. But by the last stanza, it sure sounds like more:

> I spilt the dew—
> But took the morn—
> I chose this single star
> From out the wide night's numbers—
> Sue—forevermore!

Women's letters of the nineteenth century often sound decep-
tively intimate to modern readers, but Dickinson's letters and poems
to her sister-in-law went well beyond the usual Victorian romanticism.
The sheer quantity of letters and poems for her made it plain that Susan Gilbert Dickinson was a key figure in the poet's life. Over the
course of their thirty-six-year relationship, there were 153 letters and
poems. Though few were explicitly sexual (and even then, subject to
alternative interpretations), many were clearly love letters and poems.
In one letter, for example, Dickinson compared Susan to Dante's Beat-
rice; in another, to Eden. For many scholars, Todd's picture of the
ethereal, white-dressed recluse who never ventured outside her home
was now replaced by that of a lesbian in love with her sister-in-law.
Some, among them Ellen Louise Hart and Martha Nell Smith, argued
that Todd and other members of Dickinson's family had invented the
traumatic love affair with Wadsworth in order to cover up the truth.

To be sure, the lesbian lover thesis had its problems as well.
There was the fact that the Master letters were clearly addressed to a
man: at one point, for example, she referred to his beard. And some of
Dickinson's poems were explicitly heterosexual:

> He was my host—he was my guest
> I never to this day
> If I invited him could tell
> Or he invited me.

So infinite our intercourse
So intimate, indeed,
Analysis as capsule seemed
To keeper of the seed

One possibility, of course, was that Dickinson was bisexual, and that she turned to a male Master after Susan chose Austin over her. Another, proposed by Freudian biographers such as John Cody, was that there was no Master, that Dickinson conjured him up out of her own imagination, perhaps in an effort to repress her homosexuality. Dickinson herself, in an 1862 letter to Higginson, wrote: "When I state myself, as the Representative of the Verse—it does not mean—me—but a supposed person." She was referring to her poetry, not her letters, but she was certainly encouraging readers not to take her literally.

One did not have to be a Freudian to grant the poet's right—and her manifest ability—to use her imagination. To paraphrase Robert Frost, poets don't have to go to Niagara Falls to write about falling water. Many formalist critics have gone further than that, criticizing all the attention paid to identifying Master, and arguing that it has detracted from the study of Dickinson's language.

Granted, some of the interest in Master is just a scholarly version of the local gossip Todd reported in 1881. But the relationship between an artist's work and life is surely a legitimate question, and besides, Master is a temptation impossible to resist. And, in the view of most scholars, he almost certainly did exist, in spite of Cody's provocative suggestion. In her letters to Master, Dickinson included enough details that, even if they failed to identify a particular man, made it hard to see him as pure fiction. The current consensus is that Dickinson loved both men and women, and that the Master letters grew out of an actual relationship with a man, though it may have been one-sided and unconsummated.

Regardless of who they think Master was, most scholars see the letters, like the poems, as some mix of fact and fiction. Richard Sewall, author of the most comprehensive Dickinson biography, believed Bowles was Master, but Sewall also stressed that the poet "appropriated the experience to her own creative uses." Alfred Habegger, Dickinson's most recent biographer, thought it was Wadsworth, but he also believed that the characters in poems and letters "sometimes . . . voice her private situation . . . frankly and directly [and] sometimes . . . are actors of her favorite fantasies, fictions, and projections." Habegger settled on Wadsworth for the very reasons that Sewall chose Bowles: the minister and the poet could not have met in person more than once or twice. This, Habegger believed, made him the perfect vehicle for her imagination.

Whoever he (or she) was (or wasn't), Master was certainly that.

☆ To investigate further:

Franklin, Ralph. *The Poems of Emily Dickinson.* Cambridge, Massachusetts: Harvard University Press, 1998. She may never have intended anyone to read them, but here are three volumes of them.

Johnson, Thomas, editor. *Emily Dickinson: Selected Letters.* Cambridge, Massachusetts: Harvard University Press, 1971. Includes the full texts of the Master letters.

Bianchi, Martha Dickinson. *Emily Dickinson Face to Face.* Boston: Houghton Mifflin, 1932. Dickinson's niece recalled overhearing, as a little girl, her mother talk about her aunt and "the sacrifice of her young romance."

Patterson, Rebecca. *The Riddle of Emily Dickinson.* New York: Cooper Square Publishers, 1973. Originally published in 1951. Patterson was one of the first to argue that Dickinson's lover was a woman; she concluded it was Susan Dickinson's friend, Kate Anthon.

Cody, John. *After Great Pain.* Cambridge, Massachusetts: Harvard University Press, 1971. Dickinson as psychotic.

Walsh, John Evangelist. *The Hidden Life of Emily Dickinson.* New York: Simon & Schuster, 1971. Walsh concluded Master was Judge Otis Lord, a man with whom Dickinson probably did have an affair, but many years after the Master letters.

Sewall, Richard. *The Life of Emily Dickinson.* New York: Farrar, Straus and Giroux, 1974. Sewall masterfully portrays not just Dickinson, but her family, friends, and world.

Pollak, Vivian. *Dickinson, the Anxiety of Gender.* Ithaca, New York: Cornell University Press, 1984. A fascinating combination of literary, psychological, and feminist analysis.

Wolff, Cynthia Griffin. *Emily Dickinson.* New York: Knopf, 1986. It was not a man, but God, who abandoned Dickinson (and vice versa).

Farr, Judith. *The Passion of Emily Dickinson.* Cambridge, Massachusetts: Harvard University Press, 1992. An incisive analysis of how Dickinson drew on her reading as well as life experiences.

Hart, Ellen Louise, and Martha Nell Smith. *Open Me Carefully.* Ashfield, Massachusetts: Paris Press, 1998. Emily Dickinson's letters to Susan Huntington Dickinson.

Habegger, Alfred. *My Wars Are Laid Away in Books.* New York: Random House, 2001. Insightful and elegant.

Chapter 24

Who Lost (and Who Found) the Lost Order?

As General Robert E. Lee led the Army of Northern Virginia across the Potomac River in early 1862, they were singing "Maryland, My Maryland." They had good reason to sing. They were crossing into Maryland—and into Union territory. They were confident that sympathetic slaveowners there would rally round. There was panic in Washington, and even as far north as Pennsylvania.

Indeed, the Confederates were as close to victory as they would ever be.

Reluctantly, George McClellan led the Army of the Potomac out of Washington and into pursuit. McClellan worried about leaving the capital unprotected, and he worried even more about taking on an army that had recently and soundly beaten Union troops near Richmond and then at Bull Run.

Lee halted in Frederick, Maryland, considering where to strike next. Before heading farther north, he wanted to establish a supply line through the Shenandoah Valley. That meant knocking out the federal garrison at Harpers Ferry, about twenty miles to the southwest and held by about twelve thousand Union troops.

The problem was to secure Harpers Ferry without losing his northward momentum.

Lee's solution, typically bold, was to divide his army. On September 10, he issued "Special Orders 191." Some of Lee's forces were to go north toward the Pennsylvania border, under James Longstreet. The brunt of the army, led by Stonewall Jackson, would head toward Harpers Ferry. Other divisions would spread out between Frederick and Harpers Ferry to make sure Union spies didn't find out about Jackson's movements.

This was a very risky plan. If the Union *did* find out, McClellan could strike the northern parts of Lee's army before Jackson returned. Lee's combined forces were outnumbered by McClellan's troops; spread thin from Hagerstown to Harpers Ferry, the Confederates were extremely vulnerable.

One of Lee's officers pointed out the risk.

"Are you acquainted with General McClellan?" Lee responded. "He is an able general but a very cautious one."

Lee was confident Jackson could take Harpers Ferry and reunite with the rest of the army before McClellan made a move.

Lee was not the only one who thought his opponent overly cautious. McClellan's detractors, among them Abraham Lincoln, thought his caution bordered on cowardice, or at least a ruinous immobility. The president once remarked bitterly that the Army of the Potomac should be renamed "McClellan's bodyguard."

"Place him before an enemy," said Senator Ben Wade, "and he will burrow like a wood chuck." Kenneth P. Williams, whose biography of McClellan appeared in 1949, summed up the general as a man "who sat a horse well and wanted to be President."

What Lee did not know was that fate was about to hand McClellan a break beyond any general's wildest dreams. Three days after Lee signed Special Orders 191, a "lost" copy would find its way to Union headquarters. McClellan now had in his hands a detailed description of Lee's plan, complete with routes and timetable.

"Now I know what to do!" McClellan exulted on first reading the orders. He dashed off a note to Lincoln, telling him "I have all the plans of the rebels." That evening he showed the Lost Order to General John Gibbon, saying: "Here is a paper with which if I cannot whip Bobbie Lee, I will be willing to go home."

"Castiglione will be nothing to it," McClellan added, referring to the 1796 battle in which Napoleon routed a divided Austrian army.

Not surprisingly, given the import of the Lost Order, Civil War historians have spent much time and ink on the case. Their investigations have focused on three mysteries: Who lost the Lost Order? Who found it? And how did it change the course of the war?

☆ ☆ ☆

It was no mystery whose copy of Special Orders 191 was lost. The copy, which McClellan kept among his papers after the war, was addressed to Confederate General D. H. Hill.

Confederate sympathizers were quick to blame Hill for losing not just the order but the war. One early report had Hill dropping the paper in Frederick. Another had him throwing it away, annoyed by its contents. The recollections of other Confederate generals tended to underscore how careful *they* were with their copies: General John Walker pinned his in an inside pocket, and Longstreet memorized the contents and then ate the paper.

Hill vehemently denied he had lost the order. He defended himself in an 1868 issue of the magazine *The Land We Love* and again in an 1885 letter to the Southern Historical Society. The gist of his case was the "unfairness of attributing to me the loss of a paper, solely upon the ground that it was directed to me."

As Hill explained, he'd never even gotten the orders from Lee. His copy of the orders came from Jackson (to whom he reported), not from Lee. Hill wasn't even aware anything had been lost until he read about it after the war.

Hill suggested a traitor must have stolen the lost order.

For that, he had no evidence. But Hill's alibi was perfectly credible, especially since he had kept (and eagerly showed others) the copy of the orders he received from Jackson. Most historians believed Hill; after all, he couldn't lose something he never had.

The blame for the Lost Order gradually shifted to Colonel Robert Chilton, Lee's chief of staff. Chilton had a reputation for sloppy paperwork, hardly a desirable trait in an officer whose responsibilities were largely administrative. He kept no record of who received Lee's orders, nor did he keep the receipts for the signed orders. So he had no way of knowing for sure whether Hill (or anyone else) actually received the orders. As he lamely explained in a letter to Jefferson Davis, in a "case so important," it would have been the courier's "duty to advise its loss."

Chilton also told Davis he didn't remember who was assigned to take the orders to Hill, and—not surprisingly—no one ever came forward to admit he was the courier. So the details of how the order was lost remained a mystery.

But a year after Hill wrote to the Southern Historical Society, further evidence of his innocence surfaced. It came in an 1886 account of how the Lost Order was *found*.

The earliest existing reference to the finding of the Lost Order was a note General Alpheus Williams passed on to McClellan with the order itself. Williams credited a Corporal Mitchell.

More details were revealed in 1886, when Colonel Silas Colgrove, responding to a request from the editors of *The Century* magazine, gave his account of the discovery. According to Colgrove, the Twenty-seventh Indiana Volunteers, under his command, stopped near Frederick on September 13. They set up camp not far from where D. H. Hill's division had been the night before.

"Within a very few minutes after halting," Colgrove recalled, "the order was brought to me by First Sergeant John M. Bloss and Private B. W. Mitchell . . . who stated that it was found by Private Mitchell near where they had stacked arms. When I received the order it was wrapped around three cigars [Hill was known as a cigar connoisseur], and Private Mitchell stated that it was in that condition when it was found by him.

"The order was signed by Colonel Chilton," Colgrove continued, "and the signature was at once recognized by Colonel Pittman, who had served with Colonel Chilton at Detroit, Michigan, before the war, and was acquainted with his handwriting. It was at once taken to General McClellan's headquarters by Colonel Pittman."

Pittman handed it to Williams, who brought it to McClellan.

Six years after Colgrove's account, Bloss weighed in with his own version, in which he and not Mitchell first spotted the order. Bloss's version is suspiciously self-promoting, and Colgrove's seems more credible. The only apparent error in Colgrove's story was Mitchell's rank; he was a corporal and not a private. Since both Williams's contemporaneous note and Colgrove's story credit Mitchell, it seems likely he was the first to spot the orders. And even in Bloss's version, Mitchell was clearly on the scene.

Not that it did Mitchell any good. After handing over the orders to his captain, he was sent back to his unit, in the words of historian Stephen Sears, "without even the reward of the cigars."

Besides crediting Mitchell, Colgrove's story also deflated Hill's claim that a traitor was to blame. The orders, it was now clear, had been found entirely by accident. Mitchell might very well have been more interested in the cigars than the attached paper, which he may have glanced at almost as an afterthought. As Sears put it: "Any turncoat courier or staff officer who deliberately tossed D. H. Hill's copy of Special Order 191 into a meadow near Frederick with the expectation that the Yankees might come along and somehow stumble on it, recognize it for what it was, and get it to McClellan's headquarters must rank as the war's most naively optimistic spy."

Colgrove's account was of some use to Hill, however. For if the orders were found still wrapped around the cigars (and, as McClellan recalled, still in an envelope), that meant no one had opened them before Mitchell or Bloss. Hill, had he received them, would surely have removed the cigars, and probably smoked them. As Hill argued time and again, "the paper was never received."

That it instead reached General McClellan was a remarkable stroke of luck.

☆ ☆ ☆

After getting the orders, McClellan, typically, hesitated.

Not that he doubted their authenticity; Pittman's testimony that the orders were in Chilton's handwriting took care of that. Nor did McClellan misunderstand the orders' significance. His comment to Gibbon that he could now "whip Bobbie Lee" made that clear, as did his note to Lincoln, sent a few minutes later.

In his memoirs, McClellan wrote that "on the 13th an order fell into my hands issued by Gen. Lee, which fully disclosed his plans, and I immediately gave orders for a rapid and vigorous forward movement."

In reality, he was neither rapid nor vigorous. The problem was that the one thing the Lost Order did *not* tell McClellan was how many men Lee had. Left to his own imagination, McClellan concluded the Confederates numbered about 120,000 to his 90,000 or so troops. In fact, Lee had barely 50,000, now scattered between Hagerstown and Harpers Ferry.

Still, even McClellan could not entirely squander the opportunity. Reluctantly, he attacked at Turner's Gap and Crampton's Gap on September 14—a full eighteen hours after he'd received the Lost Order. Lee ordered D. H. Hill to block the gaps, and for a day they held off the Union troops, in spite of heavy losses.

When the Union finally did break through, McClellan again hesitated. The delay saved the Confederate army. On September 15, Jackson's troops took Harpers Ferry, still following the plan set forth in the Lost Order. By September 17, they had rejoined Lee's troops at Sharpsburg, just across the Maryland border.

The stage was now set for the Battle of Antietam, or Sharpsburg, as it was known in the South. (The Northerners, mostly from urban areas, tended to be impressed by nature, such as Antietam Creek. More Southerners lived in the country, and were thus more likely to notice a town like Sharpsburg.)

Even reunited, the Confederates were still outnumbered by two to one. But Lee was unwilling to see his invasion come to naught, and he turned his army to fight. McClellan, finally, was also ready.

The battle began at dawn on September 17. Union troops gradually pushed forward, though they lost three crucial hours as the Confederates stopped General Ambrose Burnside's troops from crossing a stone bridge over the Antietam. (Burnside apparently didn't notice that his soldiers could easily have waded across the shallow creek.) By the time Burnside's men broke through the Southern lines, the last of the Confederates had returned from Harpers Ferry, and they pushed the Union back to the creek. There the battle ended.

The next morning, though he still had the numerical advantage, McClellan again hesitated. Lee took the opportunity to lead his worn-out troops back to Virginia.

Who won?

On one level, it was clearly a major Union victory, and McClellan quickly declared it as such.

"Maryland is entirely freed from the presence of the enemy, who has been driven across the Potomac," he wired Lincoln. "No fears need now be entertained for the safety of Pennsylvania."

Lee agreed it was a defeat, and he blamed it on the Lost Order, which he said allowed McClellan "to discover my whereabouts . . . and caused him so to act as to force a battle on me before I was ready for it." The Lost Order, Lee said, was "a great calamity."

Yet there is also no doubt that Lee averted a much greater calamity. Had McClellan not hesitated, had he attacked right after he read the Lost Order and before Jackson's troops returned from Harpers Ferry, the Northerners' huge numerical advantage could have overwhelmed the Confederates. And had McClellan pushed on after Antietam Creek, he might very well have prevented Lee's escape to the South.

Judging from casualties, the Union lost more men, though the South lost a higher percentage of its forces. In the bloodiest day of the war, more than 12,000 Northerners were killed or injured, and more than 10,000 Southerners.

Among the casualties of Antietam was Private Barton Mitchell, who never fully recovered from his wounds. He died in 1868, eighteen years before Colgrove published his account of how Mitchell found the Lost Order.

☆ ☆ ☆

Jackson's quick return from Harpers Ferry to Sharpsburg has led many historians to conclude that Lee found out McClellan had a copy of the Lost Order, and ordered him back. By some accounts, a pro-Confederate Maryland man was present when the order was brought to McClellan, and then passed on the news to Jeb Stuart, who told Lee. By other accounts, Lee learned about the Lost Order from the *New York Herald,* which, astoundingly, printed the news on September 14, though there's no evidence Lee read the newspaper.

In his classic 1934 biography of Lee, Douglas Southall Freeman concluded Lee didn't learn about the Lost Order until after the war. But Freeman reversed himself in his 1943 book, *Lee's Lieutenants,* after examining two accounts of conversations in which Lee referred to a Confederate spy in Maryland. In 1868, Lee again mentioned the spy, this time in a letter to D. H. Hill that explicitly said Stuart had informed him about the orders falling into McClellan's hands.

Most major Civil War historians followed Freeman's lead. Bruce Catton assumed Lee knew McClellan had the orders; so did Shelby Foote and James McPherson.

But this particular mystery about the Lost Order remains unsolved. Sears, whose book on Antietam is the standard text, disagreed with Freeman and his followers. Sears argued that the reports of Lee's conversations about the spy were secondhand and vague. As for Lee's

1868 letter to Hill, Sears contended that by then the Lost Order had been so often and so vehemently discussed that Lee must have simply become confused about when he learned about it.

Sears's strongest argument is based on Lee's behavior. Lee did *not* order Jackson back to Maryland, as he certainly ought to have done if he thought McClellan had the Lost Order. Instead, Jackson continued to follow Special Orders 191, and didn't return to Maryland until after he took Harpers Ferry.

Lee understood his opponent, and he was undoubtedly counting on McClellan's timidity when he issued the soon-to-be-lost order. But if he learned that McClellan had found the order, it would have been foolhardy for Lee to continue to assume McClellan wouldn't attack. And Lee was daring, but not foolhardy.

☆ To investigate further:

Johnson, Robert Underwood, and Clarence Clough Buel. *Battles and Leaders of the Civil War.* New York: Century Company, 1884. Volume 2 includes Hill on the events leading up to Antietam, Colgrove on the finding of the Lost Order, Confederate General John Walker's account on the capture of Harpers Ferry, Longstreet on the invasion of Maryland, and the text of Special Orders 191.

Hill, D. H. "The Lost Dispatch." *Southern Historical Society Papers,* Vol. 13, 1885. Hill's case that he didn't lose the orders is convincing, but his argument here—that losing the orders actually helped the South—is not.

McClellan, George B. *McClellan's Own Story.* New York: Charles L. Webster & Co., 1887. So determined was McClellan to tell his side that when the single copy of the manuscript was destroyed in an 1881 fire, he sat down and rewrote it in its entirety.

Freeman, Douglas Southall. *Lee's Lieutenants.* New York: Scribner's, 1944. Volume 2 includes an appendix with the correspondence which persuaded Freeman that Lee knew McClellan had the orders.

Foote, Shelby. *The Civil War: Fort Sumter to Perryville.* New York: Random House, 1958. The first volume of Foote's three-volume history, rightly acclaimed for its narrative power and rightly criticized for its pro-South bias.

Catton, Bruce. *Terrible Swift Sword.* New York: Doubleday, 1963. Volume 2 of Catton's still classic *Centennial History of the Civil War.*

Sears, Stephen. *Landscape Turned Red.* New Haven: Ticknor & Fields, 1983. This account of Antietam is remarkable in showing the perspectives of both the generals and soldiers. Sears's portrait of McClellan, whose biography he also wrote, is especially damning.

McPherson, James. *Battle Cry of Freedom*. New York: Oxford University Press, 1988. The best one-volume history of the war.

Sears, Stephen. *Controversies & Commanders*. Boston: Houghton Mifflin, 1999. Sears's essay on the Lost Order comes closer to resolving its mysteries than any other work.

McPherson, James. *Crossroads of Freedom*. New York: Oxford University Press, 2002. A succinct history of Antietam that portrays the battle as a turning point in the war.

Chapter 25

Why Did Lee Order Pickett's Charge?

On July 3, 1863, just southwest of Gettysburg, Pennsylvania, Robert E. Lee met with James Longstreet, commander of the Confederate army's First Corps and Lee's most trusted lieutenant. Lee ordered Longstreet to attack the center of the Union line on top of Cemetery Hill, about a half a mile away. Longstreet tried to dissuade Lee: the Union troops outnumbered the Confederates, were firmly entrenched behind stone walls, and had ample artillery to support them. The Confederates would have to get across more than half a mile of upward-sloping fields, during which time they would be completely exposed to Union fire. "General Lee," Longstreet later recalled telling his commander, "there never was a body of fifteen thousand men who could make that attack successfully."

But Lee overruled him. "The enemy is there," he said, "and I am going to strike him."

So Longstreet summoned General George Pickett and reluctantly ordered him to lead what has ever since been known as Pickett's Charge. At about 3 P.M., Pickett led forward his men (probably 12,000–13,000—the exact number is not known). It was a picture-book vision of the Civil War: a mile-wide parade of gray, flags waving, horses galloping, marching in perfect order across the gently rolling farmland. The elegant Pickett led the way, shouting: "Don't forget today that you are from old Virginia!"

When George Pickett stumbled back behind Confederate lines after surviving the disastrous charge that bears his name, Robert E. Lee ordered him to prepare his division to repel a Union counterattack. "General Lee," Pickett tearfully replied, "I have no division now." Lithograph by Currier and Ives. (Library of Congress.)

And then the Union forces opened fire. A few Virginians made it to the Union line but reinforcements quickly poured in and pushed them back. When the smoke cleared, nearly two-thirds of Pickett's division was gone—dead or captured. Gone, too, was the South's hope for independence. Lee would lead his army back to Virginia, and he would not surrender until almost two years later, but, most historians agree, Gettysburg was the high-water mark for the Confederacy. After Lee's defeat there and after the fall of the Confederate stronghold of Vicksburg, Mississippi, a day later, it was just a matter of time until the Union triumphed.

But a mystery remained. Why did Lee, against the advice of Longstreet, persist in ordering Pickett's charge? This was the same Robert E. Lee, after all, who a few months earlier had brilliantly masterminded the Confederate victories at Chancellorsville and Fredericksburg. Lee was renowned for his successes in drawing the Union forces into battle just when the conditions were most favorable to the

Confederacy. Yet at Gettysburg he abandoned the tactics on which he'd built his reputation and plunged ahead with the doomed attack at the Union's strongest point.

Why?

To Southern historians (and, in sharp contrast to most wars, this one was chronicled to a significant degree by its losers), Pickett's charge presented a dilemma. On the one hand, Lee was virtually the patron saint of the South—a valiant and brilliant general who could do no wrong. On the other hand, Pickett's men had also come to symbolize the courage of Southern soldiers, soldiers who these same historians portrayed as capable of carrying out any reasonable order. So, if they failed—as they did at Gettysburg—those orders couldn't have been reasonable. Yet those orders came from none other than Lee himself.

What was needed, clearly, was someone else to blame. One convenient scapegoat was Major General James Ewell Brown (known as Jeb) Stuart, commander of the Confederate cavalry. One of Stuart's major responsibilities was to act as a scout. When Lee's army crossed the Potomac and headed north into Pennsylvania, Stuart's cavalry was supposed to follow along his right flank. Stuart, however, found his path blocked by the Union army, and he had to cross the river much farther east than he'd planned. Then, when he finally did get across, he couldn't resist the opportunity to raid the Union's supply wagons. As a result, Stuart did not arrive in Gettysburg until late in the afternoon of July 2, the day after the battle began and the day before Pickett's charge.

Lee greeted him coldly: "General Stuart, where have you been?" he asked. "I have not heard a word from you in days, and you the eyes and ears of my army."

Indeed, Stuart's absence had put Lee at a disadvantage. When Stuart had failed to report, Lee had assumed it was because the Union army was still south of the Potomac. The Confederate forces were therefore dangerously spread out when they first learned that the enemy was nearby. Perhaps, had Stuart arrived earlier, Lee would have chosen someplace other than Gettysburg for the fateful battle. Still, to blame Stuart for Pickett's charge seems unfair: by the time Stuart arrived, Lee could see the Union troops massed on Cemetery Hill—and he chose to attack nonetheless.

Many historians, therefore, looked elsewhere for someone to blame for the Confederate defeat, and a great many settled on Lieutenant General Richard Ewell. It was Ewell who commanded the first Confederate troops to take on the Union troops at Gettysburg. This was on July 1—still two days before Pickett's charge—and the first day's fighting seemed to favor the Confederacy. Ewell's troops pushed Union troops under General Winfield Scott out of the town of Gettysburg onto Culp's Hill and Cemetery Hill, just south of Gettysburg. But, having won the initial battle, Ewell failed to follow up with an attack on Cemetery Hill. This, in the view of some historians, was the critical error that cost the South the Battle of Gettysburg; had Ewell pushed on and taken the heights then, before the Union troops had time to regroup and organize their defenses, the battle would have been over and Pickett need never have charged.

This, however, is unfair to Ewell. His men had suffered heavy losses in taking the town and Southern reinforcements did not reach the scene until more than a half hour after the July 1 battle—during which time the Union forces also had the opportunity to regroup. By the time Ewell's forces were ready to attack, it was very doubtful they could have succeeded. Besides, even if Ewell acted slowly on July 1, he was still no more responsible for ordering Pickett's charge than Stuart was.

The man who actually ordered Pickett to charge—and the man at whom the harshest criticism of all has been directed—was James Longstreet. This is ironic, since you'll recall it was Longstreet who most strongly advised Lee *against* the attack. But, according to some historians, Longstreet did more than disagree with Lee's plan; he undermined its chance of success. Annoyed by Lee's rejection of his alternate plan—a flanking maneuver around the Union lines to set up a defensive position there—Longstreet sulked. Even though he knew Lee had planned an early morning attack, Longstreet didn't order Pickett's division to the front until after nine in the morning on July 3. This, some historians have argued, prevented Lee from coordinating Pickett's attack on the Union center with an early morning attack by Ewell's men on the Union right. Furthermore, it gave the Union troops additional time to fortify the center.

As with the criticism of Stuart and Ewell, the criticism of Longstreet was partly valid: Longstreet was slow to bring Pickett to the front, and even slower to order him to attack. But, again, as with Stuart and Ewell, it's by no means clear that quicker action on his part would have made any difference. The Union lines were almost certainly as strong at dawn as they were at three in the afternoon. Longstreet may have carried out Lee's orders reluctantly but he did carry them out; otherwise Lee would certainly have removed him from his command after Gettysburg. The closest Lee came to criticizing him was in a conversation on the evening of July 3, in which he said the charge could have succeeded if additional troops had been sent in to support Pickett's men. But it's difficult to see where Longstreet would have found enough men to make a difference. Besides, it just doesn't make sense to blame Longstreet for the failure of an attack he adamantly opposed.

Why, then, has Longstreet so often been portrayed by Southerners as the villain, even the Judas of Gettysburg? One reason was that he had the gall to criticize Lee openly, not just at Gettysburg but years later in his memoirs. Worse, Longstreet was one of the few Southern generals who after the war became a Republican (the party of Lincoln!); he even accepted a federal job under President Grant. To Southerners, this was treason—and if Longstreet was a traitor after the war, he was probably one during the war, too.

The South never forgave James Longstreet. In 1941, on hearing that the Japanese had bombed Pearl Harbor, one of the last living Confederate veterans commented: "If Longstreet hadn't bungled at Gettysburg, we wouldn't be in this mess now."

☆ ☆ ☆

In spite of the efforts of Southern mythmakers to blame Lee's subordinates, more objective historians recognized that the critical Confederate error at Gettysburg—the plan for Pickett's charge—was made by Lee himself. Stuart *was* late; Ewell *was* timid, Longstreet *was* slow to carry out Lee's order. But the decision to send in Pickett's men was Lee's alone, and the brunt of the blame had to fall on his shoulders.

To his credit, Lee never denied this. Immediately after the battle, Lee rode among the dazed survivors of Pickett's brigade, telling them they'd fought well and their defeat was all his fault. On returning to Virginia, Lee wrote Jefferson Davis, the Confederate president, offering to resign: "I cannot even accomplish what I myself desire. How can I fill the expectations of others?" (Davis refused to accept the offer.)

Simply blaming Lee, however, didn't solve the mystery. The question remained: why would a general—a general whose reputation had been built on maneuvering his opponents into attacking him where *he* wanted—now abandon those tactics and order so desperate and dangerous a charge?

One reason was that Lee's options in Pennsylvania were much more limited than they'd been in Virginia. Having made the bold decision to invade the North, Lee had shifted the time pressure from the Union troops to his own. Now it was Lee's men who were living off the land, cut off from their supplies. The Confederate food supplies were dangerously low—so Lee felt he couldn't afford just to wait until the Union generals erred.

He could, of course, have retreated to Virginia—accepting that the two days of battle preceding Pickett's charge were nothing but a bloody draw. But this would have been an admission that his invasion had failed, that the South could do no real damage to the North and was destined to spend the rest of its days fighting on its own soil, perhaps winning some additional battles but never winning the war.

As Lee saw it, he had to attack. He hadn't come to Pennsylvania to raid a few farmhouses; he'd come for a dramatic and decisive showdown that would convince the North, once and forever, to grant the South independence. Gettysburg, though it might not be the ideal site for such a victory, was the site fate had dealt him. He'd already pushed the Union troops out of the town and, he assumed, shaken their morale. He had enough artillery, he hoped, to knock out some Union guns before the charge. At last he had Stuart's cavalry present; it could sweep around the Union lines and cause chaos among the Union troops fleeing the scene. And, above all, he had Pickett's men, who had not been used in the previous days' battles and who were rested and raring to go. Lee had tremendous faith in the abilities of Confederate soldiers; they had won other battles against odds almost as overwhelming. This confidence—this overconfidence—fatally colored Lee's judgment.

What Lee failed to take into account was that the Union soldiers were just as brave and just as committed as those of the Confederacy. The Union army had been outgeneraled in previous battles but it had not been outfought. At Gettysburg, the Union army was under the command of a new leader, General George Gordon Meade. Lincoln had appointed Meade to the top spot only days before, on June 28, but Meade was not intimidated by Lee. When Pickett's men emerged on the valley before him, he did not retreat or panic; rather, he swiftly and calmly ordered reinforcements toward the center of his line.

This is not to say Meade was a great general. In fact, he was harshly criticized after the Battle of Gettysburg for failing to counterattack after Pickett's charge failed. Lincoln was especially displeased. "We had them within our grasp," lamented the president. "We had only to stretch forth our hands and they were ours." Still, the attacks on his post-Gettysburg actions should not obscure Meade's highly competent generalship during the battle. And the Southern historians' focus on Lee and his lieutenants should not obscure the fact that the Battle of Gettysburg was not just lost by the South, but won by the North.

Pickett, who survived the charge that bears his name, recognized this. Asked after the war why the attack failed, Pickett responded: "I believe the Union army had something to do with it."

☆ To investigate further:

The War of the Rebellion: A Compilation of the Official Records of the Union and Confederate Armies. Washington, DC: Government Printing Office, 1889. Volume 27 (there are 127 in all) includes a mass of reports and correspondence pertaining to Gettysburg.

Johnson, Robert Underwood and Clarence Clough Buel. Battles and Leaders of the Civil War. New York: Century Company, 1884. Volume 3 includes Gettysburg recollections of Union and Confederate officers.

Longstreet, James. From Manassas to Appomattox. Bloomington: Indiana University Press, 1960. Originally published in 1896, this was Longstreet's answer to his critics.

Freeman, Douglas Southall. Robert E. Lee. New York: Scribner's, 1935. Though Freeman's Lee is almost superhumanly noble, this four-volume biography remains a classic. Volume 3 covers Gettysburg.

————. Lee's Lieutenants, New York: Scribner's, 1944. These three volumes complement Freeman's four on Lee. Volume 3, which covers Gettysburg, softens the unfair criticism of Longstreet in the Lee biography.

Stewart, George. Pickett's Charge. Boston: Houghton Mifflin, 1960. An objective and readable account of the charge.

Foote, Shelby. The Civil War: Fredericksburg to Meridian, New York: Random House, 1963. This second volume of Foote's three-volume history includes Gettysburg. Like the other two, it has been deservedly acclaimed for its narrative power and sweep, but equally deservedly criticized for its pro-South bias. Foote's 1994 book, *Stars in Their Courses: The Gettysburg Campaign,* is drawn from volume 2.

Catton, Bruce. *Never Call Retreat.* New York: Doubleday, 1965. This third and final volume of Catton's *Centennial History of the Civil War* covers Gettysburg. Along with the first volume, *The Coming Fury,* and the second, *The Terrible Sword,* it is among the most dramatic narrative histories ever written. Catton's 1974 book, *Gettysburg: The Final Fury,* draws from the larger work.

Coddington, Edwin. *The Gettysburg Campaign.* New York: Scribner's, 1968. A comprehensive study of the battle.

Shaara, Michael. *The Killer Angels.* New York: Random House, 1974. This novel about Gettysburg won a Pulitzer Prize and became a bestseller and the basis for the movie *Gettysburg.*

Connelly, Thomas. *The Marble Man.* New York: Knopf, 1977. Examines the evolution of Lee's image, replacing Freeman's saint with a more troubled and complex figure.

Piston, William Garrett. *Lee's Tarnished Lieutenant: James Longstreet and His Place in Southern History.* Athens: University of Georgia Press, 1987. A mostly favorable assessment of Longstreet.

McPherson, James. *Battle Cry of Freedom.* New York: Oxford University Press, 1988. The best one-volume history of the Civil War.

Waugh, John. *The Class of 1846.* New York: Warner, 1994. The West Point class of 1846 included, among other critical Civil War figures, Stonewall Jackson, George McClellan, and George Pickett. Pickett—not so incidentally, in the view of many historians—was ranked 59th in a class of 59 cadets. Here's another irony: the man whose pull got Pickett into West Point in the first place was his uncle's friend, an Illinois lawyer by the name of Abraham Lincoln.

Longacre, Edward G. *Pickett.* Shippensburg, PA: White Mane, 1995. Most historians have portrayed Pickett as an incompetent dandy: for example, Longstreet's chief of staff G. Maxey Sorrel described how Pickett's "long ringlets flowed loosely over his shoulders, trimmed and highly perfumed; his beard likewise was curling and giving out the scents of Araby." Longacre attempts, with only limited success, to portray him as a more complex and intelligent figure.

Thomas, Emory. *Robert E. Lee.* New York: Norton, 1995. A balanced biography, neither as hagiographic as Freeman's nor as cutting as Connelly's.

26

Were the Dahlgren Papers Forged?

As thirteen-year-old William Littlepage rifled through the pockets of a dead Union officer on the side of a road outside Richmond, he was hoping to find a watch. Instead, he found several documents that came to be known as the Dahlgren Papers. The dead man was Colonel Ulric Dahlgren.

Littlepage passed on the papers to his teacher, Edward Halbach. The next morning, March 3, 1864, Halbach read them. One appeared to be an address for Dahlgren's troops.

"You have been selected from brigades and regiments as a picked command to attempt a desperate undertaking—an undertaking which, if successful, will write your names on the hearts of your countrymen in letters that can never be erased," the address began.

It went on to outline Dahlgren's plan: to lead his cavalry into Richmond from the south, stopping first to release Union prisoners held on Belle Island in the middle of the James River, then continuing across "to burn the hateful city." The address also contained these instructions: "Do not allow the rebel leader Davis and his traitorous crew to escape."

A second set of orders, apparently for Captain John Mitchell, Dahlgren's second-in-command, was even more explicit: "The bridges once secured, and the prisoners loose and over the river, the bridges will be burned and the city destroyed. The men must keep together and well in hand, and once in the city it must be destroyed and Jeff. Davis and cabinet killed."

Halbach was, understandably, appalled. Dahlgren's orders seemed to cross the line from war to terrorism; bloody though the Civil War had been to that point, neither side had resorted to indiscriminate destruction or political assassination. Halbach passed the papers up the Confederate chain of command to President Jefferson Davis, the target of the Union plot.

Davis, recognizing the propaganda value of the papers, released them to the press, which quickly dubbed Dahlgren "Ulric the Hun." The *Richmond Daily Dispatch* headline read "The Last Raid of the Infernals." Another Richmond newspaper, *The Whig,* asked of the Yankees: "Are they not barbarians redolent with more hellish purposes than were the Goth, the Hun or the Saracen?"

Northerners, for their part, were equally righteous and equally adamant in calling the papers a forgery. The *New York Times* condemned "the rebel calumny on Col. Dahlgren," arguing that "no officer of the American army would ever dream of putting to death civil officers . . . and no officer in his senses, even if he were barbarous enough to contemplate such a result, would ever put such orders in writing."

The Dahlgren papers set in motion more than just propaganda. Incensed, Davis and his cabinet responded in kind, approving plans to free Confederate prisoners and let them loose in Union cities. Their hope was to stave off defeat by spreading fear and undercutting support for the war in the North. The plans failed, but the pretense of civility was now gone from the Civil War.

"In both the north and south there was fury," wrote Bruce Catton, "and the war between the sections, which once seemed almost like a tournament, had at last hardened into the pattern of total war."

The end of the Civil War brought no end to the debate over the Dahlgren Papers.

The raid on Richmond that led to Dahlgren's death originated in the mind of Brigadier General Judson Kilpatrick, an extraordinarily ambitious commander of a division of the Army of the Potomac's cavalry. Kilpatrick was known to his troops as "Kill-Cavalry," for he had few qualms about sacrificing Union as well as Confederate soldiers to achieve his objectives.

Kilpatrick knew Lincoln was impatient with his own commanders. Victories at Gettysburg and Vicksburg and Chattanooga had turned the tide in the Union's favor, but the Army of the Potomac had stalled at the Rapidan River in northern Virginia, and General George Meade appeared reluctant to push farther south. Meanwhile, stories of the suffering of Union prisoners on Belle Island and in Richmond's Libby Prison circulated through the North and in the White House.

Ignoring the normal chain of command, Kilpatrick took his bold plan directly to the president and his secretary of war, Edwin Stanton. He proposed a quick strike on Richmond. With Robert E. Lee's Army of Northern Virginia camped opposite Meade on the other side of the Rapidan, the Confederate capital had only a small contingent of home guardsmen to protect it. Kilpatrick would take his cavalry around Lee and hit Richmond before Jeb Stuart's Confederate cavalry could come to its defense. Even if reinforcements did reach the city, Kilpatrick assured Lincoln and Stanton, by then the freed prisoners would have swelled the Union ranks.

Kilpatrick got the go-ahead, and put together a force of about 3,500 cavalrymen. One was Dahlgren, whose father, Rear Admiral John Dahlgren, was a close friend of Lincoln's. At twenty-one, Dahlgren was the youngest colonel in the Union, and he craved glory every bit as much as Kilpatrick. That he had lost part of his leg chasing Lee's forces from Gettysburg did not deter Dahlgren in the least.

The operation got under way on the evening of February 28, with General George Armstrong Custer leading about 1,500 cavalry toward Charlottesville. This was meant as a diversion and it worked; while Lee worried about Custer, Kilpatrick and Dahlgren sneaked across the Rapidan to the east. At Spotsylvania, the two split. Kilpatrick continued south toward Richmond. Dahlgren led 500 men west toward Jude's Ferry, where he hoped to cross the James. The plan was for them to attack simultaneously, Kilpatrick from the north and Dahlgren from the south.

Now things went seriously awry. At Jude's Ferry, Dahlgren discovered that the past few days' rain had made the river too deep and too fast to cross. He decided to press on toward Richmond anyway, hoping to join Kilpatrick from the west instead of the south. Instead, he ran into Southern troops, and had to turn north.

Kilpatrick, meanwhile, had reached the outskirts of Richmond. He might still have managed to overrun the scant Confederate defenses there, but with no sign of Dahlgren, his nerve failed him. Faced with enemy fire, Kilpatrick decided—wrongly—that the Confederates had somehow managed to get reinforcements to Richmond. He fled toward the east, eventually reaching the Union lines at New Kent.

Edwin Forbes's drawing of Kilpatrick's troops appeared within days of their raid on Richmond. (Library of Congress.)

That left Dahlgren stranded, with the Southerners by now fully aware of his presence. Lost in the dark, he led his men into an ambush. He was shot in the head and left to die, not far from the town of Stevensville, on the road where Littlepage found him.

☆ ☆ ☆

On March 30, Lee sent a copy of the Dahlgren Papers to Meade, along with a formal protest and a demand to know whether the orders were "authorized by the United States Government." Meade, in turn, asked Kilpatrick to investigate.

Kilpatrick told Meade he had endorsed Dahlgren's address to his men—but without the offensive parts. "The alleged address of Colonel Dahlgren . . . is the same as the one approved by me," he wrote Meade, "save so far as it speaks of exhorting the prisoners to destroy and burn the hateful city and kill the traitor Davis and his cabinet. All this is false."

Kilpatrick also interviewed survivors from Dahlgren's command, all of whom insisted that Dahlgren had given no such orders.

Meade sent Kilpatrick's statement to Lee, along with his own conclusion: "Neither the United States Government, myself, nor General Kilpatrick authorized, sanctioned or approved the burning of Richmond and the killing of Mr. Davis and cabinet, nor any other act not required by military necessity and in accordance with the usages of war."

So ended the official investigation.

Privately, though, Meade had doubts. He'd never trusted Kilpatrick, especially since he'd gone over his head to Lincoln and Stanton.

In a letter to his wife in April, soon after he replied to Lee, Meade described the whole affair as "a pretty ugly piece of business." He told her he regretted implying that, if the papers were authentic, Dahlgren must have written them on his own. "Kilpatrick's reputation," Meade said, "and collateral evidence in my possession, rather go against this theory."

Indeed, relying on Kilpatrick was, as historian Stephen Sears put it, "equivalent to ordering the fox to investigate losses in the henhouse." Kilpatrick, after all, was Dahlgren's superior officer, and may have given him the orders. If so, Kilpatrick had every reason to deny they were authentic.

It's unclear what "collateral evidence" Meade meant, though he could have been referring to a conversation with General Marsena Patrick about Captain John McEntee, who served under Dahlgren and survived the raid. After talking to McEntee, Patrick wrote in his diary: "He has the same opinion of Kilpatrick that I have, and says he managed just as all cowards do. He further says that he thinks the papers are correct that were found upon Dahlgren, as they correspond with what D. told him."

It's possible Patrick told this to Meade as well as his diary. Still, McEntee was the only man who rode with Dahlgren and suggested the address could have been authentic. Moreover, McEntee's testimony is secondhand, or thirdhand, if Patrick passed it on to Meade.

One person absolutely convinced of Dahlgren's innocence was his father. The admiral was eager to clear his son's name, and in July 1864, he found some very strong evidence. While studying a photographic copy of the orders that the Confederates had made, the admiral noticed that two of the letters in his son's signature had been reversed. Instead of Dahlgren, it was Dalhgren.

It was inconceivable, the admiral argued, that his son would have misspelled his own name.

"I felt from the first . . . that my son never wrote that paper—that it was a forgery; but I refrained from giving utterance to that faith until I had seen a sample of the infamous counterfeit," he wrote. "I say now, that a more fiendish lie never was invented."

The admiral did not say who had forged the papers, but the implication was clear: someone high up in the Confederate hierarchy, perhaps even Davis himself, had framed his son. The motive may have been to create some potent propaganda, or something even more devious, such as an effort to justify the South's own plans to spread dissension and terror in the North by freeing Confederate prisoners there and letting them loose in Union cities.

It was no coincidence, Dahlgren's defenders noted, that soon after the publication of the papers, the Confederates approved their own plans to bomb the White House and kidnap Lincoln. With defeat on the battlefield only a matter of time, the Dahlgren Papers provided the perfect pretext for Southern leaders, increasingly desperate, to take the war to another level.

Dahlgren's disparagers came up with a variety of responses. In 1879, the ex-Confederate general Jubal Early pointed out that the address had been written on two sides of thin paper. The apparent misspelling, Early argued, was actually the result of ink leaking through from the back of the paper. Others hypothesized that whoever copied the papers had touched them up, and in doing so misspelled the name. Still others speculated that some other Union soldier could have written the orders for Dahlgren.

These theories get a bit convoluted, and historians might reasonably have decided the best way to resolve the questions surrounding the papers would be to examine the originals.

There was only one problem with that: no one knew where the Dahlgren Papers were.

☆ ☆ ☆

The trail of the papers leads from the Confederate archives in Richmond and then Charlotte, to the federal bureau of the adjutant general in Washington, D.C., which took over the collection after the war. In December 1865, the secretary of war requested the papers, and Francis Lieber, who headed the bureau, sent them to Stanton.

Fourteen years later, Lieber asked for them back, so that he could include them in a multivolume collection of war records he was putting together. The War Department responded that they had no record of the papers.

The mysterious disappearance has led to much speculation about why Stanton wanted the papers, and what he did with them. Some suspected a cover-up; perhaps, they argued, Stanton or even Lincoln himself had authorized burning Richmond and killing Davis. After all, the secretary of war and the president did meet with Kilpatrick, bypassing the normal chain of command.

"Perhaps it is an uncharitable thought," wrote historian James Hall in 1983, "but the suspicion lingers that Stanton consigned them to the fireplace in his office."

Stanton was pushing for a more unlimited war on the South, and it's possible he and Kilpatrick discussed the possibility of kidnapping or even killing Davis.

As for Lincoln, there's no evidence linking the president to the alleged orders, and it's not just uncharitable but unfair to imply the president had anything more in mind than freeing the Union prisoners, and perhaps sowing some chaos in Richmond. These were reasons enough for Lincoln to approve the plan, and they may very well have been all that Kilpatrick—and Dahlgren—ever intended.

Whatever its true intent, the raid on Richmond came back to haunt the Union. Confederate plots to bomb the White House and kidnap Lincoln failed, as did most of the Southern efforts to bring the war home to Northern cities. One of those recruited for the kidnapping plot, however, did not give up, even after the war was over.

His name was John Wilkes Booth.

☆ To investigate further:

Jones, Virgil Carrington. *Eight Hours Before Richmond*. New York: Henry Holt, 1957. A lot can happen in eight hours.

Hall, James. "The Dahlgren Papers." *Civil War Times Illustrated*, November 1983. An excellent summary of the mysteries surrounding the papers' origins and disappearance.

Furgurson, Ernest. *Ashes of Glory*. New York: Knopf, 1996. Furgurson uncovered an anonymous and undated paper quoting Custer as saying Dahlgren told him "that he would not take Pres. Davis & his cabinet, but would put them to death, and that he would set fire to the first house in Richmond and burn the city." As evidence of Dahlgren's guilt, that seems strained, though overall this is a very vivid portrait of Richmond during the war.

Schultz, Duane. *The Dahlgren Affair*. New York: W. W. Norton, 1998. A compelling account of the raid on Richmond and the Confederate campaign of terror that followed. Schultz makes a very strong case that the papers were, if not forged, at least altered.

Sears, Stephen. *Controversies & Commanders*. Boston: Houghton Mifflin, 1999. Includes one of the best cases for the papers' authenticity. For Sears's latest arguments, including his explicit answers to Schultz, go to www.historynet.com/acw/ bldahlgrenpapersrevisited/index.html.

Chapter 27

Did Jefferson Davis Plot Lincoln's Assassination?

W ho shot Abraham Lincoln was never in doubt. When John Wilkes Booth leaped from the presidential balcony onto the stage of Ford's Theater, he was instantly recognized as one of the best-known actors of his time. Booth made no effort to hide his identity; theatrical as always, he shouted, *"Sic semper tyrannis* [thus always to tyrants]" before dashing offstage and onto his waiting horse.

Some of Booth's co-conspirators were also easily identified. Lewis Powell, whose assignment was to kill Secretary of State William Seward, injured the secretary and a number in his household but was caught later the same night. George Atzerodt, whose target was Vice President Andrew Johnson, instead got drunk and confessed. David Herold was with Booth when Union soldiers tracked them to a Virginia farm twelve days later, killing Booth and capturing Herold.

Booth's death, however, left unsolved a greater mystery than who killed Lincoln: who did he do it *for?* Part of the solution was obvious: he did it for the Confederacy. Booth's Southern sympathies were well known, and his appropriation of Brutus's words made clear he considered Lincoln a tyrant. The assassination took place April 14, just five days after Robert E. Lee surrendered at Appomattox, and it was easy enough to surmise that Booth hoped to avenge the South's defeat. By killing not just Lincoln but also the vice president and secretary of state (who at the time was third in line for the presidency), Booth and his co-

conspirators may also have hoped to throw the Union into chaos and give new life to the Southern armies still in the field.

But the question remained: was all this Booth's idea and Booth's doing? Among Powell and Atzerodt and Herold, he was clearly the ringleader. But there were many who suspected a much broader conspiracy.

"The dreadful crime was planned by the leaders of the rebellion," wrote the *Washington Sunday Morning Chronicle.* "Such a dastardly and cowardly act is in strict accordance with their spirit."

The *Chronicle* was not alone in believing that the assassination plot originated with Lincoln's counterpart, Confederate President Jefferson Davis.

Secretary of State Edwin Stanton had no doubt Davis was guilty. Ten days after the assassination, he announced: "This Department has information that the President's murder was organized in Canada and approved at Richmond." On May 2, Johnson agreed, proclaiming that "the atrocious murder of the Late Pres. Abraham Lincoln and the attempted assassination of Hon. W. H. Seward Secretary of State, were incited, concerted and procured by and between Jefferson Davis, Clement C. Clay, Nathaniel Beverley Tucker, George Sanders, William Cleary, and other rebels and traitors."

Other than Davis, the accused were all Confederate agents stationed in Canada since 1864. There they had hatched all sorts of mostly unsuccessful anti-Union plots. These included raids across the border, spreading infectious diseases, and setting off firebombs in New York City. According to Stanton, Lincoln's assassination was just the last and most successful of their "infernal plots." The government appointed Brigadier General Joseph Holt as prosecutor, and offered rewards for the Confederates' arrests, including $100,000 for Davis.

The conspiracy trial of May and June 1865 offered a strange mix of evidence. Holt was surely out to convict the eight defendants in custody, and he succeeded in sending to the gallows Powell, Atzerodt, Herold, and Mary Surratt, whose Washington tavern was the conspirators' favorite meeting place. (Four others with less direct involvement in the murders and attempted murders received lesser sentences.) But at least as much of Holt's focus was on the Confederate leadership, even though neither Davis nor his Canadian operatives were formally on trial.

Secretary of State Edwin Stanton thought the Confederate president belonged on this broadside—and on the gallows—alongside John Wilkes Booth's co-conspirators. (Library of Congress.)

The key, for Holt, was to connect Booth to Canada, and through Canada to Davis. A number of witnesses placed the assassin in Montreal with leading rebels in the fall of 1864. Most damning by far was the testimony of Sandford Conover, a correspondent for the *New York Tribune* who had become, in his own words, "quite intimately associated" with the Southern leaders in Canada. Conover said he was in the office of Jacob Thompson, the Confederate commissioner there, when letters arrived from Davis and Secretary of State Judah Benjamin about the assassination plot. Thompson, according to Conover, read the letters and then said, "This makes the thing all right."

After the trial, Conover delivered to Holt sworn depositions from eight other witnesses, all testifying to Davis's involvement in the assassination. Davis by now was in custody at Fort Monroe, Virginia. With so much evidence accumulated, Republicans in the House of Representatives became increasingly impatient with Holt for not proceeding with a trial. In January 1866, the House Judiciary Committee decided to question Conover and his witnesses themselves.

Now the case against Davis fell apart. First, none of the witnesses could be found. Finally, a member of Holt's staff tracked down one of them, William Campbell. Campbell then blurted out: "This is all false. I must make a clean breast of it. I can't stand it any longer."

It turned out Conover had written Campbell's testimony and that of the other eight witnesses. Conover, whose real name was Charles Dunham, had made up his own testimony and then bribed the other witnesses to take revenge on Davis, by whose orders he had been jailed for six months in 1863. In the fall of 1866 Conover was convicted of perjury and sentenced to ten years.

None of this did any good for the four conspirators already hanged, nor was it really relevant to their cases. But it completely discredited the case against Davis and his Canadian commissioners. Even Holt conceded that Conover had perpetrated a "shameless fraud."

Many Southerners argued Lincoln's assassination wasn't even in the Confederacy's interest, since Johnson was expected to be harder on the South than Lincoln would have been. Davis himself took this tack, and always denied any part in the plot. "I certainly have no special regard for Mr. Lincoln," he said, "but there are a great many men whose end I would much rather have heard than his."

Two documents that surfaced in 1867 seemed to bolster the argument that Booth and his co-conspirators made their plans without any help from Virginia or Canada. A letter Booth wrote sometime in 1864 described his intention, which at that time was to kidnap Lincoln rather than kill him. Booth signed the letter as "A Confederate doing duty upon his own responsibility."

An entry from Booth's diary made clear the decision to kill Lincoln had been a sudden one. "For six months we had worked to capture, but our cause being almost lost, something decisive and great must be done," he wrote on April 14, the day of the assassination.

Both documents came to light during the trial of John Surratt, the son of the woman who'd been executed two years before. That neither was entered into evidence at the 1865 conspiracy trial was yet another indication—and not just to Southern partisans—that prosecutors had been more interested in showing there was a massive conspiracy than in determining the truth.

Davis, who had been captured by Union troops in 1865, remained imprisoned at Fort Monroe, Virginia, for two years while Stanton consid-

ered trying him for treason instead of murder. In May 1867, he was released on bail. He was never brought to trial.

With a broader Confederate conspiracy discredited, the focus shifted to
Booth himself. The picture that emerged was that of a man driven mad
by his love for the South and his desire to leave his mark on history.

A diary entry from April 21, five days before he was captured, revealed Booth's agony, not so much that the South had not risen again
but that his countrymen didn't appreciate what he'd done.

"After being hunted like a dog through swamps, woods, and last
night being chased by gun boats till I was forced to return wet, cold,
and starving, with every man's hand against me, I am here in despair,"
he wrote. "And why? For doing what Brutus was honored for. What
made Tell a Hero. And yet I for striking down a greater tyrant than
they ever knew am looked upon as a common cutthroat. . . . A country
groaned beneath this tyranny and prayed for this end, and now behold
the cold hand they extend to me."

Booth, clearly, had hoped the assassination would bring him acclaim, at least in the South. The choice of Ford's Theater was in this
respect telling. Booth was not just an actor but came from a family of
great actors; indeed, both his father and brother had achieved more
fame than he had. For his greatest moment on stage, Booth wanted to
make sure there was an audience. Powell and Atzerodt could carry out
their work in private, not Booth.

"It was all so theatrical in plan and performance," wrote essayist
Adam Badeau in 1893. "The conspiracy, the dagger, . . . the cry 'Sic
semper tyrannis'—all was exactly what a madman brought up in a theater might have been expected to conceive; a man . . . used all his life to
acting tragedy."

Booth's sister, Asia Clarke, agreed her brother was mad. Years
later, she decided it was Lincoln's visit to the theater—seemingly a celebration at the South's bleakest moment—that set him off.

Within just a few years of the assassination, Booth's madness was
as unquestioned as Lincoln's greatness. Indeed, the two were tied together. For those who revered Lincoln, it was inconceivable anyone
but a madman would have shot him.

The reputations of Davis's accusers, on the other hand, plummeted.
Johnson was impeached, the first president to suffer such ignominy. Stanton fared even worse; his enemies, North and South, charged that he had

been so eager to convict Davis that he and Holt had suppressed what was exculpatory and manufactured what was incriminating. The anti-Stanton trend culminated in 1937 with Otto Eisenschiml's *Why Was Lincoln Murdered?*, a book that argued that the secretary of war not only tried to frame Davis, but actually masterminded the assassination himself. Stanton, according to Eisenschiml, recognized that Lincoln's conciliatory approach to the South would undermine his Radical Reconstruction plans, so he recruited Booth to kill him. Then he made sure Booth was shot and the other conspirators hanged so no one could talk.

"It was to his advantage to have the President out of the way," Eisenschiml wrote. "It would mean continuance in office, increased power over a new and supposedly weak Chief Executive and a fair prospect of replacing the latter at the next election. Politically speaking, Lincoln's elimination would . . . insure the dominance of the Republican party and a more influential role for the friends and sponsors of the War Minister."

Eisenschiml's evidence, he himself conceded, was highly circumstantial. Indeed, his theory, though still believed by some diehard neo-Confederates, was nonsense. But it was merely the most extreme manifestation of the general certainty, among both the public and professional historians, that Davis and other Confederate leaders could not possibly have had anything to do with the assassination.

Then, in the late 1980s, three nonprofessional historians delved into Confederate archives anew . . . and found new evidence pointing to Davis's guilt.

☆ ☆ ☆

As a retired CIA officer, William Tidwell knew that Confederate leaders weren't likely to have left behind documents explicitly authorizing Lincoln's assassination. But he also knew that clandestine operations require funding, and that's where he picked up the paper trail.

Among the Confederate papers currently housed in the Library of Congress, Tidwell found sixty-three vouchers allocating more than $1.5 million in gold to "secret service" projects. That included $1 million for Jacob Thompson, the Confederate commissioner in Canada. The vouchers were all signed by Jefferson Davis.

In Confederate records now at the Chicago Historical Society, Tidwell found evidence of another $5 million for "secret service." In this case, the money was controlled by Confederate Secretary of State Judah Benjamin.

None of this provided a direct link between Davis or Benjamin and Booth. But it did confirm that the type of anti-Union plots witnesses described in the original 1865 conspiracy trial could have been funded by the Confederate government. In his 1988 book, *Come Retribution,* Tidwell and co-authors James Hall and David Winfred Geddy concluded that Holt and Stanton had, essentially, been right in their suspicions about the Confederate leaders' complicity. The prosecution had gone awry, of course, by depending on Conover and his fellow perjurers.

Tidwell believed prosecutors had made another, more fundamental mistake by focusing on Booth and the eight on trial, rather than on other Confederate clandestine operations more easily linked to Richmond. He pointed to an April 1, 1865, warrant issuing $1,500 in gold from a secret service account, and the capture nine days later, near Burke Station, Virginia, of a Confederate sergeant named Thomas Harney. Harney admitted to being an explosives expert, and Tidwell concluded he had been given the money to blow up the White House. It was when this plan failed, Tidwell surmised, that Booth decided to murder the president himself.

Tidwell also noted that during their post-assassination flight, Booth and Herold were aided by various Confederate agents. This, too, was not proof of Davis's involvement, but it was further evidence that the conspirators were part of a network involving more than the seven men and one woman convicted in 1865. (Among those who aided Booth was Samuel Mudd, a Maryland doctor who set the assassin's leg—injured when he leaped onto the Ford's Theater stage—and whose partisans have ever since claimed was merely obeying his Hippocratic oath. But Mudd was also an active member of the Southern underground.)

"Contrary to popular belief," Tidwell concluded, "the Lincoln assassination was . . . the result of a legitimate Confederate clandestine operation that went awry."

A majority of historians disagreed. *Come Retribution,* wrote Mark Neely of the Lincoln Library and Museum, "stacks doubtful inference on perilous surmise . . . Speculation does not lead to certainty nor, in this case, come near the truth. Assassination was an unlikely tool of war for Victorian soldiers and gentlemen like Jefferson Davis."

But the work of Tidwell and others, most notably Thomas Reed Turner and William Hanchett, has eroded the consensus view that Davis had nothing to do with the assassination. At the very least, the new research has restored a political component to the assassination.

For regardless of whether Davis or Benjamin knew of his plan, Booth was not just a crazed actor looking for the limelight. He was deeply committed to the Confederate cause. He adamantly defended independence and slavery, and he hated Lincoln for destroying both. In that sense, he was not so different from Davis, or from much of the South.

The conventional image of Booth acting alone may have helped heal the nation after the Civil War. Northerner and Southerner alike, Tidwell wrote, "could agree that Lincoln's death was a tragedy for all and get on with the business of restoring a splintered nation." But the conventional image has also obscured just how splintered that nation was.

"The shock and mourning that followed Abraham Lincoln's assassination were profound and widespread, and the martyred president quickly became the most beloved of American heroes," Hanchett wrote. "But during his lifetime Lincoln was the object of far more hatred than love."

By 1864 and 1865, Davis was no longer Neely's Victorian soldier. Perhaps in retaliation for the Dahlgren raid on Richmond, perhaps simply out of desperation, he and other Confederate leaders were willing to resort to decidedly nongentlemanly warfare. And so was John Wilkes Booth.

☆ To investigate further:

Eisenschiml, Otto. *Why Was Lincoln Murdered?* New York: Halcyon House, 1937. Stanton's most famous words, uttered soon after Lincoln's death, were "Now he belongs to the Ages." Eisenschiml, not surprisingly, thinks he never said them.

Turner, Thomas Reed. *Beware the People Weeping.* Baton Rouge: Louisiana University Press, 1982. How the public reacted to the assassination.

Hanchett, William. *The Lincoln Murder Conspiracies.* Urbana: University of Illinois Press, 1983. A critical analysis of the theories to date, including the most thorough refutation of Eisenschiml.

Tidwell, William, with James Hall and David Winfred Gaddy. *Come Retribution.* Jackson: University Press of Mississippi, 1988. The Confederate Secret Service and its role in the assassination.

Smith, Gene. *American Gothic.* New York: Simon & Schuster, 1992. An entertaining portrait of the Booth family in which father Junius and brother Edwin have as many problems staying sane as John Wilkes.

Tidwell, William. *April '65*. Kent, Ohio: The Kent State University Press, 1995. More evidence of Confederate covert action.

Rhodehamel, John, and Louise Taper. *"Right or Wrong, God Judge Me."* Urbana: University of Illinois Press, 1997. The complete writings of John Wilkes Booth.

Bak, Richard. *The Day Lincoln Was Shot*. Dallas: Taylor Publishing Company, 1998. A lavishly illustrated companion to a TNT film, this is generally sympathetic to Tidwell and includes an essay by Tidwell summarizing his position.

Steers, Edward Jr. *Blood on the Moon*. Lexington: The University Press of Kentucky, 2001. Debunks all sorts of myths that still surround the assassination, such as that Mudd was just an innocent country doctor and that Booth didn't actually die in 1865.

Swanson, James, and Daniel Weinberg. *Lincoln's Assassins*. Santa Fe, New Mexico: Arena Editions, 2001. A collection of photos, letters, documents, prints, woodcuts, pamphlets, books, and other artifacts pertaining to the trial and executions.

Winik, Jay. *April 1865*. New York: HarperCollins, 2001. The fall of Richmond, the surrender at Appomattox, the assassination of Lincoln: April 1865 was quite a month.

Chapter 28

Why Did Custer Attack?

The country's two top generals, William Tecumseh Sherman and Philip Sheridan, first heard about the Battle of Little Bighorn in Philadelphia, where they were attending a celebration of the American centennial. Their first reaction was to deny the reports.

Custer dead? His Seventh Cavalry wiped out by the Sioux and Cheyenne? It was inconceivable not just to Sherman and Sheridan but to most of America in 1876. George Armstrong Custer was the man the Northern press had dubbed the "boy general" for his precocious successes at Gettysburg, during the Wilderness campaign, and outside Appomattox, where he stopped Robert E. Lee's flight and forced his surrender. Custer's blond hair and flamboyant dress, especially the long red tie that flew behind him as he led his men to battle, added to his fame.

Out west, buckskin replaced velvet but not victories. In 1868, Custer led the Seventh Cavalry into the Washita Valley in present-day Oklahoma, where they surprised a Cheyenne village and routed Black Kettle's warriors. Smaller battles against the Sioux and Cheyenne throughout the western plains solidified Custer's reputation as the nation's premier Indian fighter.

On June 25, 1876, as Custer approached Montana's Little Bighorn River, he must have sensed his greatest victory. His scouts told him the Sioux and Cheyenne had set up a large village along the river, larger even than that on the Washita. As he did at the Washita, Custer divided his troops. He ordered Captain Frederick Benteen south to check for other

Indian camps, then to rejoin the rest of the troops near the Indian village. Major Marcus Reno, Custer's second-in-command, would attack the village from the east with 130 men. Custer himself would sweep down from the northwest with about another 220 men, catching the Indians between his forces and Reno's and preventing them from escaping.

It did not, of course, work out that way. Reno attacked, but the Indians vastly outnumbered his men: estimates put the total number of warriors in the village somewhere between 1,500 and 2,000. Reno quickly retreated across the river. There Benteen's forces joined Reno's, and together they were able to hold their position, mostly because the Indians turned west to face Custer's charge.

The next day, infantry under the command of Colonel John Gibbon reinforced Reno and Benteen's men. Slowly, they moved up the valley. The Indians were gone, they discovered, probably to their relief. To their horror, they also found that Custer and all who rode with him were dead.

How could this have happened? Why did the country's most famous Indian fighter ignore his scouts' reports about the size of the Indian village? Why did he divide his forces and then attack, when he was clearly outnumbered? Why didn't he wait for Gibbon and others under the command of General Alfred Terry, who were only a day away from the Little Bighorn?

No wonder Sherman and Sheridan didn't believe the news.

☆ ☆ ☆

Sheridan, once he got over the initial shock, wrote to Sherman: "I deeply deplore the loss of Custer and his men. I feel it was an unnecessary sacrifice, due to misapprehension, and a superabundance of courage—the latter extraordinarily developed in Custer."

President Ulysses Grant put it much more critically. He described the defeat "as a sacrifice of troops brought on by Custer himself, that was wholly unnecessary."

Granted, Grant was no fan of Custer. Custer had testified against Grant's brother during an inquiry into one of the numerous corruption scandals that plagued the administration, and Grant had not forgotten this. Indeed, much of the contemporary criticism of Custer came from Grant's supporters, defending the president's Indian policies. Custer, wrote the Republican *Chicago Tribune,* "preferred to make a reckless dash and take the consequences, in the hope of making a personal victory and adding to the glory of another charge, rather

Custer's last stand, portrayed here in Frederick Whittaker's 1876 biography, may never have happened. (Denver Public Library.)

than wait for a sufficiently powerful force to make the fight successful and share the glory with others."

Custer's critics in the military argued that he had not only exhibited poor judgment but disobeyed orders. Terry's written orders were to wait until Gibbon's troops arrived for a joint attack on the Indians. But this criticism was unfair to Custer; Terry's comments were really just suggestions, and he explicitly told Custer that he had "too much confidence in your zeal, energy, and ability to wish to impose upon you precise orders which might hamper your action when nearly in contact with the enemy." Besides, like the Republicans, the military was a little eager to deflect onto Custer any criticism of its Indian policies.

Still, his critics had a point: it was clear, at least in retrospect, that Custer would have been wise to wait for Gibbon.

The Battle of Little Bighorn also prompted critics to take another look at Custer's history, which wasn't quite as exemplary as it first appeared. The boy general's Civil War campaigns, though always daring and mostly successful, were often costly: at Gettysburg his charge halted a Confederate advance, but 481 Union soldiers were killed or wounded; during the Wilderness campaign of 1864, he lost more than a third of his brigade; even near Appomattox, Custer's command suffered 377 casualties.

Then there was the matter of Custer's 1867 court-martial for being absent without leave and for not stopping to bury the bodies of two soldiers killed while he led his troops across Kansas. Custer claimed he was rushing east to get medicine for cholera victims at Fort Wallace, but the disease had not yet hit there. It appeared more likely—to the military court that found him guilty and to most historians—that he left his post and relentlessly drove his troops simply because he wanted to see his wife, Libbie, who was waiting for him in eastern Kansas. A fine romantic gesture, to be sure, but hardly sound military strategy.

To counter her husband's critics, Libbie Custer enlisted the aid of Frederick Whittaker, a dime novelist who quickly churned out the first biography—really more a hagiography—of Custer. Errol Flynn's 1941 portrayal of Custer in *They Died with Their Boots On* had nothing on Whittaker's 1876 swashbuckler.

"Never was there a life more rounded, complete, and symmetrical than that of George A. Custer, the favorite of fortune, the last cavalier," wrote Whittaker. "To Custer alone was it given to join a romantic life of perfect success to a death of perfect heroism."

Whittaker's villains were Reno and Benteen. Had Reno not retreated when the Indians resisted, had Benteen not dawdled to the south, had either carried out Custer's plan, it would have worked. Reno was a coward and a drunk; Benteen was jealous and vindictive. Whittaker was especially harsh in his treatment of Reno, who outranked Benteen and thus made the final decision not to go to Custer's aid.

Even after the biography was published, Whittaker continued to assail Reno. In June 1878, he released a letter to the press blaming him for Custer's defeat, since "he remained idle with this force while his superior officer was fighting against the whole force of the Indians, the battle being within his knowledge, the sound of firing audible from his position, and his forces out of immediate danger from the enemy."

Reno had had enough of this. He appealed to President Rutherford B. Hayes to convene a special court where he could defend his reputation. At the army's 1879 court of inquiry, Reno and Benteen both maintained they were unaware of Custer's plight and that, even if they'd known, they were too busy defending themselves to help him. "We were at their hearths and homes," Benteen said of the Indians, "their medicine was working well, and they were fighting for all the good God gives anyone to fight for."

Those who served under Benteen defended his courage, arguing that he rallied them to defend themselves amidst the carnage. Reno's subordinates were distinctly less enthusiastic; most claimed to have seen little of him during the battle.

"I don't know whether he rose to the emergency or not," testified Lieutenant Luther Hare, when asked whether Reno was a coward. "I have not much to go upon in making an estimate."

The army court found there was nothing in Reno's conduct that merited its "animadversion." This was not the chastisement Reno must have feared after his men's halfhearted testimony, but it was hardly a ringing endorsement. Nor did it do much to solve the mystery of what caused the debacle at Little Bighorn.

What made the mystery so difficult to solve, most nineteenth-century observers agreed, was that no one had survived Custer's last stand. This was, of course, untrue: there were plenty of Indian survivors. But most of their stories were dismissed as cowardly lies.

There was more than just racism at work here. The Indian reports *were* confusing and contradictory, and often incompetently translated. Few Indians knew much about cavalry tactics and formations, making it difficult for them to analyze Custer's movements. Most spoke only after they were rounded up onto reservations, and many may have said what they thought the white interviewers wanted to hear. The reports of Custer's heroic stand were especially suspect in this regard.

Still, racism undoubtedly made it easier for late nineteenth- and early twentieth-century historians to disregard the Indian reports. So in the 1960s and 1970s historians made a concerted effort to untangle the Indian testimony. Some of their findings seemed as ideologically motivated as those of their predecessors. Instead of focusing on the Indian reports about how heroic the soldiers were, especially at the last stand, the revisionists emphasized the testimony of mass panic and disorder among Custer's troops. By 1970, the image of Custer as Flynn's swashbuckler had been replaced by Richard Milligan's buffoonish megalomaniac in *Little Big Man*. In that movie, Custer's victory over Black Kettle at the Washita is clearly meant to be seen as a parallel of the My Lai massacre in Vietnam.

"From a symbol of courage and sacrifice in the winning of the West, Custer's image was gradually altered into a symbol of the arrogance and brutality displayed in the white exploitation of the West," wrote Paul Hutton. Evan Connell agreed: "His image has fallen face down in the mud and his middle initial, which stands for Armstrong, could mean Anathema."

Yet the new attention to Indian testimony did bear fruit. Indian participants in the battle had spoken convincingly of their outrage over American Indian policy, their decision to make a united stand, and the strong leadership of such chiefs as Sitting Bull and Crazy Horse. And these factors went a long way toward explaining Custer's defeat. Wrote Robert Utley: "The simplest answer, usually overlooked, is that the army lost largely because the Indians won. To ascribe defeat entirely to military failings is to devalue Indian strength and leadership."

Further evidence of the effectiveness of the Indian warriors surfaced in 1983, after a grassfire swept across the battlefield. At first, historians treated this as a natural and historical disaster. But it turned out the fire cleared the way for a more systematic study of the site than had ever been conducted. Using metal detectors and limited excavation, Richard Fox and a team of archaeologists plotted the distribution of cartridges and bullets around the Little Bighorn. The lack of cartridges on what's now known as Custer Hill—supposedly the site of the last stand—led Fox to conclude the famous stand never happened. Overall, the pattern of artifacts revealed how quickly Custer's forces collapsed under the Indian onslaught.

"Except at the beginning of the battle, the soldiers were in disarray, without much semblance of unified purpose," Fox wrote. "Panic and fear, the prime ingredients in collapse during combat, spread throughout the tactical units.

Custerphiles again rose to defend their man and his troops. Some argued that more than a hundred years of souvenir hunting, especially around Custer Hill, had corrupted the battlefield record. Others maintained there must have been a last stand, though perhaps not at Custer Hill. But Fox's meticulous research convinced most historians that, whatever Custer's strengths or failings as a leader, he and his men were quickly overwhelmed by the Sioux and Cheyenne.

☆ ☆ ☆

Why did he attack in the face of overwhelming odds?

One theory put forward by some historians is that that he hoped a major victory would propel him to the White House. Superficially, this makes sense. Scandals had made Grant vulnerable, and Custer offered the Democrats an alternative war hero. Red Star, one of his Indian scouts, quoted Custer as saying that a victory at Little Bighorn would make him the white's "great father." But there's no other evidence Custer had political ambitions, let alone presidential ones. Red Star could have misunderstood or been misquoted.

More likely, Custer's ambitions were military. The Little Bighorn presented him with an opportunity for an even greater victory than the Washita. To Custer, the circumstances must have seemed similar. At neither the Washita nor the Little Bighorn did he know how many Indians he would face, nor did he care. He had faith that the Seventh Cavalry could whip any number of them. Besides, experience had taught him that when soldiers attacked an Indian village, the Indians tended to panic and flee. This was exactly what happened at the Washita, where Black Kettle's warriors were generally more worried about getting their families to safety than about setting up an organized defense.

Faced with a large gathering of Indians, Custer's main concern was that they not escape. Waiting for Gibbon or Terry meant not only sharing the credit for the victory, but also risking that the Indians would learn of his presence and scatter. When he spotted the village, Custer reportedly waved his hat and shouted to the troops (this according to a messenger dispatched to Benteen just before the battle): "Hurrah, boys, we've got them!"

"If indeed Custer made such a remark after sighting the greatest concentration of militant Indians in the history of North America," Connell noted, "it sounds like a joke from an old vaudeville routine." But it's perfectly possible Custer said this—or at least thought it. He was not afraid of Indians; he had, as Sheridan put it, "a superabundance of courage." His job was to track them down and attack.

And that is exactly what he did.

☆ To investigate further:

Custer, George Armstrong. *My Life on the Plains*. Lincoln: University of Nebraska Press, 1966. Originally published in 1874, the style is a bit convoluted for modern tastes but shows Custer knew how to generate good publicity for himself. Benteen referred to the book as "My Lie on the Plains."

Whittaker, Frederick. *A Complete Life of General George A. Custer*. Lincoln: University of Nebraska Press, 1993. Originally published in 1876, a biography of "one of the few really great men that America has produced."

Custer, Elizabeth. *Tenting on the Plains*. Norman: University of Oklahoma Press, 1971. Elizabeth Custer recalled her idyllic life with her husband in three books: *Tenting* covers the marriage through the court-martial (though the latter is not mentioned), *Following the Guidon* covers 1867–1869, and *Boots and Saddles* ends when Elizabeth learns about Little Bighorn. The University of Oklahoma Press reprinted *Boots and Saddles* in 1961, and the University of Nebraska Press reprinted *Guidon* in 1994.

Ambrose, Stephen. *Crazy Horse and Custer.* Garden City, New York: Doubleday, 1975. A dual biography set in a background of social and military history.

Connell, Evan. *Son of the Morning Star.* New York: Harper & Row, 1985. A meandering but always elegant and evocative narrative that brings to life not just Custer but also Reno, Benteen, Sitting Bull, and Crazy Horse.

Utley, Robert. *Cavalier in Buckskin.* Norman: University of Oklahoma Press, 2001. A revised edition of Utley's superb 1988 biography.

Gray, John. *Custer's Last Campaign.* Lincoln: University of Nebraska Press, 1991. A virtually minute-by-minute account of the battle.

Hutton, Paul. *The Custer Reader.* Lincoln: University of Nebraska Press, 1992. An anthology of classic articles.

Fox, Richard. *Archaeology, History, and Custer's Last Battle.* Norman: University of Oklahoma Press, 1993. Anyone who thinks archaeology is just for learning about ancient civilizations will find otherwise here. Highly technical but important.

Welch, James. *Killing Custer.* New York: W. W. Norton, 1994. A Native American novelist's meditation on the meaning of the Little Bighorn.

Barnett, Louise. *Touched by Fire.* New York: Henry Holt, 1996. The best parts of this biography are about Libbie Custer, and about the making of the myths surrounding her husband.

Wert, Jeffry. *Custer.* New York: Simon & Schuster, 1996. An evenhanded biography, though Utley's is better.

Michno, Gregory. *Lakota Noon.* Missoula, Montana: Mountain Press, 1997. A narrative of the battle based on Indian testimony.

Sklenar, Larry. *To Hell with Honor.* Norman: University of Oklahoma Press, 2000. The latest defense of Custer, this argues Custer's attack could have succeeded if Reno and Benteen hadn't betrayed him.

Chapter 29

Who Was to Blame for Wounded Knee?

In the year 1890, at a spot near Wounded Knee Creek in southwest South Dakota, Chief Big Foot and a band of about 120 Sioux warriors accompanied by 230 women and children, met up with 470 members of the Seventh Cavalry, commanded by Colonel James Forsyth. This was the same Seventh Cavalry that had met the Sioux at the Battle of Little Big Horn 16 years earlier; then the cavalry had been commanded by General George Armstrong Custer and the Sioux had wiped out an entire batallion.

At Wounded Knee, it was the Sioux who were almost wiped out. The battle left 25 soldiers and somewhere between 200 and 300 Indians dead, many of them women and children. It also left a number of disturbing questions: Who fired the first shot? Did the Sioux warriors conceal their weapons in order to ambush the soldiers, as many of the latter claimed? Or did the Seventh Cavalry take its revenge on a peaceful band of Sioux families? Was the Battle of Wounded Knee a battle at all—or a brutal massacre?

Eighty-five years later, while historians continued to investigate these questions, Wounded Knee was again the site of an armed confrontation between Native Americans and U.S. government forces. In 1975 two FBI agents found themselves in a shootout with members of AIM, a militant organization (its initials stand for American Indian Movement) devoted to Native American rights. When the shooting stopped this time, the two agents were dead. AIM member Leonard Peltier was convicted of murder. His supporters said he was framed by the FBI.

Once again Wounded Knee had become a symbol of Native American resistance. And once again there were disturbing questions to be answered.

The path which led Big Foot and his followers to Wounded Knee began about one hundred miles north of there, at a small Sioux village on the Cheyenne River. On the morning of December 23, 1890, the Sioux left their village, heading south toward the Pine Ridge Reservation. According to some accounts, Big Foot had been invited to Pine Ridge to settle some disputes between other Sioux factions; according to others, the Indians were going south to collect the payments due to them under the various treaties by which they'd ceded their land and moved into their reservations.

To Major General Nelson Miles, however, both Big Foot's destination and his motives were suspect. Miles was well aware that this was a period of intense unrest among the Sioux. Swarms of white settlers had killed off the buffalo, on which the Sioux depended for food. (In 1890 there were so many white settlers throughout the West that the U.S. Superintendent of the Census could no longer draw a line between those sections of the West that had been settled and those that were still wilderness; the frontier, he conceded, no longer existed.) The move to the reservations had completely disrupted Sioux institutions; major crop failures, epidemics of measles and whooping cough, and corrupt and incompetent government agents had further exacerbated their condition.

By 1890 the Sioux were near starvation. About three thousand had left the reservations and congregated in the Badlands, a stark region of plateaus and cliffs north of the Pine Ridge Reservation. There the Sioux danced the "Ghost Dance," a ritual meant to bring about a new world in which the white man would disappear and the buffalo, along with generations of past Indians, would return. The Ghost Dance was a strange mix of traditional Indian beliefs and messianic Christianity, but to a people feeling as helpless and hopeless as the Sioux, it was hard to resist.

In 1890, many whites saw the Ghost Dance as a war dance, but there's little evidence the Sioux that were killed that year at Wounded Knee were planning a battle. From an 1891 engraving by R. Taylor. (Library of Congress.)

In most of its forms the Ghost Dance religion, in spite of the apocalyptic images it called forth, did not call for violence against whites. Still, most whites—and Miles in particular—found it extremely threatening. Miles ordered the arrest of the leading Sioux chiefs who practiced the religion. On December 15, Indian policemen employed by the government arrived at the cabin of Sitting Bull—the chief who, along with Crazy Horse, had led the Sioux in the Battle of Little Big Horn. When Sitting Bull resisted, the police shot and killed him.

That left Big Foot as the most prominent Sioux chief who had taken up the Ghost Dance, and Miles ordered him arrested as well. But before the order could be carried out, Big Foot and his band slipped out of their village. The chief said he was heading to the Pine Ridge Reservation but, Miles was quick to note, the chief's destination might just as easily have been the Badlands, where he could join up with the Ghost Dancers most hostile to the whites. More disturbing still, some

of Sitting Bull's most militant followers had fled after their chief's
death and had reportedly joined Big Foot's band.

Miles ordered his forces to find Big Foot and bring him back. On
December 28, a unit of the Seventh Cavalry intercepted the Indians.
Big Foot surrendered, and the soldiers escorted the Indians to
Wounded Knee. The next morning the Indians awoke to find themselves surrounded by even more soldiers, with cannons pointing down
at them from a nearby hill. Colonel Forsyth ordered the Indians to disarm, and when the Sioux turned over only a few old guns, Forsyth sent
his soldiers in to search the Indian tepees. With tensions running high
on both sides, not much was needed to spark the conflagration.

☆ ☆ ☆

Precisely what set off the fighting is unclear. According to some eyewitness reports, an Indian medicine man named Yellow Bird began
walking among the warriors, telling them their sacred "ghost shirts"
would protect them from the white man's bullets. Reportedly, as one
of the soldiers lifted an Indian blanket to check for weapons, Yellow
Bird threw a handful of dust into the air, signaling the warriors to
draw their rifles and open fire. Other eyewitnesses told of how two
soldiers grabbed Black Coyote, a deaf warrior who'd been carrying
around his rifle, apparently without understanding what was going
on. A struggle ensued, the rifle went off accidentally, and the soldiers
then opened fire on the mostly disarmed Indians.

Which story did historians believe? It depended, at least partly,
on where their sympathies lay. For historians predisposed to finding
the Sioux deaths justifiable, the Yellow Bird story demonstrated that
the Sioux warriors, or at least some of them, had started the fight.
Moreover, it seemed as if they'd planned it in advance; witness the
simultaneous appearance of the Indians' weapons upon the signal
from Yellow Bird. And these were weapons that had been treacher-
ously concealed after Big Foot had, supposedly, unconditionally
surrendered.

For historians more sympathetic to the Indians, the Black Coyote
story corroborated their suspicions. The soldiers must have homed in
on an Indian who clearly didn't know what was going on, in order to
provoke a fight. And, as these historians were quick to remind readers,
these were soldiers of Custer's Seventh Cavalry; this was their chance
to avenge Little Big Horn.

Viewed objectively, both of these interpretations are unfair: nei-ther the Sioux nor the cavalry plotted in advance to start a fight. For the Sioux, a battle made no sense. They were vastly outnumbered and they had women and children in their midst; however desperate they were, they were not suicidal. Big Foot was suffering from pneumonia and was in no condition to plan a battle. True, he had once been one of the more ardent Ghost Dancers but he'd since lost faith in the religion; besides, he was always more of a peacemaker than a warrior. (Re-member, at least according to some accounts, Big Foot was on his way to Pine Ridge to help work out a truce between Indian factions there.)

But if Big Foot and his warriors weren't looking for a fight, nei-ther is there any hard evidence that Forsyth or his soldiers wanted trouble. Miles blamed Forsyth for deploying his troops in such fatal proximity to the Indians but this endangered the troops as well as the Indians; it was more an error of judgment on Forsyth's part than any indication that he was out for blood. Miles himself erred in his initial order to arrest Big Foot; had he left Big Foot alone, he and his follow-ers probably would have ended up on the Pine Ridge Reservation, right where Miles wanted them. But, like Forsyth, Miles hoped to avoid a fight.

So, if neither side planned to fight, who is to blame for starting it? Probably no one. In an atmosphere as highly charged as that of De-cember 29, either Yellow Bird throwing dust in the air or Black Coy-ote's gun going off could have set off the fight, without any advance planning on either side. Perhaps both events occurred simultaneously; that would surely have sufficed.

This is not to say, of course, that no one is to blame in any sense. Whatever the immediate cause of the battle, there's no denying that it was preceded by decades of broken treaties, which drove Native Americans from their land. According to an 1868 treaty—the first treaty in which the Sioux agreed to any boundaries on their land—the "unceded Indian territories" would extend, forever, from the Missouri River west to the Big Horn Mountains in Wyoming and from just be-low the Canadian border south into Nebraska. By 1890, this had been whittled down to reservations composed of fewer than 16,000 square miles. Moreover, the slaughter of so many women and children can't be attributed to the heat of battle alone; clearly the fighting released deep fears and prejudices and hatreds on the part of the soldiers. In this fundamental sense, then, the soldiers were to blame.

The fighting at Wounded Knee put an end to the Sioux uprising of 1890. Within two weeks, the remaining Ghost Dancers in the Badlands wandered back to the reservations and surrendered. Years later, a Sioux holy man, Black Elk, recalled the scene at Wounded Knee. "I can still see the butchered women and children lying heaped and scattered all along the crooked gulch as plain as I saw them with eyes still young," he said. "And I can see that something else died there in the bloody mud, and was buried in the blizzard. A people's dream died there."

In February 1973 Wounded Knee was back in the headlines. A few hundred Oglala Sioux Indians, joined by activists from AIM, seized the church at the tiny hamlet of Wounded Knee, right outside of which the bodies of Big Foot and his followers had been buried. For many of the Oglala, the occupation was a protest against the tribal council leader, Dick Wilson, whom they considered a puppet of the federal government. Wilson, they felt, was more interested in giving his cronies jobs and giving away mineral rights than in protecting the interests of the tribe. Wilson had organized vigilante squads that had terrorized his opponents. (He called his followers "Guardians of the Oglala Nation"; his opponents called them "goons.")

The leaders of AIM hoped to do more than oust Wilson. Fully aware that Wounded Knee remained a potent symbol of white injustice, they saw its occupation as a chance to publicize their broader grievances: against escalating white violence against Indians on the reservation, against exploitation of Indian lands, and against the federal government's Indian policies in general. In March, citing the long-ignored 1868 treaty, they declared Wounded Knee part of the Independent Oglala Nation.

As in 1890 the Indians of 1973 were vastly outnumbered and outgunned. Besides the Bureau of Indian Affairs police and Wilson's forces, the Justice Department sent in U.S. marshals, SWAT teams, and FBI agents. The occupiers held out for 71 days before agreeing to a peaceful settlement. Leaders of AIM had obviously failed to establish an independent nation, and they were also unable to capitalize on the national attention the occupation had generated. Like other revolutionary movements of the '60s and early '70s, AIM fell apart under the weight of its own internal divisions and under relentless pressure from the FBI. The Wounded Knee occupation turned out to be the movement's high tide.

Compared to the 1973 occupation, the 1975 shootout, reputedly involving Leonard Peltier and other AIM members, was a sordid affair. It's unclear how the fight started, or what special agents Jack Coler and Ronald Williams were doing on the Pine Ridge Reservation, but it is clear that they were shot from very close range. This was an execution, not a battle that turned out to be fatal.

In response, the FBI launched the biggest manhunt in its history. Four men were eventually indicted; of these, one was released for lack of evidence, two were acquitted by a jury, and the fourth—Peltier—was convicted of murder in the first degree and was sentenced to two consecutive life terms in prison.

AIM claimed Peltier had been set up by the FBI. Supporting this claim was the testimony of a woman named Myrtle Poor Bear. In order to extradite Peltier from Canada, the FBI presented affidavits from Poor Bear in which she claimed to have witnessed Peltier commit the murders. But later she claimed that she'd never seen Peltier in her life and that the FBI had threatened to kill her unless she testified against him. Peltier's defenders also claimed the FBI fixed the ballistics reports to show Peltier's rifle was the murder weapon.

Peltier's case became a *cause célèbre* in the 1970s and 1980s. Novelist and naturalist Peter Matthiessen wrote a book about him and Robert Redford made a movie about him. He was compared to Sacco and Vanzetti, to Nelson Mandela, and to Crazy Horse, among others. Whether Peltier deserved this lionizing is unclear; though some of the government's evidence was tainted, not all of it was. Furthermore, the cold-blooded killing of the FBI agents was no act of heroism, and the 1975 killings ought not to be conflated—as they sometimes were in the rhetoric of Peltier's defenders—with either the 1890 massacre or the 1973 uprising.

Still, there's no denying that, even if he's guilty of murder, Peltier landed in jail (where he still is) because of a federal agency's abuses of Native American rights. In that sense, his story fits all too well into the history of Wounded Knee.

☆ To investigate further:

Mooney, James. *Ghost Dance Religion and Wounded Knee.* New York: Dover, 1973. Originally published in 1896, this remains a valuable study of the Ghost Dance phenomenon.

Utley, Robert. *The Last Days of the Sioux Nation,* New Haven, CT: Yale University Press, 1963. Though too charitable to the soldiers, this remains the best book on the period leading up to and including the 1890 battle.

Brown, Dee. *Bury My Heart at Wounded Knee.* Orlando: Holt, Rinehart & Winston, 1970. The history of the West from the Indians' perspective—so much so that it refers to whites by their Indian names (Custer is at first called "Hard Backsides" because he chased the Indians so long without getting out of his saddle; later he's called "Long Hair"). A best-seller, this was not quite so original in its approach as it claimed, but it is nonetheless a powerful indictment of America's treatment of Native Americans.

S.L.A.M. Marshall, *Crimsoned Prairie: The Wars Between the United States and the Plains Indians During the Winning of the West.* New York: Scribner's, 1972. Old-fashioned both in its highly entertaining narrative style and in its extremely forgiving attitude toward army actions.

Matthiessen, Peter. *In the Spirit of Crazy Horse.* New York: Viking, 1980. Though overly long, the book argues convincingly that Peltier was framed by the FBI. Publication was delayed for eight years because of libel suits by FBI agent David Price and former South Dakota governor William Jankow, two of the book's villains.

Jensen, Richard, R. Eli Paul, and John Carter. *Eyewitness at Wounded Knee.* Lincoln: University of Nebraska Press, 1991. Photographs from before and immediately after the 1890 massacre.

Smith, Paul Chaat and Robert Allen Warrior. *Like a Hurricane.* New York: The New Press, 1996. The rise and fall of the American Indian Movement during the 1960s and 1970s.

Chapter 30

Was Sitting Bull Murdered?

By 1890, the chief who led the Sioux at Little Bighorn was in his late fifties. Sitting Bull no longer roamed the western plains. He lived in a log cabin on the Standing Rock Reservation, just below what is now the border between North and South Dakota, surrounded by his remaining two hundred and fifty or so followers. They survived, barely, on the crops they grew and meager government handouts.

To whites in the area, though, Sitting Bull remained someone to fear, especially since many of his followers were joining the "Ghost Dances" sweeping across the reservations. The dancers believed a messiah was coming, after which the buffalo would return and the white people disappear. The new religion had Christian as well as traditional Native American elements, and the Ghost Dance was not a war dance. Still, white settlers and soldiers were understandably nervous about a ritual whose purpose was to hasten their disappearance. The "ghost shirts" the Indians wore, which were supposed to protect them from any bullets, added to white discomfort.

When the Ghost Dance spread to Standing Rock, the Interior Department's agent there, James McLaughlin, blamed the most famous chief on the reservation. "Sitting Bull is high priest and leading apostle of this latest Indian absurdity," he reported to his superiors in Washington. "He is the chief mischief-maker at this agency, and if he were not here, this craze, so general among the Sioux, would never have gotten a foothold at this agency."

In November, McLaughlin paid Sitting Bull a visit, and demanded he renounce the Ghost Dance. Sitting Bull suggested the two of them take a trip in search of this messiah. As McLaughlin reported the chief's offer: "If . . . we did not find the new Messiah, as described, upon the earth . . . he would return convinced that the Indians had been too credulous and imposed upon, which report from him would satisfy the Sioux, and all practices of the Ghost societies would cease."

Sitting Bull, who was known for an ironic sense of humor, could not really have expected McLaughlin to join him. McLaughlin, in any case, had no desire to go traipsing after the Indian Messiah.

Over in the War Department, General Nelson A. Miles was also worried about the Ghost Dance. "It . . . was deemed advisable," he wrote his superiors, "to secure . . . Sitting Bull, and others, and to remove them for a time from the country."

Miles assigned Colonel William F. Cody to bring in the chief. On the face of it, this was an absurd choice. Cody, better known as "Buffalo Bill," had more experience as the star of the touring "Wild West" show than as an actual frontiersman or soldier. The ensuing confusion would have been comic had it not ended in tragedy. The *Cadron Democrat,* a Nebraska newspaper, was quick to poke fun at the War Department's approach: "Beefalo Bill," the newspaper reported on November 27, "has torn himself away from the pleasures of the Old World and the seductive company of kings, queens, jacks, and ten spots, and hastened to the scene [to] aid in the demolition of commissary cigars and government whiskey."

McLaughlin, though eager to be rid of Sitting Bull, worried that the arrival of soldiers at Sitting Bull's camp would set off violence. He also didn't like the idea of the military taking control of his reservation. He quickly wired Washington, arguing that the reservation's Indian police force could better handle the situation. "I have matters well in hand," McLaughlin wrote, "and when proper time arrives can arrest Sitting Bull by Indian police without bloodshed." Meanwhile, he dispatched a messenger to intercept Cody. The messenger told Cody that Sitting Bull was already on his way to Fort Yates to surrender, so Buffalo Bill turned around and headed back to the fort. By the time he figured out he'd been tricked, McLaughlin's bosses in the Interior Department had convinced President Benjamin Harrison to rescind Cody's orders.

In retrospect, Cody was more likely to arrest Sitting Bull peacefully than McLaughlin's police. Buffalo Bill and Sitting Bull knew each other well, since the chief had spent a year touring with Cody's Wild

"Buffalo Bill" Cody and Sitting Bull became friendly when they toured together, prompting the army to send the former to arrest the latter. (Denver Public Library.)

West show. Sitting Bull might not have surrendered to Buffalo Bill, but he probably would have politely listened to his arguments, just as he did to McLaughlin's weeks before.

Instead, just before dawn of December 15, forty-two of McLaughlin's Indian police entered Sitting Bull's cabin. As backup, McLaughlin positioned two troops of cavalry, under the command of Captain Edmond Fechet, a couple of miles from the camp. By the time the soldiers arrived, the battle was over, and fifteen Indians were dead: seven policemen, seven of Sitting Bull's followers, and Sitting Bull himself.

☆ ☆ ☆

Most whites in the vicinity of the reservation were delighted, or at least relieved. Back east, however, there were immediately accusations, at least from a few newspapers, that Sitting Bull's death was the result of more than a botched arrest.

Wrote the *Chicago Tribune* on December 17: "That the government authorities, civil as well as military, from President Harrison and General Miles down, preferred the death of the famous old savage to capture whole-skinned, few persons here, Indian or white, have a doubt. It was felt that Sitting Bull's presence anywhere behind iron bars would have been the cause of endless troubles, while should he fall victim to the ready Winchester, the thousands of Messiah-crazed Ghost dancers would rudely realize that his 'medicine,' which was to make them bullet-proof, would be worthless after all and should be forsaken."

The *New York Herald* was more explicit. "There was a complete understanding between the commanding officer and the Indian police that the slightest attempt to rescue the old medicine man should be a signal to send Sitting Bull to the happy hunting ground."

On December 28, the *New York World,* whose correspondent had accompanied Fechet's cavalry, denied Sitting Bull had been shot resisting arrest. "There was no resistance whatsoever," he maintained. "It was a crime, cruel and cowardly."

There were plenty of grounds for such suspicions. McLaughlin had chosen Lieutenant Bull Head to lead the arresting force. Bull Head was a longtime enemy of Sitting Bull. So was McLaughlin himself, who had clashed with Sitting Bull many times since the chief was assigned to Standing Rock in 1883. On his arrival, the chief demanded that he be put in charge of distributing the government rations. McLaughlin refused. In 1888 and 1889, Sitting Bull embarrassed the agent by rallying the Sioux to protest a government plan to buy large tracts of the reservation.

McLaughlin much preferred dealing with more tractable chiefs. Two months before Sitting Bull's death, McLaughlin described him in a report to Washington as "a man of low cunning, devoid of a single manly principle in his nature, or an honorable trait of character."

McLaughlin's written orders to Bull Head were to arrest Sitting Bull, but the agent added an ominous P.S.: "You must not let him escape under any circumstances."

☆ ☆ ☆

For more than forty years, it looked as if McLaughlin would have the last word on Sitting Bull's life and death. He portrayed him as not only obstructionist but cowardly, even at Little Bighorn. McLaughlin's superiors in the Interior Department, like most Americans, held Native Americans in such low esteem that they accepted this view. Nor did they doubt that Sitting Bull, who had resisted white civilization for his whole life, died, as McLaughlin claimed, resisting arrest.

In his 1910 autobiography, McLaughlin wrote: "It was not the shedding of Sitting Bull's blood I regretted so much as I did the killing of the loyal Indian policemen who were shot down by crazed fanatics on Sitting Bull's order. And he brought on the trouble which ended in his death and also the killing of much better men than he was."

Sitting Bull found a more sympathetic biographer in Stanley Vestal, whose groundbreaking work was published in 1932. Vestal interviewed Native Americans who had known Sitting Bull, and who remembered him as devoted to salvaging what he could of their way of life. He did not flaunt his courage, at Little Bighorn or elsewhere, but he was a strong leader, there and at Standing Rock. True, he was more difficult for McLaughlin to deal with than other chiefs, but that was because he consistently stood up for his people's rights. Of McLaughlin's take on Sitting Bull, Vestal wrote: "No man can rightfully claim the roles of accuser, advocate, and judge in such a case—and then write the obituary."

Vestal did not go so far as to accuse McLaughlin of plotting to assassinate Sitting Bull. But he argued that the attempt to arrest the chief was unjustified, since Sitting Bull was merely an observer of the Ghost Dances. He did not reject the new religion, but he never joined or directed the dances. The chief's suggestion that he and McLaughlin search for the messiah may have indicated a genuinely open mind on the matter. "Sitting Bull's arrest had nothing to do with the Ghost Dance," Vestal wrote. "That dance was a mere pretext . . . for McLaughlin, who was anxious to be rid of him, could think of nothing to accuse him of."

By the 1960s and 1970s, Vestal's heroic chief had replaced McLaughlin's cowardly obstructionist. A new generation of activists, led by AIM (the American Indian Movement), strove to preserve their heritage and to honor past leaders. Most took for granted that Sitting Bull had been assassinated. AIM leader Russell Means, in his autobiography, wrote that the police shot Sitting Bull on orders from McLaughlin and Miles. Literary works such as Peter Matthiessen's *In the Spirit of Crazy Horse* referred to Sitting Bull "resisting arrest" in disbelieving quotes, and even scholarly works, such as Francis Jennings's *The Founders of America,* called his killers "terrorists."

The problem was that many of these writers were more interested in righting historical injustices than in closely examining the evidence pertaining to Sitting Bull's death. Means and Matthiessen and Jennings *assumed* Sitting Bull was assassinated, and given a history of broken treaties and unbroken hostility toward Native Americans, it was a perfectly reasonable assumption. But it was not proof.

☆ ☆ ☆

It remained for Robert Utley, former chief historian of the National Park Service and author of a number of superb histories of the Indian wars, to write an unbiased biography of Sitting Bull. Utley's 1993 work depended heavily on Vestal's interviews; after all, those who knew Sitting Bull were by then long dead. Utley's portrait was not so different from Vestal's: the Sitting Bull who emerged from his pages was, if not quite the saint of the 1960s and 1970s, very much a hero. Wrote Utley: "He earned greatness as a . . . patriot, steadfastly true to the values and principles and institutions that guided his tribe."

Utley also agreed with Vestal about Sitting Bull's death: there was not nearly enough evidence to convict McLaughlin (or the police or military) of plotting to murder Sitting Bull. One witness claimed the police shot first; others said it was Sitting Bull's friend, Catch the Bear, who fired the first shot, killing Bull Head. "Rather than see him escape," Utley wrote, [the police] would kill him, as they did. But they did not plot that outcome." That the police mishandled the arrest—letting an angry crowd gather instead of whisking Sitting Bull away—also spoke against any conspiracy. Fechet, who commanded the cavalry troops that arrived too late to do any good or harm, put it this way in an 1891 report: "If it had been the intention of the police to assassinate Sitting Bull, they could easily have done so before his friends arrived."

That did not mean, of course, that the authorities were blameless. McLaughlin and many of the police had a grudge against Sitting Bull, and they surely did not mourn his death. The Interior Department and the War Department, for all their infighting, both wanted Sitting Bull behind bars, even though he hadn't committed any crime. Sitting Bull, along with his way of life, stood in the way of America's westward expansion, and fell prey to it. The Sioux's last stand came just two weeks after his death. At Wounded Knee Creek in southwest South Dakota, the Seventh Cavalry wiped out about 250 practitioners of the Ghost Dance, including many of Sitting Bull's followers and also many women and children.

This was the same Seventh Cavalry that, sixteen years earlier, had faced Sitting Bull at Little Bighorn. Their revenge was complete.

☆ To investigate further:

McLaughlin, James. *My Friend the Indian*. Boston: Houghton Mifflin, 1910. McLaughlin did not intend his title to be ironic.

Vestal, Stanley. *Sitting Bull*. Norman: University of Oklahoma Press, 1957. Originally published in 1932, this was saluted by later scholars such as Utley for "rescuing Sitting Bull's memory from the ignominy that tainted it for a generation after his death."

Adams, Alexander. *Sitting Bull*. New York: G. P. Putnam's Sons, 1973. A sympathetic synthesis of his life and times.

Utley, Robert. *The Lance and the Shield*. New York: Henry Holt, 1993. Sitting Bull's father presented a lance and shield to him when he became a warrior at age fourteen. The lance would be his favorite offensive weapon, the shield his defense against white encroachment.

Coleman, William. *Voices of Wounded Knee*. Lincoln: University of Nebraska Press, 2000. Coleman interweaves all the available (and often conflicting) sources—Sioux, military, and civilian—to tell the story of the massacre and the events leading up to it, including Sitting Bull's death.

Chapter 31

What Destroyed the *Maine*?

The U.S. battleship *Maine* arrived in Havana harbor in January 1898, amidst rising tensions between Spain and the United States. Spain was battling Cuban revolutionaries in an effort to hold on to some of its once great empire; the United States sympathized with the revolutionaries and was beginning to flex its own empire-building muscles. Officially the *Maine's* mission to Cuba was a peaceful one, but both Spaniards and Americans recognized the ship was there as a show of U.S. naval strength and resolve.

So when the ship blew up at 9:40 P.M. on February 15 and 266 crew members were killed, jingoistic Americans had few doubts who was to blame. "The *Maine* was sunk by an act of dirty treachery on the part of the Spaniards," wrote the assistant secretary of the navy Theodore Roosevelt. The February 17 edition of William Randolph Hearst's *New York Journal* ran the headline "Destruction of the Warship Maine Was the Work of an Enemy"; a front-page drawing was captioned: "The Spaniards, it is believed, arranged to have the *Maine* anchored over one of the harbor mines."

Others took a more cautious approach. President William McKinley told a friend: "We must learn the truth and endeavor, if possible, to fix the responsibility. The country can afford to withhold its judgment and not strike an avenging blow until the truth is known." (Roosevelt's response: "The president has no more backbone than a chocolate eclair.")

The navy quickly appointed a court of inquiry to determine the cause of the explosion, and in late March the court reached its verdict: the *Maine* was destroyed by a submerged mine. Though the court was unable to determine who placed or detonated the mine, the verdict released more pro-war sentiment than McKinley could resist. Even if the Spanish didn't set off the mine, it was clear to the president that most Americans considered them culpably negligent. The *Journal* had a new war cry: "Remember the Maine! To hell with Spain!" By mid-April the United States and Spain were at war.

Was the court's verdict correct? Was Spain to blame? Or did the United States go to war over what was nothing more than an accident—albeit a tragic one?

The 1898 court of inquiry was composed of four naval officers, presided over by Captain William T. Sampson. The first to testify before them was Charles Sigsbee, the captain (and obviously, a survivor) of the *Maine*. Sigsbee testified that all required safety procedures had been followed on the ship. He said that prior to the explosion he had personally checked the coal bunkers in the forward part of the ship (where the explosion had taken place) and they had not been hot enough to set off an accidental fire. The implication was clear: if it hadn't been an onboard accident, it had to have been a mine.

What really swayed the court, however, was not Sigsbee's testimony but that of the next witness, Ensign Wilfred Van Nest Powelson. Powelson had studied naval architecture and he had been working on the scene, interviewing navy divers as they came up from the wreck. He described what the divers had seen. The shattered keel of the battleship appeared to have been bent in the form of an inverted V, where the explosion had been centered. Also, a section of bottom plating had been twisted up to within four feet of the surface.

The upward bending of the metal suggested that an explosion had pushed it up from *underneath* the ship. This was the first solid evidence of a mine. It was enough to convince the Sampson court.

Meanwhile, the Spaniards were conducting their own official investigation. Not surprisingly, they reached a very different conclusion. Had the explosion been caused by a mine, the Spanish report pointed out, witnesses should have heard a dull concussion rather than the sharp report most reported. Had a mine exploded, there should have

The day after the Maine *blew up, the New York* World *was already preparing to pin the blame on the Spanish, and it didn't take long for others in the press to call for revenge. In March 1898, before a navy court of inquiry had reached any verdict, illustrator Frederic Remington asked publisher William Randolph Hearst of the New York* Journal *if he could return home from Cuba. "Please remain," replied Hearst. "You furnish the pictures and I'll furnish the war." (Library of Congress.)*

form of autonomy for Cuba. To Weyler's followers, therefore, the *Maine's* destruction was a double cause for celebration: it was a blow against both the Yankee meddlers and the spineless moderates.

Who else had reason to want the United States in the war? The rebels themselves, perhaps. Their military position had not improved during the two months previous to the explosion and could only be helped by the Spaniards having to defend themselves against the Americans. In addition, the more moderate Spanish government presented a political threat to them as well as to the Weylerites. The limited autonomy offered by the moderates was unacceptable to revolutionaries bent on full independence—and the *Maine's* destruction guaranteed that compromise would never come to pass.

Who else? Could an American eager to get us into the war be responsible? Ferdinand Lundberg, one of William Randolph Hearst's biographers, pointed a finger at the publisher. Hearst had been involved in other intrigues in Cuba, and a few days before the explosion, when his illustrator Frederic Remington asked permission to return home from Cuba, Hearst wired back: "Please remain. You furnish the pictures and I'll furnish the war." And Hearst certainly profited from the war: two days after the explosion, the *Journal's* circulation rose to over a million.

But Hearst's blustering and profiteering amounted to circumstantial evidence, at best. Without question the most likely culprits were extremists, either of the Spanish or the rebel variety. Both had reason to want to see the ship destroyed. And while it seems unlikely historians will ever know for sure whether it was Spaniards or revolutionaries—or fate—that blew up the *Maine,* almost all do agree that the forces unleashed by that explosion not only propelled us into war with Spain but into a prominent role in world affairs from which we have never retreated.

☆ To investigate further:

Message from the President of the United States Transmitting the Report of the Naval Court of Inquiry Upon the Destruction of the United States Battle Ship Maine in Havana Harbor. Washington, DC: Government Printing Office, 1898. Includes the testimony taken before the court as well as the court's report and the president's response to it.

Wilson, Herbert W. *The Downfall of Spain*. New York: Little, Brown, 1900. Wilson was the first historian to tackle the mystery; his book is a thorough examination of what was then known.

Weems, John Edward. *The Fate of the Maine*. New York: Henry Holt and Company, 1958. Leans toward a mine, but doesn't rule out the possibility of an accident.

Thomas, Hugh. *Cuba: The Pursuit of Freedom*. New York: Harper & Row, 1971. Leans toward an accidental explosion, but considers the Cuban revolutionaries the most likely candidates to have detonated a mine.

Rickover, H. G. *How the Battleship Maine Was Destroyed*. Washington, DC: Department of the Navy, 1976. Rickover's case against a mine, along with the report of his technical experts.

O'Toole, G. J. A. *The Spanish War*. New York: Norton, 1984. One of the most recent and readable histories of the war.

Blow, Michael. *A Ship to Remember*. New York: Morrow, 1992. A balanced presentation, which concludes that the *Maine*'s destruction remains an unsolvable mystery.

Samuels, Peggy and Harold. *Remembering the Maine*. Washington, DC: Smithsonian Institution Press, 1995. The case that Weyler's followers set off a mine.

Part 4

Lingering Puzzles from the Early Modern Era

1910s to 1950s

Chapter 32

What Sank the *Lusitania?*

Walther Schwieger, commander of the German U-boat that torpedoed the *Lusitania,* recorded the event, almost matter-of-factly, in his ship's log.

"Torpedo hits starboard side close abaft the bridge, followed by a very unusually large explosion with a violent emission of smoke, far above the foremost funnel," he noted on May 7, 1915. "The superstructure above the point of impact and the bridge are torn apart, fire breaks out, a thick cloud of smoke envelopes the upper bridge. The ship stops at once and very quickly takes on a heavy list to starboard, at the same time starting to sink by the bows. She looks as if she will capsize. Great confusion reigns on board."

Less than twenty minutes later, the great liner went down off the Irish coast. Of the 1,962 people on board, 1,260 died, including 128 Americans. The reaction in America was anything but matter-of-fact. "Savagery carried to its ultimate perfection," proclaimed the Minneapolis *Journal.* "Humanity is aghast," echoed Denver's *Rocky Mountain News.*

Indeed, the sinking has gone down in history as the outrage that forced the United States to enter World War I. The *Lusitania,* it was said, failed to deliver 198 American passengers to Britain, but ended up delivering two million American soldiers to the Western Front.

Germans, not surprisingly, saw things differently. For one thing, the Americans had been warned. On May 1, the day the *Lusitania* set sail from New York, the German embassy placed an ad in several New York newspapers. It stated: "Travellers intending to embark on the Atlantic voyage are reminded that a state of war exists between Germany and her allies and Great Britain and her allies; that the zone of war includes the waters adjacent to the British Isles; that in accordance with formal notice given by the Imperial German Government, vessels flying the flag of Great Britain, or any of her allies, are liable to destruction in those waters and that travellers sailing in the war zone on ships of Great Britain or her allies do so at their own risk."

The ad didn't specifically mention the *Lusitania*, but the point was ominously clear. In case anyone might have missed it, the embassy placed the ad, in some papers, on the same page as the Cunard Line's own ads for the *Lusitania*.

Moreover, the Germans maintained, the *Lusitania* was no innocent passenger liner. The ship's manifest listed 4,200 cases of rifle cartridges and 1,248 cases of shrapnel shells, along with 50 barrels of aluminum powder and 400 cases of tools and components. That was clearly destined for the British war effort. And it didn't include the items on the manifest that may have been falsified to conceal other contraband. There were supposedly, for example, 205 barrels of fresh Connecticut oysters. The oysters' shelf life would virtually have expired before they reached their destination, and besides, England had plenty of oysters of its own. There were also suspiciously large quantities of cheese.

German newspapers and diplomats argued that the *Lusitania* was fully armed, and filled with explosives and Canadian troops bound for the front. A single torpedo could not have sunk the great liner, they stressed. That second and far greater explosion that Schwieger noted could only have been the result of the torpedo striking a load of munitions hidden on board.

This was not just German propaganda. In the years since the ship went down, many historians and scientists have made similar claims. Some have gone so far as to claim that the British Admiralty, headed up in 1915 by none other than Winston Churchill, intentionally allowed the sinking in an effort to draw America into the war. Searching for answers, some investigators have delved into British archives, while others have dived into waters of the North Atlantic.

☆ ☆ ☆

The first official inquiry took place on May 8, just a day after the sinking. After some of the bodies washed ashore near the small town of Kinsale, the local coroner, John Horgan, convened a hearing before a jury of mer-

The original title of W. A. Rogers's drawing—"Those cannon on the forward deck"—derided German claims that the Lusitania *was packed with arms as well as children. (Library of Congress.)*

chants and fishermen. This made officials in London very nervous: *Lusitania* captain William Turner's testimony about what the Admiralty had (or hadn't) done to keep this ship safe was potentially embarrassing and certainly classified. The Admiralty quickly ordered the inquiry halted, but the message reached Kinsale too late. The Admiralty was, as Horgan put it, "as belated on this occasion as . . . in protecting the *Lusitania.*"

The Admiralty need not have worried. For Horgan's jurors, the guilty parties were clearly in Berlin, not London. "This appalling crime," the jury concluded, "was contrary to international law and the conventions of all civilized nations, and we therefore charge the officers of the submarine and the German Emperor and the Government of Germany, under whose orders they acted, of willful and wholesale murder."

The next official inquiry was that of the Board of Trade, the government agency responsible for merchant shipping. The hearing was chaired by Lord Mersey, a senior judge who had taken the same seat three years earlier, after the *Titanic* sank. For the *Lusitania* hearings, which opened June 15, the Admiralty wasn't taking any chances about the direction in which fingers might be pointed. Captain Richard

Webb submitted to Mersey a report that placed the blame for the disaster squarely on the shoulders of Captain Turner.

Turner, Webb charged, invited the Germans to sink his ship by completely ignoring the Admiralty's directives. As the *Lusitania* approached the Irish coast, the Admiralty warned Turner and other captains in the area that German submarines had in the past few days sunk a number of smaller boats near the coast. The Admiralty issued three directives: speed up, zigzag, and stay midchannel. Turner chose to slow down, sail a straight line, and head toward land.

"In taking the course he did, the Master of the *Lusitania* acted directly contrary to the written general instructions received from the Admiralty and completely disregarded the telegraphic warnings received from Queenstown during the hours immediately preceding the attack," Webb wrote. "The Master appears to have displayed an almost inconceivable negligence, and one is forced to conclude that he is either utterly incompetent or that he has been got at by the Germans."

Added First Sea Lord Jacky Fisher: "As the Cunard Company would not have employed an incompetent man, the certainty is absolute that Captain Turner is not a fool but a knave. I hope that Captain Turner will be arrested immediately after the enquiry."

Lest there be any doubt that Webb spoke for his superiors, Churchill scribbled his own note on Webb's report. "The Admiralty case against the Captain should be pressed by a skilful counsel," wrote the First Lord of the Admiralty. "We should pursue the captain without check."

The Admiralty's counsel was indeed skillful. He was Attorney General Henry Carson, who was best known for successfully defending the Marquis of Queensberry in a libel suit that led to the ruin of Oscar Wilde. But Turner, too, was ably represented; his lawyer was Butler Aspinall. Aspinall saw to it that Turner answered each of Webb's accusations.

Why did he slow down? Turner explained it was because of the fog and the tide. Had he pushed ahead at full speed, he would eventually have had to stop and wait for the tide to come in. That standing around he considered more dangerous than a steady eighteen knots.

He didn't zigzag, Turner said, because he thought the Admiralty's instructions were to do so after he saw a U-boat, not as a general precaution, and he never saw Schwieger's sub. Besides, zigzagging would have slowed him down even more, and speed, as the Admiralty itself said, was the *Lusitania*'s greatest defensive asset.

As for the instructions to stay midchannel, Turner argued that's what he was doing. Under normal circumstances, the *Lusitania* would have sailed within a mile or two off the Irish coast, but on her final voyage she was about twelve miles from shore. The Admiralty had never defined midchannel in a way that made Turner question his position.

Mersey's report, issued July 17, exonerated the captain. "It is certain that in some respects Captain Turner did not follow the advice given to him," Mersey wrote. "It may be (though I seriously doubt it) that had he done so his ship would have reached Liverpool in safety. But . . . the conclusion at which I have arrived is that blame ought not to be imputed to the captain.

"The advice given to him," Mersey continued, "although meant for his most serious and careful consideration, was not intended to deprive him of the right to exercise his skilled judgment in the difficult questions that might arise from time to time in the navigation of his ship. His omission to follow the advice in all respects cannot fairly be attributed either to negligence or incompetence."

Except for his refusal to scapegoat Turner, Mersey's report came as a relief to Admiralty officials. Mersey said they, too, had done everything in their power, and they deserved "the highest praise." Mersey also dismissed reports of ammunition exploding on board, in spite of one passenger's testimony that the second explosion sounded "similar to the rattling of a machine gun."

"I did not believe this gentleman," Mersey wrote.

In other words, the *Lusitania,* the Cunard Line, and the British Admiralty were all entirely innocent victims. Mersey's conclusion echoed Horgan's: "The whole blame for the cruel destruction of life in this catastrophe," he wrote, "must rest solely with those who plotted and with those who committed the crime."

The third and final official report came three years later, this time from New York. Survivors and family members of the Americans who died had sued Cunard for negligence. The decisive moment came before the case even went to trial, when the plaintiffs withdrew their allegation that the ship had carried either Canadian troops or any ammunition that might have exploded on board. Unlike the British government, which may have had an incentive to conceal troops or ammo, the plaintiffs had every reason to push for a full investigation, since the findings might add to the company's culpability. Their decision not to pursue those accusations seemed to confirm that there was, in fact, no reliable evidence of troops or ammo.

"That story is forever disposed of as far as we are concerned," said Judge Julius Mayer.

Mayer also absolved Cunard and Turner of any blame, repeating many of Mersey's arguments. By the time Mayer ruled, the United States was at war with Germany, so it was no surprise that the judge found that "the cause of the sinking of the *Lusitania* was the illegal act of the Imperial German Government."

Mayer suggested the survivors and relatives look to Germany for reparations, and in 1925, the defeated nation paid them just over $2.5 million.

Critics of the Admiralty called the official hearings a whitewash. The war muted much of the criticism, but the grumbling started as soon as the Mersey hearings ended and continued long after the war was over. Among the most vociferous critics of the official story was Colin Simpson, a *Sunday Times* reporter who reviewed the court of inquiry records (some of which weren't declassified until the 1960s) and in a 1972 book put together the case against the Admiralty.

It was not Turner, according to Simpson, who was either a knave or a fool; it was Webb, along with the Admiralty whose orders he followed. "The probability is he was both," Simpson contended. "Webb's tactical alternatives are those of a man who would appear likely to have done himself serious injury if allowed to play tactics in his bath, let alone the Western approaches."

Why, critics like Simpson asked, had Mersey and Mayer focused on what Turner did with his orders rather than the orders themselves? If submarines were active off the Irish coast, why not send a destroyer to escort the ship to safety? (Two months earlier, two destroyers accompanied the *Lusitania.*) If a destroyer wasn't available, why not reroute the *Lusitania* around the north of Ireland, away from the U-boat-infested waters? Schwieger himself wondered about the latter in his war diary. "It remains inexplicable why *Lusitania* wasn't sent through North Channel," he wrote.

To Simpson and others, the Admiralty's actions—or rather, the Admiralty's failure to act—smacked of a conspiracy. Many pointed to Churchill's February 12 letter to Walter Runciman, president of the Board of Trade. This was just after the Germans announced their intention of blockading Britain with submarines, and three months before the sinking of the *Lusitania*. Wrote Churchill: "It is most important to attract neutral shipping to our shores, in the hope especially of embroiling the U.S.A. with Germany."

To conspiracy theorists, this was proof that Churchill had deliberately exposed the *Lusitania* to danger in order to bring the Americans into the war. Kaiser Wilhelm subscribed to this theory. "England was really responsible," he told the U.S. ambassador to Germany, "as the English had made the *Lusitania* go slowly in English waters so that the Germans could torpedo it and so bring on trouble."

Was Churchill capable of such deviousness? Similar suspicions surfaced after World War II, when he was accused of withholding information from President Roosevelt about an attack on Pearl Harbor in order to bring America into that war. But, for most historians, both accusations were unproven and unfair.

The Admiralty could have ordered a destroyer escort, true, but at the time naval experts still had faith in a large liner's ability to outrun a U-boat. As for the North Channel, that appeared safer but there was no guarantee U-boats weren't there as well.

"The overriding evidence," wrote historian Diana Preston, "is that, whatever the merits of sending an escort . . . and diverting [the ship] out of harm's way, none of these actions was ever systematically considered. The reason why the tragedy was allowed to happen was that the Admiralty at senior levels was preoccupied with bigger issues."

Churchill, in particular, was busy negotiating with Italy and worrying about Britain's failing campaign in the Dardanelles. His subordinates were reluctant to take any dramatic action in his absence. Besides, most doubted the Germans would sink a large merchant ship, especially one carrying a lot of Americans.

As for Churchill's letter to Runciman, less conspiracy-minded historians could interpret it more innocently. "He merely sought to 'embroil' America in a diplomatic or commercial impasse with Germany," wrote David Ramsay. "Such a dispute would have intensified pro-Allied sentiment in America and thus have safeguarded the important munitions purchasing program."

"Far from being the subject of conspiracy," Preston concluded, "the *Lusitania,* in her last days and hours, was the victim of complacency and neglect."

In the days and hours *after* the sinking, however, there's no doubt that top officials in the Admiralty conspired to make the most of their propaganda bonanza. Not only did they try to scapegoat Turner, but they also worked to suppress any suspicions that the ship's cargo caused the second explosion. It was far better, for British propaganda purposes, that the Germans alone be responsible for the tragedy. Officials carefully selected which crew members would testify before Mersey, and they prepared statements for them emphasizing that the second explosion had been caused by a second torpedo. Many passengers who believed only one torpedo hit the *Lusitania* weren't allowed to testify, and some who did testify about a single torpedo were quickly discredited by the Admiralty's leaks to the press.

The Admiralty may also have pressured Turner to change his story. The captain told the coroner's court he thought there was a single torpedo, but by the time he testified before Mersey he thought there were two. Schwieger, for his part, was consistent. His war diary indicated two explosions, one torpedo. But his diary was, of course, just as susceptible to the manipulations of German propagandists as the testimony of the *Lusitania* crew was to Admiralty pressure.

The only way to figure out what caused the second explosion was to inspect the ship itself.

Divers had no problem locating the wreck of the *Lusitania,* three hundred feet down and twelve miles off the Irish coast. The problem was that, until the 1980s, diving technology didn't allow anyone to stay that far underwater for long. Divers who did so suffered from nitrogen narcosis, also known as the martini effect for what it did to their brains. This may have accounted for reported sightings, by U.S. Navy diver John Light and his team in the early 1960s, of a gun barrel and a large hole in the cargo area, supposedly caused by the explosion of contraband ammunition. The team's pictures showed nothing of the gun or the hole.

In 1993 Robert Ballard, who had found and explored the wreck of the *Titanic,* moved on to the *Lusitania*. Ballard had the advantage of much more sophisticated diving and lighting equipment than Light. He found no guns and no hole anywhere near the cargo area.

"We were able to inspect the entire exposed area . . . and it was clearly undamaged," he wrote. "If it held munitions, they were not the cause of the secondary explosions that sank the ship."

What did?

One clue was the coal scattered around the wreck on the bottom of the sea. Ballard's guess was that coal dust, a byproduct of the ship's boiler room, caused the explosion. The torpedo, he wrote, could have "kicked up large amounts of coal dust that blanketed the bottom of the bunkers, and that the torpedo ignited, tearing open the side of the ship for the length of one of the starboard bunkers."

Others, like Preston, maintained the torpedo ruptured a steam line. But after Ballard's findings, most historians agreed that the ship's cargo was not to blame. In this sense, Ballard's findings vindicated the British propaganda. The Germans had been telling the truth about there being only one torpedo, but the British were right that a torpedo, and not some explosive cargo, sank the *Lusitania*.

It did not take Ballard's findings, of course, to recognize that the sinking was a major propaganda victory for the British. "In spite of all its horror, we must regard the sinking of the *Lusitania* as an event most important and favorable to the Allies," Churchill later wrote. "The poor babies who perished in the ocean struck a blow at German power more deadly than could have been achieved by the sacrifice of a hundred thousand fighting men."

The United States did not enter the war until almost two years (and many sinkings) later, but Churchill was surely right that the *Lusitania* alerted Americans to the barbarism of German warfare. Back in 1915, Americans could blithely board the *Lusitania*, dismissing the German ad as an idle threat and confident that no nation would attack civilians, let alone those from a neutral country. The year the *Lusitania* sank also brought the introduction of poison gas to the front, the first air raid on civilians, and the recognition that there was no longer any such thing as civilized warfare.

☆ To investigate further:

Simpson, Colin. *The Lusitania*. Boston: Little, Brown, 1972. The case against Winston Churchill and the Admiralty; provocative and lucid, although ultimately unconvincing.

Bailey, Thomas, and Paul Ryan. *The Lusitania Disaster*. New York: The Free Press, 1975. A scholar and a seaman answer Simpson.

Ballard, Robert D., with Spencer Dunmore. *Exploring the Lusitania*. New York: Warner Books, 1995. The juxtaposition of photographs from the ship's glory days and the new underwater images is haunting.

Preston, Diana. *Lusitania*. New York: Walker, 2002. A vivid account of both the human stories and the political consequences.

Ramsay, David. *Lusitania*. New York: W.W. Norton, 2002. Ramsay is extremely thorough in dispelling the myths surrounding the ship.

Chapter 33

Did Shoeless Joe Throw the Series?

The baseball career of "Shoeless Joe" Jackson—whose talent, according to his fellow players, rivaled that of Babe Ruth—came to an abrupt end when he was banned from the game after the 1919 Black Sox scandal. That was the year gamblers bribed the heavily favored Chicago White Sox to throw the World Series.

A year later, Jackson testified before a Cook County grand jury, and the New York *Evening World* published its famous account of the player encountering a group of boys outside the courthouse.

"A man, guarded like a felon by other men, emerged from the door," reported Hugh Fullerton. "He did not swagger. He slunk along between his guardians, and the kids, with wide eyes and tightened throats, watched, and one, bolder than the others, pressed forward and said 'It ain't so, Joe, is it?'"

Jackson, according to Fullerton, gulped back a sob before answering, "Yes, kid, I'm afraid it is."

Jackson always denied this story. More to the point, he denied he ever played anything but his best, pointing to his .375 Series batting average, his five runs scored, and his six runs batted in. Since then, Jackson has become a mythic figure, sometimes a symbol of guilt and sometimes of innocence. He is the basis for the Faustian Joe Hardy in the musical *Damn Yankees* and the more sinned-against-than-sinning Roy Hobbs in the novel and movie *The Natural*. As an illiterate cotton mill worker whose natural

*Joe Jackson, wearing shoes
and (inexplicably for an
outfielder) a catcher's mitt.
(Library of Congress.)*

ability took him from a small South Carolina town to Chicago, Jackson is
a symbol of innocence; corrupted by the big city, he is a symbol of our fall
from grace. In the movie *Field of Dreams,* he emerges from an Iowa corn-
field, the perfect symbol of a lost America. Even his nickname seemed to
fit perfectly his image as bumpkin and phenom, a man without the sense
or money to wear shoes but with so much talent that he didn't need them.

Amid Jackson's apotheosis, baseball historians have continued to
debate the question of whether it actually is or ain't so. Indeed, in a
sport that thrives on debate, what Jackson did that October is baseball's greatest historical mystery.

☆ ☆ ☆

Rumors that the Series was fixed surfaced even before it began. In fact,
by the first game, so much money had been bet on the underdog
Cincinnati Reds that White Sox fans could get even odds on their
team. After the Reds won the Series, White Sox owner Charles
Comiskey offered a $20,000 reward for evidence of a fix.

Almost a year later, the reward tempted Billy Maharg, one of the
gamblers involved in bribing players, to tell his story, and a Cook
County grand jury convened to investigate. The first player to crack

was Eddie Cicotte, a pitcher who told the grand jury he'd taken $10,000 to lose two Series games.

On September 28, 1920, Jackson appeared before the grand jury, and his own testimony is among the most damning evidence against him. Jackson told the grand jury that White Sox first baseman Chick Gandil was the first to approach him about the fix. Assistant state attorney Hartley Repogle questioned Jackson:

Q: How much did he promise you?
A: $20,000 if I would take part.
Q: And you said you would?
A: Yes, sir.
Q: When did he promise you the $20,000?
A: It was to be paid after each game.
Q: How much?
A: Split up in some way. I don't know just how much it amounts to, but during it would amount to $20,000. Finally [White Sox pitcher Lefty] Williams brought me this $5,000, and threw it down.

Later the same day, Jackson seemingly contradicted himself. He told the grand jury that he'd always played his best.

Q: Did you make any intentional errors yourself . . . ?
A: No, sir, not during the whole series.
Q: Did you bat to win?
A: Yes.
Q: And run the bases to win?
A: Yes, sir.
Q: And fielded the balls at the outfield to win?
A: I did.

Still, Jackson's earlier admission, along with similar statements from Cicotte and Williams, seemed enough at least to bring the group of White Sox players, now nicknamed the Black Sox, to trial. State attorney Robert Crowe, who took over the case from Repogle, certainly expected to go to court. But when Crowe examined the grand jury's files, he discovered that critical portions of the players' testimony were missing from the record. Gone, too, were the waivers of immunity the players had signed before testifying. And Cicotte, Williams, and Jackson now denied they'd ever confessed to anything.

Crowe proceeded nonetheless, and the fraud and conspiracy trial of eight White Sox, including Jackson, opened in June 1921. Instead of the players, Crowe called to the stand Maharg and another gambler, Bill Burns, who in return for immunity described their roles in the fix. But the prosecution's case was undercut by the judge's instructions to the jury. There was no law on the books that specifically outlawed throwing baseball games. So Judge Hugo Friend explained that, to find the defendants guilty, the jurors had to be convinced the players had intentionally harmed Comiskey's business and defrauded the public. This was a difficult standard of proof for prosecutors to meet, especially since in 1920 baseball fans continued to stream into Comiskey Park, and Comiskey was making more money than ever. Besides, even if the Black Sox had thrown the Series, prosecutors hadn't presented evidence that the players were motivated by anything other than greed. It took the jury only three hours to find all eight not guilty.

The celebration, however, was short-lived. Baseball's new commissioner, Kenesaw Mountain Landis, didn't think much of the jury's verdict or of leniency in general. (As a judge, Landis once sentenced a seventy-five-year-old to fifteen years in jail. When the man said he couldn't serve that long, Landis told him to "do the best you can.")

The same evening the jurors pronounced their verdict, Landis gave his. "Regardless of the outcome of juries," he said, "no player that throws a ball game, no player that entertains proposals or promises to throw a game, no player that sits in a conference with a bunch of crooked players where the ways and means of throwing games are discussed, and does not promptly tell his club about it, will ever again play professional baseball."

Neither Jackson nor any of the seven other Black Sox would ever again play major league baseball.

☆ ☆ ☆

Jackson sued Comiskey for the salary he lost after the owner dropped him and the other Black Sox from the roster. The case went to court in January 1924. This time it wasn't enough for Jackson to show he hadn't damaged Comiskey's business; he had to convince a jury he wasn't in on the fix.

The story Jackson now told differed from the one presented to either the 1920 grand jury or the 1921 jury. Jackson claimed he knew nothing about the fix during the Series; the other players, without his permission, used his name to impress the gamblers. Indeed, Jackson went on, he did not know there was a fix until Lefty Williams gave him the $5,000 after the last game of the Series. Gamblers Maharg and Burns appeared in court again, this time to confirm that Jackson wasn't present at any of their meetings with the players. Williams also testified that he hadn't spoken to Jackson about the fix until he handed over the money.

Moreover, Jackson explained, once he learned of the fix he tried to tell Comiskey about it. With the $5,000 in his pocket, Jackson went to Comiskey's office, but the owner wouldn't see him. Jackson backed up this testimony by producing a letter he'd dictated to Comiskey suggesting that the Series was crooked. Comiskey never responded. The villain of this story was clearly Comiskey, who tried to cover up the fix to protect the value of his team. Only after Maharg blew the lid off the scandal did the owner change course and turn on the players.

Comiskey's lawyer, George Hudnall, struck back with the most startling revelation of the trial. He pulled out of his briefcase the grand jury testimony in which Jackson admitted discussing the fix with Gandil and demanding $20,000 to participate. Here was the document that had disappeared after the grand jury hearing. Jackson responded by explaining that, yes, he had sort of confessed, but only because Comiskey's lawyer had advised him no jury would believe the truth. Jackson had taken the lawyer's word that he wouldn't be prosecuted if he confessed.

If the grand jury testimony embarrassed Jackson, it was also awkward for Comiskey. How, after all, did his lawyer come to be in possession of the missing document? Questioned by Jackson's lawyers, Comiskey said he didn't know. But reporters then and historians later couldn't help but note how conveniently the grand jury testimony disappeared when Comiskey was still hoping to hold onto his star players, and how conveniently it reappeared when he was trying to avoid paying back wages to one of those players. Most historians assumed Comiskey, probably with the help of some of the gamblers, either paid off some clerk or simply stole the documents.

The 1924 jury, like the 1921 one, found for Jackson. They awarded him $16,711.04. Again, however, there was little time to celebrate. Once the jury was out of earshot, Judge John Gregory declared that Jackson was a liar. His 1921 and 1924 stories couldn't both be true, so he must have lied one of those times. Either way, Gregory wasn't going to let a perjurer walk away with a victory in his court. He immediately set aside the verdict.

After the trial, Comiskey offered an out-of-court settlement, thus precluding any more awkward questions about how he happened to have the grand jury testimony. Jackson took an undisclosed (and presumably small) amount of money and went home to South Carolina.

Comiskey's reputation, deservedly, never recovered. Many baseball historians focused on how he not only covered up the fix, but to some extent also caused it. In an era before big money baseball salaries, Comiskey paid his players significantly less than other owners paid theirs. Jackson, clearly one of the best players of all time, never made more than $6,000 a year. Cicotte, according to Eliot Asinof's *Eight Men Out,* was driven to throw the Series at least partly because of Comiskey's penuriousness. In 1917, Comiskey promised the pitcher a $10,000 bonus if he won thirty games; when Cicotte reached twenty-nine, the owner ordered him benched. (Other historians dispute Asinof's story on the grounds that Comiskey would never have promised to pay anyone $10,000.) Even before 1919, some people called his team the Black Sox, because Comiskey, unlike other owners, wouldn't pay to clean their uniforms.

Baseball historians have also done much to put the scandal in its historical context. When Landis banned the eight players, his clear implication was that he had solved the problem, that baseball's record until 1919 was pure and that it now would be again. But these were hardly the first players to get mixed up with gamblers. In addition to the eight Black Sox, fourteen others were banned from the game for similar reasons between 1917 and 1927. The record for the most thrown games probably goes to Hal Chase, a first baseman in New York, Chicago, and Cincinnati. Three of Chase's managers accused him of dishonesty before he was finally banned for bribing an umpire. With a tip of the hat to Asinof's classic, baseball historian Bill James referred to the players who were banned as the "22 men out." That figure doesn't count the many others who were allegedly involved in gambling, but against whom there wasn't enough evidence to take any action.

But back to Jackson. That some blame has fallen on Comiskey and others does not ultimately answer the question of how much belongs to Jackson. To some of his recent defenders, most notably baseball historian Donald Gropman, Jackson is blameless. The story Jackson told at the 1924 civil trial was the truth; the 1921 grand jury testimony was solely the result of an illiterate mill hand being duped by Comiskey's sophisticated lawyer. Two juries found Jackson not guilty, and so did Gropman. And, as Gropman and others have stressed, there's that .375 batting average. Jackson's twelve Series hits remained a Series record until 1960.

A majority of recent baseball historians, however, have found Jackson guilty, though to varying extents. He *did* take the $5,000 from Williams, even if we accept his word that he didn't know in advance it was coming and that he tried to tell Comiskey about it. Jackson was illiterate but not stupid. When he returned to South Carolina, he opened a successful dry-cleaning business, employed more than twenty people, and bought a home and two cars. He knew what the money was for, and he kept it.

Whether he actually earned the money by playing less than his best remains a mystery. It's possible, as some historians have suggested, that he intended to throw the games but had so much natural talent and so much love for the game that, once he took the field, he couldn't stop himself from hitting. It's also possible, as others have noted, that he was capable of playing even better than he did. His hits were plentiful, but most of them didn't come with the game on the line. He was not charged with any errors, but three triples fell near him, even though sportswriters described Jackson's glove as "the place triples go to die."

In the press box, with rumors rampant during the Series, Hugh Fullerton circled on his scorecard those plays he considered suspicious. Some involved Jackson. But, like so much else about Shoeless Joe, what Fullerton wrote has added as much to the myth as to the reality. Even Fullerton's famous story about the boy who said "it ain't so" has often been questioned, including by Jackson.

"No such word . . . was ever said," Jackson later claimed. "The fellow who wrote that just wanted something to say. When I came out of the courthouse that day, nobody said anything to me. The only one who spoke was a guy who yelled at his friend 'I told you the big son of a bitch wore shoes.'"

☆ To investigate further:

Asinof, Eliot. *Eight Men Out*. New York: Holt, Rinehart and Winston, 1963. This was a classic of baseball history long before John Sayles made it into a fine movie.

Frommer, Harvey. *Shoeless Joe and Ragtime Baseball*. Dallas: Taylor, 1992. A less thorough defense than Gropman's, though the appendix—which contains the entire text of Jackson's 1921 grand jury testimony—is useful.

Gropman, Donald. *Say It Ain't So, Joe!* New York: Citadel, 1992. Originally published in 1979, this remains the best defense of Jackson.

Fleitz, David. *Shoeless*. Jefferson, North Carolina: McFarland, 2001. A comprehensive biography that concludes Jackson was guilty.

James, Bill. *The New Bill James Historical Baseball Abstract*. New York: The Free Press, 2001. James is usually thought of as a baseball statistician, but his entertaining and provocative analysis goes way beyond the numbers.

Chapter 34

Were Sacco and Vanzetti Guilty?

No murder case—with the possible exception of O. J. Simpson's—has so sharply divided the country as that of Sacco and Vanzetti. To their supporters, Sacco and Vanzetti were, in the words of the latter, "a good shoemaker and a poor fish peddler." They were prosecuted and ultimately executed because they were radicals and immigrants in a society that would tolerate neither. That view was shared by Governor Michael Dukakis of Massachusetts, the state in which Sacco and Vanzetti lived and died. In 1977, 50 years after Sacco and Vanzetti had been executed, Dukakis declared that "any stigma and disgrace should be forever removed from the names of Nicola Sacco and Bartolomeo Vanzetti."

Revisionists have argued that Sacco and Vanzetti were indeed guilty and by the late 1960s the consensus among historians seemed to be that Sacco, at least, was probably guilty, though Vanzetti was probably not. That consensus proved shortlived, however. In the late 1980s both sides uncovered new evidence, and both sides claimed their new evidence proved they'd been right all along.

☆ ☆ ☆

The murders for which Sacco and Vanzetti were executed took place on April 15, 1920, in the town of South Braintree, 12 miles south of Boston. In the course of stealing the Slater and Morrill shoe factory's

$15,776 payroll, robbers shot and killed the paymaster, Frederick Parmenter, and his guard, Alessandro Berardelli. The crime followed a similar but unsuccessful holdup that took place in nearby Bridgewater a few months earlier; in the Bridgewater attempt, it was the L. Q. White shoe factory's payroll that the criminals were after. Both crimes took place in daylight, in front of dozens of witnesses who told police the criminals looked Italian.

Italians were on the mind of Chief Michael Stewart of the Bridgewater police for other reasons as well. The country was in the midst of what came to be known as the Red Scare. In response to the Bolshevik success in Russia as well as a series of strikes, riots, and bombings that took place in America during 1919, local police forces across the country were cracking down on radical immigrant groups. On January 2, 1920, more than four thousand foreigners were arrested, of whom more than five hundred were ultimately deported.

Among those just deported was a local anarchist named Furrucio Coaccio. Stewart recalled that Coaccio's deportation had been very easy; too easy, it now seemed. Was it possible, Stewart wondered, that Coaccio had seen his deportation as an opportunity to get out of the country quickly—with the loot from the South Braintree robbery? Stewart's suspicions were further aroused when he discovered that Mike Boda, who was now living in Coaccio's house, was an employee of the L. Q. White Shoe Company. He went to see Boda but Boda was gone.

Boda, however, had left his car behind at the local garage. Stewart asked the garage owner to let him know right away if Boda came to pick it up. Boda came by on May 5, but, before the police could get there, he took off. Left behind for the police were the two men who had accompanied him to pick up the car: Sacco and Vanzetti.

Soon the police had more reasons to suspect Sacco and Vanzetti. Both were armed, Sacco with a .32 caliber Colt automatic pistol and Vanzetti with a .38 caliber Harrington and Richardson revolver. What's more, both lied to the police; they denied knowing Boda and they denied being involved with any radical groups. Each of these claims was easily shown to be false, since the garage owner had told police they arrived with Boda and since Sacco had on him an announcement of an anarchist meeting at which Vanzetti was to speak.

The trial of Sacco and Vanzetti began on May 31, 1921. The prosecution made much of the lies the defendants had told the police, arguing that it revealed their "consciousness of guilt." More damning, perhaps, was the testimony of seven witnesses who identified Sacco as having been in South Braintree before, during, or after the shooting. No one placed Vanzetti at the shooting, but two witnesses said they saw him in the getaway car and two others said they saw him in or around South Braintree earlier in the morning of the crime.

Most damning of all was the physical evidence against the two. Not only was Vanzetti armed when he was arrested but the Harrington and Richardson revolver was the same kind of gun that the slain guard, Alessandro Berardelli, had owned; the prosecution argued that Vanzetti had taken it from him during the robbery. For Sacco, the situation was worse still: two expert prosecution witnesses, William Proctor and Charles Van Amburgh, testified that one of the bullets taken from Berardelli's body, known as Bullet III, had been fired through the Colt .32 automatic found on Sacco on the night of his arrest.

To all of the prosecution's evidence, the defense had an answer.

To the "consciousness of guilt" argument, Sacco and Vanzetti answered that, yes, they had lied to the police—but the guilt they had been conscious of was that they were radicals and foreigners. In fact, on the night they were arrested, they now admitted, they had planned to pick up Boda's car and use it to move some incriminating radical literature to a safer hiding place. No wonder they had lied to the police; in the midst of a massive roundup of radical foreigners, they assumed that's what they were being arrested for. They were concealing their involvement in a radical anarchist group, not their involvement in a murder.

As for the eyewitnesses, the defense had plenty of its own. A total of eleven eyewitnesses had placed either Sacco or Vanzetti at or near the crime scene, but plenty of other eyewitnesses had seen one or more of the robbers and failed to identify either of the defendants. The defense also attempted to impeach the testimony of the prosecution's witnesses, pointing out, for example, that one of those who identified Vanzetti stated he had spoken in clear English while in fact Vanzetti had a heavy Italian accent. Finally, the defense put on the stand witnesses who claimed to have been with Sacco and Vanzetti at the time of the crime—and nowhere near the crime scene (though the prosecution attempted to discredit the alibis by pointing out that these witnesses were friends of the defendants and fellow anarchists).

On the whole, the eyewitness testimony probably cancelled itself out. For every prosecution witness, there was a defense witness to contradict his or her story; for every defense witness, a prosecution wit-

SACCO FLAYS CAPITALISTS IN FIERY SPEECH IN COURT

Holds Courtroom Spellbound by Address---Went to Mexico to Escape War Service, He States--- Proud of Having Been a Slacker

A cap found at the murder site didn't fit Sacco, but—in contrast to those who watched O. J. Simpson struggle to get his hand into a glove—this jury was unmoved. (Boston Post, July 8, 1921.)

ness told otherwise. That made the physical evidence all the more crucial, and though the defense also had its own experts, the testimony of Proctor and Van Amburgh was persuasive. On July 14, seven weeks after the trial began, the jury found Sacco and Vanzetti guilty of murder in the first degree.

☆ ☆ ☆

But the defense had just begun to fight. Defense attorneys submitted a series of motions for a new trial. One included an affidavit from Proctor, whose testimony had been instrumental in securing a conviction. In the affidavit, Proctor stated: "Bullet number III, in my judgment, passed through some Colt automatic pistol, but I do not intend by that answer to imply that I had found any evidence that the so-called mortal bullet had passed through this particular Colt automatic."

This was a far cry from his trial testimony, where he had clearly implied that it was Sacco's specific gun that had fired the fatal bullet. Furthermore, Proctor admitted to arranging the careful phrasing of the trial testimony with the DA in order to leave the jury with the wrong impression. This was virtually an admission that he'd conspired with the DA to commit perjury; it cast doubts not only on Proctor's credibility but on the integrity of the DA. Nevertheless, on October 1, 1924, Judge Webster Thayer denied the defense's motion for a new trial.

The next bombshell came in November 1925. Celestino Madeiros, who was being held in the same prison with Sacco while appealing a conviction for murder during a bank robbery, came forward and confessed to participating in the shoe company robberies. Madeiros would not name his confederates, but he did say that neither Sacco nor Vanzetti had anything to do with the crimes. Defense attorney Herbert Ehrmann undertook his own investigation and determined that Madeiros had been working with a Providence gang under the leadership of Joe Morelli. The gang had been charged with other robberies of the same Slater and Morrill shoe company that Sacco and Vanzetti had supposedly robbed. More remarkable still was the striking resemblance between Sacco and Joe Morelli: when Ehrmann showed prosecution and defense witnesses a picture of Morelli, a number of them identified him as Sacco.

Again, however, Thayer was unmoved. In October 1926, after observing that Madeiros, when questioned, seemed unfamiliar with the scene of the crime, Thayer dismissed the defense motion for a new trial. In April 1927, he sentenced Sacco and Vanzetti to die, and on August 23, 1927 the sentence was carried out.

Still, the case would not die. Writers on each side continued to research and publish, with defenders of Sacco and Vanzetti especially prolific. These tended to emphasize the prejudices of the judge or jury, and of the country as a whole during the Red Scare.

Then in 1962, Francis Russell published one of the most influential of the revisionist studies of the case. Originally convinced that Sacco and Vanzetti were innocent, Russell came to believe that Sacco, at least, was guilty. Russell's change of heart began after he learned that Fred Moore, the primary defense lawyer during the first four years of the case, thought that Sacco was guilty. He was further persuaded when he learned that Carlo Tresca, a leading Italian-American anarchist, also thought Sacco was guilty.

But Russell still had to resolve the question of Bullet III. In 1961 he set up new tests during which ballistics experts found that Bullet III had indeed come from Sacco's gun. For Russell, this clinched the case.

But the defense had some new evidence of its own. After the Massachusetts State Police released an enormous file on the case in response to a Freedom of Information Act suit, William Young and David Kaiser discovered that Vanzetti's gun was *not* that of the guard, Berardelli, as the prosecution had claimed. More shocking still, the prosecution knew this and concealed its findings from the defense. As for Bullet III, Sacco's defenders conceded the bullet came from his gun, but noted that, according to the autopsy report and eyewitness reports in the newly released police files, the same assailant had fired all four bullets into Berardelli. How, then, could only one of the four bullets have come from Sacco's gun? To Young and Kaiser, there could only be one explanation: a bullet was shot from Sacco's gun *after the murder,* and then was substituted for one of the real bullets.

In short, according to this latest evidence, Sacco and Vanzetti were framed. Whether because they were convinced of their guilt, or just because they wanted to get rid of a couple of troublesome Italian radicals, the district attorney and his assistant used evidence they knew to be false in order to convict Sacco and Vanzetti.

For most historians, the Young/Kaiser conclusions were more convincing than Russell's. Russell assumed Moore and Tresca knew enough to determine whether Sacco and Vanzetti were guilty, but there's no way to test that evidence. Even Russell couldn't question these witnesses; he heard what each said through intermediaries. At best, Russell's evidence is hearsay; at worst, mere rumor.

The new evidence tending to exonerate Sacco and Vanzetti, in contrast, came directly from the prosecution and police files. Even before Sacco and Vanzetti were executed, the defense had questioned the state's credibility on such matters as Proctor's testimony and the reluctance to pursue the Madeiros lead. Now it became even more difficult to trust the state. The new evidence may not have proven Sacco and Vanzetti were innocent, but it certainly leaves us with reasonable doubts.

So, too, do recent studies of the pair's anarchist backgrounds. The radical organizations in which both Sacco and Vanzetti were involved were committed to violent insurrections. There's even some circumstantial evidence that Sacco and Vanzetti may have been involved in some of the 1919 bombings that led to the Red Scare (and, indirectly, to their arrest). When Sacco and Vanzetti lied to the police after their arrest, they may have been covering up more than their membership in a radical organization; it's very possible they were planning to use Boda's car to transport some explosives, rather than the radical literature they talked about at their trial. Ironically, however, this violent background also attested to the pair's innocence. Anarchists were committed to violence—but for the sake of revolution, not robbery. And there has never been any sign that the Bridgewater and South Braintree robberies were motivated by anything other than greed.

☆ To investigate further:

Frankfurter, Felix. *The Case of Sacco and Vanzetti*. New York: Little, Brown, 1927. The future Supreme Court Justice's passionate argument that the trial was unfair and that Sacco and Vanzetti were innocent.

Frankfurter, Marion and Gardner Jackson, editors. *The Letters of Sacco and Vanzetti*. New York: Viking, 1928. After reading Vanzetti's eloquent and moving letters, it's easy to see why so many believed so strongly that he could not be guilty of murder.

Fraenkel, Osmond. *The Sacco-Vanzetti Case*. New York: Knopf, 1931. Includes extensive selections from the court records.

Ehrmann, Herbert. *The Untried Case*. New York: Vanguard, 1933. How Ehrmann, one of the attorneys for the defense, put together the case against the Morelli gang.

Joughin, Louis and Edmund Morgan. *The Legacy of Sacco and Vanzetti*. New York: Harcourt Brace, 1948; reissued in 1971 by Princeton University Press (Princeton, NJ). A balanced case for the defense, which also traces how the case was represented in the press and in the arts.

Montgomery, Robert. *Sacco-Vanzetti: The Murder and the Myth*. Greenwich, CT: Devin-Adair, 1960. The first of the revisionist studies.

Russell, Francis. *Tragedy in Dedham*. New York: McGraw-Hill, 1962. Sacco was guilty, Vanzetti innocent.

Felix, David. *Protest: Sacco-Vanzetti and the Intellectuals*. Bloomington: Indiana University Press, 1965. A somewhat shrill and unfocused revisionist effort.

Ehrmann, Herbert. *The Case That Will Not Die*. New York: Little, Brown, 1969. The case for the defense, by one of the defense attorneys.

Feuerlicht, Roberta. *Justice Crucified*. New York: McGraw-Hill, 1977. A passionate case for innocence, though it adds little evidence to previous studies.

Young, William, and David Kaiser. *Postmortem*. Amherst: The University of Massachusetts Press, 1985. The latest evidence and one of the best cases for innocence.

Russell, Francis. *Sacco and Vanzetti*. New York: Harper & Row, 1986. In 1982, Russell received a letter from Ideala Gambera, the son of a radical who had known Sacco and Vanzetti. Gambera said his father had told him that everyone in the anarchists' circle knew Sacco was guilty; for Russell, this was yet more proof that both were guilty. But it's still just hearsay, and except for this letter Russell had little to say that wasn't in his 1962 book, *Tragedy in Dedham*. That first book remains the better of the two, and the best of all the revisionist studies.

Avrich, Paul. *Sacco and Vanzetti*. Princeton, NJ: Princeton University Press, 1991. Though it takes no final position on the pair's guilt or innocence, this is unique and important for its investigation of the political movement of which they were a part.

Chapter 35

Who Kidnapped the Lindbergh Baby?

Of the most famous trials of the twentieth century—those of Sacco and Vanzetti, Alger Hiss, the Rosenbergs, and O. J. Simpson—the Lindbergh kidnapping trial stands out for its lack of political significance. No one could say the accused, Bruno Richard Hauptmann, was being tried because of his politics or his race. Yet the 1932 crime and trial gripped the American press and public at least as firmly as any of these others. In the days and months following the kidnapping, sightseeing planes circled the scene of the crime, hot dog vendors lined up along the road where the body was found, and among the many thousands of letters the Lindbergh family received were 12,000 just from people eager to recount their dreams about the case.

Partly, of course, this was sheer voyeurism. The father of the kidnapped child was Charles Lindbergh, the first man to fly solo across the Atlantic. In a country which celebrated both individualism and technology, the 1927 flight guaranteed Lindbergh heroic status. This was only enhanced by his 1929 marriage to Anne Morrow, the daughter of a prominent banker and ambassador, and then by the birth of their blond-haired, blue-eyed baby, Charles Jr., a year later. But Lindbergh's status alone cannot explain the fascination with the kidnapping of Charles Jr. In the early years of the Depression, the crime tapped into deeper fears about what the future held for America's children. No wonder that Maurice Sendak, author and artist of some of the spookiest children's stories of any time, once said: "All of my books are really about the Lindbergh kidnapping."

For most Americans, therefore, the arrest, conviction, and execution of Hauptmann brought some satisfaction. But it was distinctly less satisfying that Hauptmann went to his death proclaiming his innocence. In the years since then, others have taken up his cause, contending that in their eagerness to solve such a highly publicized crime, the police arrested—and the state of New Jersey put to death—an innocent man.

☆　☆　☆

The kidnapping took place the evening of March 1, 1932, at the Lindberghs' newly finished house near Hopewell, New Jersey. Normally the family stayed there only on weekends, living the rest of the time at the Morrow family estate. But this particular week they decided to stay on. About eight o'clock Anne Lindbergh and her nursemaid Betty Gow put the baby to bed; at ten Gow went to check on him and found he was gone.

Instead, the Lindberghs found a note that read:

Have 50,000 $ redy 25000 $ in 20 $ bills 15000 $ in 10 $ bills and 10000 $ in 5 $ bills. After 2–4 days we will inform you were to deliver the Money. We warn you for making anyding public or for notify the Polise the child is in gut care.

At the bottom of the note were two intersecting circles, with the oval intersection colored red. This, the note said, was a "singnature" by which the Lindberghs would be able to recognize that future notes were from the actual kidnappers and not some other extortionist trying to cash in without actually having the child.

Indeed, the Lindberghs were soon besieged by a variety of shady characters. One was the recently jailed gangster Al Capone, who offered his services as an intermediary between the Lindberghs and the kidnappers—in return for Capone's freedom. The offer was declined.

Others were more successful in convincing the Lindberghs they could help. A former Justice Department agent, Gaston Means, claimed to know the kidnappers and convinced Evalyn Walsh McLean, the owner of the Hope diamond, to donate $100,000 to save the baby's

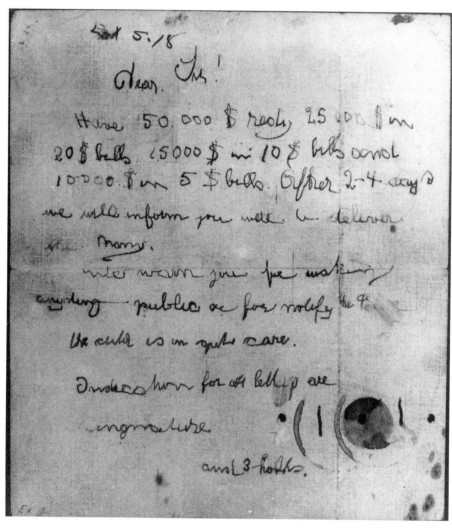

This ransom note was found on the windowsill of the Lindbergh baby's nursery. The handwriting matched Bruno Richard Hauptmann's, and the fact that it was clearly written by someone of German background (note the use of "anyding" instead of "anything" and "gut" instead of "good") was also held against the German-born defendant. (Courtesy of the New Jersey State Police.)

life—after which the money and Means promptly disappeared. (Means was eventually tracked down and convicted of embezzlement.) Another con artist, named Mickey Rosner, moved into the Lindbergh house and spent more than a week there, monopolizing their phone lines with calls to his supposed intermediaries, before the Lindberghs gave up on him and had the police throw him out.

Of all those who offered help, perhaps the most unlikely connection to the kidnappers turned out to be the most legitimate. This was Dr. John Condon, a retired schoolteacher from the Bronx. Condon was in the habit of writing eccentric letters to the Bronx *Home News,* and in one of his letters he offered his services to the kidnappers as an intermediary. Remarkably, they responded: on March 9 he received a letter with the telltale intersecting circles. This ultimately led to a rendezvous with the kidnappers at St. Raymond's Cemetery on the night of April 2. While Lindbergh remained in the car, Condon met with a man who identified himself as "John"; in return for $50,000, John gave Condon a note telling where to find the baby. Alas, a thorough search of the area described in the note turned up nothing. Seven weeks later the baby's body was found, just a couple of miles from the Lindbergh house.

Though the efforts to save the baby had been in vain, the search for the kidnappers went on. The police had noted all the serial numbers on the ransom notes Condon had given to John; moreover, the ransom was paid largely in gold certificates that, because of new currency regulations, were increasingly rare, and the police hoped this would make them easier to track. Sure enough, about two and a half years later, a gas station attendant was handed a ten-dollar gold certificate. Suspecting it might be counterfeit, he wrote down the car's license number on the certificate. And when a bank identified the certificate as ransom money the police tracked down the car's owner, Bruno Richard Hauptmann. A search of Hauptmann's garage uncovered a shoebox with $13,760 more of Lindbergh ransom money.

The evidence against Hauptmann seemed overwhelming. Handwriting experts identified Hauptmann's handwriting as the same as that on the ransom note. Condon, after some initial hesitation, identified Hauptmann as the "John" to whom he'd given the ransom money in the graveyard. Lindbergh himself identified John's voice as the same voice he'd heard from the car, as he sat waiting for Condon near the graveyard. Above all, there was the ransom money found in Hauptmann's possession.

Hauptmann's background didn't help his case. He was a German immigrant, and the spelling errors in the ransom note ("gut" for "good," "anyding" for "anything") were consistent with what might be expected from a native German speaker. Worse, Hauptmann had fled Germany to avoid sentencing for crimes that included using a ladder to enter a second-floor bedroom window (as had been the case in the kidnapping), and robbing two women who were pushing baby carriages down the street.

It seemed an open-and-shut case. Certainly the jury thought so: though five jurors favored life imprisonment instead of the death penalty, none doubted his guilt. Hauptmann was electrocuted on April 3, 1936.

And yet, to his death, Hauptmann proclaimed his innocence. Even when New Jersey's governor offered to convert his sentence to life imprisonment in return for a confession, Hauptmann refused.

Revisionists took up his cause. Anthony Scaduto in 1976 and Ludovic Kennedy in 1985 published books contending the evidence against Hauptmann was at best flimsy. Handwriting analysis was a notoriously subjective science, not the basis for a conviction, they argued. And Condon, though an impressive courtroom witness, had been extremely hesitant about picking Hauptmann out of a police lineup. To revisionists, this was best explained as the result of pressure from the authorities: the police might have threatened Condon that if he didn't identify Hauptmann decisively, they'd prosecute him as an accomplice. As for Lindbergh, he admitted he'd only heard "John" say a couple of words at the graveyard; that he identified the voice as Hauptmann's with such certainty could be another sign that the authorities had inappropriately pressured a witness, perhaps by playing on a father's fear that if he didn't come through at the trial his son's murderer would go free.

According to Scaduto and Kennedy, the case against Hauptmann was based on this kind of trumped-up evidence. The police and prosecutors—under tremendous pressure to solve the most widely talked about crime of the age—had railroaded through a conviction. Scaduto also claimed that the police had interrogated Hauptmann mercilessly, even beaten him, in a vain effort to elicit a confession.

But what about the ransom money? Even if we concede that the authorities trampled on Hauptmann's rights as a defendant, how could revisionists explain the money in his possession? Well, Hauptmann himself always maintained that a friend, Isidor Fisch, had asked him to hold on to the shoebox with the money while Fisch returned to Germany to visit his parents. Only accidentally did Hauptmann discover the box was full of money, and only because Fisch owed him money had Hauptmann spent some of it. Fisch, alas, had died shortly before the arrest.

To revisionists like Scaduto and Kennedy, this was as good an explanation as any. To most historians, however, the Fisch story was just that—a fish story, made up by Hauptmann in a desperate attempt to save himself. A 1987 book by Jim Fisher, a former FBI agent who'd gone through the newly opened New Jersey State Police archives, concluded that, although the police might have violated some of Hauptmann's rights, there was no evidence that they'd cooked up any evidence against him. Most historians have agreed with Fisher—and with the jury—that Hauptmann was guilty.

Many, however, have questioned whether he acted alone. Might Fisch have been a co-conspirator? Or was there another conspirator somewhere inside the Lindbergh house? If not, how could Hauptmann have known the layout of the house? More tellingly, how could he have known that the Lindberghs would be staying there on that particular Tuesday, contrary to their usual custom?

All this pointed to inside help, perhaps from one of the Lindbergh servants. Colonel Norman Schwarzkopf of the New Jersey State Police (the father of the Desert Storm commander) suspected an inside job from the start, but Lindbergh refused to let Schwarzkopf question the servants. He steadfastly maintained they were entirely trustworthy.

Lindbergh's motives for standing in Schwarzkopf's way are unclear. Perhaps it was because he'd been taken in by the various con men claiming to know the kidnappers. One can understand how a desperate parent would want to believe in anyone offering hope. Perhaps, too, it was reassuring to Lindbergh to think that his son was in the hands of professional gangsters—if they were in it just for the money, they would be less likely to harm the child. Or perhaps, as Joyce Milton suggested in her 1993 biography, Lindbergh couldn't bear to think that he'd been betrayed by servants he'd trusted.

Whatever his motives, the restrictions Lindbergh placed on Schwarzkopf frustrated not only police but historians. Because questions about inside help were not asked then, they cannot be answered now. And so, though we can be fairly sure Hauptmann was guilty, we must also suspect that others, equally guilty, went free.

☆ To investigate further:

Whipple, Sidney. *The Trial of Bruno Richard Hauptmann.* New York: Doubleday, 1937. Includes a complete transcript of the trial.

Lindbergh, Anne Morrow. *Hour of Gold, Hour of Lead.* New York: Harcourt Brace Jovanovich, 1973. A mother's heartbreaking diaries and letters.

Scaduto, Anthony. *Scapegoat.* New York: Putnam's, 1976. Even if it doesn't convince you Hauptmann was framed, it will convince you that his rights were violated.

Kennedy, Ludovic. *The Airman and the Carpenter.* New York: Viking, 1985. Kennedy's three previous books resulted in the posthumous pardon or release of convicted murderers; this one didn't succeed in overturning Hauptmann's conviction but it is the most persuasive argument for his innocence.

Fisher, Jim. *The Lindbergh Case.* New Brunswick, NJ: Rutgers University Press, 1987. The most recent and most thorough case against Hauptmann.

Milton, Joyce. *Loss of Eden.* New York: HarperCollins, 1993. A dual biography of Charles and Anne Morrow Lindbergh, including the best statement of the case that Hauptmann was the kidnapper—but not the only one.

Behn, Noel. *Lindbergh: The Crime.* New York: Atlantic Monthly Press, 1994. Contends the baby was killed in a fit of envy by Anne Morrow Lindbergh's sister, after which—to prevent a scandal—the family concocted the kidnapping story. Though an intriguing explanation for Lindbergh's refusal to let the police question the servants, it's ultimately unconvincing.

Chapter 36

Did Babe Ruth Call His Shot?

By 1932 Babe Ruth was already past his prime; at 38, his years of eating and drinking too much were catching up with him. No longer was he the best hitter in baseball, let alone the greatest player ever, as he once had been. Still to come, however, was the single most dramatic—and most disputed—moment of his career: his "called shot."

The setting was Chicago, the third game of the World Series between the Chicago Cubs and the New York Yankees. The Yankees had won the first two in New York and the Cub players and fans were restless and surly, tossing insults and lemons onto the field. In the fourth inning, with the score tied, Ruth came to bat; from the Chicago stands came cries that Ruth was old, he was fat, he was washed up. The Chicago pitcher, Charlie Root, threw two strikes and the jeering intensified.

Here's how Ruth recalled what happened next, writing in his autobiography:

I stepped back again and pointed my finger at those bleachers, which only caused the mob to howl that much more at me. Root threw a fast ball . . . I swung from the ground with everything I had and as I hit the ball every muscle in my system, every sense I had, told me that I had never hit a better one, that as long as I lived nothing would ever feel as good as this.

I didn't have to look. But I did. That ball just went on and on and on and hit far up in the center-field bleachers in exactly the spot I had pointed to.

A crucial home run in the World Series is itself a guarantee of at least temporary fame; this "called shot"—a home run before which the batter predicted not just the exact pitch he'd hit but the exact place it would land—was a story destined for immortality.

But did it actually happen?

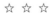

You'd think this mystery would be a cinch to solve. After all, more than 51,000 people were in Chicago's Wrigley Field when Ruth came to bat. Sportswriters from across the country witnessed the game, and the next few days' newspapers were filled with reports of the home run. In the *New York World-Telegram,* Joe Williams wrote that "with the Cubs riding him unmercifully from the bench, Ruth pointed to center field and punched a screaming liner to a spot where no ball ever had been hit before."

A couple of days later, Paul Gallico wrote in the *New York Daily News* that "Ruth pointed like a duellist to the spot where he expected to send his rapier home." A day after that, Bill Corum wrote for the Hearst newspapers that Ruth "pointed out where he was going to hit the next one, and hit it there."

Given Ruth's history as a great hitter and showman, the story seemed credible. This wasn't even the first time Ruth had called his shot. Back in 1926, another story went, he'd visited a dying boy in the hospital and promised to hit a home run for him; the next day he hit a home run and the boy miraculously recovered. The facts in that case were not quite so dramatic: in reality, the boy had been hospitalized after falling from a horse and was by no means dying, and Ruth didn't visit him in person until after he hit the home run. But he had sent the boy an autographed baseball along with a promise to hit one for him, and then he did hit the home run the next day. Not so fantastic, when you think about it: for a hitter with 714 lifetime home runs and a tremendous love of the spotlight, it was to be expected that some of the home runs were going to come after some of the promises.

Did Ruth point to the center-field bleachers before the most famous home run of his career? Depends who you ask. (Courtesy of Thomas L. Carwile.)

Still, the 1932 World Series called shot was in a class by itself. In this instance Ruth had called the specific pitch and the specific spot to which he'd hit it. The odds against success were astronomical; even Ruth, in an interview with the sportswriter John Carmichael, once admitted there was an element of luck involved.

Inevitably, there were skeptics.

Foremost among them were the two Chicago Cub players nearest the action. Gabby Hartnett, the catcher, was the only player near enough to hear what Ruth said; according to Hartnett, Ruth's words were "It only takes one to hit," referring to the one strike he had left. But Hartnett said Ruth pointed his finger at the Chicago players riding him from the dugout, *not* at the center-field bleachers.

Charlie Root, the pitcher, vehemently denied Ruth pointed to center field. Root even turned down the opportunity to play himself in a movie version of Ruth's life that included the called shot. "Ruth did not point at the fence before he swung," said Root. "If he had made a gesture like that, well, anybody who knows me knows that Ruth would have ended up on his ass."

So, it seemed, the eyewitness testimony cancelled itself out. For every witness who saw Ruth call his shot, there was one to swear he didn't. More objective evidence, in the form of a 16-millimeter home movie taken by spectator Matt Kandle Sr., was tantalizing but inconclusive: Ruth is definitely seen pointing—but whether at the pitcher, or the Cub bench, or the center-field bleachers is impossible to say.

Among serious baseball historians, however, the consensus that emerged was that Ruth did *not* point to center field. These historians pointed out that, of all the sportswriters present at the game, only one—Joe Williams, whose *World-Telegram* article is quoted above—mentioned the called shot in an article written that day. One other, John Drebinger of the *New York Times,* said Ruth "notified the crowd that the nature of his retaliation would be a wallop right out of the confines of the park," but this story didn't specify that Ruth pointed to center field. According to Ruth's premier biographer, Robert Creamer, the story that Ruth pointed to center field originated with Williams and then was picked up by Gallico and Corum and other writers who either respected Williams or who just couldn't resist such a good story.

Over time, Williams himself backed away from his initial story. It was Williams, in a February 1950 column, who quoted Gabby Hartnett's story and—though Williams still said he had "a distinct memory that [Ruth] did motion in the general direction of the stands in right center"—he admitted he now had doubts as to what that gesture meant. Fifteen years after that column, a 1965 Williams column recalled a conversation in which the sportswriter casually asked Ruth whether the called shot was the greatest thrill of his career. No, Ruth replied (according to Williams), his greatest thrill had been striking out Cobb, Crawford, and Beach with the bases loaded. Williams surmised that Ruth had deliberately ducked the question; Ruth couldn't bring himself to debunk his own legend, but he also didn't want to lie to Williams.

Not that Ruth had anything to be ashamed of. If, as Hartnett reported and as seems most likely, Ruth merely predicted he was going to hit a home run but didn't point to where it would land, this would still be a fitting capstone to his career. George Washington deserves to be a legendary figure, even if he never chopped down a cherry tree; so does Babe Ruth, even if he never pointed to center field.

☆ To investigate further:

Meany, Tom. *Babe Ruth*. New York: A. S. Barnes, 1947. An old-fashioned, anecdotal sports biography, but still fun; Meany, who once worked for Joe Williams, was an eyewitness to the called shot and a true believer.

Babe Ruth as told to Bob Considine, *The Babe Ruth Story*. New York: Dutton, 1948. This is a conventional sports autobiography for an unconventional sports figure.

Mrs. Babe Ruth with Bill Slocum, *The Babe and I*. Prentice-Hall, 1959. A loyal but surprisingly candid and often touching portrait by Ruth's second wife.

Creamer, Robert. *Babe: The Legend Comes to Life*. New York: Simon & Schuster, 1974. Not only the best biography of Ruth but one of the best biographies of any sports figure.

Wagenheim, Kal. *Babe Ruth: His Life and Legend*. Westport, CT: Praeger, 1974. A fine biography, though it had the misfortune of being published at the same time as Creamer's definitive work.

Sobol, Ken. *Babe Ruth and the American Dream*. New York: Random House, 1974. Some cynicism is called for in any biographer—and certainly in biographers of legendary figures like Ruth—but Sobol just doesn't seem to like his subject very much.

Smelser, Marshall. *The Life That Ruth Built*. New York: Quadrangle, 1975. A meandering and overly long biography that was the last and the least of the spate of mid-seventies biographies. (The rush of Ruth bios can probably be attributed to the fact that Hank Aaron was then challenging Ruth's lifetime home-run record.)

Ritter, Lawrence and Mark Rucker. *The Babe*. New York: Ticknor & Fields, 1988. An elegant pictorial biography, including stills from Matt Kandle's home movie.

Williams, Peter, editor. *The Joe Williams Baseball Reader*. Chapel Hill, NC: Algonquin, 1989. A collection of Williams's columns through which you can trace the birth, growth, and abandonment of the called-shot story.

Chapter 37

Was Amelia Earhart a Spy?

"We must be on you but cannot see you. Gas is running low."

This ominous message from Amelia Earhart reached the Coast Guard cutter *Itasca* in the early morning hours of July 3, 1937. The cutter was cruising off the coast of Howland Island, a tiny speck in the middle of the South Pacific that was to be one of the final stops on Earhart's record-breaking, round-the-world flight. But Earhart never reached Howland Island and soon lost contact with the *Itasca*. President Franklin Roosevelt ordered a massive naval search. It lasted one week, cost four million dollars (no mean sum back then), and covered approximately 250,000 miles—to no avail. Earhart, her navigator Fred Noonan, and her Lockheed Electra aircraft had disappeared.

Officials concluded Earhart had run out of gas and gone down somewhere in the ocean. In the years since then, however, the official story has been repeatedly challenged. One of the most persistent and intriguing of the alternative scenarios recasts Earhart and Noonan as spies for the United States. Their round-the-world adventure was merely cover, with their actual mission being to take pictures of Japanese installations in the Pacific. But the Japanese forced them down and (in some versions) took them prisoner or (in other versions) executed them.

The Earhart-as-spy story originated in 1943, in *Flight for Freedom*, a movie starring Rosalind Russell as a famous aviator named Tonie Carter and Fred MacMurray as the navigator she falls in love with. They plan to get lost over the Pacific to give the navy a pretext for searching the area and checking out Japanese fortifications. Just before taking off on the last leg of the journey, Carter learns that the Japanese are on to her, and that they plan to take her prisoner. So she takes off alone and ditches the plane in the ocean, sacrificing her life so the search can go on.

The movie was pure fiction. But it captured the imagination of the public and of generations of journalists, historians, and aviation buffs—some of whom set out to prove it was more than fiction.

Among the leading proponents of the Earhart-as-spy story was CBS reporter Fred Goerner. In 1960 Goerner came across a newspaper article about Josephine Blanco Akiyama, who said that while she was a girl on Saipan Island she'd witnessed a plane crash in the harbor, after which a white woman and man were taken into Japanese custody. Soon after, Akiyama recalled, she had heard shots fired.

Goerner spent six years investigating the matter, interviewing hundreds of islanders who claimed to have seen Earhart and Noonan. He concluded that the two landed somewhere in the Marshall Islands, were picked up by a Japanese fishing boat, and were then taken to Japanese Pacific military headquarters on Saipan. Some of Goerner's evidence didn't stand up on closer investigation: the remains in an unmarked grave turned out to be of non-Caucasian origin and parts of a twin-engine airplane he recovered turned out to be made in Japan. Equally problematic were that the islanders' stories about the fliers often contradicted each other: some claimed to have seen just a woman, others a man and woman; some saw the plane wrecked, others virtually undamaged; some saw the fliers summarily executed, others in jail; and the crash itself was apparently witnessed on a whole range of islands.

Still, so many islanders claimed to have seen Earhart and Noonan that their stories couldn't be dismissed out of hand. It is certainly possible, though by no means proven, that two white fliers were captured by the Japanese sometime before the war. But were these two Earhart and Noonan? And were they on a spy mission?

To answer these questions, investigators turned from the Pacific to Washington, D.C. One of these, Randall Brink, spent thirteen years analyzing documents obtained through the Freedom of Information Act. His conclusion was similar to Goerner's: Earhart was a spy. In Brink's account, Earhart's trip started as a publicity stunt but evolved into a spy mission. As a personal friend of the Roosevelts, Earhart did not hesitate to approach the president for help in arranging for refueling stops during her trip. And the president couldn't risk the temptation to use the trip for military intelligence.

To begin with, Brink pointed out, there wasn't even an airstrip on Howland Island until Roosevelt ordered the Coast Guard to build one for Earhart. This was a major construction job—at taxpayers' expense—and it would be hard to justify it as nothing more than a favor for a friend.

Brink interviewed a Lockheed technician who told him he'd cut holes in the plane so that special cameras could be installed to take pictures of Japanese installations. Brink also argued that Earhart's last-minute change in flight direction, from westward to eastward, could only be explained if hers was a spying mission. According to the original itinerary, Earhart would have flown westward over the Pacific and landed in Lae, New Guinea. There she would have been surrounded by civilians, in foreign territory, and any number of things could have gone wrong, including the discovery of the bulky camera. But by going from west to east, she would land on the isolated, U.S.-controlled Howland Island immediately after photographing Japanese installations. On Howland the film could easily be handed over to U.S. agents before she flew on to meet the crowds at Hawaii, her next stop. Earhart's explanation that she was changing the flight direction because of a seasonal change in wind patterns made no sense, Brink said; by flying from west to east she was *bucking* the prevailing wind.

In addition, Brink uncovered evidence in the files of naval intelligence that, prior to her flight, the navy had secretly installed powerful engines in Earhart's plane that would enable it to take a different, longer flight path than had been announced. This path, Brink concluded, would take her over the Japanese-controlled Marshall and Caroline Islands.

Finally, Brink found that Earhart was heard by radio operators for days after she supposedly disappeared and died. Some of these reports may have been unreliable, but as with the testimony of the islanders gathered by Goerner, there were too many to dismiss them

Those who thought Amelia Earhart was a spy for the United States pointed to her close friendship with Franklin and Eleanor Roosevelt. Here she is on a night flight over Washington with the first lady. Eleanor Roosevelt always wanted to take flying lessons, but never did. (Courtesy of the National Air and Space Museum.)

out of hand. Brink believed that Roosevelt was well aware of all the evidence that Earhart had survived, and that he ordered it covered up so that her spying activities, too, would be buried.

Brink's detractors argued that his evidence was circumstantial and that he'd overstated his case. For example, Brink cited a document in which FDR's treasury secretary, Henry Morgenthau Jr., stated that if the full story of Earhart's last flight were made public, her reputation would be ruined. Brink read that as evidence that the administration wanted to cover up Earhart's spying; Tom Crouch of the National Air and Space Museum, however, pointed out that it could just as easily be read to mean that Earhart made some errors in judgment that could have undermined her reputation as a great flier.

Some of Brink's speculation was, indeed, a bit off the wall. He gave serious consideration, for example, to a longstanding but completely unsubstantiated theory that after being captured by the Japanese, Earhart had become "Tokyo Rose," the infamous wartime disc jockey who beguiled American troops in the Pacific. At one point, Earhart's husband had made a special trip to the front lines to listen to a Tokyo Rose broadcast and had said he would stake his life that it was *not* his wife's voice.

And though Franklin Roosevelt died without ever publicly discussing Earhart's flight, Eleanor Roosevelt repeatedly denied any spy plot, stating: "Franklin and I loved Amelia too much to send her to her death." So, in the end, the spy theorists had lots of evidence, but all of it circumstantial, and lots of speculation, some of it wild.

While Brink was searching through files in Washington, other researchers continued to scour the Pacific for evidence of Earhart's landing. The best funded of them was Richard Gillespie, executive director of The International Group for Historic Aircraft Recovery (TIGHAR). In 1989 and 1991, with $750,000 of TIGHAR money, Gillespie led expeditions to the uninhabited island known as Nikumaroro. It was there that, during the initial search for Earhart, a navy pilot had reported "signs of recent habitation." But after repeated circling and zooming failed to elicit any answering wave, the pilot concluded no one was there.

Gillespie thought the pilot might have missed something, and what he found there convinced him that he was right. He returned with a number of objects, among them part of a woman's size nine shoe, consistent with the style Earhart wore; a mid-thirties cigarette lighter, which might have belonged to Noonan (who was a smoker); and an aluminum navigator's bookcase with screwholes that suggested it might have been installed on an airplane. Gillespie believed he'd solved the Earhart mystery: Earhart and Noonan had crashed on Nikumaroro.

This did not prove, of course, that Earhart died on Nikumaroro; she might still have been captured by the Japanese and she might still have been a spy. But, Gillespie claimed, here at last was some hard evidence to replace the circumstantial evidence and wild speculations of the spy theorists.

But how hard was Gillespie's evidence?

His detractors were quick to point out that even though Niku-maroro may be uninhabited now, it had been at times colonized by islanders and military personnel. Shoes might have traveled there by some means other than Earhart's feet, and the same could be said for all the flotsam and jetsam Gillespie collected. Besides, the navy pilot who'd flown over the island was a trained professional on the lookout for any signs of Earhart, Noonan, or their plane—and he'd concluded they weren't there.

So it seems, barring some yet to be discovered evidence, Amelia Earhart is destined to remain a missing person. We simply cannot say for sure where she landed, or whether she was a spy.

☆ ☆ ☆

But what if we put aside the relics of Earhart's trip and look instead at Earhart herself? What clues might be found in her past behavior? Was she the type of person likely to be a spy?

Certainly no one could doubt she had sufficient courage to be a spy. This was, after all, the first woman to fly across the Atlantic as a passenger (in 1928), the first woman to fly solo across the Atlantic (in 1932), the woman who broke her own transcontinental speed record (in 1933), the first person to fly solo from Honolulu to the mainland (in 1935). And her relationship with the Roosevelts was sufficiently close that they might very well have felt comfortable discussing top secret matters with her.

But Earhart was an ardent pacifist, likely to have resisted anything to do with the military. Besides, there were plenty of other motivations for the trip besides spying. Money, for one: Earhart's husband, the publisher George Putnam, was a master publicist with visions of lucrative endorsement contracts for his wife. Indeed, the trip generated more attention than he could have dreamed; alas, without Earhart, there was no way for Putnam to cash in.

Nor need we be so cynical to explain why Earhart took off. This was a woman who loved flying, and a flight around the world was the ultimate aerial adventure. In her journal of the flight (which she cabled to Putnam from various stops along the way so that it would be ready for publication right after the trip was over), Earhart recounted her reasons for the trip: "Here was shining adventure, beckoning with new experiences. . . . Then, too, there was my belief that now and then women should do for themselves what men have already done—and occasionally what men have not done . . . perhaps encouraging other women toward greater independence of thought and action." So feminism, too, propelled Earhart.

Her disappearance, like her motivations for the trip, can be explained without resorting to spy stories. Strictly as an aviation challenge, the trip from New Guinea to Howland Island was plenty dangerous. Howland was tiny and remote and barely above sea level; under the best of circumstances it would be difficult to find. Earhart and Noonan planned to reach it after approximately 18 hours in the air—18 hours that came after having already flown much of the way around the world, in a noisy, vibrating plane with barely room to stretch. To say that Earhart and Noonan were unlikely to be at their most alert under these conditions is no insult to either. And there is also a possibility that Noonan was drunk or hungover; though there's absolutely no evidence that this was the case, he was an alcoholic who'd been fired by by Pan American, and suspicions linger.

None of this proves that Earhart wasn't a spy. Nor does it preclude the possibility that, even if Earhart had nothing to do with it, the navy saw her disappearance as an opportunity to survey the Japanese military buildup in the region. But it's worth noting that most of Earhart's biographers have concluded she wasn't a spy. And though other investigators might have looked more carefully at the particulars of Earhart's disappearance, it was her biographers who looked most carefully at the woman herself.

☆ To investigate further:

Earhart, Amelia. *Last Flight*. New York: Harcourt, Brace, 1937. Earhart's journal, which was originally to be called "World Flight." Though it was much embellished by Putnam and other editors, and though it obviously ended before the end, it's still the closest we come to Earhart's own account of the trip.

Goerner, Fred. *The Search for Amelia Earhart*. New York: Doubleday, 1966. The story of Goerner's six-year investigation and the reasons he concluded Earhart was a spy.

Rich, Doris. *Amelia Earhart*. Washington, DC: Smithsonian, 1989. A thorough, workmanlike biography.

Lovell, Mary. *The Sound of Wings: The Life of Amelia Earhart.* New York: St. Martin's, 1989. In spite of its title, this is actually a dual biography of Earhart and Putnam.

Gillespie, Richard. "The Mystery of Amelia Earhart." *Life,* April 1992. Gillespie's own account of his Nikumaroro expeditions.

Wilkinson, Stephan. "Amelia Earhart: Is the Search Over?" *Air & Space,* September 1992. A more objective analysis of Gillespie's expedition.

Ware, Susan. *Still Missing.* New York: Norton, 1993. A feminist biography: the title refers not just to the unsolved mystery surrounding Earhart's disappearance but to her still unfulfilled goal of equality for women.

Brink, Randall. *Lost Star.* New York: Norton, 1994. Though some of Brink's speculation about what might have happened after Earhart was captured is farfetched, this presents the most thorough case that she was a spy.

Chapter 38

Who Was to Blame for Pearl Harbor?

When Franklin Delano Roosevelt declared December 7, 1941, "a date that will live in infamy," he left no question about who the infamous party was—the perpetrators of the "unprovoked and dastardly attack" on Pearl Harbor, the Japanese empire.

For many, though, Roosevelt's explanation didn't wash. The world was already at war, all diplomatic efforts to resolve tensions with Japan had failed, the entire Pacific Ocean was ready to boil over. How, with all of this going on, could our army and navy be caught sleeping?

To some revisionists, a more sinister explanation than Roosevelt's seemed called for. They've argued that the infamy belonged to Roosevelt himself. They've claimed that Roosevelt knew in advance of the attack on Pearl Harbor and deliberately withheld information about it from the U.S. commanders in Hawaii. His motive: to get the United States into the war. Eager to fight the Japanese and Germans, frustrated by isolationists in Congress and the American public, this Roosevelt was a warmonger who would stop at nothing, not even betraying his own forces, to get his way.

☆ ☆ ☆

Among the earliest to point fingers at Roosevelt were his commanders at Pearl Harbor: Admiral Husband Kimmel, the commander in chief

If FDR didn't know in advance about Pearl Harbor, he was nonetheless actively involved in the war effort. Here he is consulting with Churchill aboard HMS Prince of Wales—*four months before the attack. (Courtesy of the FDR Library.)*

of the U.S. Pacific Fleet, and Lieutenant General Walter Short, commanding general, Hawaii Department of the Army. Both, admittedly, had a strong incentive to blame Roosevelt—or, for that matter, anyone but themselves. The humiliation of the defeat at Pearl Harbor had been compounded by a presidential committee that found both Kimmel and Short guilty of "dereliction of duty."

Neither officer took this verdict lying down. Most frustrating of all was that the committee had not considered what they—and all future revisionists—considered the key evidence against Roosevelt. Namely, Magic. Magic was the code name used to refer to the brilliant work of Lieutenant Colonel William Friedman, who in August 1940 cracked the most secret of Japanese codes. From 1940 on, as a result of Friedman's breakthrough, U.S. intelligence officers were reading all of Japan's diplomatic messages.

One of these messages, which U.S. intelligence intercepted on September 24, 1941, was a "strictly secret" message from the Japanese foreign ministry to its Honolulu consulate. This came to be known as the "bomb plot" message. It read:

> With regard to warships and aircraft carriers, we would like to have you report on those at anchor . . . tied up at wharves, buoys, and in docks.

That the consulate was spying on American ships at Pearl Harbor was no surprise to anyone; the Japanese had been following U.S. fleet movements for quite a while. Now, however, they were suddenly interested in the locations of the ships in the harbor.

Why the sudden change in the Japanese spies' focus? To many who analyzed it later, including Kimmel and Short, the answer was obvious: the Japanese wanted to know the locations of ships at the harbor because they were planning to attack them there.

Yet no one in the navy or army in Pearl Harbor received a copy of the intercepted message.

Kimmel and Short felt somewhat vindicated when the navy and the army conducted their own investigations and concluded that their commanders had not been derelict. But that satisfied few. For one thing, a lot of people suspected the military was covering up the truth to protect its own people and image. And even for those who did trust the military, the question remained: if Kimmel and Short weren't to blame, who was?

This was a question too pressing to be left to historians. In 1945 a joint congressional committee opened its own investigation.

☆ ☆ ☆

Testifying about the bomb plot message, Short told the committee:

> While the War Department G-2 may not have felt bound to let me know about the routine operations of the Japanese in keeping track of our naval ships, they should certainly have let me know that the Japanese were getting reports of the exact location of the ships in Pearl Harbor . . . because such details would be useful only for sabotage, or for air or submarine attack on Hawaii. . . . This message, analyzed critically, is really a bombing plan for Pearl Harbor.

Kimmel agreed that "knowledge of these intercepted Japanese dispatches would have radically changed the estimate of the situation made by me and my staff."

The testimony mesmerized the nation. How could U.S. intelligence have failed to pass on such a critically important message to Kimmel or Short?

In the 39 volumes of testimony and documents gathered by the congressional committee, there is no definite answer. Various officers confirmed that the bomb plot message was definitely intercepted yet never reached Kimmel or Short. It *may* have reached the Washington desk of Admiral Harold Stark, chief of naval operations. Stark told the committee he didn't remember seeing the message, but he admitted that even if he had seen it he would have considered it "just another example of their [Japan's] great attention to detail." Also, he assumed (incorrectly) that Kimmel was receiving the same messages directly from Naval Communications.

The congressional committee's verdict was split.

The majority report, signed by six Democrats and two Republicans, blamed the military, both in Washington and in Hawaii. It blamed army and navy intelligence in Washington for failing to pass on this and other intercepted Japanese messages to Kimmel and Short; it blamed Kimmel and Short for failing to appreciate the considerable intelligence and other information that was available to them.

The minority report, signed by two Republicans, blamed not only the military but the administration, including Roosevelt, for failing to put the Pearl Harbor commanders on a full alert for defensive actions, given the increasing tension with Japan. Even the Republicans, however, stopped short of accusing Roosevelt of having known about the attack in advance.

Given the political pressures to which Congress was subjected, a split verdict was hardly surprising. But as time passed, most Americans came to accept the opinion of the majority report. World War II, it was generally agreed, was "the good war." So, just as Republicans dropped their prewar isolationism, they put aside their suspicions about the war's origins. As for Kimmel and Short, they continued to proclaim their innocence, but even in the military fewer and fewer people cared.

And, in retrospect, the preponderance of evidence did support the majority opinion of the committee. No one conspired to keep

Kimmel and Short in the dark. Instead, a great many people in Washington and Hawaii—including Roosevelt but also including most other top American officials—grossly underestimated the Japanese. Everyone expected that some skirmish would eventually draw the United States into war; what no one foresaw was that the Japanese would strike so suddenly and decisively. Far from being Roosevelt's pawns, the Japanese military leaders were bold tacticians. They realized war was inevitable and they determined—probably correctly—that a preemptive strike was their best chance to win it.

It was the general underestimation of the Japanese—abetted by bad communication, bad coordination, and bad luck—that was to blame for Pearl Harbor.

Yet the case against Roosevelt has popped up again and again, and it's made for some strange bedfellows. Revisionists have included both anti-communists, who felt the United States should have been fighting the Soviet Union instead of Germany and Japan, and leftist historians of the 60s, who saw sinister parallels between how Roosevelt ensnared the country into World War II and how Johnson and Nixon trapped us into Vietnam.

And in one sense, the case against Roosevelt has stood the test of time. Most historians now agree that, in his eagerness to get the United States into the war, Roosevelt was guilty both of provoking the Japanese and of overstepping his constitutional powers. In early 1941, well before Pearl Harbor and in violation of its own neutrality acts, the United States was providing covert aid to China in its war against Japan. In addition, Roosevelt's "lend-lease" plan, by which he was lending arms to the British and allowing them to pay later, was pure fiction: no one in the administration expected Britain to return the arms or to pay for them. One Republican senator, cutting through the pretense, commented: "Lending arms is like lending chewing gum. You don't want it back."

Roosevelt had no choice. Given the still-prevailing isolationism of the Congress and the public, his deceptions and manipulations were the only means he had to act against Japan and Germany. Still, there's no question that when Roosevelt described the attack on Pearl Harbor as "unprovoked," he was not telling the whole truth.

But did he know about the attack in advance? No.

After all—and this is perhaps the strongest defense of Roosevelt that can be made—Roosevelt wanted America in the war so that we could *win* the war. And it's a hell of a lot easier to win a war if your Pacific fleet is floating on, and not under, the waters of Pearl Harbor.

☆ To investigate further:

Hearings Before the Joint Committee on the Investigation of the Pearl Harbor Attack, Congress of the United States. Seventy-ninth Congress, Government Printing Office, 1946. Still the *primary* primary source.

Beard, Charles A. *President Roosevelt and the Coming of the War, 1941.* New Haven, CT: Yale University Press, 1948. Accuses Roosevelt of manipulating the American public and the Japanese, but not of actually knowing in advance about the attack.

Morison, Samuel E. *By Land and By Sea.* New York: Knopf, 1953. Includes a clear refutation of Beard's arguments.

Barnes, Harry E. *Perpetual War for Perpetual Peace.* Caldwell, ID: The Caxton Printers, 1953. Goes the whole way: not only does it claim Roosevelt wanted the attack, but that he knew about it in advance and then covered that up.

Kimmel, Husband E. *Admiral Kimmel's Story.* Washington, DC: Regnery, 1955. Kimmel's own defense.

Wohlstetter, Roberta. *Pearl Harbor: Warning and Decision.* Stanford, CT: Stanford University Press, 1962. How and why American intelligence organizations failed to understand the Japanese messages they intercepted.

Prange, Gordon W. *At Dawn We Slept.* New York: McGraw-Hill, 1981. The most thorough statement of the orthodox position and of the Japanese side of the story. This chapter is much indebted to the book.

———. *Pearl Harbor: The Verdict of History.* New York: McGraw-Hill, 1986. Refutes Toland's arguments but is otherwise a largely unnecessary reorganization of the arguments made quite well in *At Dawn We Slept.*

———*December 7, 1941: The Day the Japanese Attacked Pearl Harbor.* New York: McGraw-Hill, 1988. The third, and least necessary, of Prange's Pearl Harbor trilogy.

Toland, John. *Infamy.* New York: Doubleday, 1982. Asks some provocative questions but ultimately not a convincing revisionist statement.

Thompson, Robert S. *A Time for War.* New York: Prentice Hall Press, 1991. A compelling account of Roosevelt's efforts to get the United States into the war.

Rusbridge, James and Eric Nere, *Betrayal at Pearl Harbor.* New York: Summit, 1991. Argues that Churchill knew of the attack in advance and, in order to lure the United States into the war, withheld the information from Roosevelt.

Clausen, Henry C. *Pearl Harbor: Final Judgment.* New York: Crown, 1992. Recapitulating his 1945 investigation for the army, Clausen argues against any conspiracy. Instead, he blames uncoordinated intelligence and serious errors on the part of Kimmel, Short, and others.

Costello, John. *Days of Infamy.* New York: Pocket, 1994. Accuses FDR of gross strategic miscalculations but *not* of knowing about the attack in advance.

Chapter 39

Why Didn't the Allies Bomb Auschwitz?

For the first fifteen or so years after World War II, the Holocaust was rarely a subject of historical debate. There seemed little to debate. That the Nazis were guilty of mass murder was beyond dispute; so was the fact that the Allies had saved what was left of European Jewry. Starting in the 1960s, a string of books challenged this straightforward interpretation. The Allies were now denounced for allowing the Holocaust to happen. The revisionists' perspective was spelled out in the titles of their books: Arthur Morse's 1968 *While Six Million Died*, Saul Friedman's 1973 *No Haven for the Oppressed*, Herbert Druks's 1977 *The Failure to Rescue*, Martin Gilbert's 1981 *Auschwitz and the Allies*, Monty Penkower's 1983 *The Jews Were Expendable*. Most influential and most damning of all was David Wyman's 1984 *The Abandonment of the Jews*.

For these scholars, American apathy was the story. "America, the land of refuge, offered little succor," Wyman wrote. "American Christians forgot about the Good Samaritan. Even American Jews lacked the unquenchable sense of urgency the crisis demanded. The Nazis were the murderers, but we were the all too passive accomplices."

The consequences of American indifference, Wyman believed, were most devastatingly evident in the decision not to bomb the gas chambers at Auschwitz. The opportunity to do so was there, starting in May 1943, when the American Fifteenth Air Force began bombing German industrial complexes near Auschwitz. Nor could the administration claim they didn't know what was going on at Auschwitz; in April, two escapees had revealed the full extent of the killings there, along with detailed descriptions of the camp's layout. Some Jewish leaders, among others, pleaded that the Allies bomb the camp, or at least the rail lines bringing Jews there.

Among those persuaded was Winston Churchill. In July, he wrote Foreign Minister Anthony Eden, "There is no doubt that this is probably the greatest and most horrible single crime ever committed in the whole history of the world." He ordered Eden to study the feasibility of bombing Auschwitz, telling him to "get anything out of the Air Force you can and invoke me if necessary." But the Royal Air Force determined it was too risky, and that only the Americans might be in a position to do it.

In America, the official response came from Assistant Secretary of War John McCloy. "Such an operation could be executed only by the diversion of considerable air support essential to the success of our forces now engaged in decisive operations elsewhere and would in any case be of such doubtful efficacy that it would not warrant the use of our resources," McCloy wrote in a letter to the World Jewish Congress. "The War Department fully appreciates the humanitarian motives which prompted the suggested operation, but for the reasons stated above, it has not been felt that it can or should be undertaken, at least at this time."

"To the American military," Wyman concluded, "Europe's Jews represented an extraneous problem and an unwanted burden."

By 1993, Wyman's perspective was so common that no one was startled when it was echoed by Bill Clinton. "For those here today representing the nations of the West, we must live forever with this knowledge—even as our fragmentary awareness of crimes grew into indisputable facts, far too little was done," the president said at the dedication of the United States Holocaust Museum in Washington. "Before the war even started, doors to liberty were shut, and even after the United States and the Allies attacked Germany, rail lines to the camps within miles of militarily significant targets were left undisturbed."

Holocaust historiography, it seemed, had come full circle. The Americans, in particular the Roosevelt administration, had been transformed from the Jews' savior to a not-so-innocent bystander, even a Nazi accomplice. Not all historians, of course, agreed with Wyman. And in the years since the publication of The Abandonment of the Jews, both its detractors and defenders have scoured military and political archives to figure out why Auschwitz wasn't bombed.

☆ ☆ ☆

Wyman's first critics were military historians and aviators. Wyman may have been an expert on refugee policy and perhaps even political history, they argued, but he didn't understand the intricacies of air warfare.

True, conceded James H. Kitchens of the Air Force Historical Research Agency, American planes might have been able to reach Auschwitz in 1944, but they had neither the intelligence nor the accuracy to hit the gas chambers. "On arriving in the target area," Kitchens wrote, "attackers would have faced a dispersed, dauntingly complex objective . . . that would have had to be identified and attacked in concert with little loiter time and no release error."

"We should have no illusions that any bombing attempt would have significantly damaged the target," agreed Williamson Murray, formerly a professor at the U.S. Military Academy. In fact, there is every prospect that such bombing, given the inaccuracies of 'precision bombing,' would have killed a significant number of the Jewish inmates."

Murray noted the irony of what he called "Monday morning quarterbacking." The raid could easily have failed and killed many Jews. Then, he argued, "we would now be debating the heartless aerial attack by the Allies on Auschwitz that had only added to the terrible burden of suffering."

Richard Levy, a retired nuclear engineer, noted that many American Jewish leaders feared bombing would do more harm than good, and therefore opposed the idea. Levy also argued that, even if Allied bombers knocked out the gas chambers, that wouldn't stop the killing. The Germans could revert to shooting Jews, or they could march them to death (as they did in November 1944, when Allied armies approached Auschwitz and the Nazis destroyed the gas chambers themselves).

For all these arguments, Wyman and his followers, many with military expertise, had answers. The air force had taken photos of Auschwitz, albeit accidentally, during missions to bomb nearby oil plants; these photos provided all the intelligence pilots needed. The British had undertaken an equally difficult mission in February 1944, when they bombed a prison in Amiens to set free members of the French resistance being held there. In September, the Americans had airlifted supplies to beleaguered Polish resistance fighters in Warsaw. Some of them fell into German hands, but the operation had at least boosted Polish morale. And, yes, knocking out the gas chambers wouldn't stop all the killing, but it might at least slow it down.

The Roosevelt administration said Auschwitz couldn't be bombed. Yet American planes photographed the camp en route to nearby German oil plants. This was taken on April 4, 1944. (National Archives.)

The technical arguments about the capabilities of various planes raged back and forth. The debate sometimes seems, as historian Henry Feingold put it, "a dialogue of the deaf," and one with little hope of reaching a consensus. Some historians were also frustrated by the very idea of this kind of counterfactual analysis, better known as "what if" history. Since the Allies had decided not to bomb Auschwitz, there was no way to know for sure what would have happened if they had.

For many historians, therefore, answers would not come from military analysis but from probing the motives of the men who made the decision not to bomb Auschwitz. They were especially eager to know what Franklin Roosevelt thought about the idea.

☆ ☆ ☆

Most historians assumed Roosevelt never thought about the idea at all, because no one ever asked him. "It is likely," wrote Levy, "that widely expressed doubts about the efficacy of the proposed operation discouraged many individuals from pressing the issue at lower levels, or raising it with Roosevelt directly."

In this case, the buck seemed to stop not with Roosevelt but with John McCloy. McCloy himself insisted, in a 1983 interview, that he "never talked" with Roosevelt about bombing Auschwitz. Wrote Mc-Cloy's biographer, Kai Bird: "Repeated requests of various Jewish leaders and organizations were not lost in a bureaucratic maze; the request, together with the terrifying evidence, found their way to the right man, probably the only official in the War Department who possessed sufficient power and personal competency to persuade the government to make the rescue of European Jewry a military priority."

Bird did not defend his subject's decision. He believed McCloy was governed not by outright anti-Semitism, but by a fear that bombing Auschwitz might awaken nativist and isolationist sentiments. He didn't want to do anything, Bird believed, "that could suggest to the troops or the American public that the war was being fought in behalf of the Jews." So McCloy decided to do nothing.

The focus on McCloy succeeded in protecting Roosevelt, at least until 2002. Then historian Michael Beschloss offered surprising new evidence that the president himself made the final decision. Beschloss uncovered the tape of a private 1986 interview in which McCloy said Roosevelt "made it very clear" to him that he thought bombing Auschwitz "wouldn't have done any good," and that the president wouldn't "have anything to do with the idea."

According to Beschloss, McCloy said: "The president had the idea that [bombing] would be more provocative and ineffective. And he took a very strong stand."

That Roosevelt himself made the decision would have been supremely disillusioning for many of his Jewish supporters. So universal was Jewish support for the president that one Republican congressman said Jews had three *velten* (worlds): *"die velt"* (this world), *"yene velt"* (the next world), and "Roosevelt." In 1985, in response to Wyman's criticism of Roosevelt, historian Lucy Dawidowicz recalled that the president was "surrounded by Jewish friends and advisers with whom he talked about the terrible plight of the Jews." And Dawidowicz, whose 1975 book, *The War Against the Jews,* clearly would not have defended a president who turned his back on its victims.

Admittedly, Roosevelt had failed to change America's immigration quotas prior to the war, thus dooming many Jewish (and non-Jewish) refugees from the Nazis. But this was more Congress's doing than the president's. Besides, this was years before Auschwitz, before anyone in America could have known the full extent of Hitler's genocidal plans.

And yet, if McCloy's 1986 interview was to be believed, it was Roosevelt who, in 1944 and with plenty of evidence of what was going on there, decided not to bomb Auschwitz. Wyman had written that what governed all of Roosevelt's decisions pertaining to the Jews was "political expediency." He had the Jewish vote anyway, so why risk an anti-Jewish backlash? "An active rescue policy offered little political advantage," Wyman explained. "A pro-Jewish stance, however, could lose votes."

Perhaps. Roosevelt was, undeniably, a brilliant politician.

But it was surely possible that Roosevelt also genuinely believed, as he said to McCloy, that the bombing "wouldn't have done any good." The ongoing debate between Wyman's followers and detractors makes clear that military experts, in good faith, could disagree about the merits of bombing Auschwitz. If that's true today, it was all the more so in 1944, when Roosevelt and his generals were fully absorbed by the war effort. Though they undeniably had evidence of the Holocaust, they may not have fully comprehended it, at least as historians do today. Their attention was focused on the Normandy invasion, not a Polish concentration camp. Their objective was to defeat the Nazis, not save the Jews. Anything that distracted them from that objective, including bombing Auschwitz, was likely to get short shrift. To the extent that Allied generals thought about the Jews at all, they probably concluded that the best way to save them was to win the war as quickly as possible.

Many historians, including the Pulitzer Prize–winning Arthur Schlesinger Jr., found that logic compelling. "The best use of Allied bombing—and the best way to save the people in the death camps—was to bring the war to its quickest end," wrote Schlesinger. "FDR, more than any other person, deserves the credit for mobilizing the forces that destroyed Nazi barbarism."

In the end, there were some survivors, and they survived because the Nazis were defeated. And there probably wasn't too much more that could have been done, at least in 1944, by which time millions had already died. But, as World War II historian Gerhard Weinberg put it, "the shadow of doubt that enough was not done will always remain."

For Weinberg, bombing Auschwitz was worth trying, even though it was unlikely to succeed. "Such an action by the Western Allies would have made something of an important assertion of policy, would have encouraged desperate victims in their last days and hours, might have inspired a few additional persons to provide aid and comfort to the persecuted, and might even have enabled a tiny number to escape the fate planned for them by the Germans," he wrote.

British historian Martin Gilbert reached a similar conclusion. Auschwitz would have been a very difficult target, he conceded. But then he asked: "Difficult to hit for what end? For success against cre- matoria and railway lines? Or for morale and perhaps even morality? The latter two were often at stake during World War II as well."

What the United States could or should have done in 1944 is more than an academic question. It has resurfaced every time Americans have con- sidered military intervention to stop genocide, from Bosnia to Rwanda. Yet it's clear that the nation most entwined in the debate is Israel. The string of books condemning America's abandonment of the Jews started in the late '60s and continued through the mid-'80s, a period that encompassed both the Six-Day War and the Yom Kippur War and dur- ing which many Jews feared America might abandon Israel.

For many Jews, the message of these books was, as historian Peter Novick put it, that America had "a compelling obligation to expiate past sins through unswerving support of Israel." Wyman's villains were not just Roosevelt and his administration, but also secular Jewish leaders who, unwilling to criticize the president, didn't put enough pressure on him to act. Wyman's heroes were the religiously orthodox and politi- cally conservative Jews who pushed the hardest for bombing Auschwitz. For religiously orthodox and politically conservative Jews, here was proof that you couldn't count on liberals and Democrats like Roosevelt; here, too, was a clear justification for Israel's increasing militarism.

Ironically, Wyman's arguments appealed to many leftist Jews as well. For them, it demonstrated the dangers of trusting those in power, even liberals like Roosevelt. There was, as Novick put it, "something for everybody in the Holocaust."

None of this is to denigrate the scholarship of Wyman or others who wrote about the abandonment of the Jews. It was not Wyman, but many of his readers, who drew the parallels between Auschwitz and Is- rael. Nor is there anything wrong with drawing lessons from history, es- pecially if doing so prevents genocide. What's dangerous is using history to make a political point, without honestly and openly trying to under- stand that history. This is especially true of the Holocaust, which is too often and too carelessly invoked for contemporary political purposes.

"Whether it is done by the right or the left," wrote Peter Neufeld, a historian at the Smithsonian Institution, this "is not only ahistorical, but it will ultimately diminish the memory of those whose lives might have been saved by the bombing of Auschwitz."

☆ To investigate further:

Morse, Arthur. *While Six Million Died.* New York: Random House, 1968. An angry indictment of American apathy and bureaucratic inertia.

Feingold, Henry. *The Politics of Rescue.* New Brunswick, New Jersey: Rutgers University Press, 1970. Feingold's approach is more scholarly and dispassionate than Morse's, but his conclusions are similar.

Dawidowicz, Lucy. *The War Against the Jews.* New York: Holt, Rinehart and Winston, 1975. A superb synthesis of Holocaust history.

Gilbert, Martin. *Auschwitz and the Allies.* New York: Holt, Rinehart and Winston, 1981. What Wyman does for the American response to the Holocaust, Gilbert does for the British.

Wyman, David. *The Abandonment of the Jews.* New York: Pantheon, 1984. Even those who disagreed with Wyman's conclusions admired his scholarship and style.

Wyman, David, editor. *America and the Holocaust.* New York: Garland, 1990. Volume 12 of this thirteen-volume documentary history covers the decision not to bomb Auschwitz, including the escapees' report.

Bird, Kai. *The Chairman.* New York: Simon & Schuster, 1992. A biography of McCloy, the man whose name was synonymous with "the establishment."

Dawidowicz, Lucy. *What Is the Use of Jewish History?* New York: Schocken, 1992. Includes her 1985 essay, "Could America Have Rescued Europe's Jews?" in which she criticizes America's refugee policy but answers the question with a resounding no.

Newton, Verne, editor. *FDR and the Holocaust.* New York: St. Martin's, 1996. A useful collection of essays, though the Neufeld-Berenbaum collection is more comprehensive and up to date.

Rubinstein, William D. *The Myth of Rescue.* London: Routledge, 1997. Rubinstein's opposition to Wyman leads him to the other extreme. "No Jew," he writes, "who perished during the Nazi Holocaust could have been saved by any action which the Allies could have taken."

Novick, Peter. *The Holocaust in American Life.* Boston: Houghton Mifflin, 1999. A provocative analysis of the "uses" of the Holocaust.

Neufeld, Michael, and Michael Berenbaum, editors. New York: St. Martin's, 2000. *The Bombing of Auschwitz.* A balanced collection of essays by leading participants in the debate, including Richard Breitman, Stuart Erdheim, Henry Feingold, Martin Gilbert, James Kitchens, Walter Laqueur, Richard Levy, Williamson Murray, Deborah Lipstadt, and Gerhard Weinberg.

Beschloss, Michael. *The Conquerors.* New York: Simon & Schuster, 2002. How Roosevelt and Truman planned the postwar world.

Chapter 40

Why Did Truman Drop the Bomb?

In his 1955 memoirs, Harry Truman devoted only a few pages to his decision to drop an atom bomb on the Japanese city of Hiroshima.

"I regarded the bomb as a military weapon and never had any doubt that it should be used," wrote Truman. "The top military advisers to the President recommended its use, and when I talked to Churchill he unhesitatingly told me that he favored the use of the atom bomb if it might aid to end the war."

To end the war: this was Truman's clear and succinct rationale for using the bomb. Its devastating strength would convince the Japanese that an unconditional surrender was their only option, thus saving the lives of the American soldiers who would otherwise have to force that surrender on Japan's home ground. General Marshall had told him that an invasion might cost half a million American lives, Truman added.

Truman's secretary of war, Henry Stimson, wrote a somewhat lengthier defense of the decision to drop the bomb. Published in the February 1947 issue of *Harper's* magazine, Stimson's article recounted his activities as the chief adviser on atomic policy to both Franklin Roosevelt and Truman. In April 1945, as scientists prepared the bomb's final testing, Truman appointed Stimson head of a committee to consider the scientific, political, and military aspects of the bomb. In June,

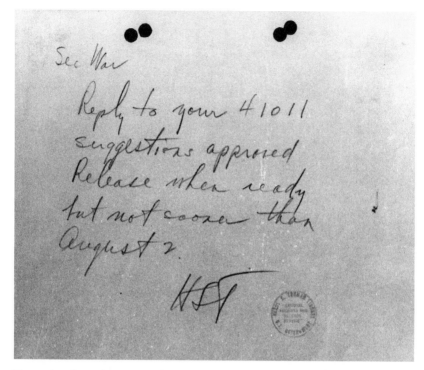

Truman's order, written in pencil to Secretary of War Stimson, to drop the bomb. (Courtesy of Harry S. Truman Library.)

the committee recommended using the bomb as soon as possible. The committee reported that scientists could envision no technical demonstration, such as dropping a bomb over a deserted island, that would convince the Japanese of its power.

On July 26, after meeting with Churchill and Stalin at Potsdam, a suburb of Berlin, Truman issued an ultimatum to the Japanese. This came to be known as the Potsdam Proclamation. Though it didn't mention the atom bomb specifically, the Proclamation warned Japan that it must surrender or face "prompt and utter destruction." Two days later, the Japanese premier responded that the ultimatum was "unworthy of public notice." That left Truman with no choice but to show he'd meant what he'd said. "For such a purpose," Stimson wrote, "the atomic bomb was an eminently suitable weapon."

From that point on, events unfolded exactly according to plan: on August 6 the first atom bomb fell on Hiroshima; on August 9 the second fell on Nagasaki; on August 14 the Japanese surrendered. Truman's and Stimson's accounts of the decision-making process seemed unimpeachable; not only had they explained clearly why they'd used the bomb, but history had proved their analysis to be correct.

Yet in the fifty-plus years since Hiroshima, revisionist historians have argued that Truman's decision to use the bomb was not nearly so straightforward as his memoirs or Stimson's article indicated. Revisionists have claimed that nowhere near 500,000 Americans would have died in an invasion; that Japan was at the brink of surrender even before the bomb was dropped; that Truman knew all of this and used the bomb anyway. His motive, according to some revisionists, was not to demonstrate American power to its Japanese enemies, but to its Russian allies. By these accounts the bomb was not the final blast of World War II, but the first blast of the Cold War.

The first to question the official explanation were hardly leftists or pacifists. Among them was Admiral William Leahy, who presided over the U.S. Joint Chiefs of Staff and was chief of staff to the commander in chief of the army and navy, serving Roosevelt in that capacity from 1942 to 1945 and Truman from 1945 to 1949. A few years after the bombs were dropped, Leahy stated: "It is my opinion that the use of this barbarous weapon at Hiroshima and Nagasaki was of no material assistance in our war against Japan. The Japanese were already defeated and ready to surrender."

Dwight Eisenhower, too, went public with his doubts. He recalled telling Stimson, before the bomb was used, "of my belief that Japan was already defeated and that dropping the bomb was completely unnecessary."

And as early as 1945, the U.S. Strategic Bombing Survey, an extensive and official study established by Stimson, published its findings that conventional bombing would have forced a Japanese surrender by the end of the year.

A variety of scholars have challenged Truman's contention that 500,000 Americans would have died in an invasion of Japan. They've pointed to U.S. military planning documents indicating that an initial landing on the island of Kyushu would have resulted in between 20,000 and 26,000 dead; the highest estimate found in these documents (based on a full-scale invasion of all Japan) was 46,000. Moreover, Truman himself used a variety of figures, with the 500,000 being only the latest and highest.

The debates over these numbers, however, only obscured the revisionists' main point: if the Japanese were at the brink of surrender, there need never have been an invasion—or an atom bombing.

In presenting their evidence, the revisionists turned to an unlikely source: a memo written by the leading defender of the decision to drop the bomb, Stimson himself. For though the secretary of war had undeniably recommended that the bomb be dropped, his proposed draft of the ultimatum to be issued to the Japanese differed in one significant point from the final Potsdam Proclamation.

In a July 2 memo to the president, reprinted right in his *Harper's* defense of the bomb, Stimson called for the ultimatum and then added: "I personally think that if in saying this we should add that we do not exclude a constitutional monarchy under her present dynasty, it would substantially add to the chances of acceptance." In other words, if the ultimatum held out the hope that the Japanese could keep their emperor, they might be more willing to surrender.

Stimson urged Truman to clarify the surrender terms to hold out the possibility of some continuing role for the emperor. So did others, including Acting Secretary of State Grew on May 28, Admiral Leahy on June 18, the State Department in a formal recommendation on June 30, Churchill on July 18, and the Joint Chiefs of Staff, also on July 18. Many pointed to intercepted Japanese documents and peace feelers the Japanese had sent out to neutral countries as evidence that Japan's leaders knew they were nearing defeat and sought only to assure that the emperor would be protected. Of the major administration figures consulting with the president on the bomb, only Secretary of State James Byrnes consistently and adamantly opposed any clarification of the surrender terms.

In the actual Potsdam Proclamation, Byrnes got his way: there was no mention of the emperor. Why did Truman go along with Byrnes—against the advice of so many of his other advisers? And why did the ultimatum not mention specifically that a new and phenomenally powerful weapon would be unleashed on Japan's cities? Wouldn't this, too, have made Japan's surrender more likely?

To some revisionists, the answer to these questions was clear: dropping the bomb was a show of force aimed not at Japan but at Russia. As further support for this thesis, revisionists noted the difference between Truman's behavior toward the Russians before and at Potsdam. Prior to the Potsdam meeting between Truman, Churchill, and Stalin, American policy had been aimed at getting Russia to go to war with Japan. On numerous occasions Truman stated that this was the primary reason he wanted to meet Stalin at Potsdam. In this, he succeeded: Stalin agreed that by the middle of August he'd declare war on Japan. In a letter home to his wife, Truman gloated: "I've gotten what I came for—Stalin goes to war . . . I'll say that we'll end the war a year sooner now, and think of the kids who won't be killed!"

But on July 16, once Truman received word that the atom bomb had been successfully tested in the New Mexico desert, American strategy suddenly changed. No longer did the president see any need for Russian help against the Japanese; no longer, in fact, did he see Russia as a wartime ally. In his mind, the Communists were now a postwar rival to be kept out of Japan and anywhere else. On July 17, Byrnes rejected Stimson's advice about including assurances about the emperor in the Potsdam Proclamation. The same day, the newly aggressive Truman faced Stalin across the Potsdam conference table and dismissed the latter's demand for bases in Turkey and the Mediterranean.

As Churchill put it, upon being told of the successful test of the bomb: "Now I know what happened to Truman yesterday. When he got to the meeting after having read this report he was a changed man. He told the Russians just where they got on and off and generally bossed the whole meeting."

The revisionist claims did not go unchallenged. Defenders of the orthodox explanation of the decision countered by arguing that Japan's peace feelers and other evidence that they might consider surrendering were a far cry from an actual surrender, and that the Japanese cabinet was at best divided on the subject. Others pointed out that even if the 500,000 figure was inflated, the cost of an invasion of Japan's home islands would still be considerable. At Okinawa, the equivalent of just three Japanese divisions had held out for one hundred days against a much larger U.S. ground force that was supported by heavy naval and air bombardment. The Okinawa campaign had left 12,520 Americans dead and another 36,631 injured and, along with kamikaze suicide raids, had left American soldiers and policymakers alike with a very vivid image of the ferocity of Japanese resistance. Under these circumstances, any American president would have to be concerned about the casualties an invasion would bring.

As for the decision not to mention the emperor in the Potsdam Proclamation, Truman may have felt bound by American public opinion. Since Pearl Harbor, Americans had sought revenge; to settle for anything less than unconditional surrender would have seemed a failure of nerve or will. Ironically, dropping the bomb may very well have allowed Truman to offer the surrender terms he couldn't beforehand. With America's mastery so completely established, he could let the emperor stay on. Hirohito remained the titular head of the Japanese nation until his death in 1989.

The debate over the bomb came to a head in 1994 when the Smithsonian Institution in Washington, D.C., prepared an exhibit commemorating the fiftieth anniversary of the Hiroshima bombing. The projected exhibition was fairly evenhanded: it stated that the war *might* have ended without the bombings if the Potsdam Proclamation had guaranteed the emperor's position, but this was by no means a strong revisionist position. Still, it was too strong for organizations like the American Legion, whose protests led the Smithsonian to remove any text from the exhibit. Instead, the *Enola Gay,* the plane that dropped the bomb, was displayed without any explanation or context.

That veterans organizations were so offended by the exhibit is ironic, given that top military leaders such as Marshall, Eisenhower, and Leahy were among the earliest to argue against the bomb's necessity. Indeed, the veterans organizations didn't seem to realize that their insistence that the bomb had won the war shifted the credit for that victory away from their own heroic efforts. But all this was lost in a debate that had become so politicized that the traditionalists could only see the revisionists as unpatriotic, and the revisionists could only see the traditionalists as callous and immoral.

What extremists on both sides have too often lost sight of is that the traditionalist and revisionist positions aren't irreconcilable. The traditionalists' claim that the bomb was dropped *solely* to save American lives was untrue—but that doesn't mean that saving lives wasn't a major concern. Conversely, though revisionists have demonstrated Truman's decision was made with an eye on Russia as well as Japan, that certainly doesn't mean he dropped the bomb *solely* to position America for the Cold War.

Truman did not drop the bomb for any single reason, traditionalist or revisionist. Many factors pushed him toward his decision—a desire to avenge Pearl Harbor and an ignorance of the bomb's full dangers, to name two more. For an inexperienced and as yet unelected president, the sheer momentum of a $2 billion project must also have been difficult to resist. "He was like a little boy on a toboggan," recalled Major General Leslie Groves, who headed up the project to build the bomb.

Might he have changed course? Perhaps. There were certainly opportunities. But the forces pushing that toboggan downward were very powerful indeed.

☆ To investigate further:

Stimson, Henry. "The Decision to Use the Atomic Bomb." *Harper's* magazine, February 1947. Written by Truman's secretary of war, this was one of the earliest and most influential of the official explanations.

Truman, Harry. *Memoirs*. New York: Doubleday, 1955. Volume 1 includes Truman's own account of his decision.

Sherwin, Martin. *A World Destroyed*. New York: Knopf, 1975. An account of the interaction between scientists and policymakers and of the origins of the arms race prior to the end of World War II.

Wyden, Peter. *Day One*. New York: Simon & Schuster, 1984. An excellent general history of the bomb, before and after Hiroshima.

McCullough, David. *Truman*. New York: Simon & Schuster, 1992. A masterful biography.

Allen, Thomas B., and Norman Polmar. *Code-Name Downfall*. New York: Simon & Schuster, 1995. A history of America's secret plans to invade Japan, and the latest defense of the traditional position.

Alperovitz, Gar. *The Decision to Use the Atomic Bomb*. New York: Knopf, 1995. The most recent and most comprehensive statement of the revisionist position, this supersedes Alperovitz's influential but more limited 1965 book, *Atomic Diplomacy*.

Nobile, Philip, editor. *Judgment at the Smithsonian*. New York: Marlowe and Company, 1995. Includes the script of the aborted fiftieth-anniversary exhibit.

Chapter 41

Was Alger Hiss a Spy?

By 1948, the House Committee on Un-American Activities seemed to have run its course. The committee had generated plenty of publicity, mostly about communist influence in Hollywood, but had little evidence to back up its more serious charge that enemy agents had infiltrated the U.S. government. Republicans as well as Democrats were beginning to say out loud that the committee should disband, that this latest red scare was, as President Harry Truman put it, a "red herring."

Then, on August 3, *Time* magazine senior editor Whittaker Chambers appeared before the committee. Chambers admitted he had, from 1934 to 1938, served in the communist underground. He could therefore offer first-hand testimony of communist infiltration into the top ranks of the Roosevelt administration. Then Chambers named names—most shockingly that of Alger Hiss. Hiss was a Harvard Law School graduate, a protégé of later Supreme Court Justice Felix Frankfurter, and a leading figure at the Yalta Conference (where, not coincidentally, critics contended Roosevelt gave away eastern Europe to the Soviets). Hiss also presided over the negotiations for the United Nations charter, and then became president of the prestigious Carnegie Endowment.

Others whom Chambers named refused to respond. Not Hiss. Two days after Chambers testified, Hiss told the committee: "I am not and never have been a member of the Communist Party." He had never even met Chambers, he added. Given Hiss's sterling reputation, the committee seemed headed toward another embarrassing dead end.

Congressman Richard Nixon, a member of the committee, was determined not to let that happen. In the absence of any evidence that

Whittaker Chambers told the House Un-American Activities Committee that Hiss was a communist. Hiss is second from the left in the second row behind him. (Library of Congress.)

Hiss was a communist, Nixon steered the investigation toward the question of whether Chambers and Hiss knew each other. Chambers, it turned out, had rented an apartment from Hiss and his wife in 1935, and even stayed with the couple briefly. Hiss had also given Chambers his old car and lent him money for a new one. On August 17, Nixon arranged a face-to-face meeting between the two.

Yes, Hiss reluctantly conceded, he had known this man, though under a different name. Chambers had introduced himself as George Crosley, a freelance journalist. Until now, Hiss had no reason to believe Crosley was someone else, let alone a communist.

Here the story might have ended, in spite of the skepticism of Nixon and others, had Hiss not sued Chambers for slander. This forced Chambers to substantiate his accusations, and on November 17, in a pretrial deposition, he did so—in the form of confidential State Department documents he claimed Hiss had given him in 1937 and 1938. He and Hiss, Chambers now asserted, had been not just communists but also spies. From 1934 to 1938, Hiss had regularly provided Chambers with documents, and Chambers had regularly passed them on to his Soviet connections.

In 1937, Chambers continued, he had become disillusioned with communism and had decided to defect from the spy network. To discourage the Soviets from coming after him, he held on to a batch of documents Hiss had given him. Some were originals, some were copies that Chambers said had been typed by Hiss's wife, Priscilla, and some were on microfilm. In true spy-story style, Chambers hid the microfilm in a hollowed-out pumpkin on his farm. There it had stayed, he explained, because he had not wanted to expose Hiss, his onetime friend, as a spy as well as a communist. Now the slander suit left him no choice. Chambers retrieved what became known as the "pumpkin papers" and, to Nixon's surprise and delight, turned them over to the committee.

Immediately, Hiss was as much a cause as a case. For conservatives, Hiss's treachery proved the dangers of communism, not just abroad but at home; for liberals, he was the innocent victim of a right-wing conspiracy aimed at undoing the New Deal. The Hiss case, wrote historian Allen Weinstein and journalist Alexander Vassiliev, "became entangled in a larger set of public issues: the meaning and merit of the Cold War, the treatment of domestic Communists, the response by intellectuals to their own radical pasts, the true extent of Communist infiltration into the United States government during the New Deal and war years, and the proper role of congressional committees in probing subversion."

There was also the issue of whether Alger Hiss actually was a spy.

Technically, Hiss couldn't be charged with espionage, since the statute of limitations was three years and the crime allegedly took place ten years earlier. But he could be charged with perjury for lying about it, and in December a grand jury indicted him for just that. The trial began in New York in May 1949.

The prosecution's star witness was, of course, Chambers, but they also had evidence to back up his story. There were the original State Department papers and the microfilm. Prosecutors also introduced into evidence Priscilla Hiss's typewriter, the copies she allegedly typed on that machine, other samples of her typing, and new samples made with the same machine. FBI experts testified that the retyped documents and the various samples had all come from the same machine.

Hiss's lawyers didn't question that the samples matched. Instead, they argued that Chambers had somehow gotten his hands on Hiss's typewriter and had made the copies himself, either back in the thirties or more recently. Besides, the defense lawyers added, their client had tracked down the typewriter (which he had given away years before) and voluntarily turned it over to the authorities, hardly the actions of a guilty man.

Hiss also benefited from an impressive array of character witnesses, including Frankfurter and Stanley Reed, another Supreme Court Justice. And defense lawyers were quick to contrast their client with Chambers, a "furtive, secretive, deceptive man" who admitted he had been a communist and who must have lied, either when he told the House committee that he and Hiss hadn't been involved in spying, or (as the defense argued) when he told the jurors that they had.

Eight jurors believed Chambers, four Hiss: a hung jury. So both sides did it all over again in a second trial that started in November. This time the defense augmented its case with the testimony of a psychiatrist. "Mr. Chambers is suffering from a condition known as a psychopathic personality," Dr. Carl Binger told the jury. The symptoms included "chronic, persistent, and repetitive lying; acts of deception and misrepresentation . . . and a tendency to make false accusations."

But the prosecution added an even more effective witness. Hede Massing testified that, like Chambers, she was once a communist spy—and that Hiss told her he was too. For the first time it was not just Chambers's word against Hiss's. Perhaps even more significantly, the political climate had changed since the first trial. In July, the State Department had cut off aid to Chinese nationalists, conceding that China had fallen to the communists. In September, the Soviet Union exploded its first atomic bomb. Under the circumstances, Americans were not taking lightly the threat of communist spies. In January, jury number two found Hiss guilty of perjury.

Hiss continued to maintain his innocence. After the verdict, he told the court, "I am confident that in the future the full facts of how Whittaker Chambers was able to carry out forgery by typewriter will be disclosed." His lawyers followed up with an appeal that suggested that the forgery was the work, not of Chambers alone, but of the FBI. According to this defense theory, Chambers didn't have to retype the State Department documents on the Hisses' old machine. Instead, the FBI designed and built a new one that could match Priscilla Hiss's typing. Hiss's lawyers went so far as to hire a typewriter expert to construct a replica.

Judge Henry Goddard didn't buy the argument. There was no evidence the FBI or Chambers or anyone else had gone to the trouble of building a phony typewriter. Besides, the retyped State Department documents matched not only the new samples from the machine but also the earlier samples of Priscilla Hiss's typing, which she herself conceded were authentic. The Supreme Court declined to hear Hiss's appeal (partly because Frankfurter and Reed, having been character witnesses in his trial, abstained from the vote). In March 1951, Hiss entered Lewisburg Federal Penitentiary, where he would spend the next three and a half years.

The "forgery by typewriter" theory took on new life in the 1970s, when Watergate undermined Nixon's credibility. Former White House counsel John Dean's 1976 book, *Blind Ambition,* explicitly tied Nixon to an anti-Hiss conspiracy. According to Dean, Nixon told Charles Colson (who went to jail for his role in the Watergate cover-up) that he had been involved in building a typewriter for the Hiss case.

In his memoirs, Hiss blamed Nixon (whom he called a "power-hungry politician"), FBI Chief J. Edgar Hoover ("the ultimate bureaucrat"), and Chambers ("the perfect pawn"). "My case," Hiss wrote, "was fabricated by [this] unholy trinity bound together by the theology of anti-communism."

Both Colson and Nixon denied Dean's story, however, and no one ever produced any other evidence of a conspiracy.

In addition to Nixon, Hiss's defenders also continued to batter Chambers's reputation. A number of psychobiographical studies expanded on Binger's analysis of Chambers as a psychopath. In 1976 the FBI released a file that included a 1949 statement from Chambers about a series of homosexual experiences he had during the same period he had been a spy. This led some of Hiss's defenders to speculate that Chambers's stories about life underground were merely a metaphor for his secret sex life. Others suggested Chambers was out for revenge because Hiss had rebuffed his friendship, or perhaps his sexual overtures. In 1976 Hiss himself described Chambers as "a spurned homosexual who testified . . . out of jealousy and resentment."

The revelation of Chambers's homosexuality, however, was not nearly as damaging in 1976 as it might have been in 1949. It might have swayed a jury then, but it hasn't changed the verdict of history. Most historians (though by no means all) have found Chambers—buttressed by the pumpkin papers—more credible than Hiss.

The opening of various KGB and other communist archives in 1992 and 1993 again raised hopes among Hiss's supporters that their man would finally be vindicated. So did the National Security Agency's 1995–1996 release of messages sent by Soviet agents during the 1940s and intercepted by American intelligence. But all these documents turned out to be inconclusive. There was no smoking gun to prove Hiss was a spy, but he was mentioned as one in at least one Romanian archive and one 1945 cable to Moscow. If anything, the new evidence pointed to Hiss's guilt.

Hard as his supporters have tried to portray him as a victim of McCarthyism, there is more evidence that Hiss was a spy than that he was framed. His conviction was not the result of the anticommunist furor that swept America during the 1950s. But there's no question that his case added to that furor. On February 9, 1950, just three weeks after the jurors in Hiss's second trial found him guilty, a Wisconsin senator, no doubt emboldened by that verdict, stood before a Wheeling, West Virginia, crowd and for the first time announced that he had in his hand a list of 205 communists in the State Department.

The era of Senator Joseph McCarthy was under way.

☆ To investigate further:

Cooke, Alistair. *A Generation on Trial*. Baltimore, Maryland: Penguin Books, 1968. Originally published in 1950, Cooke's account of the two trials remains one of the most balanced and entertaining.

Chambers, Whittaker. *Witness*. Washington, D.C.: Regnery Gateway, 1997. Chambers's autobiography, originally published in 1952, is (as his biographer, Sam Tanenhaus, put it) extraordinary both for its self-revelation and self-delusion.

Hiss, Alger. *In the Court of Public Opinion*. New York: Knopf, 1957. A defense brief.

Zeligs, Meyer. *Friendship and Fratricide*. New York: Viking, 1967. A psychoanalytic study of Chambers and Hiss; fascinating, though not always persuasive.

Weinstein, Allen. *Perjury*. New York: Knopf, 1978. An obsessively detailed account that makes a strong case for Hiss's guilt.

Hiss, Alger. *Recollections of a Life*. New York: Seaver Books, 1988. Like its author, this exhibits much logic and little passion.

Tanenhaus, Sam. *Whittaker Chambers*. New York: Random House, 1997. A superb biography; Tanenhaus believes Chambers about Hiss, but by no means about everything else his subject had to say about his life.

Hiss, Tony. *The View from Alger's Window*. New York: Knopf, 1999. Writes Alger's son in this moving memoir: "There is no way to squeeze together inside one person the translucent father I got to know and the monstrous Alger that Chambers talked and wrote about."

Weinstein, Allen, and Alexander Vassiliev. *The Haunted Wood*. New York: Random House, 1999. A history of Soviet espionage in America as seen through the once-secret KGB archives.

Chapter 42

Were the Rosenbergs Guilty?

Like Sacco and Vanzetti a generation before, Julius and Ethel Rosenberg became a symbol to those on the left of how the American government was ruled by those on the right. To the left, the conviction and execution of the Rosenbergs for "stealing the secret of the atomic bomb" revealed a society caught in the thrall of hysterical McCarthyism. So, when the Rosenbergs' sons sued the government under the Freedom of Information Act, and in 1980 obtained the FBI files on the case, those on the left assumed the couple would be finally and fully vindicated. What the files revealed, however, was not nearly so clearcut.

When the Soviet Union successfully tested its atom bomb in August 1949, the United States immediately set out to find those responsible for stealing the classified information. The search led to the British atomic scientist Klaus Fuchs, who was arrested and who confessed that he had given information to the Soviets while working on the bomb at Los Alamos in 1945. Fuchs led the FBI to his American courier, Harry Gold, who was also arrested and also confessed. Gold, in turn, led agents to David Greenglass, an army corporal who had worked in the laboratory at Los Alamos.

It was Greenglass who fingered Julius Rosenberg, his own brother-in-law. According to Greenglass, Rosenberg had dropped out of the Communist Party in 1943 in order to take on a role as Soviet spy. When Greenglass was sent to Los Alamos, Rosenberg arranged for him to pass on atomic information to Harry Gold. In fact, according to Greenglass, Rosenberg headed up a spy ring whose activities extended well beyond the theft of the atomic information.

At the 1951 trial of the Rosenbergs, the star witnesses were Gold and Greenglass. Gold testified that during the first weekend of June 1945, he traveled to New Mexico, where he met with Greenglass and gave him five hundred dollars in exchange for information on the atomic bomb. Greenglass testified that he was following instructions from his brother-in-law. The defense counsel, Emanuel Bloch, focused his efforts on discrediting Greenglass: he charged him with accusing the Rosenbergs to win leniency for his own crimes and to settle some old family grudges. Bloch did not cross-examine Gold at all since, as he explained in his summation to the jury, Gold had not claimed any direct contact with the Rosenbergs.

Later defenders of the Rosenbergs, primarily Walter and Miriam Schneir in their 1968 history of the case, were convinced that Bloch's failure to question Gold's story was a serious error. The Schneirs argued that, apart from the confessions of Gold and Greenglass, the government's sole proof that Harry Gold even met David Greenglass, when the latter supposedly passed on information to the former, was a registration card from the Albuquerque Hilton with Gold's name on it. The card had been placed in evidence during the trial. Yet, when the Schneirs examined it years later, they were shocked to find that the dates on the front and back of the card did not match. Furthermore, when the Schneirs showed the card to a handwriting expert, she expressed "some very real doubts" about whether the initials on the card were actually written by the clerk on duty at the Hilton. The Schneirs could come up with only one explanation for the discrepancies in the date and the handwriting: the card had been forged by the FBI to substantiate a Gold-Greenglass meeting that never actually took place.

Those historians who believed in the Rosenbergs' guilt were not convinced. Handwriting analysis was a notoriously imprecise science. Also, they argued, a simple hotel error could account for the different dates on the back and front of the card as easily as a botched forgery.

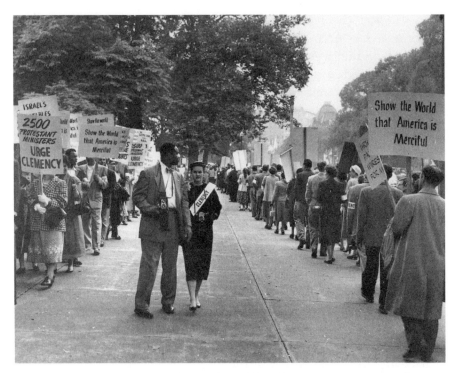

The Rosenbergs' supporters marching in front of the White House on June 15, 1953, four days before the couple's executions. (UPI/Corbis-Bettmann.)

After all, if the FBI was going to forge a registration card, it would probably have managed to forge one without any error.

So, it seemed, the evidence submitted at the trial could not change anyone's mind. Those who believed in the Rosenbergs' guilt continued to maintain that David Greenglass was telling the truth; it was inconceivable to them that Greenglass would send his own sister and brother-in-law to the gas chamber—not to mention ending up with a 15-year prison term himself—unless he and the Rosenbergs were spies. For those who believed in the couple's innocence, the Rosenbergs were scapegoats for America's anger over the loss of its nuclear monopoly. Greenglass had accused them out of fear or vindictiveness or naivete, and the government was persecuting them because they'd been members of the Communist Party.

And so matters stood until Robert and Michael Meeropol, the Rosenbergs' two sons (they'd taken on their adoptive parents' name af-

ter their parents' execution) sued the government for the release of the
FBI files on the case. When they won that case, some 250,000 pages of
FBI and other government documents pertaining to their parents' case
were suddenly open to the public.

Supporters of the Rosenbergs celebrated. Among those who assumed
the new documents would vindicate the Rosenbergs were historians
Richard Radosh and Joyce Milton, both of whom believed the couple
had been framed. Their study of the new evidence, released in a 1983
book, convinced them otherwise.

One startling revelation in the documents was that the government had not relied exclusively on Greenglass for reports of the
Rosenbergs' spying activities. Another informer, Jerome Tartakow,
had supplied a great many details about the Rosenbergs, though he
never testified in court. Tartakow, who was serving a two-year sentence for interstate auto theft, was Rosenberg's closest companion in
jail; like Rosenberg, he was a former communist and the two spent a
great deal of time playing chess together. In return for a reduction of
his sentence, Tartakow regaled the FBI with stories of Rosenberg's spy
rings. Tartakow reported that Rosenberg had admitted to him that "he
played the game and lost." He also tipped off the FBI about a photographer who had taken some passport photos of the Rosenbergs soon
after Greenglass's arrest, and whose testimony at the trial was particularly damning. Defenders of the Rosenbergs were quick to assail Tartakow's character (and even his FBI contacts were suspicious about
some of his reports). Still, it was no longer just Greenglass's word on
which the Rosenbergs' guilt depended.

The newly opened FBI files revealed other evidence against the
Rosenbergs as well, including interviews with more reliable infor-
mants who claimed to have heard, albeit indirectly, of the Rosenbergs'
spy ring. And the files traced the very suspicious disappearances of
three of Julius Rosenberg's closest friends soon after his arrest. One,
Morton Sobell, was caught in Mexico and tried and convicted (though
not executed) with the Rosenbergs. Two others, Joel Barr and Al
Sarant, later turned up in the Soviet Union.

Taken together, this new evidence, though circumstantial, convinced Radosh and Milton that the Rosenbergs were indeed spies.
The Schneirs continued to defend the Rosenbergs; they issued a
revised edition of their book in which they argued that additional

evidence from FBI files was meaningless since the FBI was perfectly capable of manufacturing or destroying evidence. But most mainstream historians sided with Radosh and Milton and now accepted the guilty verdict. In 1995, the Rosenbergs' remaining defenders received another blow, when the army released Russian cables it had intercepted and decoded in 1943. Among the Russian agents referred to was one identified as JR.

Still, the government did not emerge from the new investigations with clean hands, either. For one thing, though the new evidence against Julius Rosenberg was damning, the evidence against Ethel Rosenberg was much flimsier. David Greenglass, notably, accused only his brother-in-law and never his sister. Worse, the FBI files made clear that the only reason Ethel Rosenberg was arrested was to put pressure on her husband to confess and name names. When this strategy failed, the government upped the ante, hoping that the threat of executing Ethel would break Julius. Perhaps the most shocking document in the files revealed that FBI agents standing by at Julius Rosenberg's execution had ready a number of questions, should he choose to talk at the last moment. Among the questions was: "Was your wife cognizant of your activities?" Even as it executed her, it was clear the government remained uncertain of her guilt.

This is not to say that Ethel Rosenberg was innocent. The Rosenbergs were a very close couple, and Ethel almost certainly was aware of what her husband was up to. But there was no evidence she participated in his spying, and the government's cynical behavior in executing a wife in order to pressure a husband can hardly be considered a triumph of justice.

Furthermore, the FBI files make clear that even if the Rosenbergs were guilty of spying, the death penalty was a gross injustice. The information they were convicted of passing on to the Russians simply wasn't that important. A few months after describing the case as "the crime of the century," J. Edgar Hoover privately acknowledged to FBI agents that Soviet scientists had undoubtedly developed their bomb independent of any information they'd received through espionage. And a year after the Rosenbergs' execution, General Leslie Groves, the military chief of the Manhattan Project, told a closed meeting of the Atomic Energy Commission that "the data that went out in the case of the Rosenbergs was of minor value."

What David Greenglass passed on to Harry Gold—a crude drawing of part of the plutonium-fired implosion device—could hardly have condensed the results of the Manhattan Project in any technologically meaningful way. At most, the sketch confirmed a small part of what the Russians had already learned from Klaus Fuchs's far more sophisticated information (Fuchs, after all, was an atomic physicist) and from their own research. David Greenglass was a spy and so was Julius Rosenberg, but both were small-time amateurs. Rosenberg couldn't even hold a job, let alone run a major spy ring. To accuse him of having "stolen the secret of the atomic bomb" was either a cynical move on the part of the government, playing to the anticommunist hysteria of the period, or a sign that the government was itself caught in the grips of that hysteria.

The irony of the Rosenberg case, then, is this: the accusers and defenders of the Rosenbergs were both right. The Rosenbergs were spies, and they were also scapegoats. The Rosenbergs were not innocent, but they certainly did not deserve to die.

☆ To investigate further:

Schneir, Walter and Miriam. *Invitation to an Inquest*. New York: Doubleday, 1965. Revised edition Pantheon, 1983. Presents the case for the Rosenbergs' innocence.

Nizer, Louis. *The Implosion Conspiracy*. New York: Doubleday, 1973. A day-by-day account of the trial, somewhat biased in favor of the prosecution.

Meeropol, Robert and Michael. *We Are Your Sons*. Boston: Houghton Mifflin, 1975. The Rosenbergs' sons' own stories, including very moving letters from and between their parents, and a much less compelling argument for their innocence.

Milton, Joyce, and Ronald Radosh, *The Rosenberg File*. Orlando: Holt, Rinehart and Winston, 1983. The definitive case for the Rosenbergs' guilt.

Philipson, Ilene. *Ethel Rosenberg*. New York: Franklin Watts, 1988. Although a biography and not an investigation of the case, this portrait of the Rosenbergs as struggling working-class parents makes it difficult to believe they could have managed to do much more than just get by.

Sharlitt, Joseph. *Fatal Error*. New York: Scribner's, 1989. Concludes that the Rosenbergs were spies but that they were tried and executed unfairly.

Carmichael, Virginia. *Framing History.* Minneapolis: University of Minnesota Press, 1993. How the Rosenberg case has been portrayed in the arts; interesting more as a work of criticism than history.

Weiner, Tim. "U.S. Tells How It Cracked Code of A-Bomb Spy Ring." The *New York Times,* July 12, 1995. The latest revelations.

Chapter 43

What Has J. D. Salinger Written?

W hen a writer doesn't show his face," the famously reclusive writer Don DeLillo wrote, "he becomes a local symptom of God's famous reluctance to appear."
Not quite. But to fans of J. D. Salinger, the author's absence has sometimes seemed almost as distressing and perplexing as God's. This was the man, after all, who seemed to have all the answers. More than fifty years after its publication, *The Catcher in the Rye* continues to be a bestseller, as each new generation of teenagers discovers that Holden Caulfield speaks for them. Since 1953, when Salinger moved to the remote town of Cornish, New Hampshire, reporters and readers have sought out his fortress, hoping for a few words or at least a glimpse of the author. In the movie *Field of Dreams,* the hero seeks out a reclusive author, figuring he's the only one who can make sense of things. In the book on which the movie is based, *Shoeless Joe,* the connection is explicit: the character of the guru-author is named J. D. Salinger.

In real life, it's unlikely Salinger's visitor would have gotten through the door. Salinger is the most reclusive of authors. Unlike DeLillo or Thomas Pynchon, who have simply declined to publicize their work, Salinger has stopped publishing it.

It did not happen all of a sudden. At first, Salinger refused to deal with magazines whose editors had in one way or another offended him. He mocked the author profiles magazines ran with stories, saying that any writer who liked them was "likely to have his picture taken wearing an open-collared shirt . . . looking three-quarter-profile and tragic." Gradually, he ruled out publishing in any magazine other than *The New Yorker,* which ran no notes on contributors and was also known for its extremely sensitive editing.

There were still books, at least for a while, though they consisted of previously published stories about the fictional Glass family. Next Salinger demanded the paperbacks be published between two plain covers with no promotional copy, biographical information, or photo of the author. In 1965, there was a final story in *The New Yorker,* "Hapworth 16, 1924." And then there was nothing.

Salinger has continued to write, or so he said in the author's note to his last book, *Raise High the Roof Beam, Carpenters, and Seymour—An Introduction,* published in 1963. "There is only my word for it," he wrote, "but I have several new Glass stories coming along—waxing, dilating—each in its own way, but I suspect the less said about them, in mixed company, the better."

To the few people who have seen him since, he has also said he was still writing. In 1960, a *Newsweek* photographer found Salinger walking in Cornish. Salinger, perhaps grateful that the photographer asked his permission to shoot, explained why he couldn't allow it.

"My method of work is such that any interruption throws me off," Salinger said. "I can't have my picture taken or have an interview until I've completed what I've set out to do."

In another rare and very brief interview, Salinger spoke to a *New York Times* reporter in 1974. He did so only to stress that a collection of his stories then circulating was unauthorized, but the reporter couldn't resist the opportunity to ask why he wasn't publishing.

"Publishing is a terrible invasion of my privacy," Salinger answered. "I like to write. I live to write. But I write just for myself and my own pleasure."

What he was writing, whether about the Glasses or anything else, he would not say. He showed it to no one. This left readers to wonder, as critic John Wenke wrote, whether he was "composing masterpiece after masterpiece but refusing to publish" or "simply growing vegetables" in New Hampshire.

☆ ☆ ☆

Critics tended to look for clues in Salinger's published works. Wenke looked at Salinger's 1950 story, "For Esmé—With Love and Squalor," and

After the first two printings of The Catcher in the Rye, *Salinger demanded that his picture be removed from the jacket, and it hasn't appeared there since. This was taken by Lotte Jacobi in 1953. (University of New Hampshire.)*

found hints of the author's early frustration with writing. One character, for example, wrote "fairly regularly, from a paradise of triple exclamation points and inaccurate observations." Silence was clearly better than this.

Others noted that Salinger's work increasingly showed the influence of Eastern religions. The epigraph to his 1953 story collection was the Zen koan, "What is the sound of one hand clapping?" Perhaps, some speculated, Salinger had embraced silence as part of a Zen-like renunciation of the material world. Truman Capote said he'd heard "on very good authority" that Salinger had written five or six novels, and that *The New Yorker* had turned them down because "all of them are very strange and all about Zen Buddhism." The magazine denied this.

One of the most creative theories, from John Calvin Batchelor in 1976, was that Salinger was publishing new work under the pseudonym Thomas Pynchon. This solved two mysteries in one, since Pynchon was almost as much of a recluse as Salinger. Pynchon eventually appeared to deny the story, and Batchelor had to concede he was wrong.

New York Times reviewer Michiko Kakutani noted the solipsism of the Glass family in Salinger's later works. She blamed their solipsism on

Salinger's own. "This falling off in his work," she wrote, "perhaps, is a palpable consequence of Mr. Salinger's own Glass-like withdrawal: withdrawal feeding self-absorption and self-absorption feeding tetchy disdain."

Among the most sophisticated critics to take on Salinger's silence was the British poet and biographer Ian Hamilton. Hamilton noted that Salinger was living out Holden Caulfield's dream. In *The Catcher in the Rye*, Holden said he would "drive up to Massachusetts and Vermont, and around there" and "build me a little cabin." Hamilton also made a case that Seymour Glass, one of the main characters in a number of Salinger stories, was the author's alter ego. In the 1948 story "A Perfect Day for Bananafish," Glass—unable to survive in an imperfect world—commits suicide.

"Salinger doesn't commit suicide," Hamilton wrote, "but he does the next best thing: He disappears, he stops living in the world, he makes himself semiposthumous."

It was not, however, Hamilton's literary analysis that generated the brunt of the attention surrounding his biography, *J. D. Salinger: A Writing Life*. In the course of his research, Hamilton found stashes of Salinger's unpublished letters, which he used to buttress his conclusions. Salinger, however, was determined not to allow any of the letters, or even excerpts, to be published. In 1986, just before Random House was to release the book, he succeeded in getting a restraining order. Salinger's right not to publish—and Hamilton's right to publish—was now in the hands of the courts.

Hamilton remained confident. Partly this was because he was willing, albeit reluctantly, to pare down the excerpts from the letters to just about two hundred words. This, he assumed, would help his case. But most of Hamilton's confidence came from the realization that, if Salinger wanted to pursue the case, he would have to face the questions of Random House's lawyers. These questions would be at least as probing as any reporter's.

"I was convinced he wouldn't do it," Hamilton said. "But he did."

☆ ☆ ☆

In October 1986, Salinger was interviewed—or, more accurately, deposed—by Random House's lawyer, Robert Callagy. Some of Callagy's questions veered off from the letters to his other writings.

> *Q:* When was the last time you wrote any work of fiction for publication?
> *A:* I'm not sure exactly.

Q: At any time during the past twenty years, have you written a work of fiction for publication?

A: That has been published, you mean?

Q: That has been published.

A: No.

That much everyone already knew. Then Callagy asked whether, during the past twenty years, Salinger had written any fiction that had not been published. Salinger said he had.

Q: Could you describe for me what works of fiction you have written which have not been published?

A: It would be very difficult to do . . .

Q: Have you written any full-length works of fiction during the past twenty years which have not been published?

A: Could you frame that a different way? What do you mean by a full-length work? You mean ready for publication?

Q: As opposed to a short story or a fictional piece or a magazine submission.

A: It's very difficult to answer. I don't write that way. I just start writing fiction and see what happens to it.

Q: Maybe an easier way to approach this is, would you tell me what your literary efforts have been in the field of fiction within the last twenty years?

A: Could I tell you or would I tell you? . . . Just a work of fiction. That's all. That's the only description I can really give it. . . . It's almost impossible to define. I work with characters, and as they develop, I just go from there.

This was as close as Salinger would come to describing his unpublished fiction.

As for the unpublished letters, the first round went to Random House, but an appeals court found for Salinger. As a result, Hamilton's *J. D. Salinger: A Writing Life* was never published, though he rewrote it (minus the letters and much of the analysis of them) as *In Search of J. D. Salinger.* The book, which ended up not so much a biography as the story of the biographer's quest, was finally published in 1988.

Salinger's next biographer was Paul Alexander. Alexander's conclusions were much harsher than Hamilton's. Alexander did not discover any significant new sources, but he compiled a great deal of anti-Salinger talk. In essence, he revived Truman Capote's claim that the author hadn't published anything because he hadn't written anything worth publishing.

Alexander described the author's note in *Raise High* as "insincere," saying it "sounds as if Salinger were trying to overcompensate for the fact that he knew he had no new publishable material in development but didn't want his readers to know it." He had withdrawn from the world, Alexander suggested, to hide the fact that he was finished as a writer.

The withdrawal was even, to some extent, a publicity stunt. "By cutting himself off from the public, by cutting himself off the way he had done, he made sure the public would remain fascinated with him," Alexander wrote. "By refusing to publish any new work, by letting the public know he had new work he was not publishing, he ensured a continued fascination in the four books that were in print. . . . Salinger became the Greta Garbo of literature, and then periodically, when it may have seemed he was about to be forgotten, he resurfaced briefly, just to remind the public that he wanted to be left alone."

As Holden would have put it, Salinger was a "phony."

Even more disturbing than the idea that it was all a publicity stunt was Alexander's suggestion that Salinger really did have something to hide, namely affairs with teenage girls.

These rumors, too, were nothing new. Many readers had noticed that the wisest characters in many of Salinger's stories are young girls, such as Holden's sister Phoebe. And Salinger clearly liked the company of teenagers. When he first moved to Cornish, he hung out with local teens, Hamilton reported. In 1953, when Salinger was in his thirties, he met the nineteen-year-old Claire Douglas. They married two years later and divorced twelve years after that. In 1972, Salinger, then in his fifties, saw a *New York Times Magazine* story by eighteen-year-old Joyce Maynard, whose picture appeared on the cover. He wrote her an admiring letter. Instead of returning for her sophomore year at Yale, Maynard moved to Cornish, where she stayed for ten months.

Unfortunately for Salinger, Maynard continued to write, and in 1998 she published a memoir, *At Home in the World*. Much of it is about her relationship with Salinger.

"For most of that year I lived with him, in extreme isolation, working on a book and believing—despite the thirty-five years separating our ages—that we would be together always," Maynard wrote. "The following spring, J. D. Salinger sent me away. I remained desperately in love with him."

The Salinger portrayed by Maynard certainly continued to write. Indeed, he seemed more in touch with his fictional characters than the real world.

"He has compiled stacks of notes and notebooks concerning the habits and backgrounds of the Glasses—music they like, places they go, episodes in their history," Maynard wrote. "Even the parts of their lives that he may not write about, he needs to know. He fills in the facts as diligently as a parent, keeping up to date with the scrapbooks."

Salinger, as portrayed by Maynard, was hardly a one-dimensional figure whose sole interest was preying on young women. In fact, during their year together they never had intercourse (though they did have oral sex). But Salinger nevertheless came across as exploiting a vulnerable teenager, and as so absorbed in his work and in himself that he has no patience with anything or anyone else.

A similar view emerged from the 2000 memoir, *Dream Catcher,* by Salinger's (and Claire Douglas's) daughter Margaret. At one point, according to Margaret Salinger, her father defended himself by saying that he never neglected her, even if he was sometimes detached.

"He is detached about your pain, but God knows he takes his own pain more seriously than cancer," she concluded. "There is nothing remotely detached about my father's behavior toward his own pain, in his hemorrhages about anything personal being known about him. There is nothing remotely detached about his passionate defense of any felt infringement on his privacy or in the sanctity of his words and works."

Margaret Salinger's view of her father was by no means entirely negative. "When he chooses to make himself available, he can be funny, intensely loving, and the person you most want to be with," she wrote. "My father has . . . spent his life busy writing his heart out."

The problems arose when real people invaded Salinger's Glass world. "To get in the way of his work," Margaret Salinger wrote, "is to commit sacrilege."

Holden Caulfield imagined a big field of rye where thousands of kids would play. Nearby was a cliff, where Holden stood all day long, catching any of the kids who start to go over the edge. But Holden's creator, according to his daughter, was no catcher in the rye.

"Get what you can from his writing, his stories," she said. "But the author himself will not appear out of nowhere to catch those kids if they get too close to that crazy cliff."

☆ To investigate further:

Bloom, Harold, editor. *J. D. Salinger.* New York: Chelsea House, 1987. A useful collection of critical essays.

Hamilton, Ian. *In Search of J. D. Salinger.* New York: Random House, 1988. Hamilton may not have solved the mystery, but he came closer than anyone else—even in this much-expurgated (and therefore legal) final version of *A Writing Life.* The book is also fascinating as a study of the moral and legal dilemmas facing biographers.

Rosenbaum, Ron. "The Man in the Glass House." *Esquire,* June 1997. "In its own powerful, invisible way," Rosenbaum writes, "the silence is in itself an eloquent work of art. It is the Great Wall of Silence J. D. Salinger has built around himself." But Rosenbaum, like others, can't resist the urge to breach the wall.

Maynard, Joyce. *At Home in the World.* New York: Picador USA, 1998. Salinger's defenders bitterly attacked Maynard for making his private life public, and she didn't help matters by telling all at the same time that Monica Lewinsky did. But it was her life as well as his, and there's no denying it makes fascinating, if disturbing, reading. Salinger, of course, saw only the disturbing side. After she decided to write the book, she returned to Cornish to confront him. As Maynard described it, he pointed his finger directly at her heart. "The problem with you, Joyce," he said, "is . . . you love the world." "Yes," she answered, "I do." "I knew you would amount to this," he said. "Nothing."

Alexander, Paul. *Salinger.* Los Angeles: Renaissance Books, 1999. It's a bit of a cut-and-paste job, and it's marred by Alexander's tendency to hedge his most sweeping conclusions (such as that Salinger secretly liked attention, or teenage girls) by phrasing them as questions. Still, considering all the obstacles a Salinger biographer faces, this is a worthy effort.

Salinger, Margaret. *Dream Catcher.* New York: Washington Square Press, 2000. This must have seemed to Salinger even more a betrayal than Maynard's. It was, after all, his Holden Caulfield who said, right at the beginning of *The Catcher in the Rye,* that "my parents would have about two hemorrhages apiece if I told anything pretty personal about them . . . especially my father."

Part 5

Baffling Events of More Recent Times

1960s to 1990s

Chapter 44

Who Was to Blame for the Bay of Pigs?

In the early morning hours of April 17, 1961, about fourteen hundred Cuban exiles, trained and armed by the CIA, sailed through the Bay of Pigs and landed on the southern coast of Cuba. Two days earlier, after getting the go-ahead from President John Kennedy, Cuban pilots in eight B-26 planes supplied by the United States bombed three sites in Cuba in an effort to disable Castro's tiny air force. As the Cuban exiles came ashore, they were confident they would be backed by more American air strikes and, if necessary, American ground troops. Their goal was to overthrow the government of Fidel Castro.

It did not, of course, work out that way. The eight B-26 planes knocked out only five of Castro's planes, and on the eve of the landing, Kennedy nixed any additional air support. Instead, it was Castro's planes that took to the air, destroying the exiles' supply ships and stranding them with only limited ammunition. Meanwhile, twenty thousand of Castro's troops advanced on the beach. By nightfall of April 18, Castro's forces had killed 140 of the exiles and captured 1,189.

The Bay of Pigs was a debacle not just for the exiles but also for the president. Not only had he failed to overthrow the Cuban government, but he had driven Castro closer to the Soviet Union and enabled the dictator to consolidate his power. "How," an anguished Kennedy asked special counsel Theodore Sorensen a few days later, "could I have been so stupid, to let them go ahead?"

☆ ☆ ☆

The president made no secret of the fact that he felt his advisers, especially in the CIA, had betrayed him. In a 1965 book, Sorensen recounted his post–Bay of Pigs conversations with the president. As Kennedy explained it to Sorensen, the CIA—in particular Allen Dulles, the agency's director, and Richard Bissell, the deputy director in charge of the Bay of Pigs operation— misled him. It was crucial to act quickly, they insisted, before the Soviet Union armed Castro. And the president was willing to act, as long as it didn't mean involving American troops; such an intervention, Kennedy told Sorensen, would be "contrary to our traditions and to our international obligations." So Kennedy approved a limited amount of covert assistance for some Cuban patriots, not realizing that the Cubans and the CIA had in mind a full-fledged invasion. Kennedy hoped the exiles might seize a beachhead and perhaps provoke a general uprising, but he wasn't counting on that. As a fallback, the CIA assured him, the exiles could join up with other anti-Castro guerillas in the Escambray Mountains.

There didn't seem to be any downside. As Sorensen, paraphrasing Kennedy, put it: "If a group of Castro's own countrymen, without overt U.S. participation, could have succeeded in establishing themselves on the island, proclaimed a new government, rallied the people to their cause and ousted Castro, all Latin America would feel safer, and if instead they were forced to flee to the mountains, there to carry on guerilla warfare, there would still have been net gain."

In fact, as the CIA ought to have known, neither a general uprising nor a guerilla war was a realistic outcome. Castro already had more than enough troops and arms to suppress an insurrection from within or without. For their part, the exiles had no intention of taking to the hills. *Their* CIA contacts had led them to expect direct American support; that's why they'd joined up and that's how they'd trained. Besides, even if they wanted to go guerilla, there were eighty miles of swamps and thousands of Castro's soldiers between the Bay of Pigs and the Escambray Mountains.

Kennedy, not yet ninety days into his presidency, was still feeling his way. Fearful of being branded soft on communism, he was reluctant to quash a plan that the Eisenhower administration had set in motion. So he trusted his experts. Wrote Arthur Schlesinger, like Sorensen a member of Kennedy's inner circle as well as its historian, "Had one se-

President-elect John Kennedy with CIA director Allen Dulles, the man the president later blamed for misleading him about Cuba. (Library of Congress.)

nior adviser opposed the adventure, I believe that Kennedy would have canceled it."

Angry and humiliated, Kennedy assigned General Maxwell D. Taylor to study what went wrong. Two months later, Taylor returned with a report that must have pleased the president. The CIA ought to have made clear, Taylor concluded, that the plan couldn't work without additional American air support. The Joint Chiefs of Staff were also to blame; many had doubts about the plan, but none had voiced them, or at least none had voiced them loudly and clearly. Above all, the operation was in the wrong hands. As it grew from aiding a few freedom fighters into what amounted to an invasion of a foreign country, the CIA ought to have turned over control to the military. "The impossibility of running [an invasion] as a covert operation under CIA should have been recognized and the situation reviewed," Taylor wrote. "If a reorientation of the operation had not been possible, the project should have been abandoned."

The most scathing criticism of the CIA came from within the agency itself. CIA Inspector General Lyman Kirkpatrick spent six months putting together a report that took Kennedy entirely off the hook and faulted the agency for its "failure to advise the President . . . that success had become dubious." The Kirkpatrick report explicitly exonerated the president's decision not to authorize additional air strikes. "If the project had been better conceived, better organized, better staffed and better managed, would that precise issue ever have had to be presented for Presidential decision at all?" Kirkpatrick wrote. "And would it have been presented under the same ill-prepared, inadequately briefed circumstances?"

The invasion was doomed well before Kennedy decided against additional air strikes, and the CIA would have recognized this had they not taken on the role of advocates instead of analysts. "Timely and objective scrutiny of the operation in the months before the invasion, including study of all available intelligence, would . . . have raised the question of why the United States should contemplate pitting 1,500 soldiers . . . against an enemy vastly superior in number and armament on a terrain which offered nothing but vague hope of significant local support," wrote Kirkpatrick. "It . . . would certainly have revealed there was no real plan for the post-invasion period, whether for success or failure.

"The choice," Kirkpatrick concluded, "was between retreat without honor and a gamble between ignominious defeat and dubious victory. The Agency chose to gamble, at rapidly decreasing odds."

If Kennedy felt betrayed by the CIA, the feeling was mutual. Wrote Dulles: "In these difficult types of operations . . . one never succeeds unless there is a determination to succeed, a willingness to risk some unpleasant political repercussions, and a willingness to provide the military necessities." More bluntly, as many of the Cuban exiles themselves later put it, Kennedy lacked *cojones*.

The most comprehensive rebuttal to the Kirkpatrick report came from Bissell, who put the blame squarely on the president. Most disastrous, he argued, was the president's refusal to order additional air strikes. With control of the air, the exiles would have had the supplies they needed to hold a beachhead. And "once it could be shown to the Cubans that a Cuban force in opposition to Castro . . . was capable of maintaining itself on Cuban soil, there would be substantial defections from the Castro regime."

"Without these air strikes the plan never had a chance," Bissell concluded. "The informed military view without exception and at all times was that the complete control of the air was absolutely vital."

Kennedy's problem, according to Bissell, was not that he lacked guts. More fundamentally, he was torn between two conflicting objectives: to overthrow Castro, and to maintain the illusion that the U.S. government was not involved. That led to a series of bad decisions. For example, Kennedy insisted on using obsolete B-26 planes, because the more effective A-5 bombers would obviously be American. He moved the landing away from the Escambray Mountains, because the more remote Bay of Pigs would make for a "less spectacular" assault. Above all, of course, he backed away from additional air strikes because it would be impossible to pass them off as the work of Cuban freedom fighters and not American pilots.

Defeat, Bissell wrote, "was directly and unambiguously attributable to a long series of Washington policy decisions."

Most early historians of the Kennedy administration followed the trail Sorensen and Schlesinger blazed toward Camelot. If Kennedy erred at all during the Bay of Pigs, it was in listening to the wrong people, and he quickly learned his lesson, consulting a wider ranger of experts and taking a firm but reasonable stand, for example, during the Cuban missile crisis. Later, the Kennedy image was increasingly tarnished by revelations about secret love affairs and underworld connections. Many of his recent biographers sound much like Bissell.

"Kennedy's decisions to limit sharply the [bombing] destroyed any chance for success," wrote Thomas Reeves in 1991. "In the Bay of Pigs fiasco, Jack rejected moral and legal objections to an invasion; he lied, exhibited an almost macho temperament, became involved with military operations just enough to make them worse, and then blamed others for failure."

Kennedy's image reached a new low in Seymour Hersh's 1997 work, *The Dark Side of Camelot*. To Hersh, Kennedy's decisions about the Bay of Pigs made sense only in the context of a CIA plot to assassinate Castro. Evidence of that plot had emerged during Senate hearings in 1975.

"Jack Kennedy had every reason to believe in April 1961 that [mob boss] Sam Giancana and his men in Miami and Havana would do the deed," wrote Hersh. "That confidence perhaps made it easier for Kennedy and the men who ran the CIA to ignore their friends in the agency, the press, and elsewhere who sought to warn the administration that the secret of the . . . planned invasion was no secret." In other words, Kennedy approved an otherwise unworkable plan because he assumed that by the time the exiles landed, Castro would be dead.

The assassination plot—and Kennedy's awareness of it—also explained why the president backed away from additional bombing.

Continued Hersh: "Sorensen and Schlesinger apparently did not know the critical truths about Cuba. . . . They were not privy to one of the major reason's for President Kennedy's last-minute ambivalence about the Bay of Pigs operation: Sam Giancana's henchmen inside Cuba had been unable to murder Castro in the days immediately before the invasion." Kennedy, now recognizing the mission was hopeless, decided to cut his losses.

The problem with Hersh's argument is that, while there's no question the CIA tried to kill Castro, it's unclear whether Kennedy knew about the plot. There is no written record of anyone telling him, and those most likely to have briefed him about it have either denied doing so or been very vague about what he knew. *If* he knew, it may very well have been a factor in his decisions about the Bay of Pigs, but whether he knew remains a mystery. And if he knew about the assassination plot, it still would not have been the only factor in his decisions.

Kennedy was a complex figure, certainly more flawed than Sorensen or Schlesinger would have him, yet also more thoughtful and principled than Reeves or Hersh portrayed him. The latest scholarship about the Bay of Pigs has recognized the complexity of his character and of his decision-making. Kennedy was, as Bissell pointed out, eager to unseat Castro, but he was even more concerned about the political and moral implications of overt U.S. involvement.

The problem was that neither Bissell nor Dulles took the latter concerns seriously. As Dulles later wrote: "We felt that when the chips were down—when the crisis arose in reality, any request required for success would be authorized rather than permit the enterprise to fail."

Kennedy, faced with alternatives he considered even worse, was willing to see it fail.

☆ To investigate further:

Schlesinger, Arthur Jr. *A Thousand Days*. Boston: Houghton Mifflin Company, 1965. Besides being one of the best historians of the era, Schlesinger was one of the few Kennedy advisers to urge him not to go ahead with the Bay of Pigs operation.

Sorensen, Theodore. *Kennedy*. New York: Harper & Row, 1965. *The New York Times* called this, rightly, "the nearest thing we will ever have to the memoirs Kennedy intended to write."

Wyden, Peter. *Bay of Pigs*. New York: Simon & Schuster, 1979. How everything went wrong.

Reeves, Thomas. *A Question of Character*. New York: The Free Press, 1991. Or, as Reeves would have it, the lack thereof.

Bissell, Richard. *Reflections of a Cold Warrior*. New Haven, Connecticut: Yale University Press, 1996. The passage of time moderated Bissell's opinions, compared to his 1961 rebuttal to Kirkpatrick. On the president's decision not to authorize more air strikes, here he concedes that, important as it was, "that decision alone would not have ensured success."

Hersh, Seymour. *The Dark Side of Camelot*. Boston: Little, Brown, 1997. Compared to Hersh's Kennedy, Richard Nixon was always truthful and Bill Clinton always faithful.

Blight, James, and Peter Kornbluh, editors. *Politics of Illusion*. Boulder, Colorado: Lynne Rienner Publishers, 1998. Excerpts from a 1996 conference attended by veterans of the Kennedy White House, the CIA, and the expedition itself. To a remarkable extent, each group concluded it had suffered more from illusions about the others than from betrayals by them.

Kornbluh, Peter, editor. *Bay of Pigs Declassified*. New York: The New Press, 1998. The full texts of Kirkpatrick's report and Bissell's rebuttal, declassified thirty-seven years after they were written.

Freedman, Lawrence. *Kennedy's Wars*. New York: Oxford University Press, 2000. "For all his mistakes and misadventures," Freedman writes, "Kennedy's achievement was that he could be remembered for crises rather than hot wars."

Perret, Geoffrey. *Jack*. New York: Random House, 2001. Admirably balanced.

Dallek, Robert. *An Unfinished Life*. Boston: Little, Brown, 2003. Though media attention focused on its revelations about Kennedy's affair with an intern and his health problems, this is a comprehensive, scholarly biography. Dallek found no evidence, incidentally, that Kennedy's affair or health affected his decision on the Bay of Pigs.

Chapter 45

Who Killed JFK?

No event, save perhaps Pearl Harbor, traumatized the nation as much as the assassination of President John F. Kennedy on November 22, 1963. Not surprisingly, in both cases the public responded by questioning the official version of what happened. But while the controversy over who was to blame for Pearl Harbor has faded with time, the mystery of who killed JFK is by no means resolved in the minds of most Americans. In the more than two thousand books and tens of thousands of articles on the subject, investigators have argued that Kennedy was killed by, to mention just the main culprits: the CIA, the KGB, the FBI, the Mafia, Fidel Castro, anti-Castro Cubans, and the Joint Chiefs of Staff. Not to mention Lee Harvey Oswald.

Confronted by so much confusing and often contradictory evidence, historians have been tempted to throw up their hands and say that this is one mystery that just can't be solved. Most Kennedy scholars, in fact, have shied away from his death. But they're wrong to do so, for not only is the subject too important to ignore, but the massive accumulation of evidence has moved us a great deal closer (though not all the way) to the mystery's solution.

☆ ☆ ☆

The first official investigation into the assassination was that of the Warren Commission, headed by the Chief Justice of the United States, Earl Warren. The commission's report, released just ten months after Kennedy's death, offered a clear and simple answer to the question of who killed the president: Oswald did it, and he did it alone.

The Warren Commission concluded that Oswald had shot Kennedy from the sixth-floor window at the southeast corner of the Texas School Book Depository Building in Dallas. A construction worker across the street from the Depository saw Oswald shoot and described him to police. Forty-five minutes later, Dallas policeman J. D. Tippit stopped Oswald, who pulled out his revolver and killed Tippit. Oswald fled into a movie theater, from which he was dragged out by Dallas police. Two days later, as Oswald was being transferred from the city jail to a county jail, Jack Ruby broke through the crowds and fired a fatal shot into Oswald.

The Warren Report painted a picture of Oswald as a crazy loner, driven partly by a commitment to Marxism and partly by his own personal madness. Sent by his mother to an orphanage when he was just three, he was committed to a youth center for troubled boys when he was fifteen. He joined the marines, was twice court-martialed, went to Russia, tried to defect, and attempted suicide when the Russians decided to send him home. The Russians then relented and sent him to Minsk, where he spent two years building radios. But Oswald envisioned himself as a revolutionary leader, not a factory worker; he became as disillusioned with communism as with capitalism, and he returned to America. Back home his violent nature manifested itself in beatings of his Russian wife and in his attempted murder of right-wing General Edwin Walker. (Evidence of this previous assassination attempt only surfaced after Oswald's arrest for Kennedy's murder.)

Why did Oswald kill Kennedy? Not because of any long-felt animosity or planning. It was merely chance that Oswald happened to work in the School Book Depository Building. But when he learned that the president's limousine would pass within rifle range, he seized his opportunity. Convinced he was destined for greatness, yet a failure at everything he'd tried, Oswald grabbed his place in history.

As for Ruby, he was a failed night club and strip joint owner who, like much of the country, was grief-stricken at the assassination. But, like Oswald, Ruby loved the spotlight and, on an impulse, he too seized the chance to take center stage.

This, at least, was the scenario presented by the Warren Report.

It didn't take long for skeptics to start chipping away at the commission's credibility.

Early critics pointed out that the commission had been under tremendous pressure, both to issue its report quickly and to assure the country that Oswald acted alone. Reports of Soviet and Cuban involvement in the assassination could lead to war, after all. Besides, Lyndon Johnson didn't want any lingering questions about the assassination clouding his reelection prospects. So, though the commission supposedly worked tirelessly to find the truth, it held its hearings in secret and relied heavily on the FBI and Secret Service reports. Most witnesses appeared before staff members, rather than the commission itself; in fact, not once were all seven commission members present during questioning.

With faith in the Warren Report waning, Jim Garrison, the New Orleans district attorney, undertook his own investigation in 1966. Garrison was convinced that while Oswald was in New Orleans—where he lived before moving to Dallas—he'd hooked up with two local figures, David Ferrie and Clay Shaw. According to Garrison, all three worked for the CIA, which was behind the plot to kill Kennedy. But Ferrie died before Garrison could learn more from him, and Shaw was acquitted a mere 45 minutes after a jury retired for deliberations. And rightly so: Garrison's case against Shaw depended heavily on the testimony of a witness who admitted he had no conscious memory of anything to do with a conspiracy; only after prosecutors had drugged and hypnotized him did his story come out.

Though Garrison's conspiracy theory proved unfounded, more responsible investigators continued to undermine the credibility of the Warren Report. In March 1975 ABC aired, for the first time, the Zapruder film (film footage of the assassination taken by a spectator at the Dallas motorcade). Besides shocking the nation with its graphic detail, its image of Kennedy's head snapping back and to the left seemed to indicate a bullet fired from in front, rather than from the rear (where the School Book Depository was located).

Also in 1975, a Senate committee was shocked to learn that the CIA, with the assistance of the Mafia, had repeatedly tried to assassinate Castro during the early 1960s. Immediately this raised questions as to whether the Kennedy assassination might have been Castro's revenge, and what other information the CIA might have withheld from the Warren Commission.

In July came another bombshell: Oswald had been in contact with the FBI *before* the assassination. FBI agent James Hosty admitted that he'd received a note from Oswald shortly before the assassination and had been ordered to destroy it right after the assassination. In addition, the FBI had deleted Hosty's name, address, and telephone number when information from Oswald's address book was sent to the commission.

By 1977 the Warren Commission's credibility was in shreds, and Congress took it upon itself to launch a new full-scale investigation. In contrast to the Warren Report, the House Select Committee on Assassinations took its time, almost three years, and it explored the darkest recesses of the CIA, FBI, and other government agencies. In addition, the committee appointed panels of independent experts who used technology unavailable in 1964. These experts resolved many of the questions about autopsy reports, ballistics matches, firearms tests, and photographic evidence that critics of the Warren Report had raised over the previous 15 years.

After all this, the committee seemed convinced that, though the Warren Commission's investigation was seriously flawed, its conclusion was essentially correct: Oswald alone had killed Kennedy. Then, just before the committee was to issue its report, it heard from three acoustics experts who had analyzed the Dictabelt of a Dallas policeman's motorcycle. These experts informed the committee that they'd enhanced the recording and were 95 percent certain that they could detect four distinct shots. Because two of these shots came too close to each other for Oswald's rifle to have fired both, there must have been two riflemen. The experts also said that this additional shot came not from the Depository building behind Kennedy but from a grassy knoll in front of him.

The committee quickly revised its conclusion. In July 1979 it announced that since there were two gunmen, there must have been a conspiracy to kill JFK. But soon after the committee reached its conclusion, Dallas policeman H. B. McClain, whose radio was supposed

to be the source of the Dictabelt recordings, came forward with information that indicated that the recording hadn't been from his radio.
He'd raced along with the president's limousine to the hospital, sirens
blaring all the way—yet on the recording there are no sirens to be
heard. So, it seemed, the testimony on which the committee had based
its conclusion had been based on the careful analysis of a tape which
might have been recording a scene nowhere near and having nothing
to do with the assassination.

This latest twist had only a minor impact on public opinion. Overwhelmed by revelations that government agencies and officials had
lied—not only to the Warren Commission but about Vietnam and Watergate as well—the vast majority of the American public had become
convinced of a conspiracy. A 1983 *Newsweek* poll showed only 11 percent believed Oswald had acted alone. This conviction was hardened
with the release of Oliver Stone's 1991 movie, *JFK*, in which Jim Garrison reemerged in the form of actor Kevin Costner.

Yet, as reporters and a few historians continued to investigate the
case, their reports were increasingly less sensationalist. Though the
CIA and FBI clearly had covered up information relevant to the assassination, their primary interests had been, in the case of the CIA, to
conceal its efforts to assassinate Castro, not Kennedy; and in the case
of the FBI, to make sure its reputation wasn't tarnished by its failure to
recognize the threat Oswald posed. Gerald Posner's 1993 book, *Case
Closed*, was enthusiastically embraced, at least by the mainstream
press, for its thorough refutation of much of the evidence conspiracy
theorists had gathered over the past 30 years.

Posner was extremely effective in marshalling technical expertise,
some but by no means all of which had been presented to the House
committee. He presented, for example, a convincing explanation of the
"magic bullet." This bullet, identified as having been shot from Oswald's rifle, was found on the stretcher of Texas Governor John Connally, who'd been riding in the presidential limousine and who'd been
injured by one of the shots aimed at Kennedy. After analyzing the Zapruder film, the Warren Commission had determined that the time between when Kennedy was first hit and when Connally was first hit was
not sufficient for a single gunman to have fired two shots. Therefore,
the commission concluded, a single bullet had hit both.

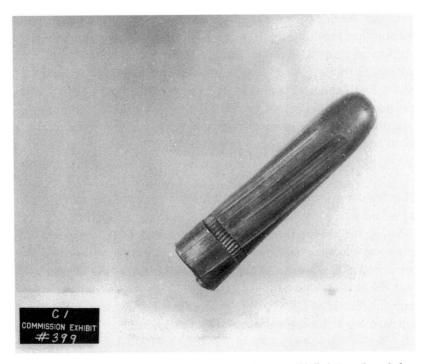

The "magic bullet," which the Warren Commission determined killed Kennedy and also went through Texas Governor John Connally. Critics of the commission couldn't believe a bullet could pass through two people and come out in such near-perfect condition. (Courtesy of National Archives.)

Critics of the commission wondered how a single bullet could have gone through both Kennedy and Connally and emerged, in nearly pristine condition, on Connally's stretcher. To conspiracy theorists, the mysterious appearance of a whole bullet from Oswald's gun smacked of a setup. A more likely explanation of how both Kennedy and Connally were hit one right after the other, they argued, was that a second bullet had been fired by a second gunman. But Posner's experts employed new technology to show that Connally's wounds and the intact bullet were the likely result of a bullet slowed by its passage through both Kennedy and Connally.

More than any technical evidence, however, what has undermined many conspiracy theories are flaws in their own logic. Consider the main candidates:

The CIA. The agency was capable of assassination—it had already admitted its attempts to kill Castro. And some high up in the agency could have feared that Kennedy, embarrassed by the CIA's bungling of the invasion of Cuba at the Bay of Pigs, might try to interfere with other CIA operations and curtail the agency's independence. *But:* This was the same Kennedy who had approved the CIA's plan to invade Cuba at the Bay of Pigs, who brought the world to the brink of nuclear war during the Cuban missile crisis, and who escalated U.S. involvement in Vietnam. Hardly a president likely to close down the Cold War or the CIA.

The KGB. Oswald was a Marxist who'd defected to Russia. *But:* Recently released KGB files indicate the Russians considered Oswald nothing but a nuisance and were delighted to be rid of him. Besides, Khrushchev would have been crazy to risk nuclear war for the sake of replacing Kennedy with the more hardline Lyndon Johnson.

Castro. Castro was aware that the CIA had tried to kill him, and in September 1963 he'd threatened revenge. *But:* Castro himself later insisted that it would have been "tremendous insanity" for him to order Kennedy's assassination and risk the full fury of all America. And, though he undoubtedly hated Kennedy, Castro wasn't insane. It is possible, however, that Oswald read of Castro's threat in the New Orleans *Times-Picayune* and took it upon himself to carry it out.

Anti-Castro Cubans. Many Cubans were unhappy Kennedy had backed away from stronger support during the Bay of Pigs fiasco; some extremists among them may have wanted the president dead. *But:* Oswald was a communist and an admirer of Castro. It's hard to imagine him working with Castro's enemies.

The Mafia. As attorney general, Robert Kennedy was cracking down on organized crime and a number of dons were undoubtedly incensed. Plus Jack Ruby had plenty of mob connections, albeit low-level ones. So, this theory went, Oswald had been hired to kill Kennedy and then Ruby had been hired to make sure Oswald didn't talk. Robert Blakey, chief counsel for the House Select Committee on Assassinations, thought the Mafia was behind the murder and the committee went so far as to discuss particular mobsters—in particular, teamster boss Jimmy Hoffa, Tampa godfather Santo Trafficante, and New Orleans godfather Carlos Marcello. All had spoken of hitting the president (at least according to witnesses of questionable reliability). *But:* There was no evidence that they'd done more than talk. Besides, couldn't the Mafia have found more reliable hitmen than Oswald and Ruby?

Of course, none of this *proves* there was no conspiracy. And, even if none of the above groups conspired with Oswald, there remains the possibility of a conspiracy between Oswald and other disaffected amateurs, some of whom may have had connections with the CIA, the Cubans, or the mob. For many Americans, Kennedy's death was so traumatic that it seemed *unfair* that he be the victim of Oswald alone; at least a conspiracy would imbue his death with some greater meaning. And, indeed, there are still too many unanswered questions about the assassination to rule out such a possibility.

But against the illogic of each particular conspiracy theory must be held up the logic, albeit twisted, of Oswald's own mind. Desperately ambitious and deeply tortured, Oswald may have seen the assassination as his chance to punish both America and Russia for not recognizing that he was a great man, destined to change the course of history—which, whether alone or with others, he most definitely did.

☆ To investigate further:

Report of the President's Commission on the Assassination of President John F. Kennedy. Washington, DC: United States Government Printing Office, 1964. Even those who disparage the findings of the Warren Commission have found its 26 volumes of testimony and evidence an invaluable source.

Weisberg, Harold. *Whitewash.* New York: Dell, 1966. The first in-depth attack on the Warren Report, this was originally self-published in 1965.

Lane, Mark. *Rush to Judgment.* Orlando: Holt, Rinehart and Winston, 1966. Another early attack on the Warren Report, this established a tradition of best-sellers on the subject. Lane also authored a 1991 book, *Plausible Denial,* which argued that the CIA killed Kennedy.

Epstein, Edward Jay. *Inquest.* New York: Viking, 1966. Of the early attacks on the Warren Report, this stands up best. Epstein presents a convincing case that the commission was unable to insulate itself from political and national security considerations. Epstein's 1968 book, *Counterplot* (Viking, NY), is also useful as a refutation of Garrison's theories, and his 1978 book, *Legend* (Readers Digest Press, NY), is an intriguing investigation of the CIA's efforts to establish whether Yuri Nosenko, a KGB officer who defected to the U.S. and who claimed to have supervised Oswald's case in Russia, was telling the truth. All three books were republished in a single volume, with new material, in a 1992 Carroll & Graf (NY) edition.

Ford, Gerald, and John Stiles. *Portrait of the Assassin*. New York: Ballantine, 1966. Consisting largely of reprints of testimony before the Warren Commission, this was the first book to defend the Warren Report. Then-Representative Ford was a member of the commission.

Summers, Anthony. *Conspiracy*. New York: McGraw-Hill, 1980. Claims that a conspiracy involved Oswald, anti-Castro exiles, Mafia members, and CIA renegades.

Lifton, David. *Best Evidence*. New York: Macmillan, 1980. Claims that Kennedy's body was stolen and surgically altered in order to eliminate evidence of a shooter in front of the president.

Blakey, G. Robert and Richard Billings. *The Plot to Kill the President*. New York: New York Times Press, 1981. Claims that the conspiracy involved organized crime and anti-Castro exiles. Blakey was counsel to the House Select Committee on Assassinations.

Davis, John. *Mafia Kingfish*. New York: McGraw-Hill, 1988.

Scheim, David. *Contract on America*. Silver Spring, Maryland: Argyle Press, 1983. Both Scheim and Davis (see above) claim the Mafia did it.

Garrison, Jim. *On the Trail of the Assassins*. New York: Sheridan Square Press, 1988. The New Orleans DA's story, which was the basis of Oliver Stone's movie *JFK*.

Posner, Gerald. *Case Closed*. New York: Random House, 1993. A thorough and compelling presentation of the case that Oswald acted alone.

Mailer, Norman. *Oswald's Tale*. New York: Random House, 1995. More a novelist's portrait of Oswald than an analysis of the evidence; nonetheless, the Oswald who emerges from the (often brilliant, if overly long) portrait is clearly a man capable of shooting the president by himself.

Chapter 46

What Happened at the Gulf of Tonkin?

Within hours of succeeding the slain John Kennedy, President Lyndon Johnson vowed: "I am not going to lose Vietnam."

That was easier said than done: the situation that Johnson inherited was already bleak and rapidly deteriorating. By early 1964 about 40 percent of South Vietnam was under Vietcong control, South Vietnamese soldiers were deserting at alarming rates, and the North Vietnamese were in the process of turning the Ho Chi Minh trail into a modern logistical system through which thousands of troops, weapons, ammunition, and other equipment were pouring south. The new regime in Saigon—the result of an assassination which preceded Kennedy's by three weeks—appeared to be even more corrupt and inept than its predecessors. Without a significant increase in U.S. support (there were currently just over 16,000 American troops there, none of whom were directly involved in the fighting), a communist victory seemed inevitable.

On the home front, Johnson was doing much better. His opponent in the upcoming election, Barry Goldwater, was talking about how satisfying it would be to lob a nuclear missile "down into the gents' room in the Kremlin." Voters panicked by Goldwater's extremism were flocking to the Democratic camp in droves, especially after the president promised that "we are not about to send American boys nine or ten thousand miles away from home to do what Asian boys ought to be doing for themselves."

But this presented a problem for Johnson. Unless he did something, Vietnam would fall. Yet, as the peace candidate, how could he escalate American involvement in the war?

Then, in the Gulf of Tonkin, off the coast of North Vietnam, came the solution to Johnson's problem. The administration reported that on August 2 and then again on August 4, while the U.S. destroyer *Maddox* was on a routine patrol mission in the Gulf, it was ambushed by North Vietnamese patrol boats. After the first attack, Johnson was restrained, promising only that patrols in the Gulf would continue and that U.S. forces would destroy any attackers. But a second attack called for a tougher response, which Johnson could now give without undermining his moderate image. He ordered planes from the nearby USS *Constellation* and USS *Ticonderoga* to attack the base of the North Vietnamese patrol boats and a supporting oil complex, and on August 5 they carried out this mission by dropping the first U.S. bombs on Vietnam. The mission was a success: eight boats were destroyed and twenty others damaged, and 90 percent of the oil depot was destroyed.

Still, Johnson and his advisers felt they might need more authority to respond quickly and decisively to the situation in Vietnam. On August 6, the president submitted to Congress legislation officially titled "Joint Resolution to Promote the Maintenance of International Peace and Security in Southeast Asia." The legislation, which was soon dubbed the Gulf of Tonkin Resolution, authorized the president "to take all necessary steps, including the use of armed force, to assist any member or protocol state of the Southeast Asia Collective Defense Treaty requesting assistance in defense of its freedom." On August 7, after Secretary of Defense Robert McNamara appeared before the Senate Committees on Foreign Relations and the House Foreign Affairs Committee to describe the unprovoked aggression against U.S. ships in the Gulf of Tonkin, the House approved the resolution by a vote of 416 to 0 and the Senate by a vote of 88 to 2.

Everything seemed to be going Johnson's way. The election was a landslide, with Johnson receiving 61.1 percent of the vote to Goldwater's 38.5 percent. And, in the Gulf of Tonkin Resolution, Congress had signed a blank check—a check which Johnson cashed in January 1965, when he ordered 100,000 ground troops to Vietnam.

The USS Maddox in 1947, seventeen years before it was involved in the battle—or rather, the alleged battle—that led to the escalation of the Vietnam War. (AP/Wide World Photos.)

But, as the United States became mired in the Vietnam War, questions arose, not only about whether we ought to be there, but also about how we got there. Some critics of the war claimed the U.S. ships had been the aggressors in the Gulf of Tonkin; others claimed that the battle there had never even taken place. Worse, some contended the administration knew these facts and intentionally misled Congress in order to extract from that body the power to go to war.

Historians of the Vietnam War, and of the Gulf of Tonkin incidents in particular, are fortunate that one of those who came to doubt the administration's story was Senator William Fulbright who, as chair of the Foreign Relations Committee, was in a position to investigate the matter.

Initially, Fulbright was one of the administration's most useful supporters, shepherding the Gulf of Tonkin Resolution through the Senate. When Senator Gaylord Nelson proposed amending the resolution to require congressional approval before the dispatch of troops to Vietnam, Fulbright convinced him that Johnson had no intention of sending the troops and that the amendment was therefore unnecessary. But as the war widened, so did the breach between Johnson and Fulbright and by 1966 Fulbright was openly critical of the president's foreign policy.

His suspicions about the Tonkin incidents were heightened in May of that year, when Assistant Secretary of State William Bundy, in secret testimony before the committee, said he'd written a draft similar to the Tonkin resolution in May or June 1964—several months before the incidents in the gulf. Bundy called the drafts "normal contingency planning," but it was clear that the administration had been preparing to escalate the war well before anything happened in the Gulf of Tonkin.

In September 1967 Fulbright authorized the committee staff to begin an inquiry into the Tonkin incidents, and he requested copies of the official logbooks of the *Maddox*. What emerged from the staff's investigations and the 1967–1968 hearings before the Foreign Relations Committee was a very different story from the one Johnson and McNamara had presented to the committee in 1964.

First, it became clear that the administration's claim that the *Maddox* was engaged in a routine patrol was at best misleading, if not downright false. Cables to and from the *Maddox* repeatedly referred to something called "34-A Operations," which, the Pentagon eventually admitted, included South Vietnamese raids on the islands in the vicinity of the U.S. ship. During the brief 1964 hearings before the passage of the resolution, McNamara had stated that "our Navy played absolutely no part in, was not associated with, was not aware of, any South Vietnamese actions, if there were any." Yet the cables indicated that the captain of the *Maddox*, John Herrick, had been aware of the operations and that his superiors might very well have been using the *Maddox* as a decoy to draw the North Vietnamese patrol boats away from the area of the 34-A Operations.

Second, though the *Maddox* had been pursued by North Vietnamese patrol boats on August 2, it was the *Maddox* that first opened fire. The North Vietnamese held their course and then did fire torpedoes at the destroyer. The torpedoes missed the destroyer but the destroyer's guns were on target; one of the North Vietnamese patrol boats sank and the others retreated back to port, briefly pursued by aircraft from the *Ticonderoga*.

It was the revelations about the August 4 incident, however, that most shocked the committee. It was this attack, remember, that had supposedly prompted Johnson to retaliate. Yet what the committee found was that the second battle almost certainly did not take place at all.

True, the *Maddox* and *Turner Joy* (another destroyer that had joined the *Maddox* after the August 2 attack) had fired four hundred rounds into the black night, dropped depth charges, and at one point tried to ram their attackers. *But not a single sailor on either vessel had actually seen or heard North Vietnamese ships or gunfire.* Nor had the pilots of the planes summoned from the *Constellation* seen the enemy. And though the *Maddox*'s sonars counted a total of 26 enemy torpedoes, none scored a hit. Even more suspicious, the sonar man on the *Turner Joy* hadn't reported any torpedoes.

Aboard the *Maddox*, Captain Herrick began to have doubts about the incident even before it ended. So once the shooting stopped, he conducted an experiment, putting the ship into high-speed turns. After each, the sonar man reported hearing torpedoes. Herrick concluded that most, if not all, of the *Maddox*'s torpedo reports were probably caused by the echo of outgoing sonar beams hitting the ship's rudders. He wired his superiors that the "entire action leaves many doubts" and suggested a "complete evaluation" before any further measures were taken.

But by then Johnson was in no mood to wait. Even as the Pentagon was sending urgent messages asking the Pacific commanders for evidence substantiating the attack, American bombers were already en route to their first North Vietnamese targets.

The navy did not invent the battle of August 4; as Herrick suggested soon after, the weather and an "overeager sonar man" might have accounted for the confusion. Nor did Johnson or McNamara invent the battle, as some later critics of the war contended; both may very well have thought the *Maddox* was attacked. But in their eagerness to use the incident to push through the congressional resolution, both ignored a good deal of evidence that the attack never took place, and both undeniably misled the public and the Congress when they described a complex and ambiguous incident as a clear, unprovoked attack. Only days after the resolution had passed, Johnson admitted he knew more than he'd told. In a private comment to George Ball, his undersecretary of state, he said: "Hell, those dumb, stupid sailors were just shooting at flying fish."

Some of the blame for what followed, however, must be shared by Congress. The Gulf of Tonkin Resolution was only the latest in a series of congressional abdications of its constitutional power to declare war. Congress had stood by as Truman sent troops to Korea without any congressional authorization; it had given permission for Eisenhower to deploy U.S. forces "as he deems it necessary" to protect Taiwan against a communist assault. Like Johnson, many Democrats in Congress were positioning themselves for the upcoming elections, and they feared Republicans would portray a vote against the resolution as unpatriotic or weak.

Later, Fulbright and others contended that they'd never intended to authorize a full-scale war in Asia. As the 1967 Senate Foreign Relations Committee report commented, "the prevailing attitude [in 1964] was not so much that Congress was granting or acknowledging the executive's authority to take certain actions but that it was expressing unity and support for the President in a moment of national crisis." Even hawks such as Senator John Stennis became disillusioned by the administration's broad use of the resolution, and in August 1966 Stennis told Secretary of State Dean Rusk that he thought the administration's deceptions might have invalidated the resolution. But Rusk dismissed the argument and Stennis's legal position was never tested. And, however much Fulbright and Stennis and others in Congress might have later regretted it, they could not deny that they'd voted for a resolution giving Johnson very broad powers; so broad, Johnson later quipped, that it was "like grandma's nightshirt—it covered everything."

☆ To investigate further:

Goulden, Joseph. *Truth Is the First Casualty.* Chicago: Rand McNally, 1969. The first of the revisionist accounts of the incident.

Galloway, John. *The Gulf of Tonkin Resolution.* Cranbury, NJ: Fairleigh Dickinson University Press, 1970. Especially useful for its inclusion of relevant documents such as the resolution itself, Johnson's addresses to the nation and to

Congress, and the transcripts of the Committee on Foreign Relations' 1968 hearings.

Windchy, Eugene. *Tonkin Gulf.* New York: Doubleday, 1971. A thorough reconstruction of the incidents.

Karnow, Stanley. *Vietnam.* New York: Viking, 1983. Given its broad scope, this cannot go into detail about the Tonkin gulf or many other aspects of the war; still, it remains the best general, balanced history of the war.

Stockdale, Jim and Sybil. *In Love and War.* New York: Harper & Row, 1984. Before becoming Ross Perot's 1992 running mate, Stockdale was a navy pilot who took off from the *Ticonderoga* to aid the *Maddox;* his book tells what he saw and what he didn't see—"no boats, no boat gunfire, no torpedo wakes— nothing but black sea and American firepower."

McNamara, Robert. *In Retrospect.* New York: Times Books, 1995. In retrospect, McNamara admits the escalation of the Vietnam War was an error, but he continues to deny (unconvincingly) that he or anyone in the administration deliberately misled Congress about the Gulf of Tonkin incidents.

Moïse, Edwin. *Tonkin Gulf and the Escalation of the Vietnam War.* Chapel Hill: University of North Carolina Press, 1996. The most recent and most thorough history of both the events and nonevents.

Chapter 47

Who Killed Malcolm X?

To most mainstream historians, the assassination of Malcolm X in February 1965 was the work of the Nation of Islam, the black nationalist religious group from which Malcolm had defected a year earlier. In the alternative presses, however, many black writers have questioned this explanation, arguing that U.S. intelligence forces played a role in the conspiracy. Compounding the problem has been the lack of extensive scholarship on Malcolm. In contrast to Martin Luther King Jr., whose life and times have been the subject of a number of major works, Malcolm is still best known through his own autobiography. And while *The Autobiography of Malcolm X* well deserves its place in the back pockets of radicals and rappers—and of any serious student of the period—it is by no means a definitive history of Malcolm's life. Nor, of course, could Malcolm cover his own death.

Does this mean Malcolm's death is destined to remain a mystery? Not entirely.

Whatever else its critics may say about the mainstream account of Malcolm's death, no one can question that the leadership of the Nation of Islam hated Malcolm X. To the Nation, Malcolm was not just an enemy but an apostate and a traitor. Malcolm had originally converted to the Nation of Islam in 1949, while serving a term in prison for burglary. The Nation redeemed him from a life of crime: no longer was he Malcolm Little (as he'd been born) or "Detroit Red" (as he'd called himself when he became a pimp and con artist); now he was Malcolm X. "The Muslim's 'X,'" he explained in the *Autobiography,* "symbolized the true African family name that he never could know [and] replaced the white slave master name . . . which some blue-eyed devil named Little had imposed upon my paternal forebears."

What the Nation offered Malcolm (and hundreds of thousands of other blacks) was a radical alternative theology. The Nation's leader, Elijah Muhammad, asserted that all whites were devils (created by an evil black scientist) whose world would be destroyed in the coming racial Armageddon. Malcolm's brilliant rhetorical skills propelled him to the forefront of the Nation, first as the minister of Harlem's Mosque Number 7, the largest in the country, and then as the Nation's national minister. He became the voice of black nationalism, the angry counterpoint to Martin Luther King Jr.'s preachings about Christian love.

So successful was Malcolm in his role as the Nation's mouthpiece that he became much better known to the press and public than Muhammad himself. This provoked the envy of others in the Nation, including its leader.

Doctrinal disagreements, too, were tearing apart Muhammad and Malcolm. Muhammad's apocalyptic vision provoked fears among whites but what he actually called for was not violence against white society but a complete withdrawal from it. Malcolm's impulses, on the other hand, were more activist. When Martin Luther King led the 1963 civil rights "March on Washington," for example, Muhammad, as part of his nonengagement policy, prohibited his followers from attending. Malcolm went along with Muhammad, *part* of the way: he derided the integrationists, branding the March the "Farce on Washington" and calling it more of a picnic than a protest. But, in blatant disregard of Muhammad's ban, Malcolm couldn't resist attending the March.

Malcolm's faith became even shakier when he learned that Muhammad had fathered a number of illegitimate children. Malcolm called a meeting of New York Muslim leaders, supposedly in order to prepare them in case the adulteries became public. In the eyes of many around Muhammad, however, this was just another example of Malcolm trying to undermine Muhammad's position.

The rift between Malcolm and Muhammad became public after John Kennedy's assassination. Muhammad had ordered all Muslims to refrain from commenting on the assassination. Malcolm, however, couldn't resist: asked for his comments, he first mentioned the many Third World leaders who'd been killed as a result of American intervention and concluded by saying that Kennedy's assassination was "a case of chickens coming home to roost."

Muhammad was outraged. Not that Muhammad was a fan of Kennedy (who was, after all, the president of a nation of white devils), but Malcolm had disobeyed his direct order. Muhammad suspended his chief minister for 90 days, and before the period was up, Malcolm had formally broken with the Nation and started his own rival organization, the Muslim Mosque, Inc.

Now Malcolm presented an even greater danger to the Nation. Not only was he preaching heresy, but he was heading a rival group and appealing to the Nation's own members. Nation ministers denounced Malcolm; he retaliated by going public with the stories of Muhammad's adulteries. So the Nation pushed up its rhetoric another notch. In a three-part series in the organization's newspaper, *Muhammad Speaks,* Minister Louis X of Boston—who had been recruited to the Nation by Malcolm and who later became known as Louis Farrakhan—condemned the "unbelievable treachery" of his former mentor. The December 4, 1964, issue of *Muhammad Speaks* contained the most suggestive attack of all: "Only those who wish to be led to hell, or to their doom, will follow Malcolm," Farrakhan wrote. "The die is set, and Malcolm shall not escape. . . . Such a man as Malcolm is worthy of death."

During the final year of his life, between his March 1964 break with the Nation and his February 1965 assassination, Malcolm was continually harassed by death threats. In his autobiography, he wrote: "Wherever I go . . . black men are watching every move I make, awaiting their chance to kill me. . . . I know that they have their orders. Anyone who chooses not to believe what I am saying doesn't know the Muslims in the NOI [Nation of Islam]."

Hostile, armed Muslims chased Malcolm in New York, Los Angeles, and Chicago. Just a week before his assassination, Malcolm's house in Queens was firebombed. Finally, on February 21, as he began to speak before his followers at the Audubon Ballroom in Harlem, he

Outside the Audubon Ballroom in Harlem, February 21, 1965. (UPI/Corbis-Bettmann.)

was shot to death by at least three and possibly (according to some witnesses in the crowd) five assassins.

☆ ☆ ☆

One of those assassins, Talmadge Hayer, was caught at the scene. The police subsequently arrested two other suspects, Norman 3X and Thomas 15X. Both Norman 3X and Thomas 15X were members of the Nation's mosque in Harlem; both had been accused of shooting Benjamin Brown, another Muslim minister who'd strayed from the fold; and both were placed at the Audubon by eyewitnesses. In March 1966 a jury found all three defendants guilty of murder.

Twelve years later, in 1978, Hayer confessed that he had, indeed, killed Malcolm, along with four fellow Muslims from the Nation's Newark Mosque Number 25. He'd stayed silent so long, he said, to protect Elijah Muhammad; since Muhammad had died in 1975, Hayer could now tell the truth. And, he emphasized, Norman 3X and Thomas 15X were completely innocent.

What to make of Hayer's story? The prosecution didn't buy it, nor did Judge Harold Rothwax, who decided that Hayer was merely trying to get his accomplices off the hook.

But many historians have found Hayer's story convincing. Clearly, Hayer was guilty—and now that he'd admitted he'd done it for the sake of the Nation, his motive was equally clear. As for Norman 3X and Thomas 15X, the case against them had never been as strong as that against Hayer. No physical evidence placed them anywhere near the Audubon on the night of Malcolm's murder and, of the hundreds at the Audubon, only a handful had identified them—this in spite of the fact that Norman 3X and Thomas 15X were well-known members of the Nation (and thus just the type of person for whom Malcolm's followers and bodyguards would have been on the lookout). Hayer's confession swayed Peter Goldman, author of the best biography of Malcolm written to date. In the original 1973 edition of his book, Goldman argued that Norman 3X and Thomas 15X were guilty but in the 1979 revision he admitted it was likely they were innocent.

All three men convicted of the murder—Hayer, Norman 3X, and Thomas 15X—have now been paroled and, barring some deathbed confessions, it seems likely that history's verdict will overturn that of the jury. Hayer was certainly guilty; Norman 3X and Thomas 15X were probably not. But more pressing historical questions remain: Who ordered the assassination? Was it Elijah Muhammad? Was it Louis Farrakhan? Or, as Hayer maintained, did he and his accomplices act for the sake of the Nation but without direct orders from any higher-ups?

Elijah Muhammad always denied giving any order to kill Malcolm. So, too, has Louis Farrakhan, though he has acknowledged that his rhetoric contributed to the atmosphere that led to the assassination. But, Farrakhan and others in the Nation have stressed that investigators wanting a full understanding of Malcolm's death should look beyond the Nation. The Nation of Islam, they argue, was not the only organization that wanted Malcolm dead.

The FBI's history of harassing Martin Luther King Jr.—which included secretly recording his extramarital affairs and threatening to send the tapes to his wife unless he committed suicide—was well documented by the 1975 Senate Select Committee on Intelligence Activities. Unfortunately, the bureau's campaigns against the Nation and against Malcolm have not been as fully investigated. Many of the files remain classified, and those that have been released include critical deletions.

But from the files that have been released, a great deal has been learned. FBI surveillance of the Nation dates back to 1956, and its actions included some of the same types of dirty tricks used against King. Between 1959 and 1962, the bureau channeled embarrassing information about Elijah Muhammad's finances and sex life to journalists. When this failed to slow the Nation's growth (perhaps because its members were not quite so puritanical or voyeuristic as J. Edgar Hoover and his agents), the bureau sent anonymous letters with additional information on Muhammad's sex life to "selected individuals" in the Nation hierarchy. Who these individuals were has been deleted from the files, but it's reasonable to assume that Malcolm was among them, and that some of the details about Muhammad's sex life that so upset him came from the FBI.

The files also indicate that at least one and possibly two FBI agents had infiltrated the Nation's top leadership, and that their job was to "plant the seed of dissension" within the organization. A February 1964 memo suggested a move that "could possibly widen the rift between Muhammad and Little and possibly result in Little's expulsion from the NOI." Again, the specifics are deleted from the file, so it's impossible to know what the plan was or even whether it was enacted. But we do know that, as the FBI desired, the rift between Muhammad and Malcolm widened.

Until more FBI files are declassified, it's impossible to say exactly what role the bureau played in Malcolm's assassination. Some, like Farrakhan, have speculated that it was an FBI agent planted in the Nation who gave the order to murder Malcolm. At this point, such speculation remains just speculation; there is no proof that anyone in the FBI actually participated in any way in the murder plot. But—and the revelations about the FBI's campaign against King and others may make this seem less shocking and appalling than it ought to be—it's quite clear that, from J. Edgar Hoover down to his agents in the field, the FBI considered its mission to be one of escalating the feud between Malcolm and the Nation. That the FBI might instead have used some of its intelligence and manpower to save Malcolm's life seems never to have occurred to anyone in the bureau.

An odd epilogue to this sordid tale must have brought at least some satisfaction to Farrakhan. Both Betty Shabazz, Malcolm's widow, and Quibilah Shabazz, his daughter, had blamed Farrakhan for Malcolm's death. In 1995 the FBI arrested Quibilah Shabazz, charging that she had tried to hire a hit man to kill Farrakhan and avenge her father's death. The key witness was a long-time government informant of dubious reliability, and prosecutors and defense lawyers ultimately struck a deal that spared them a trial and let Quibilah Shabazz off with a two-year probation.

Before the deal was struck, however, Farrakhan and Betty Shabazz spoke out together against the government's case. Ironically, this latest federal intervention in the life and death of Malcolm X had brought about what the 30 years since the assassination had not—a reconciliation between Malcolm's family and the Nation of Islam.

☆ To investigate further:

X, Malcolm, as told to Alex Haley. *The Autobiography of Malcolm X*. New York: Grove Press, 1994. A classic of African American letters.

Goldman, Peter. *The Death and Life of Malcolm X*. Champaign: University of Illinois Press, 1979. Though Goldman is a little too reluctant to accuse the authorities of wrongdoing, this is nonetheless the best biography of Malcolm. In the original 1973 edition, Goldman argues that Norman 3X and Thomas 15X were guilty; in the 1979 edition, confronted by Hayer's second confession, he concedes the others were probably innocent.

Garrow, David. *The FBI and Martin Luther King, Jr.* New York: Norton, 1981. The revelations about the FBI's war against King had come out during Senate hearings, so this book added little in the way of facts. But Garrow's analysis of the FBI's motives are provocative and convincing.

Carson, Clayborne. *Malcolm X: The FBI File*. New York: Carroll & Graf, 1991. Though it *is* missing a lot of files that have been released (as well as many still classified), what *is* here is at least suggestive of the mass of intelligence and gossip collected by the FBI.

Breitman, George, Herman Porter, and Baxter Smith. *The Assassination of Malcolm X*. New York: Pathfinder, 1991. Originally published in 1976, this is a Marxist view of the assassination. The authors argue that, after leaving the Nation, Malcolm was evolving toward socialism (for which there is some evidence) and that this provoked the CIA into some role in the assassination (for which the evidence is very circumstantial).

Perry, Bruce. *Malcolm*. Barrytown, NY: Station Hill Press, 1991. A controversial psychobiography that interprets Malcolm's life and politics as a response not to white racism but to an abused childhood. Though his analysis is often simplistic, Perry raises many issues ignored by other scholars.

Evanzz, Karl. *The Judas Factor.* New York: Thunder's Mouth Press, 1992. The Judas of the title is John Ali, a top-level Nation figure who Evanzz thinks conspired with the CIA and FBI to murder Malcolm. Evanzz raises some valid questions but doesn't answer them convincingly.

Friedly, Michael. *Malcolm X: The Assassination.* New York: Carroll & Graf, 1992. The most thorough statement of the position that the Nation of Islam was responsible for Malcolm's death, and that the FBI (although it was actively working to discredit the Nation and Malcolm) did not in any way participate in the plot.

Lee, Spike, with Ralph Wiley. *By Any Means Necessary.* New York: Hyperion, 1992. Lee's account of the making of his film about Malcolm includes his tantalizingly suggestive but ultimately frustrating interviews with Farrakhan and others involved in the case.

Gardell, Mattias. *In The Name of Elijah Muhammad.* Durham, NC: Duke University Press, 1996. The fullest account of the Nation of Islam's ideology and theology, this also includes the best account of how the FBI attempted to incite the Muslims to violence against one another.

Chapter 48

Who Won the Tet Offensive?

Tet, the lunar New Year, is a time to celebrate peace, and in 1968 both sides in the Vietnam War agreed to the traditional truce. So there was some surprise, when, on the evening of January 31, the North Vietnamese and Vietcong attacked. But the true surprise was the scope and intensity of the attacks. Just two months earlier, General William Westmoreland, the commander of U.S. troops in Vietnam, had stated that the Americans were winning the war, that American troop withdrawals might begin within two years, and that he could see "some light at the end of the tunnel." Come Tet, some seventy thousand communist soldiers stormed into more than one hundred cities and towns throughout South Vietnam, including Saigon, where they blew a hole into the wall of the U.S. embassy. Fighting was especially intense around Khe Sanh, a U.S. base in the northwest of South Vietnam where the communists had pinned down six thousand Marines.

The shockwaves were felt across America. Critics of U.S. policy in Vietnam compared the siege of Khe Sanh to that of Dienbienphu, where in 1954 the Vietnamese defeated a French garrison and forced France to abandon its former colony. "The parallels are there for all to see," Walter Cronkite told his CBS audience in early February. The light at the end of the tunnel, many commented, must have been a train headed straight at Westmoreland.

Fleeing the Tet fighting in
Hue, despite the blown bridge.
(National Archives.)

By mid-March, Senator Eugene McCarthy had come within three hundred votes of defeating the incumbent president, Lyndon Johnson, in the New Hampshire primary, and Robert Kennedy, a much stronger peace candidate, had entered the race. On March 31, Johnson ordered a halt to bombing, offered to negotiate with the communists, and—less than four years after having come out on top of one of the largest landslides in American history—declared he would not seek re-election. In May, peace talks began in Paris.

Though the talks would drag on for five years, it was clear that the Tet offensive was the war's turning point. After Tet, America was no longer looking for victory but merely a way out of Vietnam, or as President Richard Nixon put it, a "peace with honor." Except for its importance, however, there was very little else about Tet on which Americans agreed. For Vietnam doves, Tet was the moment when Americans, overwhelmed by the communists' resolve, realized the war could not be won. For hawks, not only could the war be won but the battle *was* won; in fact, they argued, Tet was a major military victory for South Vietnam and the United States, which was seen as a defeat only because of the distortions of liberals in the government and media.

The question of who won the Tet offensive, thus, went right to the heart of the question of who lost Vietnam.

Not surprisingly, among those who insisted that Tet was an American victory were those in charge of the American war effort.

"There is no doubt in my mind that the Tet offensive was a military debacle for the North Vietnamese and the Viet Cong," wrote Johnson in his 1971 memoirs. "But the defeat the Communists suffered did not have the telling effect it should have had largely because of what we did to ourselves."

"Militarily, the offensive was foredoomed to failure," agreed Westmoreland in his 1976 book. "In terms of public opinion, press and television would transform what was undeniably a catastrophic military defeat for the enemy into a presumed debacle for Americans and South Vietnamese."

To Johnson and Westmoreland, Tet was the North's "last gasp," a desperate effort to salvage a losing cause. After the initial surprise, American and South Vietnamese troops quickly routed the communists. The impact of the hole in the embassy wall was purely psychological; the communists never actually captured the compound. Only in Khe Sanh and Hue, both near the northern border, did the battle last more than a few days. In Hue, it took twenty-five days of house-to-house combat to rout the communists. At Khe Sanh, the siege lasted until early April, but the communists began to pull back in March. Unlike the French trapped at Dienbienphu, the Americans at Khe Sanh could count on the air force to carry in supplies and reinforcements, and even more crucially, to drop tons of explosives over the surrounding enemy troops. Westmoreland estimated communist losses there at between ten and fifteen thousand, compared to 205 marines. Overall, military analysts put enemy losses near sixty thousand, a devastating setback, especially for the southern communists—the Vietcong—who from then on played a comparatively small role in the war.

Johnson and Westmoreland blamed the press for turning a military victory into a psychological defeat.

"There was a great deal of emotional and exaggerated reporting of the Tet offensive in our press and our television," wrote Johnson. "The media seemed to be in competition as to who could provide the most lurid and depressing accounts. . . . The American people and even a number of officials in government, subjected to this daily barrage of near panic, began to think that we must have suffered a defeat."

There were plenty of examples of what hawks considered antiwar and defeatist coverage. On February 2, numerous newspapers, including the *New York Times* and *Washington Post,* featured on their front page a searing Associated Press photo of a South Vietnamese policeman with his arm stretched out and his gun at the head of a Vietcong captive about to be executed. On February 6, Art Buchwald parodied Westmoreland's optimism by recounting his exclusive interview with General George Armstrong Custer at the Battle of Little Bighorn. "We have the Sioux on the run," Custer told Buchwald. On February 7, Peter Arnett built a widely read AP story around a quote from an unnamed American major who, describing the shattered city of Ben Tre, explained that "it became necessary to destroy the town to save it." On February 27, Walter Cronkite—the most respected newsman and perhaps the most respected man in the country—said he was certain that "the bloody experience of Vietnam is to end in a stalemate," and called for negotiations.

The most thorough study of Tet media coverage was made by former *New York Times* and *Washington Post* correspondent Peter Braestrup. Braestrup's *Big Story* was published in 1977. In it, he lashed into his colleagues for taking Hanoi's statements at face value while questioning those of the Americans and South Vietnamese, and for promulgating speculation rather than facts. "At best, this was over-wrought instant analysis; at worst, it was vengeful exploitation of a crisis," he wrote. "Rarely has contemporary crisis-journalism turned out, in retrospect, to have veered so widely from reality."

Unlike Westmoreland, Braestrup did not accuse the press of bias. Rather, he blamed its distortions on limited resources and the pressure to sensationalize. Reporters focused on the embassy attack, for example, not just because it was a symbol of America's tottering power, but also because it took place in Saigon, where most of the correspondents were stationed. They focused on Hue and Khe Sanh, not just because that was where the enemy continued to hold the initiative, but also be-cause that's where the heaviest fighting was. They focused on the dev-astation wrought by American and South Vietnamese counterattacks for the same reason reporters are drawn to fires and earthquakes: as many an editor has put it, if it bleeds, it leads.

☆ ☆ ☆

Westmoreland and other critics of the press tended to downplay the many good reasons reporters had to distrust official sources. After all, these were the same American officials who had been proclaiming for years that victory was imminent. Westmoreland's credibility further plummeted in February, when he requested an additional 206,000 troops. The general argued that he needed the troops to take advantage of the opportunity presented by the Tet offensive, but many could not help but wonder: If Tet was such a great victory, why did the military need 206,000 more men?

As the war continued and after it ended, the military's credibility continued to erode. In 1969, investigative reporter Seymour Hersh broke the story of the My Lai massacre, during which U.S. troops killed hundreds of unarmed citizens. The investigation also raised questions about whether the huge body counts during Tet—which American officials pointed to as a sign that they had won the campaign—included civilians as well as soldiers. In 1982, a CBS exposé charged that Westmoreland doctored intelligence reports of enemy numbers to create the illusion of success. Westmoreland sued the network, but dropped the case after various military officials testified the report was accurate.

The Pentagon Papers, published in 1970 in spite of the Nixon administration's effort to suppress them, revealed that many top-level Johnson aides, military and civilian, had been extremely dissatisfied with the way the war was going. They had reached their conclusions, not because of any press reports, but through their own observations and analyses.

In 1987, Robert Komer, who had been one of the general's top deputies, recalled the mood in 1968: "What really surprised us about Tet—and boy it was a surprise, lemme tell you, I was there at Westy's elbow—was that they abandoned the time-tested Mao rural strategy where the guerillas slowly strangle the city, and only at the end do they attack the seat of imperial power directly. At Tet they infiltrated right through our porous lines."

Komer maintained that the Americans and South Vietnamese ultimately won the battle. But he conceded the offensive shook his bosses. "I mean Washington panicked," he said. "LBJ panicked. Bus Wheeler, Chairman of the Joint Chiefs, panicked."

The public, too, had had enough. Even before Tet, support for the war had been slipping, and not just among doves. Many hawks, frustrated by policies that made the military fight a war "with one arm tied behind its back," had decided it was time to get out of Vietnam.

For dove and hawk alike, the Tet offensive signaled that current strategies were not working.

"It did not matter to the American public that the platoon of sappers did not actually break into and seize the embassy building," wrote Neil Sheehan in 1988. "It did not matter in the United States that the Vietnamese Communists failed to topple the Saigon regime and foment a rebellion by the urban population. . . . What mattered to the American public was that this defeated enemy could attack anywhere and was attacking everywhere more fiercely than ever before. . . . Nothing had been achieved by the outpouring of lives and treasure and the rending of American society. The assurances the public had been given were the lies and vaporings of foolish men."

The press, then, did not deserve the blame (or the credit, depending on your perspective) for the way the public and the administration reacted to Tet. While newspaper and television reports surely had some influence, it was just as likely that many reporters—even Cronkite—were merely reflecting the increasingly prevalent disillusionment with the war.

"Rather than the press," wrote historian Clarence Wyatt in 1993, "it was the military policies of the United States and North Vietnamese governments that determined public support, or the lack thereof, for the war. . . . In the end, the American people simply tired of pouring more of their blood and money into Vietnam."

Unlike the Americans, the North Vietnamese were willing to pour into the war everything they had. They were willing to incur huge losses that, if not quite as great as Westmoreland's inflated body counts, were nonetheless a severe blow, especially to the Vietcong. For the communists, any sacrifice was worthwhile, if it struck a blow against the Americans and the South Vietnamese, as Tet surely did.

In a 1990 interview with historian Stanley Karnow, General Vo Nguyen Giap, who masterminded the Tet offensive, explained its rationale. "We attacked the brains of the enemy, its headquarters in Saigon, showing that it was not inviolable," Giap told Karnow. "Our forces destroyed large quantities of the enemy's weapons and other equipment and crushed several of its elite units. We dramatized that we were neither exhausted nor on the edge of defeat, as Westmoreland claimed. . . . We wanted to carry the war into the families of America—to demonstrate . . . that if Vietnamese blood was being spilled, so was American blood. We did all this, and more and more Americans renounced the war."

Giap was undeniably eager to justify his decisions and to claim he foresaw all of their repercussions, at home and abroad. Most likely, Giap hoped Tet would be a decisive military victory, which it most definitely was not. But his main point was credible. Devoted as he and his followers were to their cause, he was willing to sacrifice thousands of lives to strike a psychological blow against the Americans and South Vietnamese. That he did, and there is thus no reason to doubt that he therefore considered the offensive a success.

In another interview with Karnow, General Tran Do, the deputy commander of communist forces in the south during the Tet offensive, offered what seemed a completely candid analysis. "We didn't achieve our main objective, which was to spur uprisings throughout the south," the general told Karnow. "Still, we inflicted heavy casualties on the Americans and their puppets, and that was a big gain for us. As for making an impact in the United States, it had not been our intention—but it turned out to be a fortunate result."

☆ To investigate further:

Johnson, Lyndon. *The Vantage Point.* New York: Holt, Rinehart and Winston, 1971. A surprisingly frank look at presidential decision-making.

Westmoreland, William. *A Soldier Reports.* Garden City, New York: Doubleday & Company, 1976. He could have won the war—or so he says.

Oberdorfer, Don. *Tet!* New York: Da Capo Press, 1984. Originally published in 1971 and still one of the best accounts of the battles, political as well as military.

Braestrup, Peter. *Big Story.* New Haven, Connecticut: Yale University Press, 1983. An abridged edition of Braestrup's two-volume 1977 indictment of the media's Tet coverage.

Sheehan, Neil. *A Bright Shining Lie.* New York: Random House, 1988. A riveting history of the war (and of America's changing views of it), as seen through the life of military adviser John Paul Vann.

Wyatt, Clarence. *Paper Soldiers.* New York: W. W. Norton & Company, 1993. In contrast to the claims of Westmoreland and others, Wyatt argues that most of the time the press did *not* question official military reports.

McMahon, Robert, editor. *Major Problems in the History of the Vietnam War.* Lexington, Massachusetts: D. C. Heath and Company, 1995. Includes documents and essays on Tet, among them Johnson's news conference of February 2, 1968, General Earle Wheeler's military evaluation of February 27, an early communist evaluation of the offensive, and Komer's recollections.

Gettleman, Marvin, et al., editors. *Vietnam and America*. New York: Grove Press, 1995. Also a documentary history, this includes Westmoreland's report of June 30, 1968, excerpts from the Pentagon Papers pertaining to Tet, Johnson's announcement that he would curtail bombing and not run for re-election, and Hersh's report on the My Lai massacre.

Gilbert, Marc Jason, and William Head, editors. *The Tet Offensive*. Westport, Connecticut: Praeger, 1996. A collection of essays on the political and military issues surrounding Tet.

Karnow, Stanley. *Vietnam*. New York: Penguin Books, 1997. Originally published in 1983 as a companion to an Emmy Award–winning PBS series, this remains the most comprehensive and balanced history of the war.

Chapter 49

Who Killed Martin Luther King Jr.?

I 've been to the mountaintop," proclaimed Martin Luther King Jr., speaking to a crowd of striking black sanitation workers on the day before he died. "And I've looked over. And I've seen the Promised Land. I may not get there with you. But I want you to know tonight, that we, as a people, will get to the Promised Land."

Whatever premonitions King had of his death, he could not have known just how vulnerable he was there in Memphis. He could not have known, for example, that the FBI and Memphis police had been informed of three death threats within the past few days, yet had chosen—reversing their normal policies—not to inform him. He probably did not know that Memphis police would, later that same day, reassign his security detail elsewhere, and that the next day—April 4, 1968, the day of the assassination—they would pull back the tactical units stationed around the Lorraine Motel, where he was staying and on a balcony of which he would soon be shot. He surely could not have known that Edward Redditt, a black detective assigned to watch King from the fire station across the street, would be ordered off duty just hours before the assassination, supposedly because the police had received a threat to *his* life. And of course King could not have known that, hours after his death, in spite of having a description of a suspect's car, police would not yet have issued an all-points bulletin.

Even before King was buried, many suspected a conspiracy. (National Archives.)

No wonder, then, that talk of a conspiracy involving the FBI and police began right after King's murder. The arrest two months later of James Earl Ray did not quiet the conspiracy talk. Investigators had collected, to be sure, a good deal of evidence against Ray. Just a few hours before the assassination, he had rented a room with a view of the Lorraine Motel, and witnesses said the shot came from the direction of that room. Within minutes of the murder, police found a bundle in a nearby doorway; it included a gun with Ray's fingerprints on it. Police concluded Ray dropped the bundle as he fled the scene.

It was nonetheless hard to believe that a hitherto small-time robber, known to police only for having broken out of prison, had managed to strip away the police capabilities for protection and pursuit. Besides, for each piece of evidence against him, skeptics (and Ray) had answers. Most had to do with a shadowy character he claimed to know only as "Raoul." According to Ray, he met Raoul in July 1967, when the latter enlisted him to smuggle various materials across the Canadian and Mexican borders. With no other way to support himself (he was, after all, an escaped convict), Ray followed Raoul's instructions. Indeed, Raoul pretty much directed all of his movements from then on. It was Raoul who told him to buy the gun and rent the room across from the Lorraine, and it must have been Raoul, Ray asserted, who killed King or hired someone to do it. When Ray arrived on the scene and saw the area was swarming with police, he took off (again, because he was an escapee), but it wasn't until he was well out of Memphis that he learned a murder had been committed, let alone that the victim was Martin Luther King. Ray thought he was transporting the gun as part of some gunrunning scheme. He was, he insisted, merely a patsy.

In March 1969, Ray pleaded guilty to the murder and was sentenced to ninety-nine years in prison. Within hours, though, he recanted, claiming that he'd been worn down by pressure from prosecutors and his own lawyer, and that his plea was the only way he could avoid the death penalty. From that point on, Ray—and many others—never wavered in maintaining his innocence.

Ray's professions of innocence might have faded, at least from public view, had it not been for a startling series of revelations about the FBI and King. These emerged from a series of Justice Department and congressional investigations held during the early 1970s.

In 1975, former assistant FBI director William Sullivan revealed that the bureau had targeted King in what amounted to a secret war in which "no holds were barred." This included extensive taping, ostensibly to guard against communist infiltration of the civil rights movement. Agents found little evidence of that, but they found plenty of dirt on King, recording what were clearly the sounds of King having sex in a hotel room with someone other than his wife.

Bureau chief J. Edgar Hoover, whose animosity toward King was both racial and political, first tried to leak the findings to various newspapers. None bit. Hoover then took matters into his own hands. In January 1965 he ordered a spliced-together version of various bedroom tapes sent to the civil rights leader, along with an anonymous letter. The letter read in part: "King, look into your heart. You know you are a complete fraud and a great liability to all of us Negroes. . . . You are a colossal fraud and an evil, vicious one at that. . . . There is but one way out for you. You better take it before your filthy, abnormal fraudalant [sic] self is bared to the nation."

Coretta Scott King opened the tape, listened to it, and quickly passed it on to her husband. Neither had any doubt that the FBI was behind this. "They are out to break me," King said (and this, too, the FBI caught on tape).

No one aware of these dirty tricks could doubt the FBI's animosity toward King. And it did not seem such a large step from attempting to blackmail him into committing suicide to conspiring to murder him. By the mid-1970s, it was almost impossible not to suspect the FBI of some role in King's death. Former King aide Jesse Jackson later wrote: "The government, under the direction of FBI Director Hoover, did have a . . . program to discredit, disrupt, and destroy the Black movement. . . . Thus, while I do not know, I have a strong sense that there was a government conspiracy to kill Dr. Martin Luther King, Jr."

Suspicion of the FBI extended well beyond King's supporters. Said ex-FBI agent Arthur L. Murtagh: "It defies and assaults reason to think that the people who have been engaged in a ten-year-long vendetta against Dr. King are the ones who should be investigating his death."

Congress, therefore, decided to take matters into its own hands. In 1977, the House Select Committee on Assassinations called Ray to Washington for a series of interviews. These were briefly halted in June, when Ray and five other prisoners scaled a fifteen-foot wall and escaped from prison, but he was captured two days later. Back in Washington, Ray was equally ineffective in making a case that he deserved a new trial. He could not explain why his stories about Raoul had changed over time; initially, he had claimed that he drove Raoul away from the scene of the crime; now he said he was blocks away from the Lorraine when King was murdered and never saw Raoul after the murder. Nor could Ray come up with anyone who could corroborate any of his meetings with Raoul. In 1978, the committee concluded Raoul did not exist. It was Ray, not Raoul, who shot King.

Under the committee's questioning, Detective Redditt's story also fell apart. Redditt admitted that he had exaggerated his role in protecting King. In fact, his role at the firehouse was not to provide security, but to conduct surveillance. And Redditt's superiors had removed him from duty because there had indeed been a threat on his life. Similarly, it turned out, the tactical units near the Lorraine had been stationed there to prevent the striking sanitation workers from rioting, not to protect King. They left, as did the security detail, at the request of King aides, who were understandably suspicious of police intentions.

Concluded the committee: "No federal, state, or local agency was involved in the assassination of Dr. King."

That did not necessarily mean that Ray acted entirely on his own. The committee *did* suspect a conspiracy, albeit one without either the government or Raoul. There were plenty of others who wanted the civil rights leader dead, among them a racist St. Louis attorney named

John Sutherland. Sutherland, the committee learned, had a standing offer of $50,000 for anyone who killed King. Ray may have heard about the offer through his brother John, who managed a St. Louis tavern known as the Grape Vine. In fact, the committee suspected that Ray's brother might also have been part of the conspiracy.

Ray apparently never tried to collect Sutherland's $50,000, but the money may have been part of his motive. Or Ray could have been motivated by his own racism, of which there was plenty of evidence. Back in 1957, for example, while he was serving his sentence for robbery, Ray was offered a transfer to the prison farm. Most inmates preferred the farm because it allowed them more freedom. Ray, according to a prison report, turned down the transfer because the farm, unlike the rest of the prison, was integrated.

The committee, while blaming Ray and perhaps a small group of other racists, did not entirely let the FBI or Memphis police off the hook. Committee members rightly questioned why law enforcement authorities focused so much attention on their surveillance of King and so little on protecting him. The police, after all, could have overruled his aides' request that they withdraw. The police knew (as King did not) that threats had been made on his life. The police did not hesitate to remove Redditt from the scene when threats were made on his life, even though the detective objected. A security detail might not have prevented the type of sniper attack that killed King, but a more visible police presence might have deterred the killer. A quick APB might also have caught Ray before he left town.

At the very least, then, the FBI and police were incompetent. More likely, latent racism guided the decisions of some top officials. Protecting King was certainly not a priority for J. Edgar Hoover. To Hoover and all too many others, the danger King faced mattered much less than the danger he posed.

Conspiracy theories continued to proliferate, in spite of the committee's conclusion. During the 1990s, Ray's lawyer, William Pepper, promulgated one of the most far-ranging. It implicated not just the FBI and police, but also the CIA, Canadian and British intelligence, the Green Berets and National Guard, the Mafia, and the White House. Pepper charged that a military sniper team arrived in Memphis the day of the assassination, supposedly as part of a backup plan in case Raoul failed to murder King. Pepper was unable to learn more, he said, because the team's commander, Captain Billy Eidson, was dead. Pepper's credibility plummeted when Eidson appeared to deny the allegations.

Some sort of Mafia connection seemed likely in 1993, when Loyd Jowers, who owned the restaurant below the rooming house where Ray rented a room, announced that a produce dealer with mob ties had paid him $100,000 to hire the assassin. Jowers also said that Raoul (still without a last name) was in his restaurant on the day of the assassination, and that the assassin had fired from the restaurant, not the rooming house. Jowers refused to say more until prosecutors granted him immunity.

Members of the King family, who had always suspected a broad conspiracy, urged prosecutors to do so. They were convinced Ray was, as he claimed, nothing but a patsy. This led to a surreal meeting in 1997 between Ray and Dexter King, one of Martin Luther King Jr.'s four children. Dexter King emerged from the meeting as the foremost advocate of the man convicted for killing his father. In 1998, when Ray died in prison, some King relatives were among the mourners.

Dexter King urged prosecutors to grant Jowers immunity. "They don't want him to talk," he said. "They're contributing to suppressing the truth."

But prosecutors were convinced Jowers's "confession" was motivated by potential book and movie deals. "From investigating it, it looks real bogus," prosecutor John Campbell said of Jowers's story. "If we get pressured into giving him immunity, that would be a disaster. Overnight, the value of Jowers's story would skyrocket. With immunity, he could say anything he wants to. Hell, he could hold a press conference and there would be nothing anybody could do about it. . . . We are not going to help someone, or a group of people, make a financial killing with a false story."

The King family, now represented by Pepper, decided to go to court on their own. They brought a wrongful death suit against Jowers, and in 1999, after a four-week civil trial, a jury found that the restaurant owner was part of a conspiracy. The jury awarded the family $100, the token amount they'd requested, and the Kings donated the money to Memphis sanitation workers.

"It's like triumph over tragedy," said Dexter King. "History will have to be rewritten."

Most historians disagreed. However much the Kings (and the jurors) might have wanted to believe Jowers, historians generally considered the trial a farce. What made it pointless was that both sides presented essentially the same case. As plaintiffs, the Kings argued that Jowers was part of a conspiracy; Jowers's defense team agreed. No one presented the evidence that Jowers might have made up the story in order to sell it, and no one presented the state's case against Ray. King biographer David Garrow said the trial would have "zero" impact on history.

In 2000, the Justice Department agreed. After yet another investigation—prompted at least in part by pressure from the King family to take another look at the Jowers allegations—the department "found nothing to disturb the 1969 judicial determination." In other words, though a few others may have helped him, Ray was, as he pleaded in 1969, guilty.

☆ To investigate further:

Weisberg, Harold. *Frame-Up*. New York: Outerbridge & Dienstfrey, 1971. Weisberg was one of the first to argue that Ray (and also Lee Harvey Oswald) did not act alone.

Lane, Mark, and Dick Gregory. *Murder in Memphis*. New York: Thunder's Mouth Press, 1993. Originally published in 1977, when Lane was Ray's lawyer.

Garrow, David. *The FBI and Martin Luther King, Jr.* New York: W. W. Norton, 1981. Not just what the FBI did to destroy King, but why.

Garrow, David. *Bearing the Cross*. New York: William Morrow, 1986. A Pulitzer Prize–winning biography of King.

Branch, Taylor. *Parting the Waters*. New York: Simon & Schuster, 1988. A Pulitzer Prize–winning history of the Civil Rights movement that is as dramatic as the era it covers. So is Branch's 2001 sequel, *Pillar of Fire*.

Melanson, Philip. *The Murkin Conspiracy*. New York: Praeger, 1989. The CIA did it.

Ray, James Earl. *Who Killed Martin Luther King?* Washington, D.C.: National Press Books, 1992. Raoul did it.

Pepper, William. *Orders to Kill*. New York: Carroll & Graf Publishers, 1995. Everyone did it.

Posner, Gerald. *Killing the Dream*. New York: Random House, 1998. Ray did it—really.

Frady, Marshall. *Martin Luther King, Jr.* New York: Viking, 2002. A fine short biography, as long as you don't use it as an excuse for not reading Garrow and Branch.

Pepper, William. *An Act of State*. New York: Verso, 2003. Pepper's latest includes the 1999 trial and his response to the 2000 Justice Department report. The questions Pepper raises are valid, even if his answers are often unconvincing.

Chapter 50

Who Was to Blame for Altamont?

"Three weeks remained in the decade," recalled journalist Christopher Andersen, "but for those of us who were there, the sixties came to an end December 6, 1969, at the Altamont."

The Altamont Speedway, about forty miles east of San Francisco, was the site of the Rolling Stones' free concert. This was to be Woodstock West, the culmination of the Stones' American tour.

It was anything but. Unlike the idyllic New York farm that hosted America's most famous love-in, the landscape of Altamont was burnt-out grass, rusting auto metal, and broken glass. There were only a few portable toilets to serve the more than three hundred thousand fans who streamed in from across the country. Worse, there were only a few doctors for the many who were tripping on cut-price acid. Crazed, naked fans periodically stormed the stage. The Hell's Angels, a motorcycle gang hired for crowd control, used weighted pool cues to smash the heads of many of those near the stage. Knife fights broke out. Santana, then Crosby, Stills, Nash, and Young, and other bands kept interrupting their sets, trying in vain to calm things down. Jefferson Airplane singer Marty Balin saw one Angel punching a man and jumped off the stage to intervene. The Angel turned around and knocked Balin out. The Grateful Dead, which because of its San Francisco base had helped the Stones organize the concert, didn't even play. The Dead arrived at Altamont by helicopter, surveyed the scene, and promptly took off again. The Stones also arrived by helicopter. Lead singer Mick Jagger disembarked and was immediately attacked by a stoned teenager. Jagger and the Stones quickly retreated inside a trailer.

It was cold and dark when Jagger, dressed in a glowing red cape, finally took the stage. The Stones began to play "Sympathy for the Devil," and all hell broke loose. There was a small explosion at a motorcycle near the stage. Infuriated, the Angels clubbed those around them. Jagger forsook his Luciferlike persona for that of a peace-loving hippie. "Hey, people, sisters and brothers," he pleaded. "Will you cool out, everybody."

Then the Angels attacked an eighteen-year-old Berkeley youth named Meredith Hunter. In the midst of the fight, Hunter pulled a gun, and briefly pointed it at the stage. "You felt," wrote Stanley Booth, who accompanied the Stones on their 1969 tour, "that in the next seconds or minutes you could die, and there was nothing you could do to prevent it, to improve the odds for survival. A bad dream, but we were all in it."

More Angels converged around Hunter, stabbing and stomping him to death. The Stones, unaware he was dead, played on. Hunter was not the day's only victim: two other youths were killed in their sleeping bags when a car ran over them, a third drowned in a drainage ditch, and hundreds were injured. When their set was done, the Stones piled into their helicopter, as their biographer Stephen Davis put it, "leaving the damned and blasted heath of Altamont behind them, along with any lingering illusions of Woodstockian groovyness."

They also left behind, Davis added, "a significant piece of their reputation." Many blamed the Stones for hiring the Hell's Angels (by some accounts, in return for free beer). Others blamed their bad boy image and violence-laden lyrics for the mayhem. Still others found their quick departure from the scene (and the country) callous.

Even Tony Sanchez, a friend (and drug supplier) to the Stones, found the scene disillusioning. "At Altamont there were no war mongers, no businessmen, no oldies—only the pure bloody murderous reality of anarchy," wrote Sanchez. "This was the permissive society that the Stones had so long vaunted. . . . It was ugly, mindless, blind, black, and terrifying."

Was all this reasonable? Was it fair, as singer-songwriter Kris Kristofferson later called his ditty, to "Blame it on the Stones"?

☆ ☆ ☆

The Stones played "Sympathy for the Devil," and Hell's Angels attacked the crowd. (Bill Owens/Michael Ochs Archives.)

Those most directly to blame were obviously the Hell's Angels. Even the Angels' own descriptions of what went on made clear, at least in retrospect, how inane it was to hire them as peacekeepers.

"I ain't no cop," said Sonny Barger, head of the Oakland Angels, on a radio call-in show a few days after Altamont. "They told me if I could sit on the edge of the stage so nobody could climb over me I could drink beer until the show was over, and that's what I went there to do, but you know what, when they started messing over our bikes, they started it . . . Ain't nobody gonna kick my motorcycle." Barger also claimed that when the Stones stopped playing to try to calm things down, he stuck a gun in guitarist Keith Richards's ribs and told him to get on with the show.

In case anyone had any doubts about the Angels' culpability, Altamont had its very own Zapruder film. A film crew there to make a documentary about the Stones' American tour caught much of the violence on tape. After viewing the film, detectives identified Alan Passaro as one of the Angels who attacked Hunter. Passaro was charged with murder, and the film was the prosecution's main evidence at his 1970 trial.

The problem was that Passaro was just one of many Angels, most of them unidentifiable, who surrounded Hunter. It was impossible to tell whether he struck the fatal blow. Moreover, the film showed that Hunter had a gun, which let Passaro claim self-defense. The jury acquitted Passaro, and no one else was ever brought to trial.

Were the Stones to blame for hiring the Angels?

Not really. No one is quite sure whose idea it was, though some attributed it to Grateful Dead manager Rock Scully. At worst, the Stones went along with an idea that seemed to make some sense at the time.

In a 1987 interview, Mick Jagger explained the reasoning. "Everyone who lived in San Francisco . . . knew that a lot of concerts had gone on with all these same organizers, with the Hell's Angels. . . . And it may sound like an excuse, but we believed—however naively—that this show could be organized by those San Francisco people who'd had experience with this sort of thing. . . . We were still living at the end of the 'everyone's together and lovable' era, and San Francisco was supposed to be the center of it all."

Part of the Stones' naiveté stemmed from the differences between British and American Hell's Angels. The former were a considerably milder version; in fact, many British Angels attended a Stones concert in London earlier in 1969, without incident.

"The Stones don't know about Angels," said David Crosby of Crosby, Stills, Nash, and Young. "To them an Angel is something in between Peter Fonda and Dennis Hopper. That's not real, and they just found out the reality of it."

But Crosby wasn't willing to let the Stones off the hook for their general lack of concern about their fans' safety. "You can't have that big a gathering that sloppily," he said.

Many deplored that, amidst the escalating violence, the Stones nonetheless chose to keep the crowd waiting, thus upping the tension. "They behaved exactly as they always behaved . . . forcing [the audience] to grow hungry and eager for the pile driving music of the greatest rock 'n' roll band in the world," recalled Sanchez, who was with them in the dressing room. "Only this time the Stones tarried even longer than usual; this gig was to be the climax of their movie, and they needed night to fall so that Jagger's swirling costume and dazzling colored lights could create the thundering, swirling magic of an archetypal Rolling Stones concert."

The crowd waited one and a half hours before Jagger emerged, surrounded by Hell's Angels. "By allowing the Angels to stand at his side," Sanchez continued, "he was endorsing all the havoc they had wreaked." Crosby was equally harsh, accusing the Stones of "taking what was essentially a party and turning it into an ego game and a star trip."

To some extent, this was unfair. The tension at a Stones concert was part of their appeal. So, yes, the Stones did wait until dark, when the show would be more dramatic, but that would benefit the audience for the concert as well as the movie, and remember, the Stones were doing the concert for free. Besides, Jagger and Richards *did* try to defuse the situation, once they saw things were getting out of hand.

Much of the criticism of the Stones, perhaps, had less to do with their actions and more to do with their music.

It was not just conservative cultural critics who worried about the impact of the Stones' music. "The Beatles want to hold your hand," wrote Tom Wolfe, "but the Stones want to burn your town." Others noted that Charles Manson, the man who just a few months before Altamont had incited his followers to a murderous rampage, was a Stones fan. Even the names of the songs the Stones played at Altamont, like "Sympathy for the Devil" and "Street Fighting Man," conjured up images of violence. The Stones' new album was called "Let It Bleed."

Jagger himself agreed, to some extent. "The best rock and roll music encapsulates a certain high energy—an angriness," he said. "That is, rock and roll is only rock and roll if it's not safe. . . . And so it's inevitable that the audience is stirred by the anger they feel."

But Jagger insisted that the violence at Altamont was not the consequence of the Stones' music. "To me, that is the most ridiculous journalistic contrivance I ever heard," he said. "Just because it got out of hand, we got the blame."

It was this refusal to accept any responsibility that most infuriated some critics. A month after Altamont, *Rolling Stone* magazine quoted rock promoter Bill Graham: "I'll ask you what right you had, Mick Jagger . . . to leave the way you did, thanking everybody for a wonderful time and the Angels for helping out? What right does this god have to descend on this country . . . ?"

The magazine itself editorialized: "Some display—however restrained—of compassion hardly seems too much to expect. A man died before their eyes."

One can't help but agree with *Rolling Stone*. But that should not be taken to mean that Altamont had no effect on the Rolling Stones. To some music critics, Altamont spelled not so much the end of the sixties as the end of the band's influence.

"The Rolling Stones would go on to make some good-to-great work," wrote critic Mikhal Gilmore. "But after *Exile on Main Street,* the Rolling Stones would never again make music that defined our times, that helped us or even hurt us."

"What," Gilmore asked, "flattened one of the smartest, most fearsome bands that rock and roll has ever known?" What turned Mick Jagger into a "sometimes silly peacock," and Keith Richards into a "rather pampered excuse for an outlaw"?

The answer, Gilmore believed, was Altamont. The insights the Stones gained "during that naïve-but-dread-filled term of 1969," he concluded, "stunned the band into a long season of grandiose irrelevance."

☆ To investigate further:

Bangs, Lester, et al. "Let It Bleed." *Rolling Stone.* January, 21, 1970. Includes eyewitness testimony gathered by a team of reporters.

Maysles, David, Albert Zwerin, and Charlotte Zwerin. *Gimme Shelter.* 1970. The classic documentary. Say this for Jagger: he made no effort to censor the movie, even though it obviously wasn't what he had in mind when he commissioned it.

Norman, Philip. *Symphony for the Devil.* New York: Simon & Schuster, 1984. A thorough and entertaining group biography.

Booth, Stanley. *Dance with the Devil.* New York: Random House, 1984. Booth traveled with the Stones in 1969, making his biography more personal and passionate than Norman's.

Hotchner, A. E. *Blown Away.* New York: Simon & Schuster, 1990. An unsuccessful mix of oral history and investigative journalism whose main (and unoriginal) claim is that Brian Jones, the Stones' founder, was murdered.

Sanchez, Tony. *Up and Down with the Rolling Stones.* New York: William Morrow, 1979. Sordid.

Andersen, Christopher. *Jagger Unauthorized.* New York: Delacorte Press, 1993. His full (bi)sexual history.

Gilmore, Mikal. *Night Beat.* New York: Doubleday, 1998. Best known as the brother of murderer Gary Gilmore, Mikal Gilmore is also a superb music and cultural critic.

Barger, Ralph "Sonny." *Hell's Angel.* New York: William Morrow, 2000. The most shocking revelation is that he doesn't really like Harleys.

Davis, Stephen. *Old Gods Almost Dead.* New York: Broadway Books, 2001. Forty years of sex, drugs, and rock and roll.

Chapter 51

Who Was to Blame for the Kent State Killings?

In spite of its 20,000 students, Kent State University in early 1970 was virtually unknown outside Ohio. All that soon changed. On May 4 of that year, national guardsmen who'd been called in to control antiwar protests opened fire on a crowd of students, killing four and wounding nine others. From then on, the name Kent State would instantly conjure up images of slain students and horrified onlookers.

The tension that culminated in the shootings began building on Thursday, April 30, when President Richard Nixon announced on national television that he was sending American troops into Cambodia. This infuriated opponents of the war, who felt Nixon was escalating a war he'd promised to end. On Friday students threw rocks and bottles through storefronts in downtown Kent, and police had to use tear gas to disperse the crowd. On Saturday word spread around the campus of a plan to burn the army ROTC building, and a large crowd gathered there. That evening the building was burned to the ground.

Students awoke on Sunday to find the campus occupied by armed soldiers of the Ohio National Guard. Governor James Rhodes arrived in Kent for a press conference where he promptly increased the general tension by calling the protesters "worse than the brownshirts and the communist element ... the worst type of people that we harbor in America." And Adjutant General Sylvester Del Corso of the

National Guard added that "we will apply whatever degree of force is necessary to provide protection for the lives of our citizens and their property."

By Monday, May 4, student anger about Cambodia had been transferred to the national guardsmen. A noon rally attracted about two thousand students, though the vast majority just wanted to see what was going on. Guardsmen ordered the crowd to disperse; demonstrators responded by chanting "Pigs off campus" and "One, two, three, four, we don't want your fucking war." Some also started throwing rocks at the soldiers. At 12:25 a group of guardsmen crested a hill and suddenly turned, rushed back to the top of the hill, and opened fire.

To those in the antiwar movement, this was the ultimate escalation of the Vietnam War; American soldiers had branched out from killing Vietnamese to killing Americans. Hundreds of thousands of students across the country went on strike. To them, the guardsmen were murderers, guilty of conspiring with each other or their higher-ups (in some theories, as high up as the White House) to kill innocent students who were peacefully exercising their constitutional rights. Many Americans, however, thought the students got what they deserved. Richard Nixon's "silent majority" saw the students as a dangerous threat to American society and an immediate threat to the guardsmen. The guardsmen, in their view, acted in self-defense.

To cut through the heightened rhetoric of both sides, historians had to answer some fundamental questions. Were the guardsmen in danger when they opened fire, or did they just want to teach the protesters a lesson? Did someone order them to fire, or did they fire on their own? Most fundamentally of all: *Why did the guardsmen shoot?*

A series of court cases did little to answer these questions. A state grand jury indicted 25 people, mostly students, and issued a report blaming students, faculty, and the Kent State administration for the violence. But in September 1971 the state dropped almost all the charges for lack of evidence. Then a federal grand jury indicted eight guardsmen but they, too, were not convicted: in November 1974, before the case went to a jury, the judge dismissed the charges on the grounds that the government had failed to prove its case beyond a reasonable doubt.

Meanwhile, the students injured in the shootings and the parents of the slain students sued the guardsmen, the governor, and the university's president. But the civil suit was also inconclusive. The parties settled out of court, with the state of Ohio agreeing to pay a total of $675,000 to the parents and students. The defendants also signed a statement of regret about the shootings, but it was carefully worded to avoid any admission of guilt.

Among those who sympathized with the students, many suspected that these legal processes had been tainted by political considerations. Those suspicions were confirmed in May 1978, when NBC-TV revealed the existence of a 1970 memorandum from John Ehrlichman, Nixon's chief domestic adviser, to Attorney General John Mitchell. The memo, marked EYES ONLY, referred to a previous memo in which Nixon had ordered Mitchell not to convene a federal grand jury to investigate the case.

Why would Nixon try—unsuccessfully, it turned out—to squelch a grand jury investigation? With Watergate still fresh in everyone's mind, it seemed that this, too, was part of a cover-up. But what was he covering up?

One theory was that Nixon had ordered the National Guard to get tough with the students, and that he didn't want the administration to be blamed for the shootings. This seems unlikely: the National Archives has no record of a conversation between the president and Governor Rhodes or General Del Corso or anyone else connected with the killings. Nixon's sympathies undoubtedly lay with the guards, not the students, but it's hard to imagine how, sitting in the White House, he could have arranged the chaotic sequence of events that led to the killings.

Another theory, less far-fetched, was that Nixon feared a federal grand jury would find out that the government had planted its agents among the student demonstrators. The presence of government agents on campus would explain a number of other mysteries as well: for one, why the state had so suddenly dropped its case against the demonstrators, and for another, the strange circumstances surrounding the burning of the ROTC building. That the building was going to burn Saturday night was common knowledge; a large crowd had gathered to watch it by eight o'clock. Yet the police didn't show up until 9:15. Even more mysteriously, the blaze was under control when the police arrived; it did not burn out of control until *after* the police had finally chased away the demonstrators and taken custody of the building.

If government agents played some role in the fire—perhaps setting the blaze in order to give the authorities an excuse to call in the National Guard and crack down on the demonstrators—it would make sense of these strange goings-on. Still, it must be emphasized, there's no hard evidence that there were government agents on campus, let alone involved in the fire. And there are other ways to explain Nixon's interference with the Justice Department; perhaps he just didn't want to see the guardsmen prosecuted for the murder of students who were, after all, demonstrating against Nixon's policies. So, reluctantly, most historians have admitted that they cannot say for sure why Nixon tried to stop a grand jury investigation. Nor are they sure who set fire to the ROTC building; it might have been government agents, but it might also have been student or outside radicals.

But, to return to the events of May 4: Were the guardsmen in any immediate danger when they opened fire?

Spokesmen for the Guard initially claimed that the troops were retaliating to sniper fire. This was almost certainly not true. An extensive investigation by the FBI found no evidence of any bullets other than military ones.

The next and main claim made by the guardsmen was that the troops fired to protect themselves against a wild, onrushing crowd of demonstrators who were pelting them with rocks and bricks. This claim, too, was dubious. No guardsman had to be treated for any injuries after the incident. Nor were the guardsmen trapped; in fact, just before they turned and fired, they seemed about to pass out of the demonstrators' sight. Most of the witnesses interviewed by the FBI said the main body of the crowd was at least 60 yards away from the guardsmen, and photographs and television film confirmed that only a few students were any nearer. The nearest of the victims was 60 feet away, not the 20 or 30 claimed by some guardsmen.

Might the guardsmen have panicked, even if they were in no immediate danger? Possibly. Many had been on duty for nearly a week with little sleep; they'd had at least some stones thrown at them and a great many insults. But the majority of evidence contradicts this supposition as well. There were 67 shots fired—a lot more than you'd expect from a few panicked guardsmen. And dozens of witnesses told the FBI that, right before the shooting began, the guardsmen turned

The National Guard claimed it had been under attack by demonstrators at Kent State, but no photo showed any student within 60 feet of the guardsmen. (Courtesy of Kent State University.)

together to face the crowd. All this would seem to indicate the decision to shoot was just that: a decision, not a panicky accident.

So we come to the final question. Who made that decision? Some witnesses thought they saw officers on the scene giving hand signals which might be construed as an order to fire, but every officer denied giving any such order. Other witnesses reported that, just prior to the shooting, a number of guardsmen went into what they described as a "huddle." It may have been there that an officer gave the order, or that some guardsmen just decided among themselves that they'd taken enough from the students and that it was time to teach them a lesson.

No "smoking gun" was ever found at Kent State. Unless one of the guardsmen involved comes forward with some additional information, we're unlikely to learn precisely how the decision to open fire came about. But there's no question, as the president's commission on campus unrest concluded in its September 1970 report, that "the indiscriminate firing of rifles into a crowd of students and the deaths that followed were unnecessary, unwarranted, and inexcusable."

☆ To investigate further:

Eszterhas, Joe, and Michael Roberts. *Thirteen Seconds*. New York: Dodd, Mead, 1970. A quickie by two Cleveland *Plain Dealer* reporters, but with some interesting profiles of key figures, including the slain students.

The Report of the President's Commission on Campus Unrest. Washington, DC: U.S. Government Printing Office, 1970. An unbiased and authoritative report, though it leaves unanswered many crucial questions.

Michener, James. *Kent State: What Happened and Why*. New York: Random House, 1971. As always, Michener has accumulated an extraordinary quantity of information. Some of it is useful and compelling, though his narrative is colored by his strong dislike of the protesters.

Davies, Peter. *The Truth About Kent State*. New York: Farrar Straus Giroux, 1973. Davies was an insurance broker who became obsessed with one of the slain students, and who saw conspiracies everywhere. Nonetheless, it was his investigation that forced the very reluctant federal government to prosecute the guardsmen. Davies also deserves credit for his altruism: when NBC commissioned a docudrama on Kent State, it paid Michener $400,000 for the rights. Davies, on whose book NBC relied heavily, didn't ask for a cent.

Kelner, Joseph, and James Munves, *The Kent State Coverup*. New York: Harper & Row, 1980. Kelner, the chief counsel for the victims during the first civil trial, argues (self-servingly but convincingly) that the judge and jury were prejudiced against his clients.

Gordon, William A. *The Fourth of May*. Buffalo, NY: Prometheus Books, 1990. Balanced and thorough—and as close to the last word as anyone has come so far.

Chapter 52

What Did Nixon Know About Watergate?

Soon after the Watergate break-in of June 17, 1972, it became obvious this had been some sort of political operation. The burglars were caught, after all, in the Democratic National Committee (DNC) headquarters, in the Watergate office complex, and they had on them bugging devices—hardly the tools needed for a simple burglary. And then police traced the money in the burglars' possession to the Committee to Reelect the President, the aptly acronymed CREEP.

Still, no one in the White House revealed any particular concern. The president's press secretary smugly labeled the incident a "third-rate burglary." Other Republicans were equally quick to point out that no one involved in the president's campaign had any motive for being involved in such a crime. At the time of the burglary, Richard Nixon's political position seemed completely secure. Just eleven days before the break-in, Nixon had delightedly watched George McGovern win the California primary, virtually clinching the Democratic presidential nomination. Nixon realized McGovern was perceived as an ultraliberal, far to the left of the majority of voters, and his nomination made the president's reelection seem inevitable.

With Nixon's reelection virtually in the bag, what could he or anyone associated with him possibly want from the Democratic headquarters? As Nixon himself wrote in his 1978 memoirs: "The whole thing made so little sense. *Why?* I wondered. Why then? Why in such a blundering way?"

Why, indeed?

☆ ☆ ☆

To Nixon's question, some historians and journalists have answered that, indeed, neither Nixon nor anyone with his interests in mind had anything to do with the break-in. Some were convinced that the break-in was arranged by the Democrats to frame Nixon. Somewhat more plausibly, others seized on the CIA connections of some of the burglars. According to this theory, the agency felt threatened by the president's policy of détente with the Soviet Union. So its agents planned—and then sabotaged—the burglary in order to embarrass Nixon. Still others believed the Joint Chiefs of Staff were behind the crime, for much the same reason.

Of the theories exculpating Nixon, the latest was presented in a 1991 best seller, *Silent Coup,* by journalists Len Colodny and Robert Gettlin. According to Colodny and Gettlin, it was the president's counsel, John Dean, who masterminded the break-in. Why did Dean do it? Because his girlfriend (and future wife) was linked to a call-girl ring supposedly being used by the DNC.

All these theories grew out of the entirely false assumption that the DNC held nothing of interest to Nixon. True, when the break-in was planned in June he was way ahead in the polls. But the operation was planned and approved earlier in the year; at that point the front-runner for the Democratic nomination was not George McGovern but Edmund Muskie—and Muskie was ahead of Nixon in the polls.

Besides, even if the election was secure, Nixon still might have wanted to find some dirt on his opponents. According to some reports, he was especially interested in what might be found from bugging the phone of DNC chairman Lawrence O'Brien. Nixon had disliked O'Brien ever since O'Brien's days as an adviser to President Kennedy, and he'd come to hate him when O'Brien became an adviser to Howard Hughes. Nixon, too, had a relationship with Hughes, including a questionable loan from the industrialist to the president's brother that had been a big embarrassment to the president. Nixon found it galling that the O'Brien/Hughes relationship had never cost O'Brien and the Democrats politically. Nixon was so obsessed with getting O'Brien that in early August, some seven weeks after the

"He says he's from the phone company..."

(Courtesy of the Los Angeles Times.)

Watergate break-in (when it was obviously risky for Nixon to continue to go after him), the president ordered his chief of staff H. R. Haldeman to use the IRS to embarrass O'Brien.

The Watergate break-in might also have revealed how much the Democratic campaign managers knew about a Republican deal with

ITT, a corporation which had allegedly offered cash in return for a favorable antitrust ruling. Or it might have been linked to Republican efforts to find out how much the Democrats knew about illegal contributions from Thomas Pappas, a prominent businessman and Nixon supporter. Still another possibility was that the burglars were after evidence linking the Democrats to left-wing radicals.

By his own admission, the plans for the break-in were drawn up by G. Gordon Liddy, an ex-FBI agent and right-wing ideologue who was now CREEP's general counsel. On January 27 he presented his plans to John Mitchell, who was at that time the attorney general of the United States but who was preparing to resign from that office in order to run Nixon's campaign committee. Also present at the meeting was John Dean. The plans that Liddy presented included more than just wiretapping the DNC; they also called for kidnapping antiwar demonstrators and sabotaging the air-conditioning system at the Democratic convention.

According to all three present at that meeting, Mitchell rejected the plans: they were unrealistic and too expensive, he told Liddy. (That they were also blatantly illegal seemed never to have crossed the attorney general's mind.)

On March 30 Mitchell met with his deputy at CREEP, Jeb Magruder. Again, the subject was what to do about Liddy's plans. Liddy had revised them, cutting the budget from $1 million to $250,000 but still including the break-in. This time, according to Magruder, Mitchell approved the plan. Mitchell always denied he had done so, but the evidence is against him—for he soon began authorizing large payments to Liddy.

But what of Nixon himself? Did he approve the plan—or even know about it in advance?

What we know of the president's involvement comes primarily from tapes which he himself made of his White House conversations. No one investigating Watergate even knew about these tapes until July 1973, when Haldeman's aide, Alexander Butterfield, mentioned them in passing to the special Senate committee investigating the crime. From that point on, the legislative and legal investigations focused on getting hold of the crucial tapes.

Nixon considered the tapes his personal property and had no intention of turning them over to anyone. When he was ordered to do so by Judge John Sirica, who presided over the tapes litigation, the tapes started mysteriously disappearing. In October, Nixon's lawyer informed Sirica that two of the subpoenaed conversations had never been recorded. Less than two weeks later, the hapless lawyer told the judge that another of the subpoenaed tapes had an 18½-minute gap—this right in the midst of the very first White House discussion between Nixon and Haldeman on Watergate.

Who erased these crucial 18½ minutes?

Rose Mary Woods, the president's personal secretary, testified before the court that she might have caused a gap by reaching for the telephone while transcribing the tape and accidentally hitting the tape recorder's delete button. But when she was asked to demonstrate how this might have happened, she had to stretch herself into an extremely convoluted position. Stretching credibility even further was her testimony that her telephone conversation lasted only four or five minutes and therefore could not account for the remaining erasures. Nor did the testimony of Nixon's chief of staff, Alexander Haig, alleviate suspicion: it was just like a woman, he said, not to realize how long she'd been talking on the phone.

A court-appointed panel of experts concluded that the 18½-minute gap had been caused by hand operation of the controls, not the foot pedal, as Woods claimed. In addition, the panel stated that the gap had been caused by at least five and perhaps as many as nine separate erasures, and that the evidence was "consistent" with traces left by a deliberate erasure. At this point, even the conservative *National Review* threw in the towel, writing: "Believers in the accidental theory could gather for lunch in a phone booth."

The worst, for Nixon, was still to come. He eventually had to release some of the tapes Sirica requested, and on those tapes he can clearly be heard discussing payoffs and offering advice on how to commit perjury. A tape from June 23, 1972 came to be known as the "smoking gun" and it is indeed that: Nixon can be heard giving explicit instructions that the CIA should tell the FBI to lay off the Watergate investigation.

The June 23 tape proved beyond any doubt that Nixon had been guilty of obstructing justice, and once it was released, his resignation was inevitable. But, it must be stressed, it was this involvement in the crime's cover-up that brought Nixon down. Nothing on the tapes he released indicated he'd had any direct involvement or knowledge of the crime itself.

Inevitably, some Nixon apologists continued to maintain that he was innocent. The 1991 book, *Silent Coup*, became a best-seller by portraying Nixon as a victim not just of Dean (whom it accused, you'll recall, of planning the break-in to find out about his girlfriend's call-girl ring) but of Alexander Haig, the president's chief of staff. In the Colodny/Gettlin scenario, Haig was "Deep Throat," the anonymous source to whom *Washington Post* reporter Bob Woodward regularly turned when he was stumped in his Watergate investigation. When that wasn't enough to bury Nixon, Haig took it upon himself to put the final nails in the president's coffin by erasing those 18½ minutes. The missing minutes, Colodny and Gettlin speculated, included nothing at all incriminating; Haig erased them solely to embarrass the president.

Responding to *Silent Coup*, Woodward denied Haig was Deep Throat; the *Washington Post*, where Woodward still worked, ran a savage review calling the book's documentation "pathetic." More objective historians and journalists were also critical of the book, though some did admit Colodny and Gettlin raised some intriguing questions. The debate will undoubtedly go on.

But even if a somewhat revised history of Watergate ultimately emerges, some basic facts won't change. Even if Nixon's participation in the details of the Watergate cover-up turns out not to have been as central as previously thought, there is no question that he did participate—the tape of June 23, 1972, is still as smoking as ever. Furthermore, no amount of revisionism can ever explain away all the spying, dirty tricks, and other forms of harassment of enemies that characterized the Nixon presidency—and of which Watergate was only a part.

For years Nixon's operatives spied on Democrats and reporters. They attempted to break into George McGovern's office. They asked the IRS to harass Nixon's enemies. When they couldn't come up with any dirt on his opponents, they didn't hesitate to invent some—as when E. Howard Hunt forged some cables indicating the Kennedy administration had been responsible for the 1963 assassination of South Vietnamese President Diem. Long before the Watergate break-in, some of the same burglars were working for the White House

"Plumbers," a group whose quaint name came from its original task of plugging White House leaks but whose assignments included a variety of other spying jobs.

This, then, was the context of Watergate—a context in which Nixon's apparent bewilderment as to *why* anyone would want to break into the DNC can only be seen as an extraordinary performance. "In a lifetime of bold and brazen acts, this was the boldest and most brazen, as well as the most successful," wrote Nixon's premier biographer, Stephen Ambrose. "That students, scholars, and the general public continue to ask these questions, as if they were legitimate, as if there were some unsolved mystery here, constitutes a triumph for Nixon." For whatever else he knew or didn't know about Watergate, Nixon understood full well why it happened.

☆ To investigate further:

The White House Tapes. These are the primary source for any Watergate investigation. The most readily available transcripts are still Nixon's own edited version, which he made public in April 1974 and which were subsequently published in paperback by the *New York Times* and the *Washington Post*. Unfortunately, these transcripts were soon shown to be very selective—and not just because of the infamous references to "expletive deleted." As for the tapes themselves, some (though not all) can be heard at the College Park, Maryland, location of the National Archives.

Bernstein, Carl, and Bob Woodward, *All The President's Men*. New York: Simon & Schuster, 1974. How the two *Washington Post* reporters broke the story. Also worth reading is their second book, *The Final Days* (Simon & Schuster, 1976). The first book puts you inside the *Post* newsroom; the second inside the White House.

Higgins, George V. *The Friends of Richard Nixon*. Boston: Atlantic Monthly Press, 1975. For Higgins, himself a former prosecutor as well as a master of crime fiction, the heroes of the story are the prosecutors; everyone else—including not just Nixon's friends but quite a few of his enemies—is subject to Higgins's biting wit.

Dean, John. *Blind Ambition*. New York: Simon & Schuster, 1976. Almost all of the participants in the crime and cover-up penned memoirs; some more than one. Dean's two entries, this one and *Lost Honor* (Stratford Press, 1982) are invaluable.

Lukas, J. Anthony. *Nightmare: The Underside of the Nixon Years.* New York: Viking, 1976. This is one of the first and best works of Watergate investigative journalism.

Nixon, Richard. *RN: The Memoirs of Richard Nixon.* New York: Grosset & Dunlap, 1978. Though obviously self-serving, this is nonetheless highly revealing—perhaps more so than Nixon intended.

Haldeman, H. R. *The Ends of Power.* New York: Times Books, 1978. Like Dean, Haldeman produced two invaluable works, this and and the remarkably frank, posthumously published, *The Haldeman Diaries* (G. P. Putnam's Sons, 1994).

Hougan, Jim. *Secret Agenda: Watergate, Deep Throat and the CIA.* New York: Random House, 1984. Much of what made such a splash in the Colodny/Gettlin book was first published here, along with evidence that the CIA's role in Watergate was pervasive.

Ambrose, Stephen E. *Nixon (Vol. 1, The Education of a Politician,* 1987; *Vol. 2, The Triumph of a Politician,* 1989; *Vol. 3, Ruin and Recovery,* 1991). New York: Simon & Schuster. The best biography of Nixon, including (in volumes 2 and 3) a thorough presentation of the "orthodox" interpretation of Watergate.

Colodny, Len, and Robert Gettlin. *Silent Coup: The Removal of a President.* New York: St. Martin's Press, 1991. Even its detractors admit it raises some questions that ought to be pursued further.

Kutler, Stanley I. *The Wars of Watergate.* New York: Knopf, 1990. There are numerous Watergate books by journalists, but this was the first comprehensive treatment by a historian; perhaps as a result, Kutler argues that the role of investigative journalists has been much exaggerated and that most of the Watergate revelations were the result of judicial investigations.

Emery, Fred. *Watergate.* New York: Times Books, 1994. The latest history by a journalist, which restores the primacy of the journalistic and congressional investigations. *Very* thorough.

Chapter 53

Who Was Deep Throat?

gain and again, as *Washington Post* reporters Bob Woodward and Carl Bernstein delved into Watergate, Woodward would turn to a source he described as "an old friend" with an "extremely sensitive" position in the executive branch. *Post* managing editor Howard Simons named the source "Deep Throat," partly because he would provide Woodward information only on deep background (meaning he couldn't be quoted, even anonymously) and partly after a notorious porn movie. It was Deep Throat who confirmed the link between the Watergate burglars and E. Howard Hunt, a White House consultant. It was Deep Throat who told Woodward that "higher-ups" were involved in the break-in, that it was part of a larger effort to "spy and sabotage" the president's opponents, that the tapes of Nixon's conversations about Watergate contained "deliberate erasures." In an underground garage somewhere in Washington, Deep Throat provided Woodward with the information and insights that, arguably, brought down the Nixon presidency.

Other reporters couldn't help being jealous of Woodward's scoops. Even Bernstein admitted the only source he had with such comprehensive knowledge in a field was the owner of the Georgetown Cycle Sport Shop. That came in handy when his bike was stolen from a garage, but not in making sense of Watergate. "That was the difference between him and Woodward," the two reporters wrote in their 1974 book, *All The President's Men*. "Woodward went into a garage to find a source who could tell him what Nixon's men were up to. Bernstein walked in to find an eight-pound chain cut neatly in two and his bike gone."

Eventually, Woodward told Bernstein who Deep Throat was. Woodward also told *Post* executive editor Ben Bradlee. That was it: counting Woodward and the source himself, only four men knew the identity of Deep Throat. Like all reporters, Woodward had to protect his sources. But he tantalized readers of *All The President's Men* with clues. (He also quoted Deep Throat in the book, apparently disregarding the deal to use him only on deep background.) Bradlee, too, seemed to be challenging investigators to figure it out. In his 1995 memoir, *A Good Life,* he wrote: "I have always thought it should be possible to identify Deep Throat simply by entering all the information about him in *All the President's Men* into a computer, and then entering as much as possible about all the various suspects."

That's exactly what many set out to do.

Many of the early Deep Throat candidates came from the FBI or CIA. After all, Deep Throat sure acted like a spy. Besides the clandestine meetings in the garage, there was the elaborate system by which Woodward and Deep Throat signaled each other. If Woodward wanted to see his source, he would move a flowerpot with a red flag to the rear of his apartment's balcony. Deep Throat would then meet him at the garage at 2 A.M. If Deep Throat wanted to meet, he would mark page 20 of Woodward's *New York Times,* which was delivered to the reporter's apartment each morning. Woodward never knew how Deep Throat got his hands on the paper.

More tellingly, much of the information Deep Throat gave Woodward seemed to come from FBI reports. Sometimes the wording was similar. Jim Mann, another *Post* reporter, recalled that Woodward once told him he'd talked to an FBI source about Watergate. Mann concluded that Deep Throat was in the FBI. *60 Minutes* reporter Mike Wallace decided that Deep Throat was L. Patrick Gray, the bureau's acting director during Watergate. Wallace noted that Gray lived only a few blocks from Woodward, which would have made it easy for him to make a daily check of the flowerpot. Another popular choice was Mark Felt, the bureau's associate director. Felt had been a leading candidate to succeed J. Edgar Hoover, and he may have resented Nixon for choosing Gray instead. Some noted that his initials were the same as "my friend," which was how Woodward first identified his source. Felt's candidacy got a boost when a high school student named Chase

Culeman-Beckman, who had gone to summer camp with Bernstein's son, said the son had told him it was Felt. But Bernstein said he had never told his son, squelching that theory. Many suspected CIA director Richard Helms, who knew that Nixon was planning to fire him.

Deep Throat, according to these theories, had a variety of motives. Sometimes it was frustrated ambition. Other times, it was to protect the bureau or the agency from presidential manipulation, or to put an end to the unethical behavior of the president's men. Woodward himself was never sure of Deep Throat's motives, but assumed he was acting out of some sort of loyalty—not to Nixon, of course, but to the presidency. "Deep Throat was trying to protect the office," Woodward and Bernstein speculated in *All the President's Men*, "to effect a change in its conduct before all was lost."

But what if Deep Throat's motives were actually more sinister? In 1991, reporters Len Colodny and Robert Gettlin presented an alternative history of Watergate in which Deep Throat was out not to save the presidency or the country, but to take it over. According to Colodny and Gettlin's bestseller, *Silent Coup*, Deep Throat was General Alexander Haig, Nixon's chief of staff and before that a military adviser to the National Security Council. Haig's loyalty was to the military, not to the president. To cover up the military's own illegal wiretapping and to undermine Nixon's policy of détente toward the Soviet Union and China, Haig (with the help of presidential counsel John Dean) tricked an otherwise innocent president into joining the Watergate cover-up. Next, Haig made the fateful erasures on the president's tapes, not because there was anything incriminating on the tapes, but because it would embarrass Nixon. Then Haig made sure Woodward knew about the gaps.

Colodny and Gettlin traced Woodward's relationship with Haig back to the reporter's navy days, when (they speculated) he regularly briefed the general on confidential matters. Their analysis of Woodward and Bernstein's second book, *The Final Days*, indicated Haig was again an unnamed source.

Responding to *Silent Coup*, Woodward denied Haig was Deep Throat. The *Post*, where Woodward still worked, called the book's documentation "pathetic." More objective historians conceded the work was intriguing, but rejected its conclusions. Even if Nixon's role in the cover-up was not as central as once thought, the *unerased* tapes left no doubt that the president was no innocent dupe. And no amount of revisionism could explain away all the spying and dirty tricks that characterized Nixon's presidency.

Both Kissinger and Haig have been suspected of betraying their boss. (National Archives.)

☆ ☆ ☆

Most recent investigations of Deep Throat have rejected not only Haig, but also the FBI and CIA candidates. These studies have noted that Deep Throat sometimes didn't know what the FBI was doing, and once told Woodward the FBI "did not understand what was happening." Increasingly, the focus turned to White House aides.

For his 2002 book, *Unmasking Deep Throat,* Watergate conspirator turned Deep Throat detective John Dean examined the original manuscript for *All the President's Men.* One sentence read: "Significantly, he [Deep Throat] was perhaps the only person in the government in a position to possibly understand the whole scheme, and not be a potential conspirator himself." The implication, Dean believed, was that Deep Throat held a position from which he witnessed what was going on but didn't have the power to do much about it—for example, a speechwriter or press relations person. In the manuscript's margins, Bernstein queried Woodward: "Bob: too close on id of throat here?" Woodward must have thought so, because the sentence was deleted in the published book. Dean also noted that Deep Throat told Woodward he didn't want to be called at work—perhaps because there was so little privacy in the West Wing.

Also in 2002, University of Illinois journalism professor William Gaines revealed the results of a three-year class project during which his investigative reporting students noted many factors that also pointed toward a White House aide. For one thing, Bernstein regularly pestered his own FBI sources for information, which would hardly have been necessary if Woodward's source had access to bureau reports. For another, the *Post* story attributed to a White House source the information that the tapes contained gaps. Later, in *All the President's Men,* the reporters attributed the same quote to Deep Throat.

Taking up Bradlee's challenge, investigators have compared what was known about Deep Throat to what was known about the leading candidates. They've considered everything from his apparent bachelorhood (witness the many 2 A.M. meetings) to his drinking habits (Scotch). In his 2000 book, *In Search of Deep Throat,* Leonard Garment (Dean's successor as White House counsel and himself sometimes a suspect) settled on deputy counsel John Sears. Dean narrowed the field to six: presidential speechwriter (and future presidential candidate) Pat Buchanan, administrative assistant Steve Bull, speechwriter Ray Price, and press secretary Ron Ziegler. Ziegler died in 2003, but Woodward, who has said he would reveal his source's identity upon Deep Throat's death, made no comment, perhaps because the list of suspects was getting too short. Gaines's students came up with seven: in addition to Buchanan, Bull, and Price, they chose Dean assistant Fred Fielding, Nixon adviser (and later Reagan and Clinton adviser) David Gergen, White House attorney (and Woodward's Yale classmate) Jonathan Rose, and deputy press secretary Gerald Warren.

How to choose among them—or any other candidate? Some have despaired of finding a solution, and others, such as Woodward and Bernstein's former literary agent, David Obst, have concluded that Deep Throat was a composite, a character invented to make *All the President's Men* more dramatic. But this is one case where patience should pay off. Not only has Woodward promised to someday resolve the mystery, but he and Bernstein have gone so far as to make arrangements in case the reporters and Bradlee die before their source. So, unless they have been lying all along, which seems unlikely for the world's two most famous reporters, we will someday know. For now, as you read the *Post,* make sure not to skip the obituaries.

☆ To investigate further:

Bernstein, Carl, and Bob Woodward. *All the President's Men*. New York: Simon & Schuster, 1974. The book that inspired a generation of investigative reporters. In the movie, Hal Holbrook played Deep Throat.

Woodward, Bob, and Carl Bernstein. *The Final Days*. New York: Simon & Schuster, 1976. Their first book put you inside the *Post* newsroom; their second inside the White House.

Hougan, Jim. *Secret Agenda*. New York: Random House, 1984. Much of what made such a splash in *Silent Coup* was first published here.

Kutler, Stanley. *The Wars of Watergate*. New York: Knopf, 1990. Kutler was one of the first historians, as opposed to journalists, to tackle Watergate. Perhaps as a result, he argues that the role of investigative journalists has been exaggerated and that most of the Watergate revelations were the result of judicial investigations.

Colodny, Len, and Robert Gettlin. *Silent Coup*. New York: St. Martin's Press, 1991. Haig was Deep Throat and Dean masterminded the Watergate break-in because his girlfriend was linked to a call-girl ring supposedly being used by the Democrats.

Emery, Fred. *Watergate*. New York: Times Books, 1994. The latest history by a journalist, which restores the primacy of the journalistic and congressional investigations. Very thorough.

Garment, Leonard. *In Search of Deep Throat*. New York: Basic Books, 2000. Sears, Garment argues, was a secret source for Bernstein as well as Woodward, which makes his book something of a counterpoint to the composite theory: instead of turning several characters into one, Woodward and Bernstein have turned one man into two characters.

www.comm.uius.edu/spike. *Spike,* the magazine of the University of Illinois journalism department, gives the rundown on how Gaines's students chose their seven finalists. Polled by NBC's *Dateline,* the students chose Buchanan as the most likely.

Dean, John. *Unmasking Deep Throat*. San Francisco: Salon.com, 2002. Dean's book was disappointing, since he had promised to reveal the one and only, not six candidates. He was set to go with Jonathan Rose, but at the last minute Dean backed off. One advantage of an e-book is that he was able to do so. This, by the way, was Dean's third go at Deep Throat sleuthing. In 1974, he named prosecutor Earl Silbert, and in 1982 he concluded it was Haig.

Chapter 54

Were POWs Left Behind in Vietnam?

For the first time in twelve years, no American military forces are in Vietnam," Richard Nixon announced in March 1973. "All of our American POWs are on their way home."

"Operation Homecoming" brought home 591 Americans, a total that meshed with military estimates of the number of POWs. Those estimates were based on a variety of sources: battlefield reports, reconnaissance missions, letters from prisoners, and the reporting of foreign journalists in North Vietnam.

What the returning Americans had to say about their treatment also made it seem unlikely that many more could have survived in captivity. Lieutenant Commander John McCain, for example, was beaten savagely after bailing out of his navy fighter jet in 1967. He arrived in prison with two broken arms, one broken leg, a smashed shoulder, and a deep bayonet wound in his foot. He received no medical treatment until the North Vietnamese learned that his father was commander in chief of U.S. forces in the Pacific. Other prisoners undoubtedly fared worse. Most returning POWs believed they had left no comrades behind, or at least no living ones.

Two months after Operation Homecoming, the hearings of the House Foreign Affairs Committee confirmed Nixon's statement. Most witnesses, including the former POWs, testified that they didn't think any prisoners were left behind.

Hoa Lo Prison, which POWs called the Hanoi Hilton. (Department of Defense.)

In the decades since, many have questioned Nixon. Some have gone so far as to accuse him—and subsequent presidents—of covering up the continuing imprisonment of Americans in order to conceal America's secret operations in Indochina. Some real-life Rambos have taken matters into their own hands, infiltrating communist territory and returning with additional stories of American prisoners (though not with the prisoners themselves).

Even the official government numbers leave room for doubt. More than two thousand soldiers remain "unaccounted for." More than half of these, to be sure, could never have been prisoners. Though their bodies weren't recovered, it was clear that they were killed in action—for example, if their plane crashed or exploded in sight of other pilots. As for the remaining missing in action, the Defense Department has presumed that they, too, are dead.

This presumption has left many dissatisfied. For them, there is not yet—nor should there yet be—an end to the war in Vietnam.

☆ ☆ ☆

The original POW activists were family members of the unaccounted-for, who were understandably desperate to learn of their relatives' fates. This left them susceptible to all sorts of scams, and many paid lots of money for counterfeit dog tags, unidentified bones, and dubious tales of "live sightings." The movement gained momentum and followers in the late 1970s, when tens of thousands of boat people and other refugees streamed out of Vietnam, bringing with them more reports of American prisoners. Defense analysts dismissed most of these stories as at best secondhand and at worst fabricated, but there were plenty of cases where analysts simply didn't have enough information to reach a definite conclusion.

Besides, many activists simply didn't believe the Defense Department reports. In the wake of Vietnam and Watergate, government credibility was at an all-time low. If Nixon had lied to the American public about so much else, what reason was there to believe him about there being no more POWs? Many believed that North Vietnam was holding on to prisoners as bargaining chips amidst ongoing negotiations over U.S. economic aid. Others suspected the administration was covering up secret operations in Cambodia and Laos throughout and after the war. Some even argued the United States was funding its covert wars with drug money, and that the top brass feared investigators looking for POWs might stumble across proof of this.

Some hard evidence that at least one POW was still alive emerged from Vietnam in 1979, in the form of Marine Corps private and former POW Robert Garwood. Garwood was the first (and only) POW to come home after Operation Homecoming. He brought with him stories of other Americans still being held. But marine officials argued that Garwood was neither a credible witness nor a genuine POW. True, he had been held in captivity from 1965 to 1967. But at that point he had gone over to the communist side, and he had chosen to remain in Vietnam after Operation Homecoming. Garwood was court-martialed and found guilty of collaborating with the enemy, with much of the testimony against him coming from his former fellow prisoners. The result was that both the activists and the Defense Department believed Garwood's return buttressed their positions.

At this point, an ex–Special Forces lieutenant colonel named James "Bo" Gritz decided to take matters into his own hands. Gritz, who was at least part of the inspiration for the Rambo movies, was certain there were still POWs, and he planned several raids to free them. "Both Teddy Roosevelt and John Wayne are dead," he said, explaining why the job fell to him.

Only one of Gritz's operations actually made it into communist territory. In November 1982, he led a small group of Vietnam veterans into Laos. He returned to Thailand a few days later without any POWS, and was promptly arrested for an illegal border crossing.

Still, the accumulated POW sightings—even if often discredited—were further undermining the government's credibility. This was no longer a fringe movement of family members and Rambo wannabes. Ronald Reagan endorsed their cause, even if the activists were ultimately disappointed that he didn't take any decisive action. Ross Perot started to put together a presidential campaign, using the POW/MIA organizations in lieu of a traditional party. By 1991, according to a *Wall Street Journal*-NBC News poll, 69 percent of Americans believed that U.S. prisoners of war were still being held in Indochina.

Among those converted was army colonel Millard Peck, chief of the Defense Intelligence Agency's special office for POW/MIA affairs. Peck accused his own agency of having a "mind-set to debunk" reports about POWs. "The entire charade does not appear to be an honest effort, and may never have been," he said in 1991.

That same year, in response to the increasing pressure from MIA family members and the general public, the United States Senate decided to investigate.

☆ ☆ ☆

The Select Committee on POW/MIA Affairs, chaired by former senator (and Vietnam vet) John Kerry, interviewed hundreds of witnesses, ranging from Millard Peck to Bo Gritz to Richard Nixon. The committee also sent several delegations to Russia and North Korea, as well as to Southeast Asia. After a year's work, the committee issued a 1,285-page report that concluded there was no government cover-up. For the Nixon, Ford, Carter, Reagan, and Bush administrations all to have conspired to conceal POWs seemed not just unlikely but impossible.

The Kerry committee also concluded many of the POW sightings were phony, and many more were simply mistaken. Some of those sighted might have been Americans, but not prisoners; by one estimate, there were almost 250 sightings of Garwood prior to his return in 1979. Others may have been prisoners sighted before Operation Homecoming, or American civilians stranded after the fall of Saigon.

Moreover, if the North Vietnamese intended to use prisoners as some sort of bargaining chip, they had made that much more difficult by consistently denying there were any. It's tough to bargain with a chip you say you don't have.

Still, the Kerry committee left some room for doubt. The report ruled out a cover-up but not the possibility that, unbeknownst to the U.S. government, there might still be a few POWs in Vietnam. Most of the "unaccounted for," as after any war, were probably dead, but it was impossible to know for sure. Indeed, the report asserted that the issue should continue to be treated as "the highest national priority." Any final solution to the mystery, the committee concluded, had to come not from Washington but from Hanoi.

Hanoi seemed an unlikely place to look for help. The Vietnamese had denied from the start not only that they held on to any POWs, but also that they had any additional records pertaining to them. Then, in 1991 and 1992, an American researcher named Ted Schweitzer delved into Hanoi's archives.

Exactly why the Vietnamese let Schweitzer in was unclear. Schweitzer posed as a private scholar, but he actually worked for the Defense Intelligence Agency, and the Vietnamese almost certainly knew this. Schweitzer's own guess was that they opened their archives to him as a way to release the information Americans wanted without formally admitting they had it. In any case, Schweitzer was able to scan thousands of photographs and documents pertaining to POWs.

Schweitzer's access to the archives was limited, so the material he collected, like the evidence the Kerry committee compiled, could not absolutely eliminate the possibility of POWs left behind. But Schweitzer's study resolved some cases by indicating that a few of the unaccounted-for MIAs had been captured and subsequently killed. Schweitzer's informal discussions with officers in the archives confirmed this as well.

"Our darkest secret," Lieutenant Colonel Nguyen Van Thi told Schweitzer, "is that we killed many American prisoners in cold blood. They were tortured to death in prison, or simply killed outright from fear they would try to escape. . . . That is our worst secret in the MIA affair."

When Schweitzer asked how many Americans died, Thi said "perhaps hundreds."

☆ ☆ ☆

An abiding irony of the Vietnam War is that the deep mistrust of government that has sustained the POW activists was bred in the antiwar movement of the sixties and the seventies.

It's hard to imagine two more different groups. The antiwar activists were, of course, generally pacifist and leftist. The POW activists have generally been rightists and, except on this issue, pro-military. This is hardly surprising, since the main POW organizations were founded by family members of soldiers, most of whom were officers and many of whom were fighter pilots, perhaps the most glamorous job in the military. The politicians who championed the POW cause, among them Reagan and Perot, have also been mostly conservative and pro-military.

This irony has not been lost on leftist historians, some of whom struggled to hold on to their antigovernment legacy while rejecting the politics and POW theories of those they think of as "gray flannel Rambos." H. Bruce Franklin, for example, was once an antiwar activist (Stanford fired him for "urging and inciting disruption of campus activities") who subsequently wrote extensively on the POW issue. Franklin argued that, though there was neither a government cover-up nor any evidence of POWs left behind, the Nixon administration and those of the presidents who followed him were very much to blame for the POW issue.

POWs, Franklin noted, first became a political issue in 1969, when Nixon drew public attention to the communists' cruel treatment of American prisoners. To Franklin, Nixon's focus on POWs was a cynical maneuver designed to undercut the burgeoning antiwar movement, create a rationale for breaking off negotiations with North Vietnam, and continue the war indefinitely. Instead of My Lai, Americans could now concentrate on atrocities committed by the enemy.

Journalist Jonathan Schell agreed: "Following the president's lead," he wrote, "people began to speak as though the North Vietnamese had kidnapped four hundred Americans and the United States had gone to war to retrieve them."

Nixon's demand that the communists account for every American missing an action stalemated the Paris peace talks. The North Vietnamese may have known about more MIAs than they admitted, but they couldn't possibly have known about all of them. Once peace finally came and the POWs came home, Nixon continued to demand a full accounting of MIAs, the lack of which provided a convenient pretext for reneging on his promise of economic aid for Vietnam.

Subsequent administrations, according to Franklin, were equally adamant in their unreasonable demands for a full accounting, again using it as a pretext for whatever anti-Vietnam policies they preferred. The Pentagon further confused the issue by periodically redefining and combining its various lists of POWs, MIAs, deserters, and KIA/BNRs (killed in action/body not recovered). The terms were often used interchangeably, even though a full accounting of POWs, though difficult, was a reasonable goal, while for MIAs this was an impossible demand. If, for example, a pilot's plane exploded in midair, the Vietnamese were no more likely to have identified his remains than were the Americans.

"Each postwar administration has tried to exaggerate this possibility of living POWs," he wrote. "But no administration could afford to claim that there actually were POWs, because then it would be expected to rescue them."

The weakness of Franklin's argument is that it's not always clear what motives the various administrations had for making accusations against Vietnam. That Nixon used the POWs to stalemate the peace talks or renege on promised economic aid is plausible, and certainly in keeping with what else we know of Nixon. But Franklin certainly hasn't offered substantive proof. Moreover, any overarching conspiracy theory—whether the one that Franklin hinted at or that the POW activists embraced—assumes a highly unusual degree of cooperation between political adversaries. It's hard to imagine Carter getting together with Nixon or Reagan, or Bush with Clinton, in an effort to protect each other's secrets.

It seems more likely that each president at times, along with many in their administrations, moved the POWs up and down on their agendas, depending on the moment and the audience. Certainly each was aware of strong feelings about POWs, and not just among family members. Sometimes to satisfy this constituency, sometimes for foreign policy reasons (often having as much to do with U.S. relations with Russia or China as with Vietnam), each president at times demanded that Vietnam provide a fuller accounting. Even Bill Clinton, as he moved to normalize relations with Vietnam in 1995, stressed he was doing so to further "progress on the issue of Americans missing in action or held as prisoners of war."

All this undoubtedly created more confusion than clarity about the possibility of POWs, and you don't have to buy into any conspiracy theory to blame the government for that. It's possible that a full disclosure of what's in Hanoi's archives may reveal the fates of a few more MIAs, or even a few POWs. Certainly the United States should continue to push for that. But to raise expectations that these MIAs or POWs are still alive is unfair to their families and to the truth.

The cruel reality is that most MIAs have to be presumed dead, even if the details of how they met that fate remain a mystery. That is the nature of war: in World War II, the "unaccounted for" made up 22 percent of the total killed, in Korea 24 percent. In Vietnam, the unaccounted-for make up only 3 to 4 percent of the dead. Since most of their remains ended up in enemy territory, it's unrealistic to expect that number to drop much further.

☆ To investigate further:

Jensen-Stevenson, Monika, and William Stevenson. *Kiss the Boys Goodbye.* New York: Dutton, 1990. The best defense of the POW activists' position, though marred by too many anonymous or otherwise questionable sources.

Franklin, H. Bruce. *M.I.A. or Mythmaking in America.* New Brunswick, New Jersey: Rutgers University Press, 1993. Provocative and plausible, though by no means proven.

Keating, Susan Katz. *Prisoners of Hope.* New York: Random House, 1994. How charlatans, including plenty in the government, exploited the POW/MIA myth and the families of the missing.

Mather, Paul. *M.I.A.* Washington, D.C.: National Defense University Press, 1994. As a member of the Joint Casualty Resolution Center from its formation in Saigon in 1973 until 1988, Mather had an inside view of how military specialists analyzed the POW "sightings."

McConnell, Malcolm, with Theodore Schweitzer III. *Inside Hanoi's Secret Archives.* New York: Simon & Schuster, 1995. Schweitzer's own account of how he got inside and what he found.

Jensen-Stevenson, Monica. *Spite House.* New York: W. W. Norton & Company, 1997. A passionate defense of Garwood that argues not only that his court-martial was unfair, but also that American forces targeted him for assassination.

Veith, George. *Code-Name Bright Light.* New York: The Free Press, 1998. The valiant—and completely unsuccessful—efforts of the U.S. military to rescue POWs during the war.

Rochester, Stuart, and Frederick Kiley. *Honor Bound.* Annapolis, Maryland: Naval Institute Press, 1999. A thorough and often painful study of the POWs' lives in captivity, through 1973.

Franklin, H. Bruce. *Vietnam and Other American Fantasies.* Amherst: University of Massachusetts Press, 2000. Vietnam's influence on postwar American culture, from the politics of POWs to *Star Trek.*

Chapter 55

Who Killed Jimmy Hoffa?

Jimmy Hoffa left his suburban Detroit home in the early afternoon of July 30, 1975. He stopped briefly to see an old friend who ran a nearby limousine service, but the friend had already left for lunch. Hoffa then drove to the Machus Red Fox Restaurant, where he expected to meet Anthony Giacalone and Anthony Provenzano. "Tony Jack" and "Tony Pro" were also old friends, or at least old acquaintances from the days when Hoffa ran the International Brotherhood of Teamsters. At about 2:30, Hoffa called his wife to ask if she'd heard from Giacalone, and then told her it looked like he'd been stood up. It was the last she—or anyone else—heard from him.

Few doubted he was dead. Giacalone and Provenzano were mixed up with the Mafia, as was Hoffa himself. The jokes quickly circulated: Jacques Cousteau had spotted Hoffa's body, or it was under the end zone of the new Meadowlands football stadium, where the concrete had just been poured. This was, the FBI agreed, a mob-related execution.

Yet Hoffa's body was never found, Giacalone and Provenzano had airtight alibis, and neither they nor anyone else was ever charged with the murder. Hoffa's disappearance remains one of the most intriguing in American history, partly because Hoffa himself was so intriguing. Was he, as Robert Kennedy put it, the leader of a "conspiracy of evil," a union leader who had "sold out the union membership [and] put gangsters and racketeers in important positions of power within the Teamsters"? Or was he, as many Teamsters believed then and now, persecuted because he stood up for the people he represented? "For what he did for the driver, I'd take a chance on him again," one Teamster said, after Hoffa was convicted of misusing union pension funds. "If he robbed a little, what the hell."

Hoffa's connections to the mob, it was clear, were the key to solving the mysteries of his life as well as his death.

Kennedy's first efforts to connect Hoffa to the mob were distinctly unsuccessful. As chief counsel to the Senate Select Committee on Improper Activities in the Labor or Management Field, Kennedy led an investigation that called 1,525 witnesses over two and a half years. In 1957, after attorney John Cheasty testified that Hoffa had attempted to bribe him to turn over confidential committee papers, Kennedy was confident that he had the goods on the labor leader. "If Hoffa isn't convicted," he announced, "I'll jump off the Capitol Dome." Four months later, after a jury found Hoffa not guilty of conspiring to obstruct the committee's inquiry, defense attorney Edward Bennett Williams offered to send Kennedy a parachute.

The committee's final report was almost fifty thousand pages long, and resulted in the 1959 Landrum-Griffin Act and the first government regulation of internal union affairs. The investigation also led to the expulsion of the Teamsters from the AFL-CIO, and prison terms for several Hoffa associates. But Hoffa himself remained both free and in charge of the union.

When John F. Kennedy became president and made his brother attorney general, it was clear Hoffa would become a top priority of the Justice Department. ("Everyone in my family forgives," the Kennedys' father once said, "except Bobby.") The new attorney general quickly set up a special unit whose lawyers described themselves as the "Get Hoffa Squad." In 1962, prosecutors charged Hoffa with negotiating a sweetheart deal with one trucking company in return for its sending business to another, which happened to be owned by Hoffa's wife. Again, a jury found him not guilty. But that case turned out to be the labor leader's undoing when Hoffa aide Edward Partin told prosecutors that his boss had bribed the jurors. In 1964, another jury found Hoffa guilty of jury tampering. That same year, yet another jury convicted Hoffa of conspiracy and fraud having to do with a Teamster pension fund.

Hoffa was sentenced to eight years. In 1967, his appeals exhausted, he entered the federal penitentiary in Lewisburg, Pennsylvania. It was in Lewisburg, according to FBI reports, that Provenzano (who was

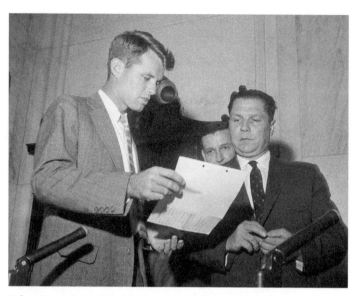

Robert Kennedy worked tirelessly to put Hoffa in jail, which was one reason Nixon was happy to commute his sentence in 1971. (Corbis.)

serving a four-year term for extortion) decided he wanted Hoffa dead. The two had once been allies. Provenzano, a member of the Genovese crime family, ran Teamster Local 560 in Union City, New Jersey, and had supported Hoffa in his rise to union presidency. At first, he also protected Hoffa from the dangers of prison, and the two regularly sat together at mealtime. The relationship went awry when Provenzano asked Hoffa for help getting credit toward his Teamster pension, which he was being denied because the Landrum-Griffin Act barred persons convicted of extortion from holding union office until five years after their incarceration. Hoffa refused, telling Tony Pro, "It's because of people like you that I got into trouble in the first place."

The feud intensified after the two men were released from prison, Provenzano in 1970 and Hoffa a year later. (The latter's sentence was commuted by Richard Nixon, one of the few men who resented the Kennedys more than Hoffa did.) The two met several times during 1973 and 1974, and Provenzano once threatened to "pull out Hoffa's guts." Provenzano's friend Giacalone was an equally threatening figure; this was a man who ran an exterminating company and was, as Hoffa biographer Arthur Sloane put it, "thought to be capable of the extermination of humans as well as animal and insect life." Even Jimmy Hoffa, not an easy man to intimidate, must have been unnerved by the promised violence of Tony Pro and Tony Jack. So when the two proposed that they all get together for a "peace meeting" at the Machus Red Fox restaurant, Hoffa must have been relieved.

He must also have been increasingly nervous when Provenzano and Giacalone failed to show up at the restaurant. Tony Pro, it turned out, was in Union City, New Jersey, playing Greek rummy in plain view of plenty of people. (Provenzano's brother later explained the game: "You knock everybody out, and when one man remains, he's the winner.") Tony Jack was at Detroit's Southfield Athletic Club, having a massage and haircut and noticed by so many people that, an FBI memo concluded, "Giacalone definitely appeared to be establishing an alibi."

According to the FBI's theory, Provenzano assigned the hit to Salvatore and Gabriel Briguglio and Thomas Andretta. Two of them picked up Hoffa at the Machus Red Fox, and killed him. FBI agents accumulated a variety of evidence, including the statements of a prison informant and of an eyewitness who thought she'd seen Salvatore Briguglio on July 30, 1975, in a car parked at the Machus Red Fox. But the Briguglio brothers and Andretta maintained they were in Union City, New Jersey, that day—playing Greek rummy with Tony Pro— and the bureau never could never shake their alibis, at least not enough to take the case to court.

In any case, many in the bureau believed Provenzano, Giacalone, and their alleged accomplices wouldn't have killed Hoffa without approval from their higher-ups. The generally accepted theory was that mob leaders had grown very comfortable with Hoffa's successor as Teamster president, Frank Fitzsimmons. True, they'd once worked quite well with Hoffa. But Fitzsimmons lacked his predecessors' temper and independent streak. So when Hoffa started making noises about making a comeback (not at all impossible, given his continuing popularity with the rank and file), the mob decided to eliminate the possibility. They turned to Provenzano because they knew he had his own reasons for wanting Hoffa dead.

Hoffa's son shared the FBI's suspicion that his father was killed to keep him from retaking the presidency. "Dad was pushing so hard to get back in office," James P. Hoffa recalled of the spring of 1975. "I was increasingly afraid that the mob would do something about it."

☆ ☆ ☆

In 1975, as the FBI investigated Hoffa's death, a Senate committee learned that the CIA, with Mafia help, had attempted to assassinate Fidel Castro. In 1977, as the FBI continued to probe Hoffa's death, a House committee investigated the death of John Kennedy. By the time the congressional committees were done, the assassinations and attempted assassinations of Castro, Kennedy, and Hoffa were all entangled, at least in the minds of some conspiracy theorists.

For starters, Hoffa hated the president. Not as much as he hated his brother, of course, but by extension, plenty. Edward Partin, the Hoffa aide who told prosecutors about his boss's jury tampering, also told them—and later the House Assassinations Committee—that his boss had talked about killing "that son of a bitch Bobby Kennedy." That wasn't the only connection between the labor leader and the president's assassination. Jack Ruby, the man who killed Lee Harvey Oswald, was the number two man in a Teamster affiliate run by a close friend of Hoffa. And Hoffa was also friendly with Tampa godfather Santo Trafficante and New Orleans godfather Carlos Marcello, both of whom were targets of the attorney general and both of whom had spoken, at least according to some witnesses, of murdering the president. Robert Blakey, the chief counsel for the House committee, believed the Mafia was behind the president's assassination, and he named three suspects: Trafficante, Marcello, and Hoffa.

For some conspiracy theorists, it was only a short jump from Hoffa-as-assassin to Hoffa-as-target. The logic went like this: The Mafia wanted Castro dead, because he was bad for their business in Cuba. The CIA wanted Castro dead, for political reasons. So Castro, in revenge for the joint CIA-Mafia attempts on his life, killed Kennedy. Alternatively, the Mafia, in revenge for Bobby's anti-organized crime efforts, killed John. Then the Mafia killed Hoffa, because they feared he might tell what he knew about either their anti-Castro or anti-Kennedy plots.

With the House and Senate both investigating, the late 1970s were the heyday of assassination conspiracy theories. Among the most persuasive was that of Dan Moldea, an investigative journalist whose 1988 book, *The Hoffa Wars*, stopped short of concluding exactly how the labor leader was involved, but suggested that the solution was "to be found in the consistent cast of characters that threaded its way through Hoffa's life—and through fifteen years of American political violence."

The men suspected of ordering Hoffa's murder, Moldea noted, were the same men suspected of plotting to kill Castro and Kennedy: Trafficante, Marcello, Provenzano, and others. "There is therefore considerable reason to believe," Moldea continued, "that Hoffa was removed for reasons more complicated than mere ambition."

Other conspiracy theorists tied Nixon to Hoffa's murder, alleging that the president feared that Hoffa, if he couldn't regain control of the Teamsters, might reveal secret union payoffs to Nixon. Still others blamed government agents for Hoffa's murder. Hoffa assistant Joseph Franco, for example, claimed in his 1987 book that he was present at the Machus Red Fox, and that he witnessed three men pick up his boss. "They were typical Ivy Leaguers," Franco wrote, "with sports jackets and shirts and ties, and you could see that they were either federal marshals or federal agents." Franco didn't say why the marshals or agents wanted Hoffa dead.

The problem with all these conspiracy theories was that there was no hard evidence to substantiate any of them. There was no evidence that Trafficante or Marcello had done anything more than talk about assassinating Kennedy, or that Hoffa had even talked about hitting the president, as opposed to his brother. Most historians eventually concluded that Oswald acted alone. And as far as Hoffa's own disappearance was concerned, the FBI didn't even have enough evidence to indict Provenzano or Giacalone or Andretta or the Briguglios, let alone other mobsters or Cubans or government agents.

In 2000, the FBI got a break in the form of DNA analysis that was not available back in 1975. They matched hair taken from Hoffa's brush with a strand found in a car owned by Joey Giacalone, Tony's son. This was a car that Hoffa's foster son, Chuckie O'Brien, had already admitted he'd borrowed from Giacalone the day Hoffa disappeared. When the DNA evidence proved Hoffa had been in the car, suspicion focused on O'Brien. O'Brien's presence that day could explain how Hoffa's murderers got him to leave the restaurant quietly. After all, the labor leader was fully aware of the dangers of dealing with Provenzano or Giacalone or anyone they sent to pick him up. But if his trusted foster son showed up, that would have at least partly allayed his fears.

The FBI suspected O'Brien might have been in on the murder, perhaps because he was angry at Hoffa's refusal to help him repay his gambling debts. Or O'Brien may have been duped by the murderers. "It is quite possible that O'Brien simply thought he was taking Hoffa to just another meeting," one government official told Moldea. "But even if that's true, O'Brien certainly became an accessory to the subsequent cover-up."

Back in 1975, O'Brien told the FBI that he never saw his foster father on the day of his disappearance, and that he borrowed Giacalone's car to run some errands. Grilled by prosecutors twenty-five years later, he stuck to his story. Ultimately, prosecutors decided that the DNA evidence wasn't enough to bring charges against him.

"It has the makings of a whodunit novel, only, unfortunately, without the final chapter being written," prosecutor David Gorcya told the Detroit *Free Press* in August 2002. "But we may someday get lucky, and someone will come forward. Someone involved in the case may want to cleanse their conscience."

How clear was James R. Hoffa's conscience? That, too, remains in dispute.

To many journalists, he was a gangster and racketeer, a Faustian criminal who sold out the Teamsters to the Mafia and who fully deserved the prosecutorial attentions Robert Kennedy heaped upon him. "Jimmy Hoffa's most valuable contribution to the American labor movement," Moldea wrote, "came at the moment he stopped breathing on July 30, 1975."

To most rank and file members of the union, however, Hoffa was a true hero, a man who dramatically improved the working conditions of millions in what had once been among the poorest paying and most dangerous of jobs. In 1998, Jimmy's son, James P. Hoffa, was overwhelmingly elected Teamster president, in spite of his notable lack of union experience. Clearly, this was a testament to the continuing power, long after his disappearance and presumed death, of James R. Hoffa.

The middle initial, by the way, stood for "Riddle."

☆ To investigate further:

Kennedy, Robert. *The Enemy Within.* New York: Harper & Row, 1960. Considering it's about a Senate committee investigation, this is remarkably dramatic and entertaining.

Brill, Steven. *The Teamsters.* New York: Simon & Schuster, 1978. Superb profiles of Teamster leaders, including Hoffa and Fitzsimmons.

Moldea, Dan. *The Hoffa Wars.* New York: Charter Communications, 1978. The many connections between Teamsters, politicians, and the mob.

Franco, Joseph, with Richard Hammer. *Hoffa's Man.* New York: Prentice Hall Press, 1987. His rise and fall, as witnessed by "his strongest arm."

Sloane, Arthur. *Hoffa.* Cambridge: Massachusetts: The MIT Press, 1991. A solid if somewhat dry biography.

Russell, Thaddeus. *Out of the Jungle.* New York: Alfred A. Knopf, 2001. Russell concedes Hoffa was corrupt, but he blames more leftist union leaders for putting politics ahead of bread-and-butter issues.

Chapter 56

Was Howard Hughes's Will a Forgery?

When Howard Hughes died in April 1976, no one was sure exactly how much his estate was worth. Partly that was because his holdings were far-flung, encompassing movies, airlines, mining claims, hotels, casinos, and thousands of acres in California and Nevada. Mostly it was because these holdings were almost all private, and Hughes had been extraordinarily secretive. There was no doubt, though, that Hughes left behind a fortune; some estimates put the value as high as $6 billion.

Within days of his death, rumors circulated that there was no will, leaving the money up for grabs. This was, on the face of it, absurd. Hughes hated paying taxes, and in the absence of a will much of the estate would go to the government.

"The tax man who Hughes spent his entire life successfully avoiding would be declared the winner," wrote his biographer Richard Hack. "If Howard Hughes were not already dead, that bit of news alone would have killed him."

The rest of the money would go to relatives Hughes hadn't spoken to in decades.

To avoid just these eventualities, Hughes had spent far more time on his will than most people, even most billionaires. He had signed a will in 1925, just before he married Ella Rice, though that was invalidated after their divorce. During the 1940s, Hughes's personal assistant, Nadine Henley, had spent numerous hours typing and retyping

Before becoming the world's richest recluse, Hughes was famous as, among other things, a pilot. In 1947, he took off in the Spruce Goose, *the largest plane ever built. (Library of Congress.)*

drafts he sent her. From the mid-1950s, he publicly spoke of his plans to leave his money to the Howard Hughes Medical Institute, a charity he set up in 1954. And during his final years, he privately promised his personal aides that he had generously provided for them in his will.

For Hughes to have died without a will seemed entirely out of character. This was not a man who left things to chance. When he wanted to date Hollywood stars like Katharine Hepburn and Lana Turner, Hughes became a movie producer. When he bought RKO, Hughes insisted on re-shooting parts of movies he didn't like. In 1967, when he was staying in the Desert Inn in Las Vegas, the owners asked him to leave because some high rollers had reserved the rooms. Hughes's response was to buy the hotel.

Indeed, Hughes's insistence on total control over his environment was famously pathological. Desperately afraid of germs, he wrote lengthy instructions for aides on how to open a can of fruit salad, how to lift a toilet seat, how to enter and leave a room. In 1955, for example, he explained how to enter his bungalow at the Beverly Hills Hilton, a process that required three men:

"Before opening the door to the room, the third man is to stand with a folded newspaper in his right hand and rapidly wave it for at least one minute to eliminate the possibility that flies will enter the room," Hughes wrote. "Using eight Kleenex placed in the left hand, the man who is rapidly waving the newspaper will knock on the door. When HRH responds, the man will open the door, using the hand with the Kleenex. The door is never to be opened further than twelve inches nor longer than ten seconds at a time. This will allow a second man enough time to enter the room."

How could a man so obsessed with power and control leave no will? That he would "die intestate and turn his empire and life's work over to the whims of countless others for dismemberment seemed," wrote the investigative reporters James Phelan and Lewis Chester, "inconceivable."

And yet, as days turned into months, there was no sign of a will.

Executives at the Summa Corporation, which included most of Hughes's holdings, undertook a national search for the will. They broke into filing cabinets and safes, where they found plenty of letters and memos referring to a will, but no will. They placed a classified ad in about forty newspapers, asking anyone with information to call. They even hired a psychic named Peter Hurkos, who claimed all he needed to find a document was a piece of its owner's clothing. The corporation supplied Hurkos with a pair of shoes; alas—maybe because Hughes had a habit of walking around not just shoeless but naked—Hurkos found nothing.

Not surprisingly, the search turned up a series of would-be heirs, among them a man who claimed to be Hughes's son and who said he communicated with his father through a radio transmitter implanted in his brain, and a woman who decided she was Hughes's daughter because she walked like him.

A woman named Martha Graves showed up with a copy of a will, dated July 1960, in which Hughes left 20 percent of his money to the Acme Mining Company, of which Graves happened to be the president and major stockholder. Graves couldn't produce the original document, she explained, because she'd packed it and the airline had lost her luggage. For her efforts, a judge awarded her a year in prison.

Somewhat more credible was the story of Terry Moore, an actress with whom Hughes had an affair in the late forties. The affair was real, and had been recorded in the gossip columns of Louella Parsons and Hedda Hopper. But according to Moore, it was more than an affair.

In her deposition for a Texas court, Moore testified she and Hughes had been married. The wedding took place on Hughes's yacht, somewhere off the coast of Mexico, and was presided over by the ship's captain. There was no license or ring, Moore conceded, but she had seen enough movies to know that a captain could marry you at sea.

Why did she keep the marriage a secret? "I was the eternal virgin," she said, describing her Hollywood image. "Howard had the reputation of being a roué, and it would be very harmful to my reputation to be married to him."

Moore's story came with no will and with one big hole in it: she had subsequently married three other men. Still, it made Hughes's relatives nervous. They stood to lose everything if by chance the court determined Moore was Hughes's widow (not to mention a bigamist). So they reached an out-of-court settlement, reportedly paying her about $350,000.

Of all the claims to the Hughes fortune, though, the one that most captured America's attention was what came to be known as the "Mormon Will." That's because it was found in the Mormon headquarters in Salt Lake City, and it gave one-sixteenth of the Hughes fortune to the Mormon Church. It also left a fourth of his assets to the Medical Institute, a fourth to establish a home for orphans, an eighth to various universities, a sixteenth to Hughes's two ex-wives (not counting Moore), a sixteenth for school scholarships, a sixteenth to be divided among Hughes's aides, a sixteenth to Hughes's cousin William Lummis—and a sixteenth to a former milkman named Melvin Dummar.

Reporters found Dummar in April 1976, working at a small gas station in Willard, Utah, and he told them he didn't know anything about the will. But he did recall that, back in January 1968, he had picked up a bum on a highway south of Tonopah and had given him a lift to Las Vegas. The bum had told him he was Howard Hughes, though Dummar certainly hadn't believed him. Dummar gave him a quarter before dropping him off.

It was easy to see why people wanted to believe Dummar's story of a good Samaritan receiving his just—and surprising—reward. Dummar wanted to be a country singer, and one of his songs was "A Dream Can Become a Reality." His dreams had carried him to three appearances on *Let's Make a Deal*, on one of which he won a car, a freezer, and a range. Now he stood to win a lot more.

Dummar's big break came when Noah Dietrich, the former Hughes executive named in the Mormon Will as executor, pronounced the handwriting and signature genuine. "It's the real thing," Dietrich told reporters.

Hughes's relatives, not surprisingly, disagreed, and they prepared to take their case to court. They pointed out that the will was riddled with spelling and grammar mistakes, even though Hughes was fairly good at both. Moreover, the will donated the *Spruce Goose* to the city of Long Beach, California. The *Spruce Goose* was the popular name for a huge flying boat Hughes had built, but it was a name he hated, and in fact he didn't even own the plane in 1968, when he supposedly wrote the will.

As for Dietrich's validation, the relatives had handwriting experts of their own to contradict it. They also noted that the executive and Hughes had split bitterly in 1957, making him an unlikely choice for executor, and that Dietrich stood to make millions in fees if the will was upheld.

Dummar's case began to fall apart in December, when investigators for the Hughes relatives found his fingerprints on a library copy of *Hoax,* a book about a failed attempt to forge a Hughes autobiography. An insert of the photographs used to copy Hughes's handwriting was missing from the book, leading investigators to suspect Dummar cut out the section. Things got worse when the FBI found his fingerprint on the corner of the envelope in which the will had been found at the Mormon headquarters. This seemed to prove Dummar a liar, since for seven months he had denied having seen the will, or even having heard of it, prior to reporters telling him about it.

In January, Dummar abruptly changed his story. He admitted he was the one who delivered the will to the church, but he continued to deny he had anything to do with writing it. His new account had a mysterious stranger in a blue Mercedes drive up to his gas station, then leave the envelope and the will on the counter. Dummar explained that he'd lied at first, because he feared no one would believe this story. Few did.

A month later, with the case seemingly lost, the stranger in the Mercedes miraculously appeared. This was Levane Forsythe, a construction worker from Alaska who, he announced, had been a secret courier for Howard Hughes. Forsythe said Hughes had given him the will in 1972, along with instructions to deliver it to Dummar after his death.

Was Forsythe telling the truth? Was Dummar? Harold Rhoden, the attorney representing Dietrich, argued they were.

"The will itself is bizarre," he conceded. "Bizarre in what it says, bizarre in the way it was written and in the way it was kept for eight years. And bizarre in the way it was delivered to the Mormon Church. But this was the bizarre way of the man who wrote it."

The eight members of the Las Vegas jury who heard their testimony didn't buy it. In June 1977, they voted unanimously that the will "was not written by Howard R. Hughes."

Dummar did not come out of the affair entirely empty-handed. His country singing career got a boost, albeit a brief one, when he was booked for two weeks in Reno. Unlike Martha Graves, Melvin Dummar was not tried for fraud. And many continued to believe his story, especially after it was turned into a popular movie, *Melvin and Howard,* in 1980, in which Hughes was played by Jason Robards and Dummar by Paul Le Mat. The real Dummar made a brief appearance as a counterman in a bus station cafeteria.

Dummar continued to dream. "What hurts me most about this will, worse than having it ruled a forgery," he said, "is that I didn't get to play myself in the movie."

Dummar's description of Hughes as looking like a bum was not far from the truth, at least in his final years. Devastated by years of drug abuse, the billionaire died with broken needles in his arms and weighing only ninety-two pounds. This led some, including Texas attorney general Rick Harrison, to suspect that his aides, perhaps with the help of his doctors, had murdered Hughes.

No one was charged with murder, though two of Hughes's doctors pleaded "no contest" to illegally supplying Hughes with drugs. And a murder conspiracy seems unlikely, especially since—in the absence of a will leaving them anything—the aides and doctors had more to gain from Hughes alive than dead.

With no will in sight, the way was clear for Lummis and various other Hughes relatives to inherit varying percentages of his fortune. The total distribution turned out to be, disappointingly, less than a billion dollars, partly because of the huge estate taxes and legal fees.

What would Howard Hughes have thought about that?

Most people pictured him turning over in his grave, distraught to see his fortune go to the government and to relatives he cared nothing about. Some suspected a valid will was destroyed, or might still turn up.

But it's also very possible Hughes never wrote one. Obsessed by his germ-phobia, he spent his final years in various hideouts around the globe. He saw increasingly few people and cared about even fewer. Why, he may have thought, should any of them get his money?

Sure, he had said he would leave the money to medical research, but there's no evidence he really cared about this. The Howard Hughes Medical Institute was in reality little more than a tax shelter; for all his talk about the charity, at no point in his life did Hughes donate any substantial sum to it. As for the promises to his aides and doctors, maybe Hughes was just stringing them along to keep them loyal. Maybe he even feared they'd kill him if he actually wrote them into his will.

"His selfish being knew nothing now of love, of tenderness, of companionship," wrote biographer Charles Higham. "Now he could really show that he cared for nothing."

"He promised [his aides he would] compose an entirely new will. Soon. But he never would," speculated journalist Michael Drosnin. "The nonexistent last testament was his last hold on power."

In the end, that power may have been all he cared about.

☆ To investigate further:

Fay, Stephen, Lewis Chester, and Magnus Linklater. *Hoax.* New York: Viking, 1972. This is the book from which Dummar allegedly cut out photos of Hughes's signature to copy. It's also the fascinating story of how Clifford Irving forged Hughes's autobiography, a scam that might have succeeded had Hughes not emerged from seclusion, briefly, to deny he had anything to do with Irving's book.

Barlett, Donald, and James Steele. *Empire.* W. W. Norton. 1979. "This is the book," wrote the *New York Times,* "Clifford Irving must wish he had written." It remains the best biography of Hughes.

Rhoden, Harold. *High Stakes.* New York, Crown, 1980. Rhoden, the attorney who represented Dietrich, believed in Dummar, even if the jury didn't.

Drosnin, Michael. *Citizen Hughes.* New York: Holt, Rinehart and Winston, 1985. Focuses on Hughes's final years, especially his political influence and his involvement in Watergate.

Higham, Charles. *Howard Hughes.* New York: Putnam's, 1993. A portrait of Hughes as ruthless, albeit drug-ridden, to the end.

Brown, Peter, and Pat Broeske. *Howard Hughes.* New York: Dutton, 1996. Everything you wanted to know about his sex life.

Phelan, James, and Lewis Chester. *The Money.* New York: Random House, 1997. The battle for the billions.

Hack, Richard. *Hughes.* Beverly Hills, California: New Millennium Press, 2001. The latest biography, and one of the most comprehensive.

Chapter 57

Did Reagan Plan an October Surprise?

From the moment Iranian students seized the U.S. embassy in Tehran and took the Americans there hostage, President Jimmy Carter was desperate to win their release. After Ronald Reagan received the Republican presidential nomination, many in his campaign were equally obsessed by the hostage crisis. The Republicans' fear was that Carter would pull off what they called an "October Surprise"—a last-minute deal that would free the hostages, boost the president's popularity, and win him the 1980 election. On January 18, 1981, Carter and the Iranians finally reached a deal, but by then it was too late to save his presidency. Two days later, which was 444 days after the Iranians overran the embassy and just hours after Reagan took office, all fifty-two hostages were on their way home.

The timing was no coincidence. The final deal, which unfroze billions of dollars of Iranian assets, was not significantly different from what Carter had offered in October. Most commentators assumed Iran's Ayatollah Ruhollah Khomeini waited until January because of his personal animosity toward Carter. Having cost Carter the election, Khomeini heaped on him the additional humiliation of waiting until Reagan took office to free the hostages.

Others, however, saw something even more sinister in the timing. They suspected the Reagan campaign had pulled off its own October Surprise, a secret deal by which the Iranians agreed not to free the hostages until after the American election, in return for which the

President Reagan greets the hostages. (National Archives.)

new Reagan administration would send them not just money but arms. If true, this was a scandal that dwarfed Watergate or Iran-contra, one that struck at the very heart of the democratic process.

"If a deal had been made by Reagan's team," wrote Gary Sick, a member of Carter's National Security Council and one of the administration's leading experts on Iran, "bartering the freedom and conceivably the safety of fifty-two Americans for political gain, the very legitimacy of the Reagan presidency was put into question."

☆ ☆ ☆

Allegations about the Reagan campaign's October Surprise evolved over a number of years, surfacing in the *Washington Post* and *New York Times* in 1986 and in later pieces in the *Miami Herald*, *The Nation*, *In These Times*, *Playboy*, and elsewhere. Sick synthesized much of this work, added a great deal of his own research, and published *October Surprise* in 1991.

Sick's take on events was especially striking because he had been a key figure in setting Carter's Iran policy without suspecting the Republicans might be conducting separate negotiations with the Iranians. Indeed, Sick's 1985 book, *All Fall Down*, recounted the events of

1979 through 1981 without even mentioning the rumors of a secret Republican deal. The 1991 book told quite a different story.

"The essence of the arrangement from the start," Sick wrote, "was for Iran to hand the hostages over to the Republicans (rather than Jimmy Carter) in return for some arms immediately (via Israel) plus the promise of future arms and political benefits once the Reagan administration came into office." Sick was convinced the Republicans not only struck a deal but carried it out: "Almost immediately [after Reagan took office], the flow of arms to Iran intensified."

The man behind the deal, according to Sick, was William Casey, Reagan's campaign manager and later director of the CIA. In February 1980, Casey approached Jamshid Hashemi, an Iranian arms dealer, to arrange a meeting with the ayatollah's representatives. Campaign and Iranian officials met that summer in Madrid and that fall at the L'Enfant Plaza Hotel in Washington. They closed the deal in October in Paris.

October, Sick noted, was also when the Iranians, for no apparent reason, temporarily stopped negotiating. "Khomeini and the Iranian leadership had what they considered to be a more attractive offer if they were willing to wait," Sick wrote. "Jimmy Carter had been extremely uncooperative in Israel's efforts to restore an arms relationship with Iran whereas the Reagan-Bush campaign held out the prospect of improved relations, at least at the covert level, and a steady supply of military equipment through Israel."

Sick's main sources were five Iranians and Israelis who allegedly participated in these meetings, including Hashemi. Former Iranian Prime Minister Abol Hassan Bani-Sadr also said he believed there was a secret deal, though he didn't participate directly in the talks.

From the American side, there were quick denials, except from Casey, who died in 1987, four years before Sick's book was published. Reagan's aides said they were nowhere near Paris or Madrid at the time of the alleged meetings. Two campaign foreign policy advisors, Richard Allen and Laurence Silberman, admitted they'd discussed the hostages with an Iranian representative at the L'Enfant Plaza. But they stressed they were merely collecting information; in fact, they claimed, when the Iranian representative (whose name they didn't know) offered to trade the hostages for arms, Allen and Silberman abruptly ended the meeting.

The furor over Sick's allegations forced Congress to step in. In August 1991, the House and the Senate launched separate but parallel investigations into the October Surprise.

The Senate's Committee on Foreign Relations finished first, issuing its report in November 1992. The Senate report criticized the Reagan campaign for failing to report what it knew, such as what the Iranian representative told Allen and Silberman at the L'Enfant Plaza. More seriously, the report stated Casey was "fishing in troubled waters." (That was the phrase used by Ahmad Madani, one of the Iranian officials questioned by Senate investigators, to describe Casey's behavior.) On the most serious charge, that of delaying the release of the hostages through a secret deal, the report concluded there was not "sufficient credible evidence."

The House report followed in January 1993, and was generally considered more significant, since its task force interviewed more than 250 people across the world and reviewed tens of thousands of documents. The House provided the Reagan campaign with a more complete, though not absolute, vindication. Most of the Iranians and Israelis who were supposedly at the meetings testified they hadn't been in either Madrid or Paris, and the documentary evidence—hotel and telephone records, personal calendars, passports—backed up their stories. The Ritz Hotel in Paris, supposedly the site of one of the final meetings, didn't have any conference facilities matching the descriptions in the allegations.

Hashemi, it turned out, had been under FBI surveillance during 1980, and the FBI turned over its tapes to the task force. After listening to twenty-one thousand of Hashemi's secretly recorded conversations, the task force found no mention of the Madrid or Paris meetings. Under oath, Hashemi backed away from his earlier statements that he had attended the meetings. Three other Sick sources also testified that they didn't know anything about the meetings. Two stuck by their earlier stories, but couldn't present any corroborating evidence. The task force concluded they were liars.

As for the Americans, most were able to prove to the task force's satisfaction that they hadn't been in either Madrid or Paris. The Secret Service corroborated that then–vice-presidential candidate George Bush, who one of Sick's sources placed at the Paris meetings, was actually in Washington at the time. It was more difficult to trace Casey's itinerary for the summer and fall of 1980, since he was no longer alive. Casey left for London on July 27 to attend a conference on World War II, and returned to the United States two days later. The task force decided that did not leave him time for a side trip to Madrid.

The House report also believed the Reagan aides' account of the L'Enfant Plaza meeting, though they faulted Allen and Silberman for not reporting it to Carter administration officials.

It was impossible, the task force concluded, to "prove a negative" and to absolutely rule out the possibility that there was a secret meeting. But "in almost all instances, the evidence clearly establishes the presence of major alleged participants . . . to be someplace else, doing something else."

☆ ☆ ☆

The Reagan administration, though it publicly supported an embargo on arms sales to Iran, was clearly more willing than Carter's to turn a blind eye toward them. In fact, the House task force noted, Iran bought more than $4 billion in arms from various countries during Reagan's first two years in office. Even more damaging to Reagan's reputation was the 1986 revelation that the administration itself sold arms to Iran, and then illegally used the profits to support the Nicaraguan contras.

So it was not surprising that the House report did not dispel all suspicions. In a 1993 op-ed piece in the *New York Times*, Sick wrote that the "concern expressed by Senate investigators that Mr. Casey was 'fishing in troubled waters' remains." The *Times* itself editorialized that "from the outset, the Reagan administration considered using U.S. arms to bolster supposed 'moderates' in Iran, and . . . that's the mentality that led to the Iran-contra affair, which was very definitely not the concoction of conspiracy-mongers."

But most historians, including Sick, accepted the report's conclusion that, whatever else they may have done, Reagan's campaign aides did not trade arms for the hostages. The task force interviewed many of the dealers who sold arms to Iran in 1980 and 1981, and all denied any link between their sales and the hostages. The dealers' sole reason for selling arms to Iran, they explained, was to make money.

If there was no deal, why did the Iranians wait until Reagan took office to free the hostages?

One possibility, as many commentators immediately assumed, was that Khomeini hated Carter a lot more than he hated Reagan. But there were historical as well as personal forces at work. In 1979, when Iranian students first stormed the embassy, Khomeini was just one of many who aspired to rule the country. With no one in control, there was no one with the power to free the Americans. By the second half of 1980, Khomeini was firmly in charge. And unlike his more moderate opponents, he didn't have to worry that, if he let the hostages go, he'd be accused of being pro-American.

The final push for their freedom came from Saddam Hussein, who invaded Iran in September 1980. To fight Iraq, Iran needed money and weapons, and Khomeini must have realized it was time to let the hostages go. The ayatollah's final delay, from September to January, may have been intended to cost Carter the election. He may also have wanted, as historian David Patrick Houghton speculated, to demonstrate his power over America. In 1953, after nationalists took over Iran, a CIA-backed coup put the Shah back on the throne. Twenty-seven years later, Khomeini showed that Iran, too, could decide who would be its enemy's leader.

☆ To investigate further:

Sick, Gary. *October Surprise.* New York: Times Books, 1991. Sick, more than anyone else, forced Congress to investigate.

The "October Surprise" Allegations and the Circumstances Surrounding the Release of the American Hostages in Iran. Washington, D.C.: U.S. Government Printing Office, 1992. The Senate report.

Joint Report of the Task Force to Investigate Certain Allegations Concerning the Holding of American Hostages by Iran in 1980. Washington, D.C.: U.S. Government Printing Office, 1993. The House report.

Walsh, Lawrence. *Iran-Contra: The Final Report.* New York: Times Books, 1994. Though the October Surprise and Iran-contra investigations were separate, one can't help but notice that many of the same figures keep cropping up in both.

Houghton, David Patrick. *U.S. Foreign Policy and the Iran Hostage Crisis.* New York: Cambridge University Press, 2001. A useful if somewhat theoretical analysis of the Carter administration's decisions.

Chapter 58

What Did Reagan Know About Iran-Contra?

Throughout the early 1980s, Congress was engaged in a heated debate over whether to support the contra rebels in Nicaragua. Supporters of the contras, among them President Ronald Reagan, portrayed them as anticommunist freedom fighters; opponents decried them for being more interested in profiteering than in democracy or human rights. In the summer of 1984, the contras' congressional opponents prevailed. Capitalizing on public fears that support for the contras could enmesh the nation in another Vietnam, they passed the Boland amendment, which banned any further military aid to the contras. Then in October 1986, Nicaraguan soldiers shot down a cargo plane carrying arms to the contras. The captured pilot, Eugene Hasenfus, confessed that he was part of a covert U.S. government-supported operation—an operation in clear violation of the Boland amendment.

Not true, Reagan assured reporters. Although he adamantly supported the contra cause, his administration had had to abide by the will of Congress. Hasenfus was a private citizen working on behalf of other private citizens. "There was no government connection with that at all," Reagan stressed.

A month later, just as the furor over Hasenfus's statement was dying down, a Lebanese newspaper reported that the Reagan administration had shipped arms to Iran in an effort to win the freedom of

American hostages being held in Lebanon. Again the White House was plunged into crisis. In this case, the problem was not so much that such arms shipments were illegal (though they were a violation of the Arms Export Control Act), but that they directly contravened the administration's own oft-stated policy of not negotiating with terrorists. In fact the Reagan administration had been actively pressuring other countries to join an arms embargo against Iran. If the arms-for-hostages story were true, the administration looked like hypocrites, or worse, like fools—for once Iran had the weapons in hand, what was to prevent the terrorists from seizing more hostages?

The administration's response again was to deny the story. Yes, the president said in a televised talk on November 13, the United States had been in contact with some groups in Iran, but this had been purely an effort to bolster those moderates in their efforts to seize power from Ayatollah Khomeini. "We did not—repeat—did not trade weapons or anything else for hostages, nor will we," Reagan said.

Then, on November 25, the president opened a press conference by admitting he had not been "fully informed" of the nature of his administration's dealings with Iran. At that point Attorney General Edwin Meese took the podium and announced that some weapons had indeed been sold to Iran. Even more shocking, Meese continued, was that the profits from these arms sales—approximately $12 million—had been used to finance the contra war efforts. So the Iran and contra stories were not only true, they were linked.

The man responsible for the "diversion" of the $12 million, Meese said, was a mid-level staffer at the National Security Council, Lieutenant Colonel Oliver North. North had now been "relieved of his duties" and his superior, National Security Adviser John Poindexter, had resigned. But if Meese thought that would put an end to the scandal, he was mistaken. Over the next seven years a series of investigations delved deeper and deeper into the Iran-contra affair, attempting to find out who knew what—and when. Above all, what they wanted to know was this: Did Reagan himself know about—or authorize—the covert operations of his National Security Council?

☆ ☆ ☆

Eager to make clear there was no cover-up, the president quickly appointed a commission to investigate the affair. The Tower Commission (named after its chairman, ex-Senator John Tower) interviewed key figures, including Reagan. On the subject of aid to the contras, Reagan was clear: he told the commission he had not known about the activities of the National Security Council staff. On Iran, he was more confused. In his first interview, he said he had approved a shipment of arms to Iran; in his second interview, he retracted this position. Then in a letter to the commission, Reagan wrote: "The simple truth is 'I don't remember.'"

The commission accepted the president's word. After all, Reagan's reputation had always been that of a hands-off manager, one who set broad policy but paid little attention to the details. It was easy to imagine his being oblivious to the actions of the NSC staff members. The Tower Commission report was highly unflattering to the president—the forgetful, confused figure who emerges in the report's pages was hardly the image Reagan wanted to project—but it exonerated him of any wrongdoing or knowledge of wrongdoing.

Next up were the House and Senate, each of which appointed a select committee to investigate the Iran-contra affair. The most dramatic testimony before the joint committee was that of North. Having been granted "use immunity" by Congress—which meant nothing he said could be used against him in any future criminal proceedings—North admitted he'd shredded documents, falsified evidence, and participated in other illicit activities intended to aid the contras and cover up the arms-for-hostages deals. But in spite of these admissions, North emerged from the hearings a star—and, to many, a hero. His patriotic fervor, his military bearing, his all-American looks made him seem far more likeable than his congressional inquisitors. Also working in North's favor was the fact that the committee had decided to avoid any substantive discussions on the merits of contra aid (and that seventeen of the twenty-six committee members had voted *for* aid). North could speechify about freedom fighters without fear of being contradicted.

In addition, North emphasized he was no lone ranger; he was a loyal soldier following orders. When the Boland amendment was passed, North's boss, National Security Adviser Robert McFarlane (who preceded Poindexter in the job), came to him with instructions directly from the president. These instructions, North told the committee, were to keep the contras together, "body and soul." McFarlane, in his testimony, confirmed that Reagan had said this to him, and that he had passed it on to North.

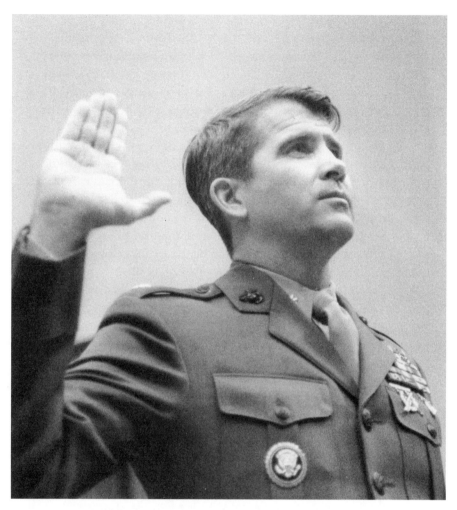

A man so good at following orders that a fellow marine once said: "Ollie North's commanding officer should never even think out loud." (UPI/Corbis-Bettmann.)

Did this mean President Reagan had ordered the diversion of funds from the Iran arms sales to the contras? North didn't know. Neither did McFarlane, who had been replaced by Poindexter before the diversion. And Poindexter testified that he had *not* told the president about the diversion. "The buck stops here with me," he told the congressional committee.

After Poindexter's testimony, the committee eased up on Reagan. Its report was harsher than that of the Tower Commission—the president was blamed for creating or at least tolerating an environment where those who did know of the diversion could easily believe they were carrying out the president's policies. But on the key question of whether he ordered the diversion or even knew about it, he was off the hook.

In retrospect, many have speculated about why the committee backed away from investigating what else Reagan did or didn't know, what else he did or didn't order. After all, the diversion was merely the point at which the Iran and contra scandals intersected; it was hardly the entirety of either scandal. Why didn't the committee take a deeper look at Reagan's role in the Iran arms sales themselves, or in the overall National Security Council effort on behalf of the contras? Why did the diversion become the focus of the investigation?

In his autobiography, North suggested one reason why the administration chose to focus on the diversion:

> This particular detail was so dramatic, so sexy, that it might actually—well, *divert* public attention from other, even more important aspects of the story, such as what *else* the President and his top advisers had known about and approved. And if it could be insinuated that this supposedly terrible deed was the exclusive responsibility of one mid-level staff assistant at the National Security Council (and perhaps his immediate superior, the national security adviser), and that staffer had acted on his own (however unlikely *that* might be), and then, now that you mention it, his activities might even be *criminal*—if the public and the press focused on *that,* then maybe you didn't have another Watergate on your hands after all. Especially if you insisted that the President knew nothing about it.

In other words, the administration used the diversion as a diversion.

Still, the congressional committee went along with the focus on the diversion. This can be explained partly by the committee's makeup. Its members were, by and large, moderates; they had no desire to uncover information that might bring them uncomfortably close to a discussion of impeachment. And partly, the committee was following the lead of the public, which just wasn't that interested in the scandal. At one point, the *New Republic* tried to stir things up by holding a contest to come up with a jazzier name for the "Iran-contra affair." Entries included "Contraversions," "Ronnybrook," and the winner, "Iranamok." None caught on.

The underlying problem was that, in contrast to the dark and brooding Nixon, Reagan remained ever cheerful and popular. The committee's members had no desire to undercut that popularity. Moreover, the committee had early on set a ten-month timetable by which they wanted their hearings and report finished, and time was running out. So the hearings ended and the report came out—with many questions unanswered.

Lawrence Walsh, the independent counsel appointed by a three-judge panel to prosecute any illegal activities associated with Iran-contra, was not burdened by the political or time pressures felt by the congressional committee. His investigations continued until 1993 and resulted in criminal charges against fourteen individuals. Among these were McFarlane, who pleaded guilty to four counts of withholding information from Congress; North, who was convicted of altering and destroying documents, accepting an illegal gratuity, and aiding and abetting in the obstruction of Congress; and Poindexter, who was convicted of conspiracy, false statements, destruction and removal of records, and obstruction of Congress.

But though Walsh was not burdened by the political or time pressures on the congressional committee, he was bound by its grants of immunity. North and Poindexter appealed the convictions, arguing that witnesses at their trials had to have been influenced by the highly publicized congressional testimony. The appeals court admitted that was possible and reversed the convictions. North then declared himself "totally exonerated." But that was nonsense. The only reason North went free was that the crimes he'd been charged with were crimes he'd admitted to while under immunity.

The North and Poindexter reversals did not dissuade Walsh from pushing on—up into the highest levels of the Reagan administration. After a lengthy investigation, Walsh concluded that then Vice President George Bush was not nearly as "out of the loop" as he later claimed. Bush was regularly briefed on the Iran and contra operations, though he probably didn't know about the diversion. In the end though, Walsh decided not to prosecute Bush. Unlike the Tower Com-

mission or the congressional committees, whose job had been to uncover the truth, Walsh's mandate was more limited. His responsibility
was merely to prosecute criminals, and Walsh did not have enough evidence to prove that the vice president had violated any criminal
statute. Still, the investigation kept Bush on the defensive throughout
the presidential elections of 1988 (when he defeated Michael Dukakis)
and 1992 (when he was defeated by Bill Clinton).

Walsh also investigated the roles of Secretary of State George
Shultz and Secretary of Defense Caspar Weinberger. Shultz and Weinberger, Walsh admitted, were peculiar targets. They were the only
high-level members of the Reagan administration who had consistently *opposed* the arms deal with Iran. But Walsh argued they'd known
what was going on and conspired to cover up the Iran arms sales in order to protect the president.

In the case of Shultz, Walsh eventually decided there was a reasonable doubt as to whether he'd willfully given any false testimony
and Walsh decided not to prosecute. In the case of Weinberger, Walsh
charged him with four counts of false statements and perjury. Then on
the eve of the trial in December 1992, President Bush took his revenge
on Walsh. In one of his final acts before turning over the Oval Office to
Clinton, Bush pardoned Weinberger. In doing so, Bush argued that
Walsh was prosecuting officials because he disagreed with their policies, not because of any actual criminal activities. Walsh, in turn, accused Bush of pardoning Weinberger to cover up his own role, and
that of Reagan, in the Iran-contra affair.

Objective observers, including Theodore Draper, the leading
Iran-contra historian, have criticized both Walsh and Bush. Walsh was
faulted for pursuing a Shultz and Weinberger conspiracy theory that
was never entirely clear or convincing and that was, in any case, tan-
gential to the main Iran-contra issues. And Bush's action was suspiciously self-serving: Had the Weinberger case gone to trial, Bush
would certainly have been called as a witness and his claims to have
been out of the loop would have been strenuously contested.

As for Reagan, he had slipped beyond Walsh's grasp well before
the pardons. Reagan's testimony (via videotape) at the Poindexter trial
and his subsequent interviews with Walsh revealed a man who seemed
genuinely unable to recall even the main events of Iran-contra. Perhaps, in retrospect, Reagan was already suffering from the early stages
of Alzheimer's disease (which was later diagnosed). In any case, Walsh

concluded, Reagan's conduct, like Bush's, "fell well short of criminality which could be successfully prosecuted."

Nonetheless, of the three official reports on Iran-contra, Walsh's came down the hardest on Reagan. "The President's disregard for civil laws enacted to limit presidential action abroad," Walsh wrote, "created a climate in which some government officials assigned to implement his policies felt emboldened to circumvent such laws." By directing McFarlane to keep the contras alive "body and soul," by disregarding the warnings of Shultz and Weinberger against selling arms to Iran, by openly encouraging individuals and other countries to fund the contras during the ban on U.S. aid, Reagan set the stage on which Oliver North acted. In this sense, there is no question that the man responsible for Iran-contra was Ronald Reagan.

☆ To investigate further:

Tower, John, Edmund Muskie and Brent Scowcroft. *The Tower Commission Report.* New York: Times Books, 1987. The first official report.

U.S. House of Representatives Select Committee to Investigate Covert Arms Transactions with Iran and U.S. Senate Select Committee on Secret Military Assistance to Iran and the Nicaraguan Opposition. *Report of the Congressional Committees Investigating the Iran-Contra Affair.* 1987. The second official report.

Cockburn, Leslie. *Out of Control.* New York: Atlantic Monthly Press, 1987. Contends that well before the Boland amendment was passed, the administration was involved in a wide range of activities that circumvented congressional restrictions on aid to the contras. Also presents evidence that the contras were involved in drug smuggling and that the CIA knew about it.

Cohen, William, and George Mitchell. *Men of Zeal.* New York: Viking, 1988. Two senators on the Iran-contra committee tell, among other things, how the television cameras affected their inquiries and why they gave Ollie North immunity.

Segev, Samuel. *The Iranian Triangle.* New York: The Free Press, 1988. Focuses on Israel's role in the Iran-contra affair and on the Israeli side of the triangular U.S.-Iran-Israel relationship.

Reagan, Ronald. *An American Life.* New York: Simon & Schuster, 1990. The president's own version, or at least that of one of his better ghostwriters.

North, Oliver. *Under Fire.* New York: HarperCollins, 1991. The number one best-seller from the man so good at following orders that a fellow marine once commented: "Ollie North's commanding officer should never even think out loud."

Draper, Theodore. *A Very Thin Line.* New York: Hill and Wang, 1991. A thorough reconstruction of the Iran-contra affair and the numerous crossings of the thin line that separates the legitimate from the illegitimate exercise of government power.

Wroe, Ann. *Lives, Lies and the Iran-Contra Affair.* New York: I. B. Tauris & Co., 1991. A British journalist's provocative perspectives on the moral and political philosophies underlying the affair.

Kornbluh, Peter, and Malcolm Byrne. *The Iran-Contra Scandal: The Declassified History.* New York: The New Press, 1993. A useful documentary history.

Walsh, Lawrence E. *Iran-Contra: The Final Report.* New York: Times Books, 1994. The results of the independent counsel's seven years of investigations.

McFarlane, Robert. *Special Trust.* New York: Cadell & Davies, 1994. Like the books of most of the principals (almost all of whom wrote one), McFarlane's is somewhat self-serving, but his has more pathos—and perhaps more credibility—since he was the only figure involved to show some remorse about his role in the affair. So much remorse, in fact, that in February 1987 he attempted suicide.

Timberg, Robert. *The Nightingale's Song.* New York: Simon & Schuster, 1995. An elegant multiperson biography, which traces Iran-contra back to its origins in the experiences of McFarlane, Poindexter, and North at the Naval Academy in Annapolis and later in Vietnam.

Chapter 59

What Caused Gulf War Syndrome?

It was, journalist Seymour Hersh observed, "the perfect war." In just a few weeks of bombing and a few days of ground fighting, the United States drove the Iraqis out of Kuwait and forced Saddam Hussein to concede defeat. "We've kicked the Vietnam syndrome," said the first President George Bush.

Yet within a few years the Gulf War had given its name to a syndrome of its own—a mysterious illness that befell about 100,000 of the 700,000 veterans who served in the Persian Gulf. The most common symptoms were headaches, rashes, muscle and joint pain, diarrhea, loss of memory, shortness of breath, insomnia, and exhaustion—in many cases severely debilitating.

Many vets, naturally, looked to the Gulf for the cause. Some suspected it was something in the air, perhaps the soot or something else from the spectacular oil well fires that burned out of control for months. They dubbed the pollution "Agent Oil," after Agent Orange, the herbicide American forces used in Vietnam and later implicated in the chronic health problems of some vets. But there were very few respiratory complaints of the type the soot or other particles would likely have caused, so doctors ruled out the oil fires as the source of the problems. Other possibilities moved to the fore. Perhaps it was some bacterium or virus, or a pesticide or vaccine used in the Gulf, or depleted uranium, a radioactive material used during the war (for the first time) in U.S. weapons. Or perhaps the vets were suffering the effects of Iraqi chemical or biological weapons.

The Pentagon denied any of these were the problem. Indeed, defense officials denied there was a problem. A 1992 report by the Walter Reed Army Institute of Research concluded there was "no objective evidence for an outbreak of disease." As more and more vets came forward with complaints, officials had to acknowledge they were sick, but they continued to maintain the symptoms had nothing to do with the Gulf, or at least with any toxic agents there. Many of the first to complain were with reserve units; perhaps, officials surmised, they had been less able than regular soldiers to handle the stress of war. Veterans Administration doctors suggested psychological counseling.

This managed only to enrage the sick vets, who were certain the problem wasn't in their minds. They accused officials of trying to avoid paying them war-related benefits, or of trying to protect the image of a war won virtually without casualties. "This is not a mental problem with the veterans," said Michigan Senator Donald Riegle, one of the vets' strongest advocates. "It may be a mental problem over at the Defense Department."

The first Gulf War was over, but the battle over the syndrome that bears its name raged on.

☆ ☆ ☆

Riegle's position as chair of the banking committee proved surprisingly relevant, since it enabled him to investigate the sale of weapons to Iraq in the 1980s, when the U.S. supported Saddam Hussein's war against Iran. Among the exports from American companies was a stock of anthrax. Here was another incentive for a government cover-up: the United States had supplied Hussein with weapons that he could use against American GIs. In 1993, Riegle's staff issued the first of a series of reports blaming biological and chemical weapons for the vets' ailments.

Defense officials quickly denied the allegations, arguing there was no evidence that any American soldiers had been exposed to anthrax. The vets' symptoms, they pointed out, didn't match those of anthrax or other biological agents. These weapons are designed to quickly kill or disable their victims. Many vets, in contrast, didn't become sick until months or years after the war.

Riegle's focus then switched to chemical weapons. The Bush administration, it turned out, had supplied Iraq not only with biological pathogens but also with the chemicals needed for nerve gas, and United

Nations inspectors in Iraq after the war determined American intelligence had vastly underestimated Hussein's chemical weapon capability.

Defense officials responded much as they had to the allegations of biological warfare: there was no evidence chemical weapons were used against Americans, the symptoms didn't fit, the reactions would have been acute and immediate, not chronic and delayed.

In December 1996, a committee of scientists appointed by President Bill Clinton weighed in. Basically, the committee sided with the Defense Department experts. The most likely culprit remained stress, which the committee described as "an important contributing factor to the broad range of illnesses currently being reported by Gulf War veterans."

It was not the committee's conclusions, however, that received the most attention. The most startling revelation to come out of its research was that, contrary to all the Pentagon's denials, American soldiers *had* been exposed to nerve gas in Iraq.

The exposure, the Pentagon now admitted, came just after the war ended. In March 1991, U.S. forces blew up an ammunition depot at Khamisiyah in southern Iraq. Though military officials didn't realize it at the time of the bombing, a 1986 CIA report left no doubt that Khamisiyah contained artillery shells filled with the nerve gas sarin.

For suspicious veterans and their advocates, the Khamisiyah revelations proved the government couldn't be trusted. "It's clearly a cover up," said Connecticut Congressman Christopher Shays, another veterans advocate. "The DOD [Department of Defense], the VA [Veterans Administration], the CIA, and even the FDA as it related to their involvement with the DOD, has no credibility with me."

"It's hard for me to imagine that some people in the CIA who had firsthand knowledge would be unable to recognize that this would be helpful information," Shays continued. "Forget having Congress know. The soldiers. Think how outraged you would be as a soldier to learn, five years later, that you might have been exposed to chemicals, and that if they knew sooner you might have been able to be in a treatment program and yet you weren't given that information."

The CIA argued that a communications breakdown was to blame. Investigative journalist Seymour Hersh accepted that explanation, concluding that Khamisiyah "was a criminally negligent mistake, but it was not a cover-up." Hersh interviewed Generals Colin Powell and Norman Schwarzkopf, both of whom denied having known there was nerve gas at Khamisiyah. "There is no reason to doubt their word," Hersh decided. "Even the military's harshest critics in the Gulf War veterans' groups and Congress acknowledge that no American commander would ignore firm evidence of nerve gas exposure and thus put his troops at risk."

Whoever was to blame, there was no longer any denying that U.S. soldiers—perhaps as many as a hundred thousand, according to some estimates—had been exposed to nerve gas. And many of the sick vets were now sure this was the cause of their ailments. So the medical experts reexamined the issue.

"We went back and looked at all our clinical [data]," said Dr. Stephen Joseph, Assistant Secretary of Defense for Health Affairs from 1994 to 1997. "I mean, there's the best example of what a bombshell, no pun intended, was."

Ultimately, Joseph "didn't really see that the Khamisiyah revelation invalidated anything we'd done." Most medical experts agreed. The amount of gas released must have been very small; otherwise the soldiers nearest the facility would certainly have suffered immediate symptoms, such as gagging or gasping.

"The levels of exposure calculated from the Khamisiyah event," stated a 2000 report prepared for the secretary of defense, "are so low that enduring responses would not be expected, and indeed, the exposure may have been at the no-effect level."

Still, the 2000 report conceded: "There is very little literature on the long-term effects of exposure to doses below those that would cause any acute clinical symptoms. The possibility that such exposure could possibly produce chronic health effects cannot be ruled out."

The report concluded by calling for more research in this area.

☆ ☆ ☆

Another area on which researchers are focusing is a possible connection between Gulf War syndrome and similar illnesses, such as chronic fatigue syndrome, fibromyalgia, and multiple chemical sensitivity. These illnesses have much in common: they're chronic but not fatal, their symptoms are often similar, and doctors have been unable to use conventional and objective methods of diagnosis.

In one sense, linking these illnesses merely piles one mystery on another, since scientists have neither a cause nor a cure for any of them. Nor are most sick vets happy about the search for these links,

The war made heroes of President Bush and General Norman Schwarzkopf, but not among veterans who suffered from Gulf War syndrome. (George Bush Library.)

since all these illnesses have often been tied to stress—still a dirty word to those whose symptoms are all too physical.

Increasingly, doctors have tried to reassure patients that stress can cause physical symptoms, and that saying so doesn't turn them into neurotic malingerers. Their suffering is real, regardless of its cause. "Too many of us think that to suffer stress is to admit weakness," argued Dr. Philip Landrigan, who was a member of the presidential advisory committee and who also investigated Agent Orange. "I mean, war is hell. People that go to war are heroes, and they suffer enormously. It's not surprising that when they come home, they have symptoms."

Dr. Kenneth Hyams, an infectious disease specialist and Desert Storm vet, examined decades of military and medical records and found that symptoms similar to Gulf War syndrome have recurred in veterans of every war. Gulf War vets were not exempt, just because theirs was a quick victory. "It was not a low-stress war," Hyams said. "There was less direct combat for a shorter period of time than in previous wars. But . . . there was a lot of anticipation, a lot of anxiety and worry about the outcome of the war and about the use of chemical weapons or other types of weapons of mass destruction."

That doesn't mean that stress is the complete explanation, or that research shouldn't continue on the effects of low-level exposure to nerve gas, as well as other areas. Another 2000 report to the secretary of defense, for example, found that mycoplasmas, microorganisms that can cause disease in plants and animals, were present in a number of vets with Gulf War syndrome. "We're not saying it's all psychological," Hyams said, "because there may be subsets of organic disease. But it's the most unifying explanation."

☆ To investigate further:

www.pbs.org/wgbh/pages/frontline/shows/syndrome/analysis. Based on a *Frontline* report, the PBS website includes excerpts from the presidential advisory committee report and revealing interviews with Shays, Joseph, Landrigan, Hyams, and other doctors, veterans, and advocates.

Eddington, Patrick. *Gassed in the Gulf.* Washington, D.C.: Insignia, 1997. The case, ultimately unconvincing, for a conspiracy against the veterans.

Hersh, Seymour. *Against All Enemies.* New York: Ballantine, 1998. A highly critical and effective summary of the politics and epidemiology of Gulf War syndrome.

Augerson, William. *Chemical and Biological Warfare Agents.* Santa Monica, California: RAND, 2000. One of a series of reports prepared for the secretary of defense and reviewing the scientific literature on Gulf War illnesses. Others in the series cover infectious diseases, pyridostigmine bromide (a drug given to U.S. troops as protection against nerve gas), immunizations, stress, oil well fires, depleted uranium, and pesticides.

Wheelwright, Jeff. *The Irritable Heart.* New York: W. W. Norton, 2001. A strong case for linking Gulf War syndrome and other mysterious (and stress-related) illnesses such as chronic fatigue syndrome. The title comes from a similar-sounding malady suffered by Civil War veterans.

Chapter 60

Was O. J. Simpson Guilty?

Even before the trial began, most Americans—certainly most white Americans—believed O. J. Simpson murdered his ex-wife, Nicole, as well as an unfortunate bystander, Ron Goldman. After all, 95 million television viewers followed the slow-motion chase of the white Ford Bronco that ended in his arrest. In the Bronco were O. J.'s passport, a fake goatee and mustache, and more than $8,000 cash, all pretty clear indications that he wasn't heading for the nearest police station. The jury had not yet been selected when a book by Nicole's friend Faye Resnick soared to the number one spot on the bestseller lists, knocking Pope John Paul II down to number two and informing Americans of Simpson's history of beating his wife. And once the trial finally got under way, Americans saw a parade of expert witnesses present the physical evidence: shoeprints, matching a pair O. J. owned, stamped in the blood at the murder scene; Nicole's blood on a sock in his bedroom; Goldman's blood in O. J.'s Bronco; O. J.'s hair on a cap next to the bodies and on Goldman's shirt; the bloody gloves, one found between the bodies and the other, still holding the victims' hair, outside O. J.'s house. One DNA expert testified that the blood found near the victims, which matched O. J.'s, would match only 1 out of 170 million people. The blood on the sock, which matched Nicole's, would match that of only 1 out of 6.8 billion people—more people, author Dominick Dunne noted, than there are on earth.

So when, after more than nine months of testimony, the jury took under four hours to reach its unanimous verdict, the reason seemed clear: race. The case was lost, *Newsweek* explained, "virtually the day the predominately African-American jury was sworn in." Pros-

If it doesn't fit . . . (Corbis.)

ecutor Christopher Darden agreed: "I could see in their eyes the need to settle a score," he said.

Even defense attorney Robert Shapiro jumped on the band-wagon. "Not only did we play the race card," he told Barbara Walters on the day the verdict was announced, "we dealt it from the bottom of the deck."

In October 1995, when the jurors decided Simpson was not guilty, it seemed certain that time would confirm their bias and his guilt. But the verdict of history has turned out to be far from unanimous.

☆ ☆ ☆

Resnick's book, *Nicole Brown Simpson: The Private Diary of a Life Interrupted,* was published in October 1994, five months after the murders and right in the middle of jury selection. In one sense, it obviously helped the prosecution by providing a clear motive for the murders. Resnick portrayed O. J. as a womanizer and wife beater, whose jealousy only increased after the divorce. "I can't take this, Faye," Resnick quoted Simpson. "I mean it. I'll kill that bitch." Though Judge Lance Ito temporarily suspended jury selection and pleaded with the television networks to cancel interviews with Resnick, this only made people—including would-be jurors—all the more eager to read it.

Ironically, Resnick's book may have done more for the defense than for the prosecution. Prosecutor Marcia Clark was furious with Resnick for having joined the parade of potential witnesses who took "cash for trash." Moreover, Resnick's tales of her own (and Nicole's) drug abuse tainted her credibility and the victim's image. Fearing what defense attorneys would do with this, Clark decided not to put Resnick on the stand.

The prosecution's case suffered another blow when Ito ruled inadmissible some of the evidence of O. J.'s abuse. This included Nicole's call to the Sojourn Counseling Center, a battered women's shelter in Santa Monica, to complain that O. J. was stalking her. Nicole called the center on July 7, just five days before her death.

Still, Ito did allow some evidence of Simpson's abuse, and that's what prosecutors led with when the trial finally got under way in January 1995. The jury heard about a 1989 beating for which Simpson received a suspended sentence and was ordered to pay $500 to the Sojourn Center. They also heard about a 911 call Nicole made in 1993.

Having established Simpson's propensity to violence (at least in their minds), prosecutors moved on to the physical evidence, which culminated in the trial's most dramatic moment. This was on June 15, when, as millions watched, Simpson put on the pair of gloves police found at the murder scene and at his own home—or, rather, tried to put on the gloves. After struggling with the right-hand glove, he turned to his attorney Johnnie Cochran and told him they were too tight. The moment inspired Cochran's most famous line to the jury: "If it doesn't fit, you must acquit."

Prosecutors maintained the gloves *did* fit, and that Simpson's struggle was an act. "I hoped everyone could see that, hoped the jury could see it," Darden said later. But Clark knew the prosecution was in trouble. She recalled: "I looked down at the bloody, weathered leather, and I said to myself, that's it. We just lost the case."

As if that wasn't enough, prosecutors next had to deal with Mark Fuhrman, the detective who had found the second glove at Simpson's home. Questioned by defense attorney F. Lee Bailey, Fuhrman denied having used the word "nigger" during the previous ten years. Then, in July, the defense got their hands on twelve hours of taped interviews between Fuhrman and aspiring screenwriter Laura Hart McKinney. McKinney had interviewed Fuhrman as part of her research for a screenplay about Los Angeles police. On the tapes, Fuhrman said the word forty-one times.

Fuhrman claimed he was merely playing a role for McKinney, and Ito ruled the jury could hear only two of the excerpts in which the detective used the word. That was damaging enough. Hollywood never showed any interest in McKinney's work, but now her tapes reached a wider audience than any movie. More to the point, even in their much-edited form, the jury could hear that Fuhrman was a liar and a racist. Defense attorneys were quick to accuse Fuhrman of taking the glove from the murder scene, wiping some of Simpson's blood on it, and then planting the bloody glove at Simpson's house. How Fuhrman got his hands on Simpson's blood wasn't clear, but the strategy was brilliant: with Fuhrman's credibility shattered, the gloves, once among the prosecution's strongest evidence, were now a cornerstone of the case for the defense.

The defense team went after other prosecution witnesses besides Fuhrman. Criminologist Dennis Fung, for example, hadn't noticed any blood on Simpson's socks during his initial investigation, and an FBI lab found that some of the blood contained a preservative called EDTA, which is more often found in laboratories than in humans. Someone must have put Simpson's blood on the sock in the lab, the defense concluded. Fung had also neglected to secure Simpson's Bronco at the crime scene, casting doubt on any evidence found there.

Some of the tainted evidence, the defense conceded, might have been the result of sloppy police work rather than a conspiracy to frame Simpson. But it was tainted nonetheless. And, if the police were either crooked or incompetent, *none* of their evidence could be trusted. Forensic scientist Henry Lee, a defense witness, put it this way: "While eating . . . spaghetti, I found one cockroach. . . . No sense for me to go through the whole plate of spaghetti. . . . If you found one, it's there."

Immediately after the verdict was announced, the fingers started pointing.

Fuhrman blamed Clark for not standing by him, as well as other detectives for mishandling both the physical evidence and their questioning of Simpson. Other detectives blamed Fuhrman for his racism, and Clark for failing to introduce any evidence pertaining to the Bronco chase. Clark defended her decision, arguing that bringing up the chase would have given Simpson's attorneys the chance to counter that he was not fleeing justice but planning suicide—and that the police had driven him to it.

Some blamed Clark for focusing too much on domestic violence, saying she should have introduced other possible motives. What if, some suggested, a jealous Simpson killed Nicole because he suspected she was having an affair? Faye Resnick said Nicole was having an affair with O. J.'s friend and fellow football star Marcus Allen, though Allen denied it. Fuhrman, among others, believed Nicole was having an affair with Goldman. But Clark insisted this was a case of escalating domestic violence. Critics suggested this was because she wanted to keep the victims' images pure, or because Clark herself was in the midst of an ugly (though not violent) divorce. In any case, the jury wasn't buying the connection between the earlier incidents and the murders.

"This was a murder trial, not domestic abuse," juror Brenda Moran told reporters after the trial. "If you want to get tried for domestic abuse, go in another courtroom."

For her part, Clark blamed Darden for demanding that Simpson try on the gloves. (Darden must have been "on a testosterone high," she said.) She blamed Ito for excluding some of the evidence of domestic violence and for allowing Simpson—in a brief statement waiving his right to testify—to tell the jury he was innocent, without having to take the stand and face any cross-examination. She blamed the media for turning the trial into a circus.

Above all, of course, prosecutors blamed the defense team, especially Johnnie Cochran, for making race an issue, and the jury for choosing race over justice. "It wasn't a Dream Team that would acquit O. J. Simpson," said Clark. "It was a Dream Jury." Millions of white Americans shared Clark's outrage.

Gradually, though, these passions subsided. Civil libertarians argued that the jury had plenty of nonracial reasons for its verdict. Two members of the dream team, Barry Scheck and Peter Neufeld, were specialists in the evidentiary use of DNA, and defense experts such as Lee were very effective on the stand. Clark herself conceded that the prosecution had made a fiasco of the glove demonstration and that Fuhrman was a racist. For the jurors to have some doubts about a case in which Fuhrman was a key witness was perfectly reasonable. It did not necessarily mean that they freed Simpson because of his race, or even that they thought he was innocent. It may merely have meant that they had doubts—reasonable doubts—about his guilt. And any criminal jury has an obligation under those circumstances to find a defendant not guilty.

Alan Dershowitz, himself a member of the Dream Team, reflected this emerging consensus in his book *Reasonable Doubts*. Jurors, he argued, were not supposed to be historians.

"The discovery of historical and scientific truths is not entrusted to a jury of laypeople selected randomly from the population on the basis of their ignorance of the underlying facts," Dershowitz wrote. "The task of discovering such truths is entrusted largely to trained experts who have studied the subject for years and are intimately familiar with the relevant facts and theories."

Like historians, jurors are supposed to figure out what happened, but it's by no mean their only goal. "If it were," Dershowitz continued, "judges would not instruct jurors to acquit a defendant whom they believe 'probably' did it, as they are supposed to do in criminal cases."

At least one juror, a white woman named Anise Aschenbach, was apparently thinking along these lines. She said after the trial that she thought Simpson was probably guilty, "but the law wouldn't allow a guilty verdict."

The law did, however, allow the families of Nicole Brown Simpson and Ron Goldman to sue Simpson, and in February 1997 a civil jury found him liable for the deaths and awarded the victims' families $33.5 million. To some, like Dershowitz, this confirmed that the system worked. The civil jury heard much of the same evidence as the criminal one, but its verdict was based on a different standard of proof. The civil jury had only to find that a "preponderance of evidence" pointed to Simpson's liability. In this case, reasonable doubt was not enough to save Simpson.

The civil libertarian view of the Simpson case is comforting. "O. J. didn't get away with anything," wrote Gerry Spence, seemingly one of the few famous defense attorneys who didn't join the Dream Team. "The system worked. It revealed his guilt and, at the same time, preserved its safeguards for us."

Similar analyses went a long way to ease the tensions that flared up after the criminal verdict, when blacks across the country cheered and whites looked on in horror. It was much safer to see the verdict as an expression of reasonable doubt than of African Americans' contempt for the justice system. Besides, O. J. was no Rodney King. It was one thing for blacks to protest the acquittal of the police officers who beat up the helpless King, quite another for them to rally round a football and movie star who, as the legal scholar Jeffrey Abramson put it, was "more at home on white golf courses than in the black community."

And yet, much as we might like to deny it, this case clearly was about race.

There were other issues, to be sure. Marcia Clark was not wrong to recognize the dangers of domestic violence. Yet, as Brenda Moran's statement made clear, this was not what was foremost in jurors' minds.

Money, too, was an issue. Few defendants, black or white, could have afforded the Dream Team. Few could have hired a renowned expert like Henry Lee, or the private investigators who uncovered the Fuhrman tapes. No wonder critic Diana Trilling argued that the "m" word was as crucial to the outcome of the trial as the "n" word.

Above all and undeniably, though, the issue was race. Shapiro was correct to say the defense had played the "race card," though perhaps wrong to lay the blame on Cochran. Simpson was no Rodney King, but the black community's mistrust of the Los Angeles Police Department was based on a pattern of abuse, not a single beating. Simpson, to many blacks, was merely another victim, though one with the means to fight back.

"Race had been there all along," commented the legal scholar Paul Butler, "or at least as soon as Fuhrman reported to the scene of the crime."

"Race is not a card," agreed the cultural historian Michael Eric Dyson. "It is a condition shaped by culture and fueled by passions buried deep in our history that transcend reason. That's why many white folk are angry at the verdict, while many black folk feel joy."

Or, as Cochran put it: "I just want to say something about this 'race card.' Race plays a part in everything in America."

☆ To investigate further:

Resnick, Faye, with Mike Walker. *Nicole Brown Simpson: The Private Diary of a Life Interrupted*. Beverly Hills, California: Dove Books, 1994. Ito halted jury selection so he could read the book.

Simpson, O. J. *I Want to Tell You*. Boston: Little, Brown, 1995. Simpson's responses to letters he received in jail.

Abramson, Jeffrey, editor. *Postmortem*. New York: Basic Books, 1996. A wide-ranging and provocative collection of essays by lawyers, political scientists, historians, and others who address what the case revealed about race, domestic violence, law, money, and the media.

Bosco, Joseph. *A Problem of Evidence*. New York: William Morrow, 1996. According to Bosco, Simpson was guilty *and* framed.

Bugliosi, Vincent. *Outrage*. New York: W.W. Norton, 1996. The man who prosecuted Charles Manson tells how Clark and company bungled the case.

Darden, Christopher, with Jess Walter. *In Contempt*. New York: Regan Books, 1996. The trials of the case's sole black prosecutor.

Dershowitz, Alan. *Reasonable Doubts*. New York: Simon & Schuster, 1996. Why the verdict was reasonable.

Schiller, Lawrence, and James Willwerth. *American Tragedy*. New York: Random House, 1996. This behind-the-scenes look at the squabbles and strategies of the defense team is surprisingly balanced, considering that Schiller co-authored Simpson's own book.

Shapiro, Robert, with Larkin Warren. *The Search for Justice*. New York: Warner Books, 1996. Shapiro is eager to portray himself as the Dream Team's quarterback—except when it came to playing the race card, when he was equally eager to hand the ball to Cochran.

Toobin, Jeffrey. *The Run of His Life*. New York: Random House, 1996. Authoritative treatment.

Clark, Marcia, with Teresa Carpenter. *Without a Doubt*. New York: Viking, 1997. Somewhat self-serving (and not just because Viking paid $4.2 million for the book), but nonetheless a fascinating look behind the scenes of the prosecution's case.

Dunne, Dominick. *Another City, Not My Own*. New York: Crown, 1997. A pointlessly fictionalized memoir of the trial. Stick to his 2001 book, *Justice*, if you like Dunne's take on celebrity murders.

Fuhrman, Mark. *Murder in Brentwood*. Washington, D.C.: Regnery, 1997. "The world does not know me," Fuhrman writes. But we know what he said.

Lange, Tom, and Philip Vannatter, with Dan Moldea. *Evidence Dismissed*. New York: Pocket Books, 1997. Lange and Vannatter were the lead detectives on the case.

Spence, Gerry. *O.J.: The Last Word*. New York: St. Martin's Press, 1997. Well . . . maybe Spence's last words.

Petrocelli, Daniel, with Peter Knobler. *Triumph of Justice*. New York: Crown, 1998. Petrocelli, the lawyer who represented the Goldman family, tells the story of the civil suit, including his confrontation with Simpson on the witness stand.

Dunne, Dominick. *Justice*. New York: Crown, 2001. Dunne's *Vanity Fair* essays chronicle life among the rich and famous and murderous. About half the book is devoted to Simpson's trial, about which Dunne offers plenty of entertaining celebrity gossip, though not nearly as many insights as he thinks.

Index